Dart in Actio

Dart in Action

CHRIS BUCKETT

MANNING

Shelter Island

For online information and ordering of this and other Manning books, please visit
www.manning.com. The publisher offers discounts on this book when ordered in quantity.
For more information, please contact

> Special Sales Department
> Manning Publications Co.
> 20 Baldwin Road
> PO Box 261
> Shelter Island, NY 11964
> Email: orders@manning.com

Manning Publications Co.
20 Baldwin Road
PO Box 261
Shelter Island, NY 11964

Development editor:	Susanna Kline
Technical proofreader:	John Evans
Copyeditor:	Tiffany Taylor
Proofreader:	Toma Mulligan
Typesetter:	Gordan Salinovic
Cover designer:	Marija Tudor

ISBN 9781617290862
Printed in the United States of America
1 2 3 4 5 6 7 8 9 10 – MAL – 17 16 15 14 13

brief contents

        13 ▪ Server interaction with files and HTTP 283

        14 ▪ Sending, syncing, and storing data 308

        15 ▪ Concurrency with isolates 331

contents

foreword

When I heard that we were starting work on Dart, a structured and scalable language with a fast virtual machine, a powerful editor, and a compiler to JavaScript, at first I didn't believe it. "Could this be the project to make web programming easier for developers like me?" I hopefully wondered. Coming from a structured language background, and used to powerful developer tools, I'd been waiting for a more productive way to build larger modern web apps. The Dart project sounded like just what I was looking for. I grew up on object-oriented languages like C++, Java, and Ruby as I first built interactive websites and then later rich client-side web apps. I learned to be productive with classes, objects, and modular code. I appreciated IDEs for their analysis, refactoring, and navigation capabilities because they helped me write more complex, larger applications. Life was great. Looking for a new opportunity, I was lucky enough to get a job working with the Chrome team. For the first time, I learned how to exploit the modern browser, and I dove into the many HTML5 features. The modern web evolves very quickly and reaches so many people that it's an exciting place to be. Life was even better.

Although I loved the iterative and fast-paced nature of web development, I was missing my structured languages and helpful tools. I wanted a way to build for modern browsers with IDEs that could perform code completion, languages that had real classes, and more.

So when I heard about Dart, I jumped at the opportunity to help out. Build for the most exciting platform with a development experience that I'm familiar and productive with? You bet!

I wasn't the only developer who immediately joined the fun. The author of this book, Chris Buckett, is one of our earliest adopters of Dart. He started the Dartwatch blog on the day that Google announced Dart, and it's still going strong. Chris has been with the project since the beginning, so it's only natural that he is one of the first to write a book to help other developers learn Dart.

Chris is some sort of super author, for he has been able to write this book as the project was going through numerous changes to its libraries and language. He's done a great job covering the many different aspects and features of the Dart project. I especially enjoyed his numerous examples of not only the core language features, but also the more advanced HTML5 features. Chris embraces the single-page app and shows how to use Dart to build modern browser-based apps. You'll even learn how to program server-side Dart with this book!

After a year of hard work, tens of thousands of commits, thousands of bugs, and great community feedback, the dream of structured web programming is a reality. Although Dart isn't done yet, thanks to Chris's book, together we can have fun building great apps for the modern web. Enjoy!

SETH LADD
DEVELOPER ADVOCATE
GOOGLE

preface

In October 2011, rumor became reality when Google released a new language aimed at developing complex, Google-scale web applications. An internal Google email titled "Future of JavaScript" had appeared on the web a month earlier, indicating that a language, possibly to be known as Dash, was undergoing development within Google, with the aim of being a better language for the web than JavaScript. Born out of frustration with the slow progress in evolving JavaScript, partly caused by the numerous interested parties and committees, this new language aimed to be everything JavaScript could be if it were invented now. Its key goal was to "maintain the dynamic nature of JavaScript, but have a better performance profile and be amenable to tooling for large projects." It would also be able to cross-compile to JavaScript. This language was released as a technical preview to the wider world and given the name Dart.

I had just come out the back of a major GWT project at my employer, creating a bespoke document-referencing application designed for touch screens that would be deployed in non-computer-friendly environments. Google Web Toolkit (GWT) is a technology that Google created for cross-compiling Java to JavaScript. GWT lets developers benefit from the structure, type-safety, and tooling provided by Java, while still being able to target browsers natively without requiring plug-ins such as Flash or Silverlight. Having spent the last two years writing GWT code and coordinating developers across three countries, I knew the value of being able to use tooling to validate code at integration points—something that was lacking when trying to achieve the same with JavaScript. The ability to reuse code on both the client and the server also appealed to me—I had seen the benefit.

Keen to know more about this new Dart language, I read all the documentation that was available. At the time, this consisted of the source code, some sample projects, and the language specification. It seemed that if I were to make the effort of getting the knowledge into my head, it would be worth sharing with the wider community through blog posts. I started the Dartwatch blog and shared a series of simple descriptions of how to achieve common tasks in Dart, such as how to organize a project, how to create classes, and how to interact with the browser. One thing led to another, and I was approached by Manning about the possibility of writing a book on Dart. Just over a year later, the result is in print.

Over the last year, Dart has had time to mature, and its developers have been listening and responding to feedback. Dart's Milestone 1 release is imminent, and there have been many changes to the original language specification as a result of real-world use by the language's early adopters. A community of these early adopters has also been creating tools and libraries such as database drivers, 2D and 3D graphics libraries, and MVC frameworks, many of which can be found on GitHub or on the Dartwatch website.

Dart Milestone 1 is a major achievement and gives Dart developers the chance to build on the core Dart language to create a great set of libraries and APIs to turn Dart into the "batteries included" language that the team at Google envisages. Every day, Dart improves; and thanks to its open source nature, you can watch (and even contribute to) the commits by many developers into the Dart source code repository. I hope that this book helps you build great Dart apps.

acknowledgments

It turns out that writing a book isn't as straightforward as I first thought, and without the guidance and effort of the all who were involved at Manning, it's unlikely you would be reading this book today. Thanks to Michael Stephens for setting me on this path in the first place; it's been a fun project. Many people behind the scenes at Manning have contributed by proofreading, editing, preparing images, and performing the myriad other tasks that go into producing a book such as this—thank you all.

A special mention must also go to two people at Manning. First, thanks to Bert Bates, whose mentoring in the early days showed me how to turn what could otherwise have been a dry reference manual into something that is more pleasing to read. In the back of my mind when writing each chapter was the mantra, "Tell Bert why he should care about this subject..." Second, thanks to my editor, Susanna Kline, who kept each chapter focused and helped keep me motivated and on schedule for the best part of a year.

Dart has a vibrant developer community centered around the dartlang mailing list and Google+. From that community, John Evans and Kevin Moore deserve thanks for their technical proofreading of the subject matter, along with Adam Singer, Matthew Butler, and Ladislav Thon, whose contributions are always welcome.

Also from the developer community, thanks to all those readers who provided valuable feedback by reviewing the book at its various stages of development: André Roberge, Carl Taswell, Chad Davis, Craig Lancaster, Dylan Scott, Glenn Stokol, Jon Skeet, Olivier Nouguier, Rick Goff, Rodney Bollinger, Rokesh Jankie, Steve Pretty, Terry Birch, and Willhelm Lehman.

Thanks also to all the contributors to the book's bulletin board, who helped spot the inevitable typos, and to the readers of Manning's Early Access Program (MEAP).

Finally, thanks to all those on the Dart team, including Seth Ladd, who helped me and many other early adopters keep up to date with the various changes as Dart evolved from its initial release to the language you see today. Special thanks to Seth for kindly contributing the foreword to the book.

about this book

This book will help you learn the Dart language, understand the Dart ecosystem, and write Dart code targeted to run in modern web browsers and on the server. You'll use the latest HTML5 technologies to build apps capable of running disconnected in the browser and create Dart servers capable of two-way communication with browsers.

As a structured language, Dart is ideal for building large-scale apps in distributed teams. And with tools to enable automatic checking and validation of your and your fellow developers' code, Dart helps make your life as a developer easier.

Audience

This book is aimed at developers who have been frustrated by the lack of structure and tooling available to them when building browser-based apps. If you have a working knowledge of Java, C#, or JavaScript, then you'll be able to dive right in and get working with Dart.

Whether you prefer to build interactive user interfaces or are happier creating efficient back-end code, you'll find that Dart, combined with modern browser technology, brings the structure of the server to the front end, and the flexibility, dynamism, and speed of browser development to the back end.

Whether you're a novice web developer or are experienced with writing structured code, this book will help you get up to speed with Dart language concepts. The book uses an example-based format, with examples throughout each chapter to introduce new concepts. The text indicates Dart's similarities to other languages such as Java and JavaScript, as well as shows its differences.

Like Java, Dart has great tools; and like JavaScript, Dart doesn't require a compile step, which means that with this book you can quickly get ready to start building client and server Dart applications.

Roadmap

This book is structured to get you working with Dart as quickly as possible. It's split into four parts. Part 1 includes overview chapters designed to get you up and running with Dart:

- Chapter 1 provides an overview of the language features and concepts and why Dart exists. If you've ever been exasperated by the lack of typing and documentation that could be encoded in a browser-based language, this chapter will help you to understand the philosophy behind Dart. This base will give you an idea of the types of large-scale web apps you can build with Dart.
- Chapter 2 discusses the wider Dart ecosystem, including the rich tooling you get by choosing a structured web-development language created by a market-leading web company. With the technical resources to concentrate on a whole-developer experience, rather than just the language, Google has created an IDE, a custom Dart browser for rapid development, a server-side virtual machine, and other tools to help you build quality code.
- In chapter 3, you'll build an example web app, getting a taste of how Dart interacts with the browser. You'll build a user interface, listen for browser events, and create unit tests to confirm the validity of your code.

Part 2 covers the core language features:

- Chapter 4 examines functions, which are first-class objects in Dart. JavaScript developers will be familiar with some of the techniques of functional programming, but Java and C# developers will find many new ideas that are common practice in browser-based web development.
- Chapter 5 moves on to building the structure of your app by using Dart's library system, and shows how that relates to privacy. Dart's privacy mechanism might surprise Java and C# developers and will be a welcome treat to those experienced with JavaScript.
- Chapters 6, 7, and 8 explore Dart's class and interface structure. Classes form the backbone of any reasonable-size app, and knowing how to effectively build class hierarchies and use library classes provided by other developers is an essential skill.
- Chapter 9 returns to functional programming to explore the asynchronous nature of web APIs. You'll learn how to work with future values, that is, variables that will have a value at some point in the future. This will leave you ready to start working with the APIs provided by Dart's client and server libraries.

Part 3 discusses building client-side browser apps:

- In chapter 10, you'll learn about Dart's event loop and create a user-interface in Dart.
- Chapter 11 builds on the structure of your app to add browser-based navigation, persistent client-side storage, and interaction with the JSON data format.
- By chapter 12, you'll be ready to start connecting your app to external systems, such as external JavaScript and third-party server APIs. Although Dart is targeted at all modern web browsers, in this chapter you'll also learn how to package your app for deployment as a Chrome app in Google's Web Store.

When you reach part 4, you'll be ready to hook up your app with the server side:

- Chapter 13 introduces building a command-line Dart application, accessing the filesystem, and serving HTTP data to build a simple file server.
- Chapter 14 builds on client-side communication by connecting the client side to a server-side database and performing two-way communication with Web-Sockets technology to push data to the client.
- In chapter 15, knowing how to interact with the server, you'll be ready to learn how Dart achieves concurrency through its system of isolates, a message-passing threading model that provides a safer means of concurrency than the equivalent in Java or C#. You'll also use the isolate system to load Dart code dynamically into your running application. This gives you a great basis for building plug-ins and extensions into your app.

The appendixes provide a concise reference to and examples of the core Dart language, giving you a quick guide to Dart's specific syntax idiosyncrasies and quirks.

Code conventions and downloads

All the source code in the text uses a `fixed width font like this`. The text contains many code snippets and diagrams, and there are complete, annotated code listings to show key concepts. These code listings, snippets, and diagrams usually relate to the surrounding body text and are a key part of learning Dart.

In some cases, code has been reformatted to fit the page, but in general, the code has been written to take page width into account. Although the examples are often simple in order to to show a key concept or example, the body text and code annotations provide additional depth.

Source code for the examples in this book is avaiable for download from the publisher's website at www.manning.com/DartinAction.

Software requirements

Working with Dart requires at the very least the Dart SDK, which is available from www.dartlang.org. The Dart SDK is included in the Dart Editor download, which also includes the custom Dart browser, Dartium (essential for rapid Dart development), and the Dart to JavaScript converter. This download is available for Windows, Mac, and Linux.

Author Online

Your purchase of *Dart in Action* includes free access to a private web forum run by Manning Publications, where you can make comments about the book, ask technical questions, and receive help from the author and from other users. To access the forum and subscribe to it, point your web browser at www.manning.com/DartinAction. This page explains how to get on the forum once you are registered, what kind of help is available, and the rules of conduct on the forum.

Manning's commitment to its readers is to provide a venue where a meaningful dialogue among individual readers, and between readers and the author, can take place. It's not a commitment to any specific amount of participation on the part of the author, whose contribution to the forum remains voluntary (and unpaid). We suggest you try asking the author some challenging questions, lest his interest stray!

The Author Online forum and archives of previous discussions will be accessible from the publisher's website as long as the book is in print.

About the author

Chris Buckett is a technical consultant responsible for delivering enterprise-scale, web-based business applications. Chris runs the popular Dartwatch.com blog and is an active contributor to the dartlang mailing list.

about the cover illustration

The figure on the cover of *Dart in Action* is captioned an "Island Woman from Zadar, Dalmatia." The illustration is taken from the reproduction published in 2006 of a 19th-century collection of costumes and ethnographic descriptions entitled *Dalmatia* by Professor Frane Carrara (1812 - 1854), an archaelogist and historian and the first director of the Musuem of Antiquity in Split, Croatia. The illustrations were obtained from a helpful librarian at the Ethnographic Museum (formerly the Museum of Antiquity), itself situated in the Roman core of the medieval center of Split: the ruins of Emperor Diocletian's retirement palace from around AD 304. The book includes finely colored illustrations of figures from different regions of Croatia, accompanied by descriptions of the costumes and of everyday life.

Zadar is an historic town located on the Adriatic coast of Croatia; its orgins date to the Stone Age. Zadar faces the islands of Uglian and Pasman, from which it is separated by the narrow Zadar Strait. The promontory on which the old city stands used to be separated from the mainland by a deep moat which has since become landfilled. The region is rich in influences of the many nation states that ruled it through the centuries, from the Greeks and Romans to the Venetians and Austrians. Today, the city is part of the Republic of Croatia.

Dress codes have changed since the 19th century and the diversity by region, so rich at the time, has faded away. It is now hard to tell apart the inhabitants of different continents, let alone different towns or regions. Perhaps we have traded cultural diversity for a more varied personal life—certainly for a more varied and fast-paced technological life.

At a time when it is hard to tell one computer book from another, Manning celebrates the inventiveness and initiative of the computer business with book covers based on the rich diversity of regional life of two centuries ago, brought back to life by Carrara's pictures.

Part 1

Introducing Dart

Dart is a great language for developing web apps. In chapter 1, you'll get an overview of why Dart was created and how Dart solves some of the problems experienced by many developers coming to web development. You'll discover some of the features the language offers and see why single-page web applications are a good architecture for building apps in Dart.

In chapter 2, you'll start to come to grips with the rich tool ecosystem that comes with Dart. Dart is more than a language—it's an entire development toolset, including an IDE, a custom developer browser for testing and debugging, and a Dart to JavaScript converter.

In chapter 3, you'll build a simple Dart app, learning how to create a browser-based, single-page web app. Through this example application, you'll be introduced to the language, including Dart's classes, functions, and variables. By the end of the chapter, you'll have a Dart project with a functioning user interface and accompanying unit tests, and you'll be ready to start learning about the core Dart language in Part 2.

Hello Dart 1

This chapter covers

- Basics of the Dart development platform
- A look at the Dart language
- Tools for building Dart applications

Dart is an exciting language that raises the possibility of building complex web applications more quickly and accurately than ever before. In this chapter, you'll find out how the Dart language and its tool ecosystem fit together, you'll discover some of the key features of the Dart language, and you'll see how you can you use Dart to begin building single-page web applications.

1.1 What is Dart?

Dart is an open source, structured programming language for creating complex, browser-based web applications. You can run applications created in Dart either by using a browser that directly supports Dart code or by compiling your Dart code to JavaScript. Dart has a familiar syntax, and it's class-based, optionally typed, and single-threaded. It has a concurrency model called *isolates* that allows parallel execution, which we discuss in chapter 15. In addition to running Dart code in web browsers and converting it to JavaScript, you can also run Dart code on the command line, hosted in the Dart virtual machine, allowing both the client and the server parts of your apps to be coded in the same language.

The language syntax is very similar to Java, C#, and JavaScript. One of the primary goals for Dart was that the language seem familiar. This is a tiny Dart script, comprising a single function called `main`:

```
main() {

    var d = "Dart";

    String w = "World";

    print("Hello ${d} ${w}");

}
```

Single entry-point function main() executes when script is fully loaded

Optional typing (no type specified)

Type annotation (String type specified)

Uses string interpolation to output "Hello Dart World" to browser console or stdout

This script can be embedded in an HTML page's `<script type="application/dart">` tags and run in the Dartium browser (a Dart developer edition of Google's Chrome web browser). You can convert it to JavaScript using the dart2js tool to run it in all modern browsers, or run the script directly from a server-side command line using the Dart Virtual Machine (Dart VM) executable.

There's more to Dart than just the language, though. Figure 1.1 shows the ecosystem of tools, which includes multiple runtime environments, language and editor tools, and comprehensive libraries—all designed to improve the developer's workflow when building complex web applications.

In addition to a great tool ecosystem that helps you build applications, Dart is designed to seem familiar, whether you're coming from a server-side, Java and C# world, or a client-side, JavaScript or ActionScript mindset.

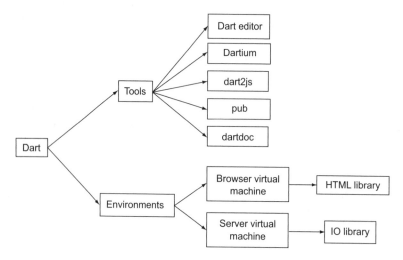

Figure 1.1   Dart is more than just the language. The Dart project has an entire ecosystem.

A key tool for Dart developers is Dartium, which lets you write or edit Dart code and see it running by loading the file and refreshing the browser. When Dartium is combined with the Dart Editor, you get the additional benefit of round-trip debugging.

1.1.1 *A familiar syntax to help language adoption*

One of the key design decisions was that Dart should be familiar to both JavaScript and Java/C# developers. This design helps developers who are new to Dart pick up the language quickly. If you're familiar with these other languages, you'll be able to read and understand the intent of Dart code without much trouble.

Java and C# developers are generally comfortable with type systems, classes, inheritance, and other such concepts. JavaScript developers, on the other hand, range from UI designers who copy and paste code to add interactivity to a web page (and have never used a type) to seasoned JavaScript programmers who understand closures and prototypical inheritance. To help with this developer diversity, Dart has an *optional typing* feature, which allows developers to specify absolutely no types (by using the var keyword, as in JavaScript), or use type annotations everywhere (such as String, int, Object), or use any mixture of the two approaches.

By using type information in your code, you provide documentation about your intent, which can be beneficial to automated tools and fellow developers alike. A typical workflow when building a Dart application is to build up the type information progressively as the code takes shape. Adding or removing type information doesn't affect how code runs, but it does let the virtual machine validate your code more effectively. This allows Dart's type system to bridge the gap between JavaScript's dynamic type system and Java's and C#'s static type system.

Table 1.1 provides some comparisons among Dart, Java, and JavaScript.

Table 1.1 High-level feature comparison among Dart, Java, and JavaScript

Feature	Dart	Java	JavaScript
Type system	Optional, dynamic	Strong, static	Weak, dynamic
First-class citizen functions	Yes	Can simulate with anonymous functions	Yes
Closures	Yes	Yes, with anonymous classes	Yes
Classes	Yes, single inheritance	Yes, single inheritance	Prototypical
Interfaces	Yes, multiple interfaces	Yes, multiple interfaces	No
Concurrency	Yes, with isolates	Yes, with threads	Yes, with HTML5 web workers

Dart is a general-purpose language, and like JavaScript or Java you can use it to build many different types of application. Dart really shines, though, when you're building complex web applications.

1.1.2   *Single-page application architecture*

The single-page applications Google Mail, Google Instant Search, and Google Maps are typical of the type of web application that Dart was designed to build. The source code for the entire application (or at least all the use cases for a major portion of the application) is loaded by a single web page. This source code, running in the browser, is responsible for building a UI and requesting data from the server to populate that UI, as shown in figure 1.2.

Single-page applications use a fast client-side virtual machine to move processing from the server to the client. This allows your server to serve more requests, because the processing involved in building the layout is moved onto the client. By using Dart's HTML libraries to incorporate modern HTML5 browser-storage and -caching technologies, applications can also cache data in the browser to improve application performance further or even allow users to work offline.

Each Dart script has a single entry-point function called main() that is the first function executed by the Dart VM. Thus you can rely on all code that defines an application when the main function is called; you can't define and execute a function within running code as you can with JavaScript—there is no eval() or other monkey-patching of executing code. This single feature helps you write Dart applications that fit the single-page application architecture, because you can be sure your code will execute as a single, known unit of code. The Dart VM uses this feature to improve application start-up time, using heap snapshots to load apps much more quickly than the equivalent JavaScript application.

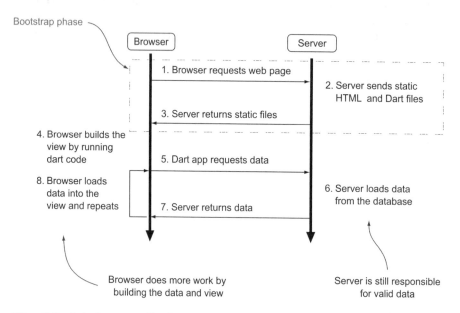

Figure 1.2   A single-page application runs in the browser, only requesting data from the server.

> **Remember**
> - Dart is a language for web development and has a familiar syntax.
> - Dart's tool ecosystem provides greater productivity than equivalent dynamic languages.
> - Dart's optional type system bridges the gap between JavaScript's dynamic typing and Java's static typing.
> - Type annotations can greatly aid the development process among teams of developers by allowing tools to validate source code.
> - Dart is ideal for developing single-page web applications.

Now that you've been introduced to Dart as a development platform, it's time to get hands-on with some of the key features of the Dart language.

1.2 A look at the Dart language

Dart is a fully featured, modern language. It has its roots in Smalltalk and is influenced by many other languages including Java, C#, and JavaScript. This section provides a grounding in some of the core concepts and highlights several complex pieces of the language that the book covers in detail.

> **Dart is an evolving language**
>
> At the time of writing, the Dart language is at a transition point between the experimental "technical preview" phase and a release that Google calls Milestone 1. Milestone 1 isn't version 1 but a line in the sand to allow features such as extended libraries surrounding the core language to be developed and enhanced. The Dart platform is intended to be a fully featured "batteries included" development environment, containing everything you need to build complex web applications. And Google, along with members of the Dart community, is now focused on building these libraries.
>
> Milestone 1 also provides a neat baseline to enable you to start building applications, knowing that the breaking changes to the language syntax will be infrequent. Changes to the surrounding libraries, however, are likely, and the Dart Editor contains a helpful Clean-up tool that you can use to apply language and core library changes to your code.

1.2.1 String interpolation

Strings are used in many places throughout web applications. Dart provides a number of ways for you to convert expressions into strings, either via the `toString()` function that's built into the base `Object` class or by using string interpolation.

String interpolation uses the $ character or ${ } expression within single or double quotes. When you want to convert an expression to a string, you use the variable name with the $ prefix, such as $name. If you want to use an expression that needs to be evaluated, such as a calculation or method call, include the curly braces:

```
"The answer is ${5 + 10}"
```

You can create multiline strings by using three double quotes; and you can write string literals (which ignore the $ evaluation) by prefixing the string with an r character, such as r'literal string'. There is no + concatenator to join two strings together. You must use string interpolation such as $forename $surname or, if they're known string values, place them next to each other. For example,

```
var title = "Dart " "in " "Action";
```

produces a single string variable containing "Dart in Action".

The following listing shows the things you can do with strings using Dart's built-in print function, which outputs to standard output, server-side, or the browser debug console when run in a browser.

Listing 1.1 String interpolation in Dart

```
void main() {

  var h = "Hello";
  final w = "World";
  print('$h $w');                              $ evaluates
                                               simple variables
  print(r'$h $w');                             r prefix outputs literal string
                                               without interpolation
  var helloWorld = "Hello " "World";           Adjacent string constants
  print(helloWorld);                           are concatenated

  print("${helloWorld.toUpperCase()}");        Evaluated expressions need
  print("The answer is ${5 + 10}");            to be within braces ${ }

  var multiline = """                          Multiline strings ignore first
<div id='greeting'>                            line break following """
  "Hello World"
</div>""";                                     Multiline strings can contain
  print(multiline);                            both single and double quotes

  var o = new Object();                        String interpolation automatically
  print(o.toString());                         calls toString() function
  print("$o");

}
```

The output from this listing is

```
Hello World
$h $w
Hello World
HELLO WORLD
The answer is 15
<div id='greeting'>
  "Hello World"
</div>
Instance of 'Object'
Instance of 'Object'
```

You'll use string interpolation and the print function a lot when experimenting with Dart, logging variables to help with debugging, and inserting values into HTML snippets.

1.2.2   *Optional types in action*

One of the key differences between JavaScript and Dart is that Dart has the concept of types baked into the language. Fortunately, by using Dart's *option typing*, you can get the benefit of strong typing through type annotations where you use them.

Optional type annotations are used in variable declarations, for function parameter definitions and return types, and in class definitions. The following snippet shows four ways of declaring the string variable message. The first two have no type annotations, and the second two provide the String type annotation, indicating to developers and tools that you intend a string value to be used in the variable:

```
var messageA;
var messageB = "Hello Dart";

String messageC;
String messageD = "Hello Dart";
```

No type annotations provided

Type annotations provided

In the previous snippet, two of the variable declarations initialize the value of message at the time it's declared. If the value won't change after declaration, then you should use the final keyword, as shown here:

```
final messageE = "Hello Dart";
final String messageF = "Hello Dart";
```

Uses final with no type annotation

Uses final with type annotation

Const

We'll cover the final keyword in more detail later in the book.

As an example of how you can benefit from using optional typing, consider the following block of code, which has a trueIfNull() function that takes two parameters and returns true if both are null (and false if not). This code has no type annotations at present, but we'll explain how you can use type annotations to show intent:

```
trueIfNull(a, b) {
    return a == null && b == null;
}
main() {
    final nums = trueIfNull(1,2);
    final strings = trueIfNull("Hello ", null);
    print("$nums");
    print("$strings");
}
```

Function takes two values

Stores "false" in dynamic variable nums

Outputs variables nums and strings to console

Stores "true" in dynamic variable strings

No type annotations are provided in the snippet, which means that when reading this code, you have no idea about the developer's intent. The trueIfNull(a,b) function could mean that trueIfNull(a,b) should take two int types and return a bool (true/false value), but the developer could have intended something else—for example, to return the string "true" instead of a bool. Dart's optional typing allows the developer to provide documentation in the form of type information about the parameters and return types:

```
bool trueIfNull(int a, int b) {
  return a == null && b == null;
}
```
Adds return type and
parameter types

```
main() {
  final bool nums = trueIfNull(1,2);
  final bool strings = trueIfNull("Hello ", null);
  print("$nums");
  print("$strings");
}
```
Adds type information
about variable declarations

> **NOTE**   The previous example contains a `bool` type. In Dart, unlike in JavaScript, there is a single false value: that of the keyword `false` itself. Zero and null don't evaluate to false.

Adding this type information doesn't change the running of the Dart application, but it provides useful documentation that tools and the VM can use to validate the code and find type errors. Dart can be said to be *documentary typed* because the code will run the same without the types. Any type information provided can help the tools during static analysis (in the Editor or from the command line as part of a continuous build system) and at runtime. Future developers who may maintain your code will also thank you.

> **TIP**   Use specific types (for example, `String`, `List`, and `int`) where doing so adds documentary value, such as for function parameters, return types, and public class members; but use `var` or `final` without type annotations where it doesn't, such as inside function bodies. The Dart style guide available at www.dartlang.org recommends this approach. You should get used to seeing a mix of code like this, because it's the way Dart was intended to be written.

Optional typing is core to many of Dart's mechanisms and appears throughout the book, where the syntax is different enough from Java and JavaScript to warrant explanation. Functions are covered specifically in chapter 4.

1.2.3   *Traditional class-based structure*

Dart uses classes and interfaces in a traditional and unsurprising object-oriented way. It supports single inheritance and multiple interfaces. If you aren't familiar with class-based OO programming, it would probably be useful to read about the subject at one of the many resources on the web. At this point, it's enough to point out that Dart's OO model is similar to Java/C# and not similar to JavaScript. We'll look at classes and their features in greater depth in chapters 6 and 7.

All Dart classes inherit by default from the `Object` class. They can have public and private members, and a useful getter and setter syntax lets you use fields interchangeably with properties without affecting users of the class. The next listing shows a quick example of a class.

```
Listing 1.2   A simple class in Dart
class Greeter {                              ◁── class keyword defines new class
  var greeting;      ──◁── Public property
  var _name;    ◁─── private                           ◁─
                                                         Private property
  sayHello() {                     ◁── Public method    denoted by _
    return "$greeting ${this.name}";          ◁─
  }                                             Uses String
                                                interpolation

  get name => _name;                           Getter and setter with
  set name(value) => _name = value;            shorthand syntax
}
                                               new keyword creates
main() {                                       new instance of Greeter
  var greeter = new Greeter();      ◁─
  greeter.greeting = "Hello ";                 Assigns values to fields and
  greeter.name = "World";                      setters with same syntax
  print(greeter.sayHello());
}
```

This simple class contains a lot of functionality. Private members are indicated by prefixing the name with the _ (underscore) character. This convention is part of the Dart language, with the benefit that you can instantly tell when you're accessing a method or property in private scope when you're reading code.

The getter and setter syntax is also useful because you can use the fields of a class the same way you use getters and setters. Thus a class designer can expose the property (such as greeting, in listing 1.2) and later change it to use a getter and setter (such as in name in the example) without needing to change the calling code.

The this keyword, which causes a lot of misunderstanding in the JavaScript world, is also used in a traditional OO fashion. It refers to the specific instance of the class itself and not the owner of the class (as in JavaScript) at any given point in time.

Classes are optional

Unlike in Java and C#, classes are optional in Dart. You can write functions that exist in top-level scope without being part of a class. In other words, you don't need to declare a class in order to declare a function. If you find that you're writing classes that contain utility methods, you probably don't need a class. Instead, you can use Dart's top-level functions.

1.2.4   Implied interface definitions

Dart has interfaces just like Java and C#, but in Dart, you use the class structure to define an interface. This works on the basis that all classes define an implicit interface on their public members. Listing 1.3 defines a class called Welcomer and a top-level sayHello() function that expects a Welcomer instance. In addition to using the extends keyword to implement inheritance of the sort found in Java and C#, you can also use the interface defined on each class by using the `implements` keyword. The `Greeter` class implements the public methods of `Welcomer`, which allows it to be used in place of a `Welcomer` instance. This lets you concentrate on programming against a class's interface rather than the specific implementation.

Listing 1.3   Every class has an implicit interface

```
class Welcomer {
  printGreeting() => print("Hello ${name}");       Welcome class can be
  var name;                                        created and inherited
}                                                  from ...

class Greeter implements Welcomer {                ... but also has an
  printGreeting () => print("Greetings ${name}");  implied interface that
  var name;                                        Greeter implements.
}

void sayHello(Welcomer welcomer) {                 Expects Welcomer
  welcomer.printGreeting();                         argument
}

main() {
  var welcomer = new Welcomer();
  welcomer.name = "Tom";
  sayHello(welcomer);

  var greeter = new Greeter();                     Because Greeter
  greeter.name = "Tom";                            implements a Welcomer
  sayHello(greeter);                               interface, it can be used
}                                                  in place of Welcomer.
```

This ability to implement a class that doesn't have an explicit interface is a powerful feature of Dart. It makes mocking classes or providing your own custom implementation of a class relatively straightforward; you don't need to inherit explicitly from a shared base class.

1.2.5   *Factory constructors to provide default implementations*

In addition to having a constructor syntax similar to Java and C#, Dart has the concept of *factory constructors*. This lets the class designer define a base class to use as an interface, and supply a factory constructor that provides a default concrete instance. This is especially useful when you intend a single implementation of an interface to be used under most circumstances.

Listing 1.4 shows an `IGreetable` class that has a factory constructor to return an instance of a `Greeter` class. The `Greeter` class implements the interface defined on `IGreetable` and lets users of the interface use the default `Greeter` implementation without knowing they're getting an implementation of `Greeter`. Thus the class designer can change the specific implementation without users of the `IGreetable` interface being aware of the change.

Listing 1.4 Factory constructors for default implementations

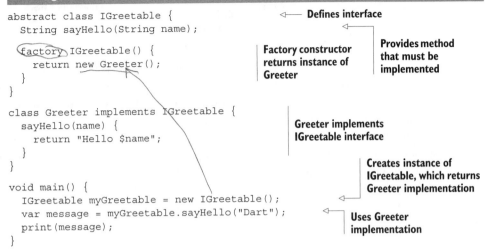

```
abstract class IGreetable {                    ← Defines interface
  String sayHello(String name);
                                                   Provides method
  factory IGreetable() {        Factory constructor  that must be
    return new Greeter();       returns instance of  implemented
  }                             Greeter
}
class Greeter implements IGreetable {
  sayHello(name) {              Greeter implements
    return "Hello $name";       IGreetable interface
  }
}                                                Creates instance of
                                                 IGreetable, which returns
void main() {                                    Greeter implementation
  IGreetable myGreetable = new IGreetable();  ←
  var message = myGreetable.sayHello("Dart");  ←  Uses Greeter
  print(message);                                 implementation
}
```

Because of this ability, it's important to note that a number of the core classes are interfaces—for example, `String` and `int`. These have specific implementation classes that are provided using factory constructors. I cover classes, interfaces, and their interaction with the optional type system at length in part 2 of the book.

1.2.6 *Libraries and scope*

Dart has the ability to break source code files into logical structures. It's possible to write an entire Dart application in a single .dart file, but doing so doesn't make for great code navigation or organization. To address this issue, Dart has libraries baked into the language. A *library* in Dart is a collection of source code files that *could* have been a single file but have been split up to aid human interaction with the code.

I mentioned earlier that classes are optional in Dart. This is so because functions can live in the top-level scope of a library. In Dart, a library is one or more .dart files that you group together in a logical fashion; each file can contain zero or more classes and zero or more top-level functions. A Dart library can also import other Dart libraries that its own code uses.

A library is defined using the `library` keyword, imports other libraries using `import`, and refers to other source files using `part`, as shown in the following listing.

Listing 1.5 Libraries and source files

```
library "my_library";                            Declares that
                                                 file is a library
import "../lib/my_other_library.dart";  ←

                                                 Imports another library
part "greeter.dart";      Includes other source files  from a different folder
part "leaver.dart";       (containing Greeter class)

greetFunc() {                              Defines function in top-
                                           level library scope
```

```
    var g = new Greeter();
    sayHello(g);
}
```

◁─┐ **Uses class from**
     greeter.dart file

◁─┐ **Calls function in**
     top-level scope of
     my_other_library

From the listing, you can see that it's possible to define a method in the top-level scope of a library—that is, without it being part of a class. Therefore, you need to define classes only when you need to instantiate an object, not when you just need to collect a group of related functions.

Libraries can pull a group of source files into the same scope. A library can be made up of any number of source files (including zero), and all the source files put together are equivalent to having a single library file containing all the separate files' code. As such, each source file can reference code that's in another source file, as long as both source files are part of the same library. Each source file can also reference code that's exposed by importing other libraries, as in the example my_other_library.dart in figure 1.3.

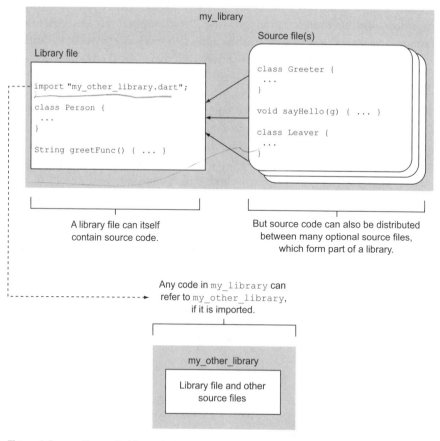

Figure 1.3 **my_library.dart is made from greeter.dart and leavers.dart and uses another library called my_other_library.dart (which in turn is constituted from various source files).**

To avoid naming conflicts, such as when a library that you're writing and a library that you're importing both contain a class called Greeter, you can apply a library prefix such as

```
import "../lib/my_other_library.dart" as other;
```

and then refer to classes in that library using the form

```
other.otherLibFunction("blah");
```

Thus it's possible to ensure that you name your classes and methods sensibly without having to worry about polluting a global namespace.

A library can form the entry point of your application, but if it does, it must have a main() function. You can have multiple libraries, each with its own main() function, but it's the main function in the library referred to in the <script> tag that's executed.

Any functions or classes in your library are made available to any importers of your library; that is, they're public. To stop importers of your libraries from using specific functions or classes, mark them as private.

CLASS AND LIBRARY PRIVACY

Although libraries and classes can be useful to modularize your application, good practice dictates that you keep the workings of your class or library private. Fortunately, Dart provides a simple method for making things private: prefix the name of a method, function, class, or property with an underscore (_). Doing so makes the item library private, or private within the scope of a library.

PRIVATE, BUT ONLY WITHIN A LIBRARY

In our ongoing example, if something is marked as private with the underscore, it means that if class Greeter and class Leaver are in the same library, they can access each other's private elements (similar to package private in Java). It also means that a property or function _greeterPrivate() is accessible from any other class in the same library. But when Greeter is imported via another library, it isn't visible to that other library, as shown in figure 1.4.

Private elements can include top-level (library) functions, classes, class fields, properties and methods (known as members), and class constructors. From within a library, privacy is ignored, such that any part file can access private elements in another part file if the library brings those source files into the same library. Users of the library can't access any private elements of that library (or private elements of classes within that library).

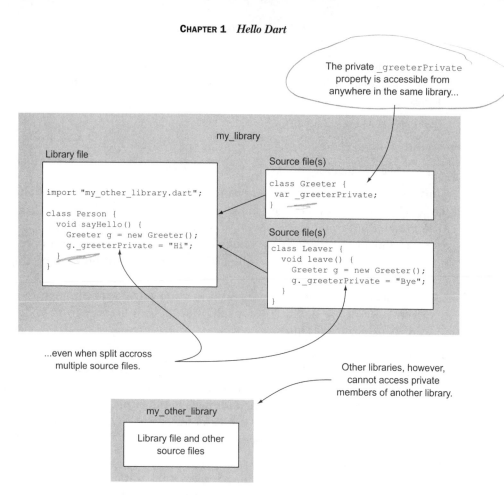

The private `_greeterPrivate` property is accessible from anywhere in the same library...

Figure 1.4 **Private elements such as fields, methods, library functions, and classes are private within a library. Privacy is indicated by an _ prefix. Users of the library can't access private elements.**

1.2.7 *Functions as first-class objects*

You can pass around functions in Dart as objects, in a manner similar to in JavaScript: you can pass a function as a parameter, store a function in a variable, and have anonymous (unnamed) functions to use as callbacks. The next listing gives an example of this feature in action.

Listing 1.6 Functions as first-class objects

```
String sayHello(name) => "Hello $name";

main() {
  var myFunc = sayHello;

  print(myFunc("World"));

  var mySumFunc = (a,b) {
    return a+b;
  };
```

➊ Declares function using function shorthand

➋ Assigns function into variable

Calls function stored in variable

Defines anonymous function

```
    var c = mySumFunc(1,2);
    print(c);                        ◁───┐  Calls anonymous
}                                        │  function
```

❶ is a single-line function that uses => shorthand to return a value. The following two functions are identical:

```
String sayHello(name) {
  return "Hello $name";
}

String sayHello(name) => "Hello $name";
```

With a function defined, you can get a reference to it and store it in a variable ❷. You can pass this around like any other value. Anonymous functions such as the one stored in the variable mySumFunc are often used in event-handler callbacks. It isn't uncommon to see a block of code like

```
myButton.on.click.add((event) {
  // do something
});
```

(with the anonymous function indicated in boldface).

1.2.8 *Concurrency with isolates*

Dart is a single-threaded language. Although this design may be at odds with current hardware technology, with more and more processors being available to applications, it means that Dart has a simple model to code against.

In Dart, the *isolate* (rather than the thread or process) is the unit of work. It has its own memory allocation (sharing memory between isolates isn't allowed), which helps with the provision of an isolated security model. Each isolate can pass messages to another isolate. When an isolate receives a message, which might be some data to process, an event handler can process that message in a way similar to how it would process an event from a user clicking a button. Within an isolate, when you pass a message, the receiving isolate gets a copy of the message sent from the sending isolate. Changes to the received data aren't reflected on the sending side; you need to send another message back.

In a web page, each separate script (containing a main() function) runs in its own isolate. You might have scripts for different parts of your application, such as one for a news feed, one for offline syncing, and so on. Dart code can spawn a new isolate from running code in a way similar to how Java or C# code can start a new thread. Where isolates differ from threads is that an isolate has its own memory. There's no way to share a variable between isolates—the only way to communicate between isolates is via message passing.

Isolates are also used for loading external code dynamically. You can provide code outside of your application's core code that can be loaded into its own memory-protected space and that will run independently of your app, communicating via message passing. This behavior is ideal for creating a plug-in architecture.

The Dart VM implementation may use multiple cores to run the isolates, if required. And when isolate code is converted to JavaScript, they become HTML5 web workers.

> **Remember**
> - Dart has optional (or documentary) typing.
> - Libraries help you break up source files and organize code.
> - Privacy is built into the language.
> - Functions are first-class and can exist without classes.
> - Dart understands concurrency using message-passing isolates.

Now that you've seen a high-level view of what Dart looks like, let's look at how you can use it to program the web.

1.3   Web programming with Dart

One of Dart's aims is to improve the life of developers. And because Dart is ultimately a programming language for the web, a significant amount of effort has gone into turning the browser DOM-manipulation API into something that's a joy to use. In JavaScript, accessing the browser DOM was a chore until jQuery was created, which made it feel natural to work with the browser. Similarly, the dart:html library was written to ease the writing of browser code in Dart.

1.3.1   dart:html: a cleaner DOM library for the browser

At the time of writing, no UI widget library is available for Dart. Although the Dart team has publicly stated that they expect Dart to be a "batteries included" language, the early public release of Dart means that they need to spend some time getting the language working perfectly before the focus moves to higher-level abstractions. But they have built what could be considered the equivalent of jQuery core, in the form of dart:html.

If you've used a framework like jQuery, then you'll be familiar with using CSS selectors to access DOM elements such as DIVs with id="myDiv" or all the <p> elements. The dart:html library makes this work easy. Rather than including a number of different calls to get elements, such as getElementsById() and getElementsByName(), as you would with native DOM APIs, dart:html has only two methods for selecting elements: query(), which returns a single element, and queryAll(), which returns a list of elements. And because the dart:html library uses Dart lists, you can use all the standard list functions such as contains() and isEmpty(), and array syntax such as element.children[0]. The following listing shows some interaction with the DOM via the dart:html library.

Listing 1.7   Interacting with the browser

```
import 'dart:html';                                Imports dart:html
                                                   library
void main() {
  var button = new Element.tag("button");          Creates new
                                                   button element
```

```
button.text = "Click me";
button.on.click.add((event) {
  List buttonList = queryAll("button");
  window.alert("There is ${buttonList.length} button");
});

document.body.children.add(button);
```

Adds anonymous function (in bold italic) as event handler to on.click event

Adds button to HTML body

The listing uses a named constructor to create a button. The button is given an event handler (using an anonymous function) and added to the document body. Running this example produces the output shown in figure 1.5.

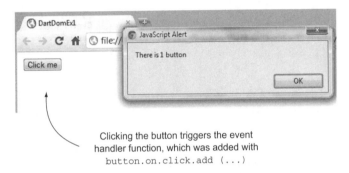

Clicking the button triggers the event handler function, which was added with `button.on.click.add (...)`

Figure 1.5   The output from clicking the button in listing 1.7

By interacting with the browser in this fashion, you can create complex UIs entirely in Dart code and CSS. We'll explore this in chapter 4.

> **TIP** When you're writing browser code, remember that the print function used in print("Hello World") sends output to the browser console, not to the page. You can access the browser console in Chrome under the Wrench > Tools > JavaScript Console menu option.

1.3.2   Dart and HTML5

Just as you can interact with browser elements directly, the dart:html library also exposes HTML5 elements such as the canvas, WebGL, device motion events, and geolocation information. The output shown in figure 1.6 is produced by the code in listing 1.8, which uses the HTML5 Canvas API.

The Dart code that draws this output to the canvas adds an HTML5 <canvas> tag to the browser DOM and then uses it to get a 2D drawing context. The Dart code then writes text and shapes onto the drawing context.

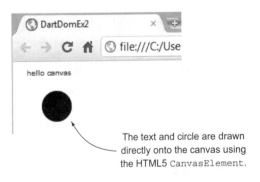

The text and circle are drawn directly onto the canvas using the HTML5 CanvasElement.

Figure 1.6   Drawing on the browser canvas

Listing 1.8   Drawing on the browser canvas

```
import 'dart:html';
import 'dart:math';

void main() {
  CanvasElement canvas = new Element.tag("canvas");        Creates new
                                                           CanvasElement
  canvas.height = 300;
  canvas.width = 300;                           Adds canvas to
  document.body.children.add(canvas);           document body

  var ctx = canvas.getContext("2d");                  Gets drawing
                                                      context from canvas

  ctx.fillText("hello canvas", 10, 10);            Writes text

  ctx.beginPath();
  ctx.arc(50, 50, 20, 0, PI * 2, true);            Draws filled
  ctx.closePath();                                 circle
  ctx.fill();
}
```

By creating a CanvasElement and adding it to the page, you get an area that you can draw directly onto using the standard drawing methods such as drawImage, fillText, and lineTo. We'll look at this in more detail in chapter 10.

With the dart:html library, you have ready access to all the standard browser elements that you'd expect to code against. And because the DOM library, which forms part of the dart:html library is generated from the WebKit IDL (Interface Definition Language), you can be sure of getting access to the up-to-date browser functionality available in Dart.

Remember
- dart:html provides a Dart view of the browser DOM.
- HTML5 support is a core part of the Dart language.

Now that you have some knowledge of Dart running in the browser, it's time to look at the tools available to help you write Dart.

1.4   *The Dart tool ecosystem*

The Dart tools are considered a feature of the Dart platform and as such are undergoing development as rapid as that of the language. As developers, we tend to experience any particular language through the available tools (or lack thereof), and Google is putting a lot of effort into this area. The place to start is editing code.

1.4.1   *The Dart Editor*

Although you can use any text editor to write Dart code, you'll get the best experience when you use the Dart Editor. The Dart Editor is built using the Eclipse Rich Client Platform (RCP), a framework for building customized code editors. In the Dart Editor,

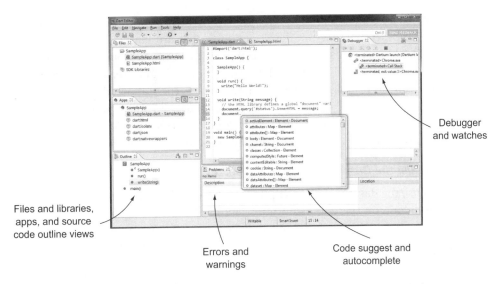

Files and libraries, apps, and source code outline views

Errors and warnings

Code suggest and autocomplete

Debugger and watches

Figure 1.7 **The Dart Editor, showing a simple browser application and the code-completion window**

you get the usual features such as code completion, navigation, and code outlining, along with static analysis such as warnings and errors. The static-analysis tool is also available as a standalone command-line tool that you can use in your continuous-build system to provide early indication of errors in the code. Figure 1.7 shows a typical view of some of the features in the Dart Editor.

Using the Dart Editor, you can write code; and if that code is associated with an HTML page, you can convert the code into JavaScript and open it in a browser of your choice by using the dart2js tool. In the Dartium browser, which is Chrome with the Dart VM embedded, you can skip the conversion to JavaScript and execute the code directly in the browser. Dartium also communicates back to the Dart Editor to allow round-trip, step-by-step debugging.

If your code isn't associated with an HTML page, the editor will run the code as though it were executed from the command line, outputting to the stdout console.

1.4.2 *Dart virtual machine*

The Dart VM is the core of the Dart language. One use is as an executable on the command-line VM (which allows you to run Dart code on the console), such as to start up an HTTP server or run a simple script (equivalent to a batch file or shell script), or any other console-based use of Dart. Another use is to embed it in another application, such as Dartium.

1.4.3 *Dartium*

Dartium is a customized build of Chromium (the open source version of Google Chrome) with the Dart VM embedded in it. It recognizes the script type application/

dart and executes Dart code natively in the browser without requiring conversion to JavaScript. It includes the developer tools that are familiar to many web developers who build websites and web applications with Chrome. Coupled with the Dart Editor, it provides step-and-continue debugging: you can add breakpoints to the editor and then refresh your app in the Dartium browser; the Editor's debugger will stop on the correct breakpoint, allowing you to inspect variables and step through instructions.

The Dartium browser makes developing Dart as simple as developing JavaScript. A simple browser refresh is the only step you need to run your Dart code.

1.4.4   *dart2js: the Dart-to-JavaScript converter*

You use the dart2js tool to compile Dart into JavaScript, from within the Dart Editor or standalone on the command line. The dart2js tool compiles all the various libraries and source code files that make up a Dart application into a single JavaScript file. The code it outputs is fairly readable, although when you use Dartium to develop natively in Dart, you'll seldom need to read it.

dart2js also produces JavaScript source maps, which allow you to hook back from the output JavaScript to the original Dart code. This recent innovation is also used successfully in other languages that convert to JavaScript, such as CoffeeScript and Google Web Toolkit (GWT).

> **NOTE**   dart2js is the third Dart-to-JavaScript converter. The first was dartc, and the second was a tool called frog. You may see these names in various older documents and blog posts; they're all tools to convert Dart to JavaScript.

1.4.5   *Pub for package management*

Package management is a key feature of any language, with Maven for Java, NuGet for .NET, and npm for node.js being common examples. Dart has its own package manager called pub. Pub lets library developers define package metadata in a pubspec file and publish their libraries in code repositories such as GitHub.

When you use a library, you can use the pub tool to download all the various libraries that your app requires, including versioned dependencies. We'll discuss this more and show an example of using pub in chapter 5 when we look at Dart's library structure.

Remember
- The Dart tool ecosystem forms a core part of the Dart project.
- The Dart Editor provides rich tooling for developers.
- Dartium makes developing in Dart as simple as a browser refresh.
- Dart is designed to be converted to JavaScript.

1.5 *Summary*

At first glance, Dart might be seem like just another language. But when you take into account the entire Dart ecosystem, Dart represents an exciting prospect in the world of web development. With applications becoming more complex and requiring larger development teams, Dart and its associated tools and environments promise to provide some structure in the previously overly flexible world of JavaScript.

Single-page applications hosted in a browser (such as Google Plus) become more achievable with a language like Dart, because maintaining a large client-side code base becomes less fragile. Dart—with its ability to either run natively or be converted to JavaScript—coupled with HTML5 is an ideal solution for building web applications that don't need external plug-ins to provide features.

In the following chapters, you'll play with the Dart ecosystem, explore the core language, and use Dart to develop single-page web applications that target modern HTML5-capable web browsers. By the end of the book, you'll be developing Dart applications that run offline in the client, are served from a Dart file server, and connect to a Dart server to persist data in a database.

"Hello World" with Dart tools

2

This chapter covers

- Discovering the Dart tool set
- Building apps with the Dart Editor
- Tools for debugging apps
- Running apps in the browser
- Deploying apps to JavaScript

Dart has a rich tool ecosystem that enables you to write, run, and debug Dart code in a variety of environments. Google takes a "batteries included" approach to the Dart tools and fully intends to provide all the tools you'll require to build complex applications. The Dart tools are currently available for Windows, Mac, and Linux platforms; you can find them on Google's dartlang.org website.

The Dart tool set starts with the Dart Virtual Machine (Dart VM). The virtual machine exists in two guises. First, it's on the server as a command-line runtime environment, similar to a Java, Python, or Ruby VM; you'll use this version to run a simple "Hello World" application. In its second incarnation, it's embedded in a version of the Chrome web browser called Dartium, where it has access to the browser document object model (DOM). You'll see Dartium when you use the Dart Editor to edit and run the same "Hello World" application in the browser, but this time hosting the Dart script in an HTML file.

You'll also use the Dart Editor, which is capable of building applications that run both in the browser and on the server, to enable debugging and refactoring of the "Hello World" app. Here, you'll use the dart2js tool, which compiles the various Dart source files and libraries into a single JavaScript application.

You'll use the dartdoc tool to generate formatted HTML API documentation from your code's comments. This is the same tool that creates Google's own Dart API documentation website, and you'll use it to produce documentation for your "Hello World" app.

When you choose Dart as a platform for writing web apps, you get more than language features: you get to use the tools developed by Google for Google. Download the Dart Editor, which bundles all the tools you need, including the Dart software development kit (SDK) and the Dartium browser, and we'll start exploring.

2.1 The command-line Dart VM

There are versions of the Dart VM for Windows, Mac, and Linux platforms. This allows you to write Dart code that runs without a web browser and accesses the capabilities of the machine, including the filesystem and socket-level network I/O. The VM uses an asynchronous, event-loop model, similar to Node.js (which is a server-side VM based on the Chrome JavaScript VM). The Dart event-loop model runs your code to completion and then passes control to the event loop, which notifies your code when something interesting happens, such as a file becoming open or data being retrieved from a TCP socket.

Let's start with a basic Dart script—the simplest "Hello World" script, in fact, that you can achieve in a single line that outputs the string `"Hello World"` to the console.

Listing 2.1 HelloWorld.dart

```
main() => print("Hello World");        ⟵ print command outputs to stdout
```

This single-line function, called `main()`, is the entry point for all Dart applications. You can also write it using the more traditional function syntax, with the function body surrounded by curly braces:

```
main() {
  print("Hello World");
}
```

To run this code, save it in a text file, give it a .dart file extension, and pass it as a parameter to the Dart binary found in the downloaded Dart-SDK's bin\ folder. On Windows, this is dart.exe. The output is shown in figure 2.1.

The Dart VM can also be embedded in other applications, but this topic is outside the scope of this book. Possible applications include providing a Dart scripting environment in a text editor, similar to the way the Python runtime is embedded in popular editors such as Sublime Text.

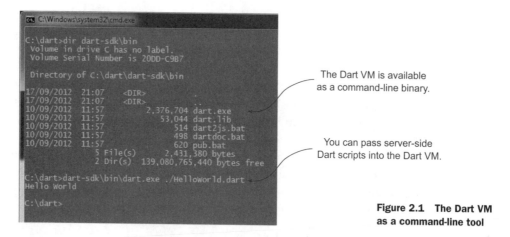

The Dart VM is available as a command-line binary.

You can pass server-side Dart scripts into the Dart VM.

Figure 2.1   The Dart VM as a command-line tool

Although you can run Dart scripts from the command line—and you'll run server-side Dart applications in a production environment from the command line—it isn't ideal as a development tool. Fortunately, the Dart Editor, which we'll look at next, lets you run command-line Dart VM executables in the Dart Editor, along with running Dart in the browser-hosted Dart VM.

We'll look in much more depth at server-side programming, including the event loop and accessing server-side resources such as files, in part 4 of this book, where you'll build a web server and use HMTL5 web sockets to communicate with Dart running in the browser.

> **Remember**
> - The Dart VM is available as a server-side binary that runs from the command line.
> - The server-side Dart VM has full access to server-side APIs, such as the filesystem and network sockets.

2.2   *"Hello World" with the Dart Editor*

The Dart Editor has a growing number of essential tools to help you develop and debug Dart code. Some of these are code navigation, code autocomplete, refactoring, and information about errors and warnings. Although Dart—like many dynamic, interpreted languages—can be written in just about any text editor, the Dart development team has put significant effort into providing a fully featured developer experience that is often missing from other JavaScript alternatives.

You'll start by using the Dart Editor to run the same HelloWorld.dart script in the server-side Dart VM, this time launched from the Dart Editor. Then you'll modify the script to enable it to be hosted in an HTML page and run in the browser-based Dart VM, which is built into the Dartium web browser that comes bundled with the Dart Editor.

Figure 2.2 shows the Dart Editor that you'll be working with throughout the rest of the book.

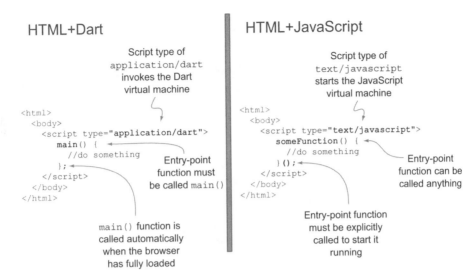

HTML+Dart

Script type of
`application/dart`
invokes the Dart
virtual machine

```
<html>
  <body>
    <script type="application/dart">
      main() {
        //do something
      };
    </script>
  </body>
</html>
```

Entry-point
function must
be called `main()`

`main()` function is
called automatically
when the browser
has fully loaded

HTML+JavaScript

Script type of
`text/javascript`
starts the JavaScript
virtual machine

```
<html>
  <body>
    <script type="text/javascript">
      someFunction() {
        //do something
      }();
    </script>
  </body>
</html>
```

Entry-point
function can be
called anything

Entry-point function
must be explicitly
called to start it
running

Figure 2.2   The Dart Editor is a lightweight version of the Eclipse tool.

2.2.1   *Exploring the Dart Editor tools*

The Dart Editor provides the standard range of developer tools such as method and property autocomplete, refactoring, code navigation, and syntax checking and debugging. When you edit your app with the Dart Editor, your code, and the code of all the external libraries that make up your application, is validated for errors and warnings. Internally, the Dart Editor uses the dart_analyzer tool to provide static analysis of the Dart code. This tool can also be used on the command line—for example, to integrate it into a continuous-build system such as Hudson, CruiseControl, or Bamboo.

> **NOTE**   At the time of writing, the command-line version of the dart_analyzer tool is available only on Mac and Linux platforms. The Windows version is still under development.

You can use the output from dart_analyzer in the Dart Editor to highlight lines of code that that may contain errors or could be considered warnings, as shown in figure 2.3.

This error-checking also allows the Dart Editor to provide some quick-fix capabilities. For example, the Editor gives you the option to create a new prnt (String string) function stub based on its knowledge of the missing prnt() method. The warning shown in figure 2.3 is telling you that a + method is missing on the String object. This may be valid code, as you'll see when we look at handling noSuchMethod() in chapter 7, so it's flagged as a warning rather than an error. You can execute code that contains warnings; you can't execute code that contains errors.

When you run the "Hello World" script, its output is redirected to the Dart Editor's own console instead of running in a separate console window. The Dart Editor is using the same Dart VM binary that you used in the previous section when you ran the

Trying to concatenate
two strings with a
+ operator produces
a warning. This code
will be allowed to run
but may cause
a runtime exception.

A straightforward typo,
trying to call a `prnt()`
function instead of a
`print()` function,
is highlighted as an error.

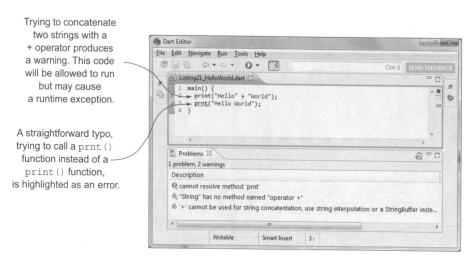

Figure 2.3   Errors and warnings are shown in the Dart Editor.

"Hello World" script from the command line. Figure 2.4 shows the output in the Editor's console window.

The Dart Editor contains a number of tools to help you navigate around code: your own code and any external libraries you're using, whether brought in from the Dart SDK or open source libraries.

CODE NAVIGATION AND THE STANDARD LIBRARIES

The Dart project is open source. That philosophy is baked into the language, and as such, all the standard library code is open source, too. Thus, using the Editor's code-navigation features, if you want to see what the `dart:html` ButtonElement class looks like or examine the `dart:core` List code structure and comments, they're right there at your fingertips in plain text.

You can navigate directly from your code to the declaration site by using the Open Declaration (F3) command. This command works for both your own code and any other libraries you import. It's useful, for example, to be able to navigate a hierarchy of method calls throughout several libraries to discover the underlying reason for a particular bug or way of working—especially when you're developing in a team and

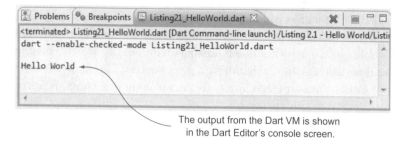

The output from the Dart VM is shown
in the Dart Editor's console screen.

Figure 2.4   The Dart VM produces output in the Editor console.

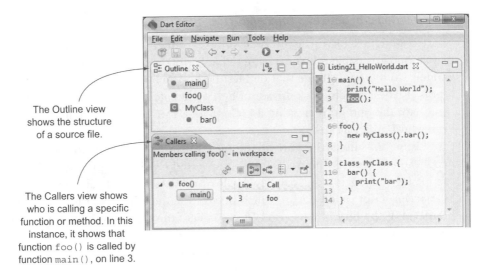

The Outline view shows the structure of a source file.

The Callers view shows who is calling a specific function or method. In this instance, it shows that function `foo()` is called by function `main()`, on line 3.

Figure 2.5   The Dart Editor Callers and Outline views

someone else has implemented an underlying library or you're using third-party libraries from the web.

The Dart Editor also has useful Outline and Callers views. The Outline view lets you visualize the outline of your source file, showing top-level functions, classes, and class members. The Callers view, which you activate on a specific function or method, shows which location in your code calls that function. This is similar to Find References in Java and C# tools. Figure 2.5 shows an example.

CODE SUGGEST AND AUTOCOMPLETE

Code autocomplete, although not always needed if you know the source and libraries well enough, is incredibly useful when you're learning a new library and its features. It lets you see the available methods immediately, in the code, under the cursor. Is there a Sort method on the List class? Is there a way to get a list of char codes from a String? Code autocomplete will tell you this without your needing to leave the Editor—in fact, without leaving the text Editor pane.

This feature is useful when you're working with someone else's code, whether it was written by someone else on your team or taken from other projects that you're using. It could be said that you should not need autocomplete if you knew all the methods and their parameters by heart, but the reality of today's open source frameworks is that they change rapidly, and having method and parameter information directly in your code can only help.

Code navigation, autocomplete, and error information are common tools that many developers have used elsewhere, and they're unsurprising in their use. They're worth noting because few JavaScript editors have these features. One of Dart's design goals is to make developers' lives better when developing web applications, and these three tools help to achieve this.

2.2.2   *The relationship between Dart and HTML files*

Dart is designed to run in the web browser, either as native Dart or converted to JavaScript. To enable this conversion to JavaScript, your application needs to exist separately from the HTML file that defines the host web page. Fortunately, the Dart Editor is also designed to work this way: when you create a new project in the Dart Editor, you have the option of creating a boilerplate HTML file that contains a script tag to run your Dart application.

Listing 2.2 shows the bare-minimum HTML that you need to enable your Dart application to run as either a Dart or a converted JavaScript application. It contains a script tag linking to your existing HelloWorld.dart script. It also contains another JavaScript script called dart.js, which detects whether the host browser contains the Dart VM. If the host browser isn't Dart enabled, the script modifies any application/dart scripts to application/javascript and appends a .js suffix to any `src` properties in those script tags: for example, it changes HelloWorld.dart to HelloWorld.dart.js. The following JavaScript version of your Dart app, as you'll see shortly, is created by the dart2js tool.

> **Listing 2.2   HTML file that can run your Dart app in both Dart and JavaScript**

```
<!DOCTYPE html>
<html>
  <body>
    <script type="application/dart" src="HelloWorld.dart"></script>
    <script src="http://dart.googlecode.com/
              svn/branches/bleeding_edge/
              dart/client/dart.js"></script>
  </body>
</html>
```

Script referencing your Dart application file

dart.js JavaScript file allows non-Dart-enabled browsers to link to HelloWorld.dart.js instead

The code built into the linked dart.js, which is included in the HTML, contains a snippet of JavaScript that checks to see whether the function `navigator.webkitStartDart` exists in the browser. You can also use this check in your code to determine whether you're running in a Dart-enabled browser.

Figure 2.6 shows the relationship between the host HTML file and your "Hello World" Dart script.

2.2.3   *Running "Hello World" with Dartium*

From the Dart Editor, you can run this app the same that you did with the Dart VM version. The Dart Editor detects that there is an associated HTML file and loads the app into the Dartium web browser, served from its own built-in server. This built-in server lists all the Dart applications that are currently available in the Editor, as shown in figure 2.7.

"Hello World" uses the `print()` function to output a message. When running in a web browser, `print()` outputs to the browser's debug console, similar to the JavaScript

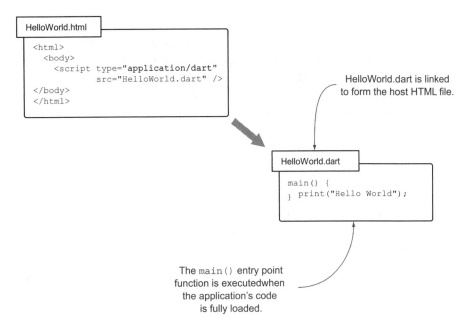

Figure 2.6   HTML links to external Dart files

console.log() function. The Dartium web browser can communicate with the Dart
Editor, and any text that appears in the Dartium debug console is sent back to the
Dart Editor's console. Dartium also knows about breakpoints in the Dart Editor, and
code will pause execution in the Dart Editor when a specific breakpoint is reached.
We'll look at this debugging feature a little later in the chapter.

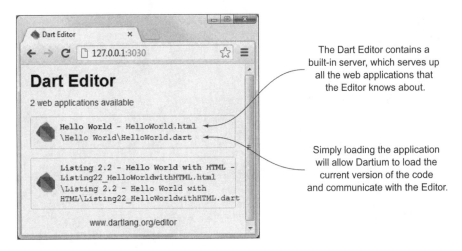

Figure 2.7   Viewing the Dart Editor's web server from Dartium

2.2.4 *Using dart2js to convert to JavaScript*

When your application user doesn't use a browser that runs Dart natively, they must use the JavaScript version of your app. Fortunately, you can convert Dart code to JavaScript using the dart2js tool (more on that later), which outputs a .js (JavaScript) file that contains a compiled version of the .dart app. The dart2js tool actively removes redundant code, so you can import as many external Dart libraries as you wish, safe in the knowledge that only the code that's used in your app ends up as JavaScript. You access the dart2js tool from the Editor by selecting Tools > Generate JavaScript from the Editor's menu.

The complete output of your "Hello World" application contains the readable JavaScript shown in the following listing. It includes the code to start a Dart isolate (the execution unit in Dart) and the print() functionality from the core Dart libraries. The dart2js tool also outputs a sourcemap file, which modern browsers can use to show the original Dart file. Thus although you can view the output JavaScript, you don't need to.

Listing 2.3 HelloWorld.dart.js: output of dart2js

```
// Generated by dart2js, the Dart to JavaScript compiler.
// The code supports the following hooks:
// dartPrint(message)   - if this function is defined it is called
//                         instead of the Dart [print] method.
// dartMainRunner(main) - if this function is defined, the Dart [main]
//                         method will not be invoked directly.
//                         Instead, a closure that will invoke [main] is
//                         passed to [dartMainRunner].
function Isolate() {}
init();

var $$ = {};
var $ = Isolate.$isolateProperties;
$.Primitives_printString = function(string) {
  if (typeof dartPrint == "function") {
    dartPrint(string);
    return;
  }
  if (typeof console == "object") {
    console.log(string);
    return;
  }
  if (typeof write == "function") {
    write(string);
    write("\n");
  }
};

$.print = function(obj) {
  $.Primitives_printString(obj);
};

$.main = function() {
  return $.print('Hello World');
};
```

main() function with
print statement

```
var $ = null;
Isolate = Isolate.$finishIsolateConstructor(Isolate);
var $ = new Isolate();
//
// BEGIN invoke [main].
//
if (typeof document != 'undefined' && document.readyState != 'complete') {
  document.addEventListener('readystatechange', function () {
    if (document.readyState == 'complete') {
      if (typeof dartMainRunner == 'function') {
        dartMainRunner(function() { $.main(); });
      } else {
        $.main();
      }
    }
  }, false);
} else {
  if (typeof dartMainRunner == 'function') {
    dartMainRunner(function() { $.main(); });
  } else {
    $.main();
  }
}
//
// END invoke [main].
//
function init() {
Isolate.$isolateProperties = {};
Isolate.$finishIsolateConstructor = function(oldIsolate) {
  var isolateProperties = oldIsolate.$isolateProperties;
  var isolatePrototype = oldIsolate.prototype;
  var str = "{\n";
  str += "var properties = Isolate.$isolateProperties;\n";
  for (var staticName in isolateProperties) {
    if (Object.prototype.hasOwnProperty.call(isolateProperties, staticName))
      {
        str += "this." + staticName + "= properties." + staticName + ";\n";
      }
  }
  str += "}\n";
  var newIsolate = new Function(str);
  newIsolate.prototype = isolatePrototype;
  isolatePrototype.constructor = newIsolate;
  newIsolate.$isolateProperties = isolateProperties;
  return newIsolate;
};
}
//@ sourceMappingURL=HelloWorld.dart.js.map
```

Linked sourcemap file

Now that you have your application code available as both Dart and JavaScript code (from a single Dart source), it's possible to let the browser switch between the Dart implementation of the app and the JavaScript version. If the browser understands Dart, it will load the .dart code. If not, it will get the .js version of the code.

NOTE   Unlike Google's Java-based Google Web Toolkit (GWT) product, which outputs different JavaScript files for each targeted browser, dart2js outputs a single JavaScript source. Dart is designed to convert to a single JavaScript output for running in modern web browsers.

2.2.5   *Generating documentation with dartdoc*

Also in the Editor's' toolset is the dartdoc tool, which you can use to generate API documentation. If you add a doc comment to your `main()` function, as shown in the following snippet, you can generate the appropriate API doc:

```
/// This is the entry point function
/// and outputs Hello World to the console
main() {
  print("Hello World");
}
```

Function documentation read by dartdoc

The API documentation that's output is the same as that used by the Dart API docs hosted at http://api.dartlang.org. The dartdoc for the "Hello World" app is shown in figure 2.8.

2.2.6   *Debugging Dart with breakpoints*

The Dartium browser and the Dart Editor work in conjunction to enable breakpoints and step-by-step debugging. When you set a breakpoint in the code and run your app with Dartium, two-way communication between the Dart Editor and Dartium allows the Dart Editor to break when your code reaches the breakpoint. In this respect, you get functionality similar to what you might expect from Java or C# application development. You can watch variables, browse the stack, and step over and into method and function calls, all from the Dart Editor.

Figure 2.8   Generated dartdoc for your "Hello World" application

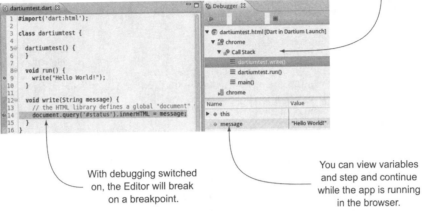

The call stack shows the function and method calls taken to get to this point.

With debugging switched on, the Editor will break on a breakpoint.

You can view variables and step and continue while the app is running in the browser.

Figure 2.9 Setting breakpoints and debugging in the Dart Editor

Figure 2.9 shows this behavior in action, with the source code on the left and the debugger with the call stack and local variables running on the right.

> **Remember**
> - The Dart Editor comes bundled with the Dart SDK and the Dartium browser.
> - Many code navigation and editing tools are available in the Editor, including code refactoring, the Callers view, and the Outline view.
> - The dart_analyzer tool is used for static analysis of the code. It produces errors and warnings that appear in the Dart Editor.
> - You can create an HTML-formatted API document from your code comments using the dartdoc tool.
> - The Dart Editor and Dartium communicate with each other to provide an integrated, round-trip debugging solution.

Live debugging of web apps is a powerful tool. Having the ability to set breakpoints directly from either the Dart Editor (in which you have a quick edit, save, and refresh cycle) is a powerful aid to getting your app working perfectly.

You've seen how to edit Dart using the Dart Editor tools and run Dart in the Dart Editor. It's time to look at using Dart to drive a user interface.

2.3 *Importing libraries to update the browser UI*

In this section, we look more at how Dart communicates with the browser DOM using the dart:html library. Using the Dart Editor and Dartium to provide quick updates of your code, you'll modify your HTML file to contain a single <div> element with a DOM

ID of "status". You'll reference this status <div> in your "Hello World" script, updating the content of the script with a "Hello World" string. The following listing shows the new status <div> you're adding.

Listing 2.4   HelloWorld.html with status <div>

```
<!DOCTYPE html>
<html>
  <body>
    <div id="status">Waiting for Dart...</div>                  You'll modify the content of
    <script type="application/dart" src="HelloWorld.dart"></script>   this <div> in your Dart app.
    <script src="http://dart.googlecode.com/
                svn/branches/bleeding_edge/dart/client/dart.js"></script>
  </body>
</html>
```

Now that you have an element in your HTML page, you can modify your Dart script to update it. You'll replace the print statement with one that gets the <div> element from the page. In order to do this, you need to use one of the built-in libraries, called dart:html. The dart:html library is designed to provide all the HTML APIs that you expect from the browser DOM, but in a consistent manner, with Dart-style API access; you'll see much more of this library throughout the book. If you're used to using jQuery with JavaScript, then the dart:html library should feel familiar.

2.3.1   Importing Dart libraries

To import a library, you use the import statement. The import statement comes in three variations, which we'll look at in more detail in chapter 5. The first is used to import core libraries, such as dart:html. In this case, you use the dart: prefix, in this form:

```
import "dart:html";
```

Because this library is built into the Dart SDK, the tools know automatically where to find it.

The second flavor of import is used to import third-party dependencies. It uses the package: prefix:

```
import "package:unittest/unittest.dart";                 We look at Dart's unit-test
                                                         framework in chapter 3.
```

Libraries imported using the package: prefix are resolved using pub, Dart's package-manager tool, which is available for use on the command line or in the Dart Editor.

Pub can pull dependencies from the internet using code repositories such as GitHub or Dart's own pub.dartlang.org repository. In this form, it serves a purpose similar to that of Java's Maven, .NET's NuGet, and node.js's npm tool. The most important commands are as follows:

```
pub install
pub update
```

The first command installs the dependencies required, and the second updates them. Pub is a new tool and will likely evolve to provide a number of features, such as setting up boilerplate websites and frameworks.

The final flavor of the `import` statement imports your own local or other local libraries by file path, for example:

```
import "./myLibraries/helloLibrary.dart";
```

This form uses an implicit URI to access Dart libraries, which should be accessible by the Dart tools. When you convert Dart to JavaScript, all these imported libraries are pulled together into a single JavaScript file, containing only the code that is used.

2.3.2 Accessing DOM elements with dart:html

Figure 2.10 adds `import "dart:html";` into your Dart code and shows the modified `main()` function, which updates the `status` `<div>` with the text `"Hello World"`. The `dart:html` library provides the `query()` function shown.

The `query()` function is similar to jQuery's `$()` function, which queries the browser DOM by using CSS selectors.

CSS selectors

CSS selectors are patterns you can use to pick items out of the browser DOM, and the two most common are `#id` and `.class`. There are plenty of tutorials available on the web, but the following is provided as a reminder.

Given the following two lines of HTML

```
<div id="firstLine" class="myTextBlock">This is div number 1</div>
<div id="secondLine" class="myTextBlock">This is div number 2</div>
```

you can select both lines by using the CSS selector `.myTextBlock` (because they both share the same class), but you select the lines individually by using their ID values `#firstLine` and `#secondLine`. IDs should be unique, but multiple elements can share a class.

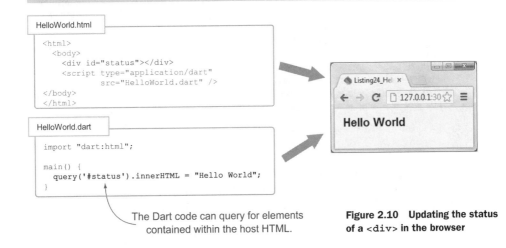

The Dart code can query for elements contained within the host HTML.

Figure 2.10   Updating the status of a `<div>` in the browser

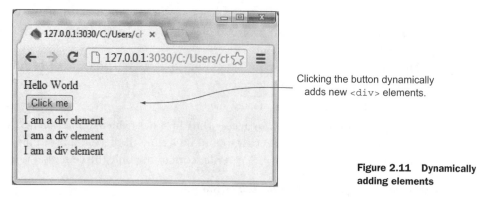

Clicking the button dynamically adds new <div> elements.

Figure 2.11 Dynamically adding elements

2.3.3 *Dynamically adding new elements to the page*

You've seen how you can modify elements that already exist in the HTML page that's hosting the Dart app, but a single-page application is responsible for building its own user interface from code. This means you need to be able to dynamically create elements. Let's modify the "Hello World" app once again: this time, add a button that, when clicked, adds a new <div> containing the "Hello World" string. The output will look like figure 2.11.

All browser elements inherit from a base Element object. You have a number of ways to create elements dynamically, by using a tag name, an HTML string, or, for common elements such as Buttons, a specific ButtonElement class. We'll look again at creating elements in the next chapter and in much more detail in part 3 of the book, when we deal with building client-side web apps.

The next listing shows the modified "Hello World" app, which builds up the user interface.

Listing 2.5 HelloWorld.dart: creating elements dynamically

```
import "dart:html";

main() {
  query("#status").innerHTML = "Hello World";      // Modifies existing #status element

  var button = new ButtonElement();                // Creates new button element
  button.text = "Click me";                        // Sets text property on button
  button.on.click.add( (e) {
    var div = new Element.html("<div>I am a div element</div>");   // "on click" event-handler function creates <div> from HTML string
    document.body.elements.add(div);
  });

  document.body.elements.add(button);              // Dynamically adds button to page
}
```

In this snippet, you created some browser elements dynamically and hooked up your button to an event handler. This event-handler function is an example of an anonymous function, which we'll look at in more detail in chapter 4.

Remember

- Dart uses the `dart:html` library to provide access to browser DOM APIs and elements.
- Your app can create elements dynamically and add them to the browser DOM.
- You can use the pub package-management tool to import external libraries.
- You can import libraries directly on the filesystem.

2.4 Summary

In this chapter, we've examined the tools that are available to the Dart developer. Many languages have the same aims as Dart, but few of them provide the rich tool set that goes along with the language:

- The Dart Editor, Dartium, and the Dart VM provide tools to help you write, run, and debug Dart code.
- dart2js converts Dart code to JavaScript, which targets modern web browsers.
- Dart has built-in libraries that let you interact with the web browser's DOM in a friendly manner.

Using the Dart Editor and Dartium together should aid you as you learn and experiment with the Dart language and core libraries. The quick develop-and-run cycle that you get by being able to run Dart code directly in the Dartium web browser, without needing a compile step, gives you a great productivity boost, because it becomes simple to try parts of the language and see your results immediately.

In the next chapter, you'll start to build a real client-side Dart application. We'll take a high-level look at some of the Dart language concepts you'll see again in more depth throughout the rest of the book, including optional typing and classes. You'll also see how you can use Dart's unit-test framework to begin testing your app.

Building and testing
your own Dart app

3

This chapter covers

- Building a user interface in the browser
- Reacting to user events
- Reusing code with functions
- Getting familiar with Dart classes
- Writing simple unit tests

It's time to get your hands on some real Dart code. Using the core language constructs of variables, functions, and classes, you'll build a simple browser-based packing-list app called PackList to let users keep track of things to take on their vacations. One of Dart's design goals is to be familiar; this chapter should help you feel comfortable with the Dart functionality around variables, functions, and classes before we get to the more surprising and interesting features in later chapters.

Instead of building the simple user interface in raw HTML, you'll build it using `Element` classes from the built-in `dart:html` library. At the time of writing, no GUI or widget library is available as part of the Dart SDK, although various open source

PackList is a client-side app that lets a user add items to take on holiday and cross them off as they're packed.

It can be served from any web server as static .html and .dart files (or dart2js converted JavaScript), because there is no server-side processing involved.

Figure 3.1   The PackList application

third-party libraries are in development. It's the Dart development team's goal to make Dart a "batteries included" solution, and a UI library will eventually be included in the SDK. For now, though, you can build user interfaces by manipulating HTML elements in Dart code; knowledge of how to do this will also help you when a UI library does appear, because you'll be more confident with the underlying mechanisms behind the widgets.

Although the PackList example app is straightforward and simplistic for example purposes, in the real world you would also create a single-page web application this way. The simple UI will contain an input text box to take some input from the user, a button for the user to click, and a <div> to display the list of items that the user wants to take on holiday. Your application will react to user events by adding event-listener functions that allow the user to add items to the list and mark them as packed. Finally, you'll create a class to hold the item (and whether it has been packed). This design provides the code with structure and reusability.

The PackList example isn't concerned with the server-side part of a web app—the app can be run in a browser directly from a local file (although you could also host the files on a web server). PackList runs only in the client; I'll discuss sending data back and forth between the client and the server in a chapter 14. The app should end up looking like figure 3.1.

By the end of the chapter, you'll have a working browser-hosted, single-page application and a set of simple unit tests that you can use to validate your code.

3.1   Building a UI with dart:html

A single-page application like the PackList app builds its UI by executing code in your web browser to create and manipulate HTML elements. This approach has the advantage of keeping the UI display logic in the browser (such as making layout decisions based on the state of the user's data), which can ultimately free up server resources to serve more users. In the single-page application design, the server would send the Dart application code to the browser as static files and then send data to the browser once the app starts running.

You'll build the PackList app from an entry-point HTML file that hosts the Dart script, and a Dart code file that creates and attaches HTML elements to the HTML document in the browser.

3.1.1 *Entry-point HTML*

All browser-based Dart apps must be hosted by an HTML file. This is your entry-point HTML file, which references your app's .dart file using an HTML <script> tag. The .dart file contains the main() function of your application, which is called automatically when the Dart code is fully loaded and ready to start. The minimal HTML file needs to contain a <script> tag referencing the Dart source code, which looks like the following:

**Dart <script> tag loads .dart file
and starts main() function running**

```
<html>
  <body>
    <script type="application/dart" src="packList.dart"></script>
  </body>
</html>
```

The Dart Editor can create these files for you when you use the New Application Wizard and select the Web Application option. The HTML file that's created also has a useful JavaScript tag that loads the packList.dart.js (JavaScript version) of your app if the browser doesn't natively support Dart.

> **TIP** *Dart isn't running?* The Dart Editor Wizard creates a sample HTML file and a sample .dart file. Before you start writing your application, remove the example class from the .dart file and the <h1> and <h2> tags from the .html file; otherwise, you'll see the "Dart is not running" message when you run your app in the browser.

Now that you have the entry-point HTML file, which contains a <body> and a <script> tag to load the Dart app, it's time to look at the how you can populate the <body> with HTML elements from within Dart code.

3.1.2 *Creating dart:html elements*

When you're building a UI in Dart, use the dart:html library, which is one of the Dart libraries in the Dart SDK. dart:html provides a standardized way for you to interact with the browser by abstracting away a number of the idiosyncrasies of the browser DOM (in a manner similar to the jQuery library that's popular with JavaScript). Using dart:html, you can create HTML elements (such as buttons, <div>s, and so on) and attach them to the browser. HTML elements are represented using the parent Element class (and subclasses, such as DivElement and ButtonElement), and you get programmatic access to all the properties and methods available on the HTML elements. Elements can contain child elements, have IDs and styles, and have event listeners attached.

TIP Actually, you're working with an implementation of the `Element` (and `DivElement` and `ButtonElement`) interfaces, but this is transparent to you, the coder—you have an instance of something that "looks like" an `Element`. I'll talk more about interfaces and their relation to classes in chapter 6.

There are two ways of creating HTML elements in Dart; one creates an empty HTML tag that you need to populate programmatically, such as `<div></div>`. The other produces a prebuilt HTML tag, as in

```
<h2 id="title">Pack<em>List</em></h2>
```

To create a new `Element`, call the `dart:html` `Element` constructor using the new keyword. This step creates a new `Element` object for you to store in a variable and then attach to the body. The first way that `dart:html` allows you to create elements creates an empty HTML tag:

```
var myElement = new Element.tag('div');
```
◁— **HTML tag name**

The second way constructs an element containing the child elements and properties that you specify in the snippet:

```
var myElement = new Element.html(
           '<h2 id="title">Pack<em>List</em></h2>');
```
◁— **HTML tag**

Both approaches have their advantages, and we'll look at them in this section as you build up your app's UI.

The PackList application will have an `<h2>` title heading, a text box, a button, and a `<div>` element, to contain each of the items to take on holiday. You'll create each of these elements in Dart code and add them to the document body; the resulting HTML will look something like figure 3.2.

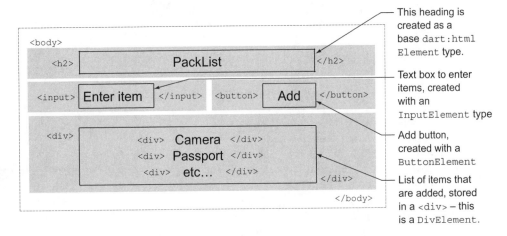

Figure 3.2 The layout of the PackList application

3.1.3   *Creating a new Element from HTML snippets*

Creating `Elements` with the constructor `new Element.html("...some html...")` is useful when you want to provide a string of HTML to create an element and one of the following is true:

- You know in advance what the element (and its child elements) will look like.
- You don't need to reference each child element individually as a variable in Dart (you can still access them later by querying for them).

You can pass any string of HTML into the `Element.html` constructor, as long as it results in a single top-level HTML element:

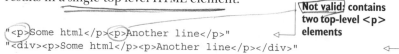

```
"<p>Some html</p><p>Another line</p>"
"<div><p>Some html</p><p>Another line</p></div>"
```

Not valid: contains two top-level `<p>` elements

Allowed because both paragraph elements are wrapped in a single `<div>` element

---

Declaring strings in Dart

When you declare a string in Dart, you have a number of choices. You can declare a multiline string by using a triple quote, such as

```
var myString = """<div>
   <p>a multiline string</p>
</div>""";
```

This stores a string that's formatted as follows:

```
<div>
   <p>a multiline string</p>
</div>
```

When you declare a multiline string, the string is stored exactly as defined, including any whitespace, which can affect readability. Thus this string

```
var myString = """<div>
                  <p>a multiline string</p>
               </div>""";
```

outputs the following string (which probably isn't what was intended):

```
<div>
                  <p>a multiline string</p>
               </div>
```

Fortunately, for HTML snippets, we don't care whether the final string is multiline, but we do care about readable code. Dart lets you automatically concatenate adjacent string literals (if you have two strings next to each other, even across line breaks, they'll be concatenated). Therefore, the following two string declarations store identical (but not multiline) values:

```
var myString = "<div>" "<p>a string</p>" "</div>";
var myString = "<div>"
                  "<p>a string</p>"
               "</div>";
```

The second `myString` makes for nice, readable code but doesn't affect the HTML output.

An ideal use for the `Element.html` constructor is something like

```
var paragraphContent = "Some about box text";
Element infoBoxDiv = new Element.html("""
<div id='infoBox'>
   <h3>About PackList</h3>
   <p>$paragraphContent</p>
</div>""");
```

Creates multiline string with triple quotes

Embeds paragraphContent variable into HTML snippet with $ prefix

This is an ideal set of elements, because you don't need to reference the child elements of the `aboutBox` `<div>` and the text is relatively static. The `paragraphContent` variable is embedded within the multiline string.

> ## Embedding variables into a String declaration
> Dart also provides an easy way to embed a variable into a string: `$variableName` or `${expression}`. This feature lets you declare a string as follows:
>
> ```
> var myValue = 1234;
> var myString = "<p>$myValue</p>";
> var myOtherString = "<p>${myValue + 1}</p>";
> ```
>
> These examples store the value `"<p>1234</p>"` in `myString` and `"<p>1235</p>"` in `myOtherString`.

When you create an element using the `Element.html` named constructor, you can still access all the properties and methods on the element variable, as in

Adds another child element to the infoBox

```
infoBoxDiv.children.add(new Element.html("<p>a second paragraph</p>"));
var id = infoBoxDiv.id;
```

Reads `<div id='infoBox'>` value

The second way to create HTML elements is to use the `Element.tag()` constructor, which provides you with an empty element that you can populate and manipulate in Dart code.

3.1.4 Creating elements by tag name

Sometimes you want to define all the properties dynamically at runtime. The second way of creating an `Element` is by tag name, which gives you an empty tag ready for manipulation, as in the following code:

```
var itemInput = new Element.tag("input");
```

This example create an `InputElement` that maps to the HTML:

```
<input></input>
```

You can then populate some of the HTML element's properties using the `itemInput` object's fields:

```
itemInput.id = "txt-item";
itemInput.placeholder = "Enter an item";
```

This creates HTML that looks like the following:

```
<input id="txt-item" placeholder="Enter an Item"></input>
```

TIP The placeholder text in an input box is the light-gray text that disappears when you start typing in the text box.

Whether you use `Element.tag()` or `Element.html()`, you get back an object that looks like a `dart:html Element`. Sometimes, though, it's useful to access the extra properties available on specific element types, such as `InputElement` or `ButtonElement`. With Dart's optional typing, the running code doesn't care if you specify the actual type of the element, but it can be useful to declare specific types of element so the type checker can help by providing warnings if you try to use the element in ways that don't make sense for that particular object. For example, you could use any of the following to create a new text box:

```
var itemInput = new Element.tag("input");
Element itemInput = new Element.tag("input");
InputElement itemInput = new Element.tag("input");
```

The third line, which specifies that the `itemInput` is an `InputElement` (rather than something else, like a `ButtonElement` or `DivElement`) lets the tools (and other readers of your code) confirm that you intend to deal with an `InputElement`. You also get handy code-completion with specific properties and methods for the `InputElement` from the Dart Editor.

All the elements that you expect to find in HTML have an equivalent type defined in the `dart:html` library, including the latest HTML5 elements such as `CanvasElement`.

TIP Dart also provides the `dart:dom` library. It provides direct access to the browser DOM and acts as an equivalent to JavaScript DOM manipulation, at the expense of losing the ability to work with a consistent Dart `Element` interface.

Now that you can create elements using the `Element.tag()` and `Element.html()` constructors, you can add them to the HTML document to show them in the browser.

3.1.5 Adding elements to an HTML document

An HTML document's visible content is contained within its `<body>` tags. When you create elements with the `dart:html` library, you add these elements to the document's `<body>` tag. `dart:html` defines a `document` property in the top level of the library, which itself contains a `body` element property. Reference this `document.body` property in code, using the form

```
document.body.children.add(...some element...)
```

TIP The top-level document also defines a `document.head` property, which is useful for dynamically attaching elements such as `meta-keywords` or document `title` elements into the HTML page header.

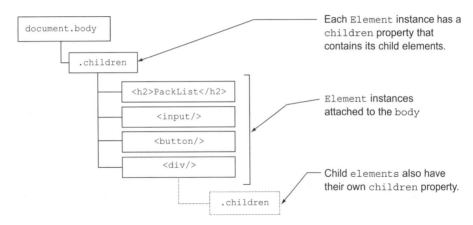

Figure 3.3   The body element has a number of child elements.

document.body itself is an Element, and all Elements have their own children property, which allows you to build up parent/child hierarchies of elements as shown in figure 3.3.

The PackList app requires that you add a title, wrapped in an <h2> tag, and you'll use the Element.html() constructor for this. Also create the input text box and the button using the Element.tag() constructor. The following listing shows the lines of code you need, wrapped in the main() method (which is called automatically when the application starts running).

Listing 3.1   Adding a new Element to the document body

```dart
import "dart:html";                    // Imports dart:html library

main() {
  var title = new Element.html("<h2>PackList</h2>");   // Creates title element from HTML snippet
  document.body.children.add(title);                    // Adds title to document body

  InputElement itemInput = new Element.tag("input");    // Creates and adds input text box
  document.body.children.add(itemInput);

  ButtonElement addButton = new Element.tag("button");  // Creates and adds Add button
  document.body.children.add(addButton);

  DivElement itemContainer = new Element.tag("div");
  document.body.children.add(itemContainer);
}
```

When the application starts running, you get HTML that contains the following snippet:

```html
<body>
  <h2>PackList</h2>        // h2 node added to HTML body
  <input></input>          // Input text box added to body
  <button></button>        // Button added to body
</body>
```

In addition to adding the elements to the body, you need to populate some properties on your new elements, such as these:

```
inputButton.placeholder = "Enter an item";
addButton.text = "Add";
addButton.id = "add-btn";
```

It doesn't make any difference whether you do this before or after the element is added to the browser body—the browser will update as required to reflect the current state of the HTML elements.

Finally, to complete your UI, you need to add a <div> element to contain your list of holiday items. By using some element.style properties (shown in listing 3.2), you can apply styling information directly to the <div> (in the real world, use CSS for layout formatting).

When you run your app, it produces the UI shown in figure 3.4. The following listing shows the full code to create this UI, which creates the four elements and sets the properties.

Listing 3.2 Building the PackList UI

```
import "dart:html";

main() {
  var title = new Element.html("<h2>PackList</h2>");
  document.body.children.add(title);

  InputElement itemInput = new Element.tag("input");      ⟵ Sets properties on
  itemInput.id = "txt-item";                                  InputElement
  itemInput.placeholder = "Enter an item";
  document.body.children.add(itemInput);

  ButtonElement addButton = new Element.tag("button");    ⟵ Sets properties on
  addButton.id = "btn-add";                                   ButtonElement
  addButton.text = "Add";
  document.body.children.add(addButton);

  DivElement itemContainer = new Element.tag("div");      ⟵ Sets properties
  itemContainer.id = "items";                                 on DivElement
  itemContainer.style.width = "300px";
  itemContainer.style.border = "1px solid black";
  itemContainer.innerHTML = " ";                     ⟵ Sets content of <div> to
  document.body.children.add(itemContainer);                 be a single nonbreaking
}                                                             space ( )
```

Figure 3.4 The PackList UI

This code is somewhat contrived for the purpose of example. By using the `Element`
`.html` constructor, you could also create the `itemContainer` `DivElement` more con-
cisely, as follows:

```
DivElement itemContainer = new Element.html('<div id="items"
              style="width:300px;border:1px solid black"> </div>');
```

You now have a UI built from Dart code using the `dart:html` library. These are the
building blocks for all Dart UIs.

Remember

- You can create `Element` types using either `Element.html(...snippet...)` or
  `Element.tag(...tag name...)`.
- The `dart:html` library defines all the elements that a modern browser
  understands.
- The Dart Editor can help provide you with autocomplete information for the properties (and the API documentation at api.dartlang.org can help provide more detail).
- Elements become HTML tags in the browser. Properties are attributes on those
  tags.
- All elements (including the `body`) have a `children` property that contains the list
  of its child elements.

The current code in your app only builds a static UI, though. It doesn't react and
change when the user interacts with it. To handle the user clicking the Add button
and add the item entered into the list, you need event listeners, which are a type of
function that we'll look at in the next section.

3.2 *Building interactivity with browser events*

To let your UI react to user events, such as a button click, use event listeners. A
`dart:html` event listener is a function that takes a single `event` parameter, which is a
type that implements the `Event` interface, such as the one in the following snippet:

```
myEventListenerFunction(Event event) {
  window.alert("Look - an event has been triggered");
};
```

The event parameter provides extra information about the event. As with the `Element`
and `ButtonElement` types, `Event` is a general-purpose type. You can handle specific
types of event depending on the element that created the event. For example, if it's a
`MouseEvent`, the event parameter contains a flag to indicate whether the left or right
button was clicked. The PackList app doesn't need to know this, though—it needs to be
aware only that the Add button was clicked, so the general-purpose `Event` object is fine.

3.2.1 *Adding the PackList item from a button click*

The PackList app contains an input box, a button, and a `<div>` in which to put your
PackList items. The basic use case is that when a user clicks the `addButton`, you take

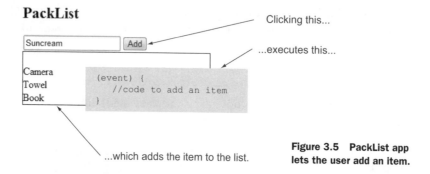

Figure 3.5 PackList app lets the user add an item.

the text from the input box and add it into the `itemContainer`. You should then clear the `inputBox`. This flow is shown in figure 3.5.

You can do this in the click listener for the `addButton` by using the following code, which creates a new `<div>` (of class `item`) containing the `packItem` and adds it to the item container. You need to look out for two pieces of code:

- Where you add a click listener to the `addButton`
- The click listener function itself:

```
main() {
  // ...snip ui element creation code...
  addButton.on.click.add((event) {                    Adds click
    var packItem = itemInput.value;                   listener
    var listElement =
      new Element.html("<div class='item'>${packItem}<div>");    Click listener
    itemContainer.children.add(listElement);                    function body
    itemInput.value= "";
  });
}
```

This code should be added within, and at the end of, the existing `main()` method. Every time a user clicks your Add button, your app now adds their item to the list.

There's a lot of syntax in that new block of code, so let's pull back a bit and see what's going on. We'll look at some of the different ways you can create functions in Dart and how the click listener function is defined, and then we'll examine some of the ways you can specifically use these as click listeners.

3.2.2 *Event handling with Dart's flexible function syntax*

Partly due to Dart's optional typing and partly to provide syntactic sugar, which can save on typing and aid readability, Dart provides a number of ways to define functions. You should get used to spotting them.

TIP Syntactic sugar is a feature of a language that makes things nicer to read or express.

At the highest level, a function in Dart can be declared in either longhand form, which is similar to that in JavaScript, Java, or C#, or shorthand form, which can contain only a single statement and uses the `=>` (lambda) operator to execute and return a single statement.

The longhand form looks like this:

```
void myEventListener(Event event) {
  // do something
  window.alert("an event");
}
```

And the shorthand (or single-line) form looks like this:

```
void myEventListener(Event event) => window.alert("an event");
```

As usual in Dart, the return type and the parameter types are all optional and have no impact on the running of the application. You don't even need to write `void` as a return type.

The single-line function syntax is useful when you want to set a value or call another function. It's also worth noting that the single-line function syntax implicitly returns the value of the call, whereas the longhand version must specify the return value. The two functions here are equivalent:

```
int addValues(int a, int b) {
  return a+b;
}

int addShorthandValues(int a, int b) => a+b;
```

=> operator implicitly returns value of the expression. If no value is created by the expression, it returns null.

It's important to also note that although all the type information is optional, such as the return type and parameter types, the parameters themselves must be named (unlike in JavaScript, in which all parameters are optional). Also unlike in JavaScript, there's no `function` keyword—even the function name is optional. An anonymous function (one without a name) can be stored in a variable or passed directly into another function as a parameter, which is what you're doing with the event handler.

In your PackList app, the line `addButton.on.click.add( )` takes a function as its parameter, and you can pass in your event handler without first giving it a name, as in

```
addButton.on.click.add( (event)  {
  // function body
});
```

or

```
addButton.on.click.add( (event) =>  ...single statement... );
```

You can also store the function in a variable first, as in

```
var myEventListener = (event) {
  // function body
};
addButton.on.click.add(myEventListener);
```

or

```
var myEventListener = (event) => ...single statement... ;
addButton.on.click.add(myEventListener);
```

Longhand (multiline) function syntax	Shorthand (single-line) function syntax
```int someFunction(int a, int b) { return a+b; }```	```int someFunction(int a, int b) => a+b;```
```someFunction(int a, int b) { return a+b; }```	```someFunction(int a, int b) => a+b;```
```someFunction(a, b) { return a+b; }```	```someFunction(a, b) => a+b;```
```var someFunction = (a, b) { return a+b; }```	```var someFunction = (a, b) => a+b;```
```(a, b) { return a+b; }```	```(a, b) => a+b;```

Figure 3.6   Identical functions in both longhand and shorthand form, with varying levels of type information

You'll use functions in Dart in many places, such as to provide reusable blocks of code, and we'll discuss functions in more detail throughout the book.

To help you spot functions when they appear, figure 3.6 shows a list of identical functions written with varying levels of type information, in both longhand and shorthand form. They all perform identically when called (they return the result of a + b).

> **Remember**
> - Functions have a multiline syntax and a shorthand syntax.
> - Function return type information and parameter type information are optional.
> - Anonymous functions can be passed as parameters and stored in variables.

Now that you can create event listener functions, you can continue with the PackList app as we look at some of the events that dart:html can provide.

3.2.3   *Responding to dart:html browser events*

The dart:html library provides a way to handle all the events that a browser can raise on an element. You access this list of events through the element.on property, which in turn contains all the events that an element can react to. For example, some of the events your button could raise include the following:

```
addButton.on.click
addButton.on.drag
addButton.on.mouseMove
```

Each of these events is in fact another list (specifically, an `EventListenerList`) that contains a list of event listeners. You can add your event listener function to that list by using the list's `add()` method, either by function name

```
addButton.on.click.add(myEventListenerFunction);
```

or inline

```
addButton.on.click.add((event) {
  window.alert("I handle events as well");
});
```

or inline by using shorthand function syntax:

```
addButton.on.click.add(event) => window.alert("Me too!"));
```

All three functions show a browser alert dialog. Because the click event is an `EventListenerList`, it's perfectly valid to add all three. Each function will be fired in turn when you provide a single click to the button.

If you wanted to remove the `myEventListenerFunction` (you have a handle to it by name), you could similarly call

```
addButton.on.click.remove(myEventListenerFunction);
```

which would remove the same function from the event listener list.

Your PackList app currently uses an anonymous function to handle the button click event, but you can make that function work harder by giving it a name and using it when you get a keyboard event. You need to do some refactoring.

3.2.4   *Refactoring the event listener for reuse*

It would also be useful to allow the application to add an item to the list when the user presses Enter. Adding an event listener to the text box to detect the Enter key is relatively straightforward:

```
itemInput.on.keypress.add( (event) {              keyCode 13 is
  if (event.keyCode == 13) {                   ◁── the Enter key.
    var packItem = itemInput.value;
    var listElement =                                           Copy of block
➡      (new Element.html("<div class='item'>${packItem}<div>");   of code from
    itemContainer.children.add(listElement);                      button click
    itemInput.value= "";                                          listener
  }
} );
```

But you've copied the block in the `if` statement from the `addButton` event handler. Copying a block of code is poor practice. You should extract that block of code into a separate function outside of the `main()` function so it can be reused around the application:

```
addItem() {
  var packItem = itemInput.value;
  var listElement =                                          Block of extracted code
➡      new Element.html("<div class='item'>${packItem}<div>");  from click listener, put
  itemContainer.children.add(listElement);                      into function called
  itemInput.value = "";                                         addItem()
}
```

You can now modify the event listener functions to call the newly extracted `addItem()` function:

```
addButton.on.click.add( (event)  => addItem());

itemInput.on.keypress.add( (event) {
  if (event.keyCode == 13) {
    addItem();
  }
});
```

**addButton
click listener**

**itemInput
keypress listener**

This is great, except that the `addItem()` function no longer works. Because the `inputItem` text box and the `itemContainer` `<div>` variables were declared in the `main()` function, they're now out of scope in the `addItem()` function.

You need to use another feature of the `dart:html` library to allow you to reference these two HTML elements—the ability to query for elements in the browser using CSS selectors.

3.2.5 *Querying HTML elements in dart:html*

You'll often have elements that exist in the browser HTML but to which you don't currently have a variable reference. These might be elements that were added as a result of using the `Element.html()` constructor, or perhaps you've added elements in a different part of your application and you need to retrieve them from the browser. Fortunately, `dart:html` elements have two useful functions: `element.query(...)`, which returns a single element, and `element.queryAll(...)`, which returns a list of matching child elements.

In your PackList app, you need to get a handle to both the `itemInput` text box (to retrieve the user's item) and the `itemContainer` `<div>` (to add the user's item). These elements are both child elements of the body, as shown in figure 3.7.

The following example snippet uses the `queryAll()` function to return all input tags that are children of the body (there will be only one) and retrieve the specific single `items` `<div>` by ID (using the CSS selector #items).

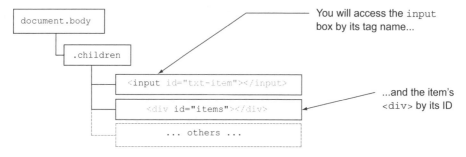

Figure 3.7 The input text box and the `items` `<div>` can both be queried for from the document body.

To get references to the input box and the item container <div>, you need to add the following lines to the top of the addItem() function:

Queries for all input tags that are children of body tag

```
addItem() {
  var itemInput = query("input");

  InputElement itemInput = itemInputList[0];

  DivElement itemContainer = query("#items");
  // ... snip ... rest the function body.
}
```

Selects first (and only) one into itemInput variable

Queries for element with ID #items

In the real world, you'd access these two items both by #id. The # is a CSS ID selector, which should always return a single element. By contrast, using the line itemContainer.queryAll(".item") returns a list of elements that match the CSS class .item regardless of their specific element type—in this case, they'd be all the PackList item <div>s that the user has added.

The complete app listing so far, which now reacts to events by letting your user add items by either clicking the mouse or pressing Enter, is shown in the next listing.

Listing 3.3 PackList that reacts to user events

```
import 'dart:html';

main() {
  var title = new Element.html("<h2>PackList</h2>");
  document.body.children.add(title);

  InputElement itemInput = new Element.tag("input");
  itemInput.id = "txt-item";
  itemInput.placeholder = "Enter an item";
  itemInput.on.keyPress.add( (event) {
    if (event.keyCode == 13) {
      addItem();
    }
  });
  document.body.children.add(itemInput);

  ButtonElement addButton = new Element.tag("button");
  addButton.id = "btn-add";
  addButton.text = "Add";
  addButton.on.click.add((event) => addItem());
  document.body.children.add(addButton);

  DivElement itemContainer = new Element.tag("div");
  itemContainer.id = "items";
  itemContainer.style.width = "300px";
  itemContainer.style.border = "1px solid black";
  itemContainer.innerHTML = " ";
  document.body.children.add(itemContainer);

}
addItem() {
  var itemInputList = queryAll("input");
  InputElement itemInput = itemInputList[0];
```

addItem() function called when user presses Enter

addItem() function called from a button click

Extracted addItem() function

```
      DivElement itemContainer = query("#items");
      var itemText = itemInput.value;
      var listElement =  new Element.html("<div
                      class='item'>${itemText}<div>");
      itemContainer.children.add(listElement);
      itemInput.value = "";
}
```

Code from original button click listener

You now have a client-side app that lets the user add items to the PackList. It contains a number of `dart:html` elements and a function to allow you to query for the input and output elements; this function is called when the user clicks the mouse or presses Enter. The next step is to let users tick off items as they're packed; in the next section, you'll add a `PackItem` class to wrap this functionality and allow for even better code reuse.

> **Remember**
> - An event listener in `dart:html` is a function that takes a single `event` parameter.
> - You can add multiple event listeners to listen to a single event being raised.
> - `dart:html` allows you to query for a single element with CSS selectors using the `query()` function.
> - Query for multiple child elements with the `queryAll()` function.

3.3 *Wrapping structure and functionality with classes*

The final step in your PackList app is the ability for a user to tick off items that are packed. A user should be able to toggle between an item being packed and not packed by clicking the item.

The simplest way to do this is to add another click listener to each of the items in the list. When the user clicks the item, your click function will add a CSS style to add a strikethrough style to the item.

To do this, refactor the app to add a simple `PackItem` class that does the following:

- Wraps the functionality of each packed item by implementing a toggle between packed and not packed
- Stores some data about the item (its name and whether it's packed)

Figure 3.8 shows the new flow.

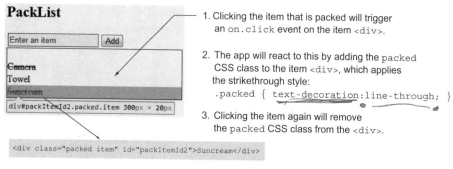

Figure 3.8   The app reacts to the user clicking a packed item by adding a strikethrough.

In order to support the strikethrough, you need to add the following CSS styles to the HTML file (at the top of the <body> section is fine):

```
<body>
  <style type="text/css">
      .item { cursor:pointer; }
      .packed { text-decoration:line-through;  }
  </style>
... etc ...
```

All pack items have a pointer cursor to indicate that they're clickable.

When item is assigned CSS .packed class, text has ~~strikethrough~~ styling.

Now that you have some simple styles in your host HTML file, you can start to create the PackItem class. Put it somewhere above or below your main() function (but not inside):

```
class PackItem {

}
```

3.3.1 Dart classes are familiar

One of Dart's design goals is to be familiar, which is apparent in its class syntax. If you've used classes in C# or Java, then the Dart class structure will seem familiar. Of course, Dart adds a couple of nice features in addition to being a standard, single-inheritance, multiple-interface, class-based language.

One of these features that you may have already noticed is that classes aren't mandatory (unlike in C# and Java). Functions can exist without being wrapped in a class; the main() and addItem() functions exist in the top-level scope without being part of a class. Also unlike in C# and Java, you can put as many classes as you want into a single Dart file—there's no restriction, but you can break your code into separate files to keep your source code organized, a topic covered in chapter 5.

That aside, classes in Dart have constructors, methods, and properties that can be public or private, and they have a special syntax for getters and setters. We'll deal with the constructor first, which will allow you to create PackItems.

3.3.2 Constructing the PackItem class

The basic functionality required for the PackItem class is to store the itemText passed to it from your addItem() function. You can do this using the code in listing 3.4, which defines the class itself and an itemText property and initializes that property with a value passed to the constructor. You also need to add the UI element that will be attached to the UI. Look out for the constructor initializer shorthand for initializing the itemText property (the constructor is a function with the same name as the class).

Listing 3.4 Basic class structure

```
class PackItem {
  var itemText;        ← itemText property
  var uiElement;

  PackItem(this.itemText) {
    //empty constructor body
  }
}
```

(Currently uninitialized) UI element that will be attached to UI

Constructor that accepts single itemText parameter (which also initializes itemText property)

> **WARNING**   Best practice alert! It isn't generally good to mix UI behavior and business logic behavior in the same class as the examples here do by adding the data and the UI element in the same class. It makes unit testing your app harder and represents a tightly coupled application design; but for the purpose of example, the single example class will contain both the UI behavior and the business logic (is it packed or not?). A better design would have two classes: one responsible for UI layout and the other to hold and manipulate your data. You could then loosely couple one to the other, a technique I use later in the book when discussing client apps in Dart in greater depth.

You can create a new instance of this class with a line like the following:

```
var somePackItem = new PackItem("Suncream");
```

This is the same `new` keyword that you used when creating `Elements` from the `dart:html` library. It calls the `PackItem` constructor and passes in the item text (which you'll get from user input).

Some lessons were learned from how constructors are used in C# and Java, and these have been incorporated into Dart. One of them is that a common use for constructor parameters is to populate class properties—in this case, the `itemText` property.

Dart allows you to write the constructor in this typical (for Java developers) form:

```
PackItem(itemText) {
  this.itemText = itemText;
}
```

But Dart also lets you shortcut this by indicating in the parameter list that all you'll do is initialize a property. You can then write the constructor as follows:

```
PackItem(this.itemText) {     }
```

This syntax is handy, and you can mix and match standard parameters and initializer parameters:

```
PackItem(this.itemText, color, quantity) {
  this.color = color;
  this.quantity = quantity;
}
```

Now that you have your basic class, you can begin to refactor the `addItem()` method as shown in listing 3.5. `addItem()` now constructs the `PackItem`, passing in the item text, and reads the `uiElement` property to add it to the `itemContainer`. The `uiElement` will ultimately contain a `<div>`, but for the moment your class leaves that unspecified with the var keyword.

Listing 3.5   Refactoring the addItem method to use your class

```
addItem() {
  var itemInputList = queryAll("input");
  InputElement itemInput = itemInputList[0];
  DivElement itemContainer = query("#items");
```

```
var packItem = new PackItem(itemInput.value);
itemContainer.children.add(packItem.uiElement);
itemInput.value = "";
}
```

Creates instance
with PackItem
constructor

Gets uiElement property of class
and adds it to itemContainer

Although the refactoring is valid, it has one vital problem: the uiElement property isn't yet initialized and therefore contains a null value. You can fix that by converting it from a property to a getter (with no further refactoring of addItem() required).

3.3.3 *Wrapping functionality with property getters and setters*

Fields, getters, and setters in Dart can be used interchangeably with no change to the calling code. This means the line

```
itemContainer.children.add(packItem.uiElement);
```

has no knowledge as to whether it's reading a value from a getter or from a property. A getter (or setter) is a method that's prefixed with the get (or set) keyword. A getter must take no parameters, and a setter must take a single parameter, as in the following code:

```
class PackItem {
  var _uiElement;

  DivElement get uiElement => _uiElement;

  set uiElement(DivElement value) => _uiElement = value;
}
```

uiElement
property renamed
to _uiElement

Getter using shorthand
function syntax to
return _uiElement

Setter also using
shorthand function
syntax to set _uiElement

You may have noticed that the example code renames the original uiElement to _uiElement (adds the underscore prefix). This change has a particular significance that I'll discuss in chapter 5 when I talk about libraries and privacy; for the moment, you can treat this as a private property by convention.

> **TIP** Remember that optional typing means you don't need to specify type information. But it's useful to users of your class to provide type information on the public properties and methods that callers can use (as is done here). Type information is documentation for humans and tools.

Users of your class can use code such as this:

```
var packItem = new PackItem("Sunscreen");
packItem.uiElement = new Element.tag("div");
itemContainer.children.add(packItem.uiElement);
```

Sets value on
uiElement via
setter

Gets value of
uiElement via
getter

Because getters, setters, and properties are interchangeable, the library designer can start with simple properties like these

```
class  PackItem {
  var uiElement;
}
```

and then change them to getters and setters as greater functionality is required, without the caller needing to change their code.

> **WARNING**   A good class designer will design getters and setters in such a way that they execute swiftly. It's good practice to allow a user of the class to *think* they're reading a property, even if lazy initialization or some other processing is going on in the getter or setter.

READ-ONLY PROPERTIES WITH GETTERS

The `PackItem uiElement` should be read only—that is, only code in your class should expect to be able to modify it. Because `addItem()` currently reads the `uiElement` property, you can replace this item with a getter in the class and no setter (which effectively means you can only read the value and not write a new `uiElement` value). Use your getter to "lazy initialize" the `uiElement` private property as shown in the following listing. The first time the getter is called, it creates the `<div>` element and stores it in the `_uiElement` private property. Each subsequent time, it returns the same `_uiElement`.

Listing 3.6   Adding a `uiElement` getter

```
class PackItem {
//snip... other code
  var _uiElement;                        uiElement has
                                         been renamed
                                         to _uiElement

  DivElement get uiElement {                           If private
    if (_uiElement == null) {                          _uiElement isn't
                                                       yet initialized ...
      _uiElement = new Element.tag("div");
                                                       ... initializes it with
      _uiElement.classes.add("item");                  new <div> element

      _uiElement.text = this.itemText;         Adds CSS .item class
    }                                          so it gets a pointer
                                               mouse style
    return _uiElement;
  }                                   Sets text that you'll
}                 Returns _uiElement   show on item
                         to caller
```

Your app now runs and provides the user with a nice "click here" mouse pointer when the mouse is moved over one of the added items. The pack-list items still don't toggle when someone clicks them, but you're getting closer. The next step is to store some state data in the `PackItem` class, in the form of a Boolean `isPacked` property, and to add a click listener to toggle `isPacked`, as described in figure 3.9.

UPDATING THE UI STATE THROUGH A SETTER

Once again, you'll use a setter and a getter to represent the `isPacked` property. There's a requirement to perform an action (updating the UI) when you set the `isPacked` value, which you can do by adding the additional CSS class `.packed` to the `uiElement` property. The `.packed` CSS class specifies `text-decoration: linethrough` in the CSS styles that you added to your HTML file earlier.

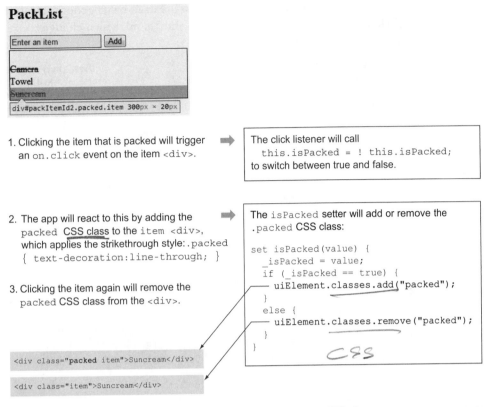

Figure 3.9   The `isPacked` property adds or removes the `.packed` CSS class.

First, add the private _isPacked property and the setter and getter, as shown next.

Listing 3.7   Adding the `isPacked` property, getter, and setter

```
class PackItem {
//...snip... other code
  var _isPacked = false;

  bool get isPacked => _isPacked;

  set isPacked(value) {
    _isPacked = value;
    if (_isPacked == true) {
      uiElement.classes.add("packed");
    }
    else {
      uiElement.classes.remove("packed");
    }
  }
}
```

Private _isPacked property, initialized with false (rather than null, which is the default)

Shorthand getter function syntax

Longhand setter function syntax

Adds and removes CSS .packed class

Your final task is to add a click listener to the `uiElement` to perform the toggle between packed and not packed. The `uiElement`, as a `<div>`, can react to `on.click` events, so you need to add a click listener into the `uiElement` getter. The code in bold is the click listener itself, defined in function shorthand, which changes the `isPacked` value from true to false, and vice versa:

```
DivElement get uiElement {
    if (_uiElement == null) {
        _uiElement = new Element.tag("div");
        _uiElement.classes.add("item");
        _uiElement.text = this.itemText;
        _uiElement.on.click.add( (event) => isPacked = !isPacked);
    }
    return _uiElement;
}
```

> **Uses ! (not) operator to reverse isPacked value. Has the effect of calling isPacked setter with new value.**

And with that final flourish, you now have a working client-side app that can be converted to JavaScript and deployed on any web server as a set of static files to run in all modern browsers. It uses a single Dart class containing a constructor and getters and setters.

> **Remember**
> - Dart classes are similar to C# and Java classes.
> - Constructor parameters can automatically initialize property values.
> - Getters and setters are interchangeable with properties.
> - It's good practice to use type information on getters, setters, and properties and other methods that you expect people to use.

3.4   Unit-testing the code

Testing the code that you've written is a standard best practice in software development. The Dart tools provide static analysis of the code, with help from the type information provided, but being able to run repeatable unit tests both in the browser and in server-side code from the console helps verify the quality of your code. In Dart, a unit-test suite is another app that you write that sits alongside your actual app. You can then run your unit-test app in the browser, where it executes each test and outputs the results to the browser.

Let's look at some code. You'll add a new app to your source folder to sit alongside the PackList.dart and PackList.html files. Your unit-test PackListTest.html file is straightforward and minimal, containing only a script reference to the PackListTest.dart unit-test application, and is shown in the following listing.

> **Listing 3.8   PackListTest.html: entry-point HTML file for your unit test**

```
<!DOCTYPE html>

<html>
  <head>
    <meta charset="utf-8">
    <title>PackListTest</title>
```

```
  </head>
  <body>
    <script type="application/dart" src="PackListTest.dart"></script>    ◁—┐
  </body>
</html>                                                                   **Link to PackListTest.dart**
                                                                          **application entry-point file**
```

Now that you have the test app's HTML file, you can start to add code to PackList-Test.dart. This file imports the PackList.dart application, which you'll be testing, and also imports Dart's unit-test framework and a unit-test configuration script that's provided by the unit-test framework. The unit-test configuration links the unit-test library to a set of output functions, which outputs the results either into the browser window or into the server console.

> ## Client vs. server restrictions
>
> Although Dart can run in the browser (client side) and on the server, a number of specific libraries can run only on the client side, and some are valid only on the server. The `dart:html` library interacts with the browser DOM and is available for use only when Dart is running in the web browser. The `dart:html` library won't run on the server-side Dart executable, because no browser DOM is available.
>
> Testing any code that imports `dart:html` won't work as a server-side test, because the server-side virtual machine doesn't contain the browser DOM for HTML interaction.

Listing 3.9 shows the minimal code required to get a client-side test suite app up and running. When you import the real PackList.dart app, you need to provide an import prefix, because otherwise there'd be a clash between the two top-level `main()` functions—one in the PackList app and one in the PackListTest app. The `import` prefix lets you differentiate the two different `main()` functions. (We'll visit this topic in more depth in chapter 5.) Import the unit-test framework using the `pub install` command from the command line or Dart Editor menu option.

Listing 3.9 PackListTest.dart: client-side test suite boilerplate code

```
import "package:unittest/unittest.dart";    ◁— Imports unit-test framework

import "package:unittest/html_config.dart";

// import "package:unittest/vm_config.dart";

import "PackList.dart" as packListApp;

main() {
  useHtmlConfiguration();

  // useVmConfiguration();

  // todo: Add tests here
}
```

Imports client-side HTML configuration

If you were testing on the server-side VM, you'd import the VM configuration.

Imports library that you're testing

Sets up client-side HTML configuration

If you were testing on the server-side VM, you'd set up the VM configuration.

This is where you'll add tests.

To enable package management, you need to specify that you're using the unit test dependency in the pubspec.yaml file created by the Editor. Chapter 5 discusses the pub package manager and `pubspec` syntax in greater detail. For this test, you just need to add a dependency section to your application's pubspec.yaml file, as shown in this snippet:

```
dependencies:
  unittest: any
```

Then run `pub install` from the Editor's menu to pull the unit-test dependency into the project.

3.4.1 Creating unit tests

You now have all the boilerplate necessary to start writing unit tests. A *test* is a function that you create and that is passed into the `test()` function, which comes from the `unittest` library, which comes as part of the unit-test framework. We'll look more at passing functions around in the next chapter; for the moment, the syntax for creating a test is shown in figure 3.10.

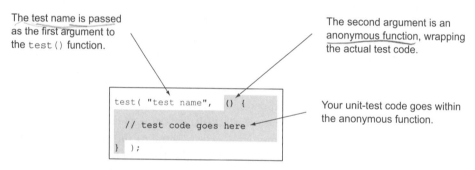

The test name is passed as the first argument to the `test()` function.

The second argument is an anonymous function, wrapping the actual test code.

Your unit-test code goes within the anonymous function.

```
test( "test name",  () {

   // test code goes here

}  );
```

Figure 3.10 The code required to set up a unit test

3.4.2 Defining test expectations

In your unit test, you can call any valid Dart code. Typically, unit tests should check expectations—for example, that a value isn't null, or that an object's property is assigned correctly. For this, you use the `expect()` function (also provided by the `unittest` library), which takes two parameters: the actual value you've generated in your test and a matcher that lets you provide the value you expect. A simple version of this setup is shown in listing 3.10, which contains two tests. The first expects that a newly created instance of `PackItem` isn't null, and the second validates that the `itemText` value assigned in the constructor is correctly returned by the property on the class.

Listing 3.10 Testing for expectations in unit tests

```
// snip boilerplate imports
main() {
  useHtmlConfiguration();
  test("PackItem constructor", () {
```

Defines unit test

```
    var item = new PackItem("Towel");
    Expect.isNotNull(item);
  });
```

→ **Expects that new item isn't null (using static isNotNull method)**

→ **Standard Dart code to create PackItem**

```
  test("PackItem itemText property", () {
    var item = new PackItem("Towel");
    expect(item.itemText, equals("Towel"));
  });
}
```

→ **In second test, creates another PackItem**

→ **Expects that itemText has been correctly assigned the value "Towel" using the built-in equals() function**

You can see the output of this code in figure 3.11. The output of each test is displayed in the browser window, along with a stack trace for failing tests.

Automating test runs

Browser-based unit tests can be automated with the aid of an external client-side test framework, such as Selenium (www.seleniumhq.org), which you can launch from a continuous build server. Selenium can navigate the unit-test page in your app, where the unit tests run in the browser. You can configure Selenium to pass or fail based on the browser content rendered. Dart also provides Selenium web-driver bindings, allowing Selenium scripts to be written in Dart directly. See the Dart webdriver API at api.dartlang.org for more details.

The isNotNull and equals matchers are built into the unit-test framework. Table 3.1 lists some other built-in matchers.

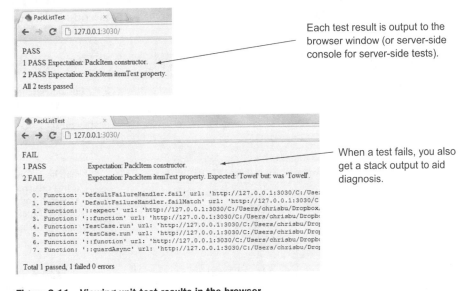

Each test result is output to the browser window (or server-side console for server-side tests).

When a test fails, you also get a stack output to aid diagnosis.

Figure 3.11 Viewing unit test results in the browser

Table 3.1   Provided unit-test matchers

Matcher	Description
isNull isNotNull	Expects the actual value to be null or not null
isTrue isFalse	Expects the actual value to be true or false
same(expected)	Expects the actual object to be the same object instance as the expected object
equals(expected)	Expects the actual object to be equal to the expected object
isEmpty contains(expected)	Expects the actual list to be empty or contain a specific expected object
throws throwsNullPointerException	Expects that any exception was thrown Expects that a specific exception was thrown (other matchers exist for other core exceptions)
anything	Expects any value

3.4.3   Creating a custom matcher

Creating a custom matcher is a matter of extending the provided BaseMatcher class. We'll look more at extending classes in chapters 6 and 7, but to extend the base matcher, you can create a class that provides two functions: a matches() function and a describe() function. The matches() function returns a bool value depending on whether the expectation was matched. The following listing shows a custom matcher class that validates whether two different PackItems contain the equivalent itemText value.

Listing 3.11   Creating a custom PackList matcher

```
// snip boilerplate

class CustomMatcher extends BaseMatcher {        CustomMatcher
  PackItem _expected;                            extends BaseMatcher

  CustomMatcher(this._expected);                 Constructor that takes
                                                 expected value
  bool matches(PackItem actual) {
    if (_expected.itemText == actual.itemText) {  matches() function,
      return true;                                which returns true if
    }                                             expected and actual
    else {                                        item text match
      return false;
    }
  }

  Description describe(Description description) {  Adds description
    description.add("itemText");                   for use in UI
  }
}
```

```
main() {
  useHtmlConfiguration();

  test("PackItem custom", () {
    var packItem1 = new PackItem("Towel");
    var packItem2 = new PackItem("Towel");
    expect(packItem2, new CustomMatcher(packItem1));
  };
}
```

> **Uses custom matcher
> in unit-test code**

This section has offered you a quick look at unit tests in Dart. By creating unit tests alongside your code and running them when your code changes, unit tests become another tool in your toolbox for creating correct code that runs as expected.

Remember
- You can run unit tests in the browser or on the server.
- Browser-based unit tests can import libraries that use `dart:html`.
- Server-side unit tests can't import libraries that use `dart:html`.
- Unit tests use the `expect()` function in conjunction with a matcher to validate your test's expectations.
- You can build custom matchers by extending the `BaseMatcher` class.

3.5 *Summary*

You now know about constructs such as classes and the shorthand function syntax that I'll use throughout the book. We've covered a lot of ground in this chapter, touching the surface of a number subjects that we'll return to in greater depth. Let's summarize what's been discussed:

- The `dart:html` library provides a neat way to interact with the browser, using Dart classes, properties, and lists to allow you to create and manipulate browser DOM elements.
- `dart:html` defines a number of events that event-listener functions can listen to. Event listeners are functions that take a single event parameter, and you can add multiple event listeners to listen to a single event.
- Dart functions have a single-line shorthand that also automatically returns the result of the expression.
- Classes in Dart are similar to classes in Java and C# and have properties and methods. They also have special `get` and `set` keywords to define getters and setters.
- Getters and setters on classes can be used interchangeably with properties by calling code, which has no knowledge of whether it's using a property or a getter or setter.
- We looked at unit tests in Dart, which can run in the browser and on the server. You use unit tests to create expectations around your code, and you match the actual output against the expected output using either a built-in or a custom matcher.

In the real world, you'd add the ability to store the data across browser sessions, perhaps in browser local storage, and to send data back to the server. These topics are covered in parts 3 and 4 of the book, which discuss building applications in greater depth.

Now that you've seen the basics of a web app in Dart, it's time to change tack a little and examine Dart language concepts in more detail. These concepts are equally applicable for Dart in the browser or on the server. In the next chapter, we'll examine functions in Dart, which are the building blocks of any application; for instance, you'll find that functions can also be variables.

Part 2

Core Dart

In this, the largest part of the book, you'll learn about the core concepts, language features, and structure required for building Dart applications.

Chapter 4 introduces functions and closures, key concepts in Dart that will be new to developers more familiar with class-based languages such as Java and C#. Functions are core to the language, and anonymous functions are used everywhere, such as handling events from the browser or other systems.

In chapter 5, you'll see how to create structured Dart applications by organizing your Dart project into libraries. Although Dart is a class-based language, libraries form the smallest unit of privacy in a Dart codebase, rather than classes; you'll see how this can be used to good effect.

Chapters 6 and 7 introduce and expand on Dart's class and interface structure and how you can achieve duck typing with Dart's optional type system. Dart's `dynamic` and `Object` types will make an appearance, and you'll see how you can build rich type inheritance hierarchies.

Chapter 8 builds on the previous two chapters to show how you can overload the standard operators and build generic, general-purpose versions of your classes. It also explains how this technique is used in the generic collection classes and how you can use generics in your own apps.

By chapter 9, you'll be familiar enough with Dart's syntax to revisit functions. This time we'll look at their use in asynchronous programming, where function callbacks and Dart's `Future` type are used to make async programming more structured.

By the end of this part of the book, you'll have the core knowledge of the Dart language and structure that will let you effectively use APIs provided by the Dart ecosystem that will help you build web apps.

Functional first-class functions and closures

This chapter covers

- Declaring functions and return types
- Specifying mandatory and optional parameters
- Storing first-class functions in variables
- Using functions as closures

Dart is similar in many ways to languages such as Java and C#, but its function syntax is more similar to that found in JavaScript than in more strongly typed languages. In Dart, everything is an object, including functions, which means you can store a function in a variable and pass it around your application the same way that you might pass a `String`, an `int`, or any other object. This is known as having *first-class* functions, because they're treated as equivalent to other types and aren't second-class citizens in the language.

First, we'll examine Dart's function syntax options, which have a longhand and a shorthand notation and various forms, depending on how much optional type information you provide. You'll take these functions and use them as variables and pass functions around as parameters and return types.

Once you have a grounding in using functions as first-class objects by storing them in variables, we'll look at how you can define function types to provide strong type information. These definitions help the type system validate that functions you're passing around your application match the developers' intentions.

Finally, we'll look at closures, which occur when a function is created and uses variables that exist outside of its own scope. When you pass that function (stored in a variable) to another part of the application, it's known as a *closure*. This can be a complex topic; it's used extensively in JavaScript to emulate features such as getters and setters, and class privacy—features that are already built into the Dart language.

> **NOTE** In general, everything you'll discover about functions is also applicable to methods, which are a special type of function that's associated with a class. We'll look in detail at classes in chapter 6.

4.1 *Examining Dart functions*

A computer program is a list of instructions or steps that the computer must execute in a certain order, sometimes using the output of one step as the input to another step. In the real world, you perform functions with inputs and outputs all the time. For example, when mixing concrete for a garden project (I often find myself doing more garden construction than tending to actual plants), I follow this recipe to make great general-purpose concrete. Each function takes inputs and outputs, and the functions I perform are highlighted in bold:

1 **Measure** the quantity of cement (the cement volume).
2 **Measure** the quantity of sand as twice the cement volume.
3 **Measure** the quantity of gravel as three times the cement volume.
4 **Mix** the cement and sand to create a mortar mix.
5 **Mix** the mortar mix with the gravel to create a dry concrete mix.
6 **Mix** the concrete mix with water to create wet concrete.
7 **Lay** the concrete before it sets.

The `measure()` and `mix()` functions are reused throughout these steps, taking the input of a previous step to produce a new output. When I mix two ingredients, such as cement and sand, this gives me a new ingredient (mortar) that I can use elsewhere in the recipe. There is also a `lay()` function, which I use only once. The initial volume of the starting quantity of cement depends on the job; for example purposes, I use a bag as an approximate unit of measure.

You can represent these functions in Dart using the code in listing 4.1. The listing omits the various `Ingredient` classes that the functions return, but for this example, they're unnecessary (you can find them in the source code associated with this book). The set of concrete-mixing instructions is followed in the `main()` function, which is the first function to execute in all Dart applications.

Listing 4.1 Mixing concrete in Dart

```
Ingredient mix(Ingredient item1, Ingredient item2) {
  return item1 + item2;
}

Ingredient measureQty(Ingredient ingredient,
                      int numberOfCementBags,
                      int proportion) {
  return ingredient * (numberOfCementBags * proportion);
}

void lay(ConcreteMix concreteMix) {
 // snip - implementation not required
}

main() {
  Ingredient cement = new Cement();
  cement.bags = 2;
  print(cement.bags);

  Ingredient sand = measureQty (new Sand(), cement.bags, 2);
  Ingredient gravel = measureQty (new Gravel(), cement.bags, 3);

  Ingredient mortar = mix(cement, sand);
  Ingredient dryConcrete = mix(mortar, gravel);

  ConcreteMix wetConcrete = new ConcreteMix(dryConcrete, new Water());
  lay(wetConcrete);
}
```

Both mix() and measureQty() functions output ingredients.

measureQty() returns a new ingredient by calculating a proportion based on number of cement bags.

Enter starting number of bags of cement.

Calculate amount of other ingredients based on number of bags of cement.

Mix ingredients, using output of previous function as input to the next.

Dart functions are similar in declaration to Java and C#, in that they have a return type, a name, and a list of parameters. Unlike JavaScript, they don't require the keyword `function` to declare that they're functions; unlike Java and C#, the parameter types and return types are all optional, as part of Dart's optional type system.

Now that some example functions are defined, let's look at some other ways these functions could be defined in Dart, taking into account Dart's optional typing and longhand and shorthand function syntax. Chapter 3 briefly examined Dart's longhand and shorthand function syntax: the shorthand syntax allows you to write a single-line function that automatically returns the output of the single line. Dart's optional typing also means the return type and the parameter types are both optional. Figure 4.1 shows various combinations of type information for the longhand and shorthand versions of the `mix` functions.

You can use Dart's shorthand function syntax only for single-line functions, whereas you can use the longhand function syntax for single or multiline functions. The shorthand syntax is useful for writing concise, clear code. And as you'll see in the following section, shorthand functions automatically return the result of the single line.

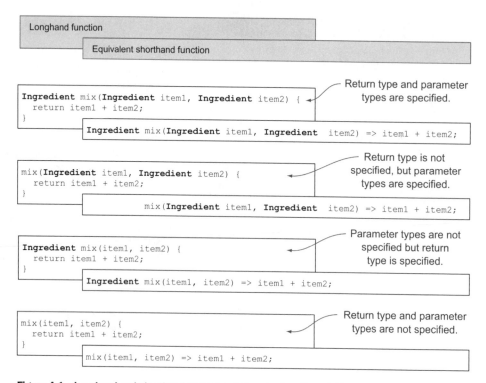

Figure 4.1 Longhand and shorthand versions of the `mix` functions in Dart

4.1.1 *Function return types and the return keyword*

All Dart functions return a value. For single-line shorthand functions, this value is always the result of the single-line expression. For longhand functions, the return value defaults to `null` unless you actively return a value.

Single-line shorthand functions automatically return the result of the single-line expression; for example, the shorthand `mix(item1, item2)` function returns the result of `item1 + item2` without explicitly stating that the function will return a value. The shorthand syntax, which uses the form

function_name() => expression;

can be read as "return the result of the expression." This is always the case for shorthand syntax functions, even if the expression doesn't obviously produce a value, such as calling another function with no return value. Because the default return value is `null`, you always end up with a `null` value returned in the absence of any other value.

Longhand functions, on the other hand, always return the default `null` if you don't actively return another value by using the `return` keyword. The `return` keyword can also specify an optional value to return (which replaces the `null` default), such as in this longhand `mix()` function:

```
return item1 + item2;
```

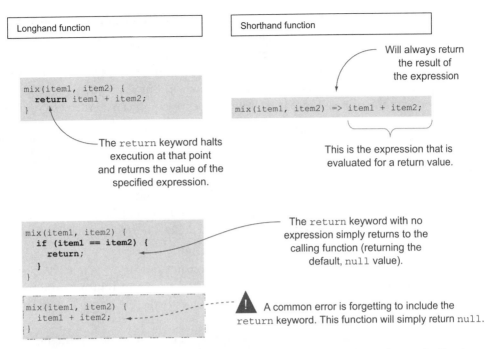

Figure 4.2 Longhand functions require the `return` keyword to return a value, whereas shorthand functions return the result of their single-line expression automatically.

When `return` is used, it immediately returns the result to the calling code. If a longhand function does explicitly return a value with the `return` keyword, then the function returns `null`. Figure 4.2 shows the `return` keyword used in a longhand function and the expression that's evaluated for a return value in the shorthand style. It also shows a common error that can occur in your code: forgetting to use the `return` keyword.

SPECIFYING A RETURN TYPE

You can specify the return type of the function by prefixing the function name with the type you're expecting to return. Dart's optional typing means if you don't explicitly specify a return type, then you're returning a dynamic type, as in

```
Ingredient mix(item1, item2) {...snip...}
mix(item1, item2) {...snip...}
dynamic mix(item1, item2) {...snip...}
```

Return type can be specified for function.

No return type specified = specifying dynamic return type.

When you specify a return type, the tools can validate code in three ways: first by providing a warning if you haven't explicitly returned a value in longhand functions (using the `return` keyword), and second by validating that the type you're returning is the type that was expected to be returned—for example, that you're indeed returning an `Ingredient` object. The third validation method is provided to users of your function. Because Dart's type system provides documentation, the explicit return type is used to validate that the calling code is correctly handling the return type. For example, you might try to assign the result of mix(), which is an Ingredient, into a ConcreteMix type variable, which you might then try to lay. Without a return type specified, this code would be valid but incorrect. But when you document your function with the proper Ingredient return type, the tools can alert you to your error:

```
Ingredient mixture = mix(new Sand(), new Gravel());
lay(mixture);
```

Sand and gravel alone aren't a solid base for construction.

Tools will warn you that type Ingredient isn't assignable to type ConcreteMix.

The mix() function explicitly returns an Ingredient type, but the lay() function explicitly expects a ConcreteMix type. Without the explicit type information, Dart would allow this code to run (until the code failed later in another flow).

USING THE VOID TYPE TO INDICATE NO RETURN VALUE

This behavior raises a new problem: how do you explicitly state that you aren't expecting to return a value from a function? All Dart functions return a value, but you can provide documentation to the type checker with the void type to indicate that you aren't expecting to return a value.

Imagine that you're going to use a small cement mixer to do the mixing for you. You can create a function to start the mixer that returns no value:

```
startMixer(speed) {
  Mixer.start(speed);
}
```

returns null

Because all Dart functions return a value, this code automatically returns a default null value to the calling code. Users of the startMixer() function as it's currently declared can't tell whether the designer of that function intended a null value to be returned or left out the return keyword in front of the call to Mixer.start() (which might be a coding bug). When you try to store the return value of startMixer, it contains null:

```
var runningMixer = startMixer("slow");
```

runningMixer variable contains null because startMixer() function doesn't explicitly return a value.

Fortunately, when you use the explicit return type void, you provide documentation to the user that you didn't intend to return a value. Doing so also provides the type checker with information that it can use to provide warnings if you try to use the return value. It doesn't stop the function from returning the default null value, but it does warn you that you shouldn't be using that returned value. You can modify the function as follows:

```
void startMixer(speed) {
  Mixer.start(speed);
}
```

void keyword explicitly declares that you aren't returning a value

Providing `void` as a return type also validates that the function code doesn't use the `return` keyword to return a value.

4.1.2 *Providing input with function parameters*

In addition to returning values, Dart functions take parameters as inputs. Unlike in JavaScript, you must specify all the parameter names in a function definition. In JavaScript the parameter list is optional, because all the arguments passed to a function can be accessed dynamically using an internal arguments variable. Dart is much more structured, requiring all the parameters to be defined in the function definition in a manner similar to that of Java or C#. Dart doesn't have function (or method) overloading, but it does have optional parameters.

> **TIP** There is no difference in the parameter definitions for longhand and shorthand functions, so the examples show only the longhand syntax in this section, but they apply equally to either syntax.

The `measureQty(ingredient, numberOfCementBags, proportion)` function currently takes three parameters: `ingredient`, `numberOfCementBags`, and `proportion`. The function can use them in the same way it would use variables in the scope of the function. The typed and untyped versions of the function signature look like the following:

```
measureQty(Ingredient ingredient,
              int numberOfCementBags,
              int proportion) {
    // ...snip...
}
```
Typed version indicates parameter type information

```
calculateQty (ingredient,
              numberOfCementBags,
              proportion) {
    // ...snip...
}
calculateQty (dynamic ingredient,
              dynamic numberOfCementBags,
              dynamic proportion) {
    // ...snip...
}
```
Untyped and dynamic versions are equivalent

When you provide type information such as `Ingredient` and `int` for function parameters, you're declaring that the input types should have an *is-an* relationship with `Ingredient` and `int`, respectively. This allows the type checker to validate that the calling code is passing correctly typed arguments to the `measureQty()` function. Calling code must pass all the arguments in the same order in which they appear in the function declaration; in the example, this means `ingredient` must come first, then `numberOfCementBags`, and finally `proportion`:

```
var sand = measureQty(new Sand(), cement.bags, 2);
```

ARGUMENTS ARE PASSED BY REFERENCE

When you call the `measureQty()` function to pass in arguments, each argument—for example, a sand ingredient—contains a reference to the value passed in. Therefore,

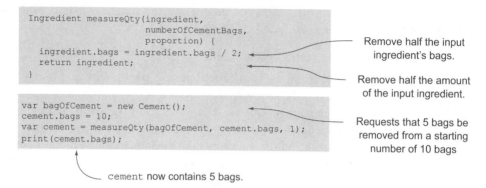

Figure 4.3   When you pass an object by reference, you can change the properties of that object but not the object itself.

you can change the properties of the ingredient (such as the quantity remaining) but not the ingredient itself, as shown in figure 4.3.

For example, what happens if you create a new bag of sand in the `measureQty()` function, realize that the bag passed in doesn't contain enough, and grab some more from the store? It turns out that in this case, the original bag of sand remains untouched. The following listing demonstrates this concept in action.

Listing 4.2   Checking parameters passed by reference

```
Ingredient measureQty(ingredient, numberOfCementBags, proportion) {
    if (ingredient.bags == 0) {                        Function detects
        ingredient = new Ingredient();                 if not enough of an
        ingredient.bags = numberOfCementBags * proportion;   ingredient is passed in.
        return ingredient;
    }                    ... but does so only in the scope of the    New ingredient
}                        function. Original bag is still empty.      overwrites one
                                                                     passed in ...
main() {
    var emptyBagOfCement = new Cement();    Pass empty bag of
    emptyBagOfCement.bags = 0;              cement anyway.        Original
                                                                  emptyBagOfCement
    var cement = measureQty(emptyBagOfCement,1,1);                is unmodified
    print(emptyBagOfCement.bags);                                 outside the function.
}
```

This code works the same regardless of whether you're modifying an object, such as the `ingredient` instance, or a more primitive type, such as an `int`. You lose the reference to the new type on return because everything is an object (as discussed in the previous chapter); when you change the reference to the object being passed in, all you're doing in the function is losing the original reference and creating a new reference. The code outside the function still has a handle on the original object reference.

OPTIONAL POSITIONAL PARAMETERS

Dart functions can have optional parameters with default values. When you're creating a function, you can specify parameters that calling code can provide; but if the calling code chooses not to, the function uses the default values.

When measuring out the quantity of ingredients, which are proportional to the number of bags of cement, you call the `measureQty()` function, which returns a new ingredient based on the number of bags of cement and the required proportion. Sometimes you want a 1:1 ratio between the number of bags of cement and your input ingredient. Without using optional parameters, you can modify the function to check if `numberOfCementBags` and `proportion` are `null` and then default them to 1 as follows:

```
measureQty(ingredient, int numberOfCementBags, int proportion) {
    if (numberOfCementBags == null) numberOfCementBags = 1;   Default to
    if (proportion == null) proportion = 1;                    I if null
    return ingredient * (numberOfCementBags * proportion);
}
```

The calling code needs to know the number of bags and proportion values to pass into the `measureQty()` function. This is true even if the calling code wants to pass in a standard, default value, such as a proportion of 1. Calling code can make calls like this:

```
measureQty(new Sand(), null, null);
measureQty(new Sand(), 1, null);
measureQty(new Sand(), null, 1);
measureQty(new Sand(), 1,1);
```

These are known as *positional arguments*; their position in the calling code matters. For example, the third argument is the proportion, and the first is the ingredient.

It would be better if the calling code could pass in only the values it needed to, such as the ingredient and the proportion, without passing in the number of bags if it wasn't required. Dart lets us achieve this with optional parameters. Optional parameters must appear in a block together after all positional parameters are defined. The optional parameters block is defined within a pair of square brackets and, like positional parameters, is a comma-separated list. For example, you can change the example function to support optional parameters (shown in bold) as follows:

```
measureQty(ingredient, [int numberOfCementBags, int proportion]) {
    // ... snip ...
}
```

Now calling code can provide values for `numberOfCementBags` and `proportion` only if it needs to.

You can refer to optional parameters by position, by providing arguments for them in the order in which they're declared:

```
measureQty(new Sand(), 2, 1);        Optional parameters may
measureQty(new Sand(), 2);           be omitted if not required.
measureQty(new Sand());
```

Of course, in this code the parameter values will still be initialized to `null` if they aren't provided, which means `measureQty()` still has to check for `null` values and default them to 1. Fortunately, you can also provide default values as part of the named parameter's function declaration:

```
measureQty(ingredient, [int numberOfCementBags=1, int proportion=1]) {
    return ingredient * (numberOfCementBags * proportion);
}
```

**Provide default values
for optional parameters.**

Now calling code can opt to either provide the parameters or not, and your function is simplified by not requiring a null check on the parameters. As noted earlier, the mandatory parameters must all be passed in, and in the correct order. But this isn't true for optional parameters. Calling code can use optional parameters in one of two ways:

- Not provide values at all. The function uses the default value or null if no default value is specified.

- Provide a value for each optional parameter in the order in which they're declared, reading from left to right. The calling code can provide arguments to populate each of the optional parameters. Any parameters not populated default to null or the specified default value.

OPTIONAL NAMED PARAMETERS

An alternative to optional positional parameters is to use optional named parameters. These allow calling code to specify the parameters into which it's passing values, in any order. As before, mandatory parameters come first, but this time the optional parameters are specified between curly braces, with default values provided in this form:

```
measureQty(ingredient, {int numberOfCementBags:1, int proportion:1}) {
    return ingredient * (numberOfCementBags * proportion);
}
```

**Optional named parameters
are specified in curly braces.**

Note that unlike the optional positional parameters, the default values for optional named parameters use a colon (:) to separate the parameter name and value. Calling code can now call the measureQty() function, passing in the mandatory ingredient argument and optionally the numberOfCementBags and proportion arguments, in any order:

```
measureQty(new Sand(), numberOfCementBags: 2, proportion: 1);
measureQty(new Sand(), numberOfCementBags: 2);
measureQty(new Sand(), proportion: 1);
measureQty(new Sand());
```

**Named optional
arguments passed by
calling code use the
parameter name.**

Unlike optional positional parameters, calling code must specify the parameter name for all supplied optional named parameter values. This means the following function call isn't valid

```
measureQty(new Sand(), 2, 1);
```

because the optional values must be named.

> **NOTE** With mandatory positional parameters, calling code has no knowledge about the parameter names. Optional named parameters, on the other hand, form part of your code's API, so you should spend as much time naming optional parameters as you'd spend on other API names, such as function and method names. Changing the name of an optional parameter once you've released your code could affect other users of your code in the same way as changing a function name.

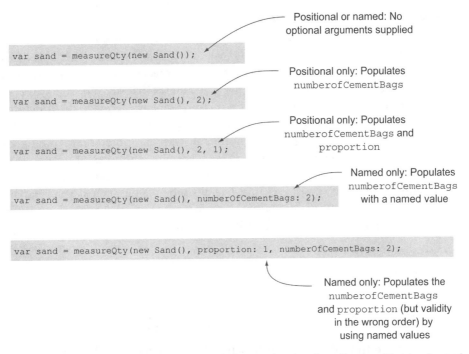

Figure 4.4 The different ways that calling code can supply values for optional positional and named function parameters

You can't define both optional named parameters and optional positional parameters in the same function definition. You should make a choice based on the likely use cases for your function.

Figure 4.4 shows different ways to call the `measureQty()` function.

Remember
- Shorthand functions automatically return the value created by the single-line expression that forms the function body.
- Longhand functions should use the `return` keyword to return a value; otherwise, `null` is automatically returned.
- You can tell the type checker that you aren't intending to return a value by using the return type `void`.
- Type information on parameters is optional.
- You can declare optional parameters as a comma-separated list within square brackets after the mandatory parameters are declared.
- Calling code can refer to optional parameters by name, using a *name*: *value* syntax.

Now that you know what a function looks like, how to call it, how to specify return types, and how to use and mandatory and optional parameters, it's time to look at what else you can do with functions: specifically, how to store functions in a variable and pass them into other functions as function arguments.

4.2 *Using first-class functions*

The term *first-class functions* means you can store a function in a variable and pass it
around your application. There's no special syntax for first-class functions, and all functions in Dart are first class. To access the function object (rather than call the function),
refer to the function name without the parentheses that you'd normally use to supply
parameters to the function. When you do this, you have access to the function object.

Consider the `Ingredient mix(item1, item2)` function from earlier in the chapter.
You can call it by following the function name with parentheses and passing values for
the function arguments, such as `mix(sand,cement);`. You can also refer to it just by
name, without the parentheses and parameters; this way you get a reference to the
function object that you can use just like any other value, such as a `String` or an `int`.
Once you have the function object stored in a variable, you use that new reference to
call the function again, as shown in the following snippet:

```
var mortar = mix(sand, cement);
```
Calls mix function and stores its return value in mortar variable

```
var mixFunction = mix;
```
Stores function itself in mixFunction variable

```
var dryConcrete = mixFunction(mortar, gravel);
```
Calls mixFunction variable to return more mortar

```
print(mix is Object);
print(mix is Function);
```
Function is an Object and a Function, so it prints true.

You can see from the example that the `mix()` function (and the `mixFunction` variable) has an *is-an* relationship with both the `Object` type (remember, everything *is-an*
object), and it also has an *is-an* relationship with a class called `Function`, which represents the function type.

This concept raises an interesting possibility. If you can store a function in a variable, do you need to declare the function in the top-level scope first? No, you can
declare a function inline (within another function body) and store it in a variable,
rather than declare a function in the top-level library scope. In fact, there are three
ways to declare a function inline and one way to do so in the top-level library scope, as
shown in figure 4.5; the function declarations are highlighted in bold. We'll go
through each of these examples in the next few pages.

> ### Function scope vs. library scope
> The largest block of scope in Dart is the `Library`, and all functions that aren't
> wrapped inside another block, such as another function or a class definition (where
> they're called *methods*), exist in library scope. These are considered to be at the top
> level of the `Library`.
>
> You can also declare functions inside another function. These are considered to be
> in function scope like any other variable declared in a function, such as a `String` or
> an `int`. You can access these function-scoped functions only in the block where they
> were declared, unless you pass them to another function as a parameter or return
> value (just like other variables). You'll see examples of this when we discuss closures
> later in the chapter.

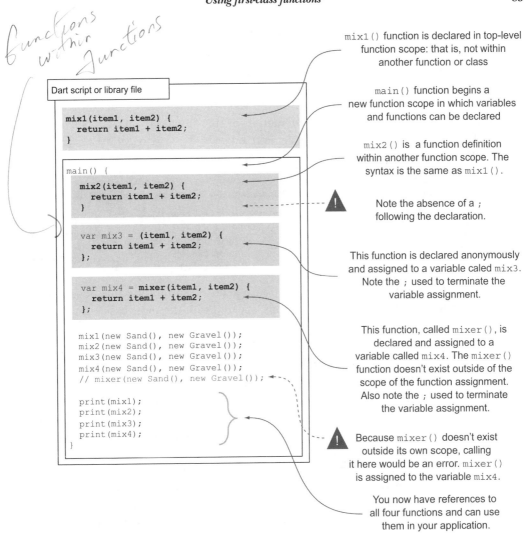

functions within functions

Dart script or library file

```
mix1(item1, item2) {
  return item1 + item2;
}
```

```
main() {
  mix2(item1, item2) {
    return item1 + item2;
  }

  var mix3 = (item1, item2) {
    return item1 + item2;
  };

  var mix4 = mixer(item1, item2) {
    return item1 + item2;
  };

  mix1(new Sand(), new Gravel());
  mix2(new Sand(), new Gravel());
  mix3(new Sand(), new Gravel());
  mix4(new Sand(), new Gravel());
  // mixer(new Sand(), new Gravel());

  print(mix1);
  print(mix2);
  print(mix3);
  print(mix4);
}
```

mix1() function is declared in top-level function scope: that is, not within another function or class

main() function begins a new function scope in which variables and functions can be declared

mix2() is a function definition within another function scope. The syntax is the same as mix1().

Note the absence of a ; following the declaration.

This function is declared anonymously and assigned to a variable caled mix3. Note the ; used to terminate the variable assignment.

This function, called mixer(), is declared and assigned to a variable called mix4. The mixer() function doesn't exist outside of the scope of the function assignment. Also note the ; used to terminate the variable assignment.

Because mixer() doesn't exist outside its own scope, calling it here would be an error. mixer() is assigned to the variable mix4.

You now have references to all four functions and can use them in your application.

Figure 4.5 The four different ways to declare a function. mix1() is in the top-level scope, and the other three are declared in a function body.

You've already used the top-level library scope to declare functions such as mix1(), which is known as a *library* function. The other three function declarations, all within the body of another method, are known as *local* functions, which need more explanation. They're a part of Dart that looks deceptively simple but, like closures, can be complex.

4.2.1 *Local function declarations*

Local functions are functions that you declare within the body of another function. Unlike library functions, you can't explicitly reference them outside of the function in which they were declared. But you can pass them into other functions and use them as return values from the function you declared them in and store them in a list so that some code block can dynamically execute them in turn.

Listing 4.3 defines and uses the `combineIngredients()` function, which takes a mixing function and a pair of ingredients as its parameters. By accepting an arbitrary mixing function as a parameter, the `combineIngredients()` function allows you to mix ingredients with any implementation of that function you want, such as mixing with a shovel or mixing with a cement mixer. I'll refer to `combineIngredients()` throughout this section.

Listing 4.3   Function that takes a function object as a parameter

```
Ingredient combineIngredients(mixFunc, item1, item2) {     ◁──┐   First parameter defines
                                                                mixing function that will
    return mixFunc(item1, item2);     ◁──┐                      be used. Other parameters
                                          mixFunc() function    are items to be mixed.
}                                         mixes two items and
                                          returns the result.
```

Now that you have a use for a function object stored in a variable, let's look at the three ways of declaring local functions, starting with the most basic: the simple local function declaration. In the following sections, the examples all use the longhand syntax, but the rules apply equally to the shorthand function syntax.

SIMPLE LOCAL FUNCTION DECLARATION

The simple local function declaration shown in figure 4.6 shares the same syntax as library functions declared in the top-level scope, except that they happen to exist within another function. Their name is also their reference, as with `mix2()`; and their own name exists in their own scope, so they can be recursive (I'll discuss recursive functions a little later in this chapter).

When you're declaring a simple local function in the scope of another function, you don't need to provide a terminating semicolon, because the closing brace provides the terminator—it's the same as declaring a function in the top-level scope. This is an important point, because the other two methods of declaration—which explicitly assign a function to a variable—do require a semicolon following the closing brace.

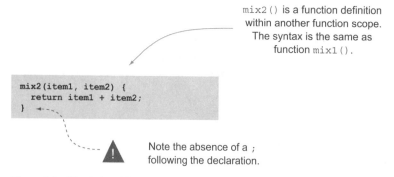

`mix2()` is a function definition within another function scope. The syntax is the same as function `mix1()`.

```
mix2(item1, item2) {
    return item1 + item2;
}
```

Note the absence of a ; following the declaration.

Figure 4.6   Simple local function declaration syntax

You can strongly type a function by providing type information in the same manner as top-level, library-scoped functions. The following listing defines a strongly typed function mix2() within the main() function, which is passed into the combineIngredients() function.

Listing 4.4 Outer `main()` function uses the inner `mix()` function

```
main() {
  mix2(item1, item2) {
    return item1 + item2;
  }

  var cement = new Cement();
  var sand = new Sand();

  var mortar = combineIngredients(mix2, cement, sand);

  var dryCement = mix2(mortar, new Gravel());
}
```

- Local function defined as mix2(), which creates a function object
- Can pass mix2 function object into other functions in the same way as other variables
- Can also call mix2() directly in declaring function's scope

The method name mix2() exists in the scope of the mix2() function itself. This setup allows mix2() to call itself (creating recursion) or refer to its own function object.

Recursion

A *recursive* function is a function that calls itself. It's a technique often used in sort and search functions to traverse trees of data. Consider the following recursive function called stir(), which calls itself while the stir count is less than 10:

```
stir(ingredient, stirCount) {
  print("Stirring $ingredient")
  if (stirCount < 10) {
    stirCount ++;
    stir(ingredient, stirCount);
  }
}
```

- If current stirCount is less than 10 …
- … increment stirCount …
- … and call stir() again (recurse).

There are a number of good resources on the internet about recursion as a computer science topic—it isn't a technique found only in Dart. What's important is that for this technique to work, the name of the function must be available in its own scope; that is, the method stir() must exist and must be valid to refer to it when it's called. Simple local function declarations, in common with top-level, library-scoped function declarations, have their own name in scope and can therefore recurse.

ANONYMOUS FUNCTION DECLARATION

An anonymous function is declared without a function name; see figure 4.7. Like any other function declaration, you can assign it to a function object variable, pass it directly into another function, or use it as the return type of the declaring function. But you can't use it recursively, because the function has no name for itself in its own scope.

The longhand version of this function requires a terminating semicolon because you're assigning a value to a variable (mix3), and that variable assignment statement needs to be terminated before the code can move onto the next statement.

```
var mix3 = (item1, item2) {
  return item1 + item2;
};
```

> This function is declared anonymously and assigned to a variable called `mix3`. Note the `;` used to terminate the variable assignment.

Figure 4.7   Anonymous function declaration

An anonymous function starts with the opening parenthesis and continues to the end of the function body. With function shorthand, you can declare an anonymous function in the following form:

```
() => null;
```

This function, declared as is, can never be called, because it has no name to reference it by. But this is a valid anonymous function that takes no parameters and returns a null value.

Anonymous functions are often used to pass a function directly into another function as a parameter or store functions in a list. These two methods work because the reference to the function object is preserved by either the parameter name of the receiving function or the element in the list. Listing 4.5 shows this concept in action by creating a list of anonymous functions for processing extra ingredients. You then call each function in the list in turn. The anonymous functions are highlighted in bold, and longhand and shorthand versions are shown. The anonymous functions are passed as parameters into the `List.add()` method, where they can be referred to later (just like a `String`, an `int`, or any other object).

Listing 4.5   Storing anonymous functions in a list

```
main() {
  List taskList = new List();

  taskList.add( (item) => item.pour() );          ◁── Adds shorthand anonymous
                                                        function to list

  taskList.add( (item) {
    item.level();                                  ◁── Adds longhand anonymous
    item.store();                                       function to list
  } );

  var aggregate = new Aggregate();

  foreach(task in taskList) {                      ◁── Iterates through list
    task(aggregate);                               ◁── Calls each
  }                                                     function in turn
}
```

This pattern is used extensively with the browser event handlers. You can add multiple functions to specific events, such as `button.on.click.add()`, which takes a function as its parameter and adds that function to a list of handlers that are called when the button is clicked. You can still use this pattern by passing in a reference to a function by name, but often—especially for single-line functions—it's simpler and more readable to pass

This function, called `mixer()`, is declared and assigned to a variable called `mix4`. The `mixer()` function doesn't exist outside of the scope of the function assignment. Also note the `;` used to terminate the variable assignment.

```
var mix4 = mixer(item1, item2) {
  return item1 + item2;
};
```

Figure 4.8 Named function assignment declaration

the function in anonymously, as in the following call to `combineIngredients`, which takes a function as a parameter. The anonymous function is in bold:

```
combineIngredients( (item1, item2) => item1 + item2, sand, gravel);
```

You're still able to provide type information for the parameters in the parameter list but not for the return type, because Dart thinks any text to the left of the opening parenthesis is the function name (thus making it a named function rather than an anonymous function). The following would be a function called `Ingredient`, rather than an anonymous function that returns an ingredient:

Doesn't provide a return type because it thinks the function name is Ingredient

```
Ingredient (item) => item.openBag();
```

This issue can be resolved with the third and final way of declaring local functions: function assignment.

NAMED FUNCTION ASSIGNMENT DECLARATION

The third way of declaring a function is a hybrid of both of the previous versions in that it declares a named function and immediately assigns that function to a variable. Because this is an assignment, like the previous example, you must also terminate this assignment with a semicolon, as shown in figure 4.8.

This approach has the advantages that you can declare the return type and you have a function name that's in the scope of the function, allowing recursion if required. In this example, the function name in the scope of the function is `mixer()`, and this name is available *only* in the scope of the function. To refer to the function elsewhere, you must use the name `mix4`.

You can rewrite the `mix4()` function to use recursion and provide type information if you pass it as an argument to the `combineIngredients()` function, as shown next.

Listing 4.6 Recursive, typed, named function

```
main() {
  var mix4 = Ingredient mixer(Ingredient item1,
                              Ingredient item2) {
    if (item1 is Sand) {
      return mixer(item2, item1);
    }
    else (
      return item1 + item2;
```

Function is declared with name mixer(), with return and parameter type information provided, and assigned to variable mix4.

Function name mixer() is in scope, which allows you to use recursion.

```
        )
    }
    var sand = new Sand();
    var gravel = new Gravel();
    combineIngredients(mix4, sand, gravel);
}
```

> Passes in mix4() function, which is your reference to mixer() function

The name `mixer()` is essentially a throwaway. It's available only in the scope of the function and isn't valid elsewhere. When you declare the `mixer()` function directly into another function as an argument, you can't refer to `mixer()` anywhere but within itself. This example looks nearly identical to the simple, local function declaration that we looked at first but is subtly different by virtue of the function being assigned implicitly to the parameter of the `combineIngredients()` function, as shown in figure 4.9.

We've looked at declaring functions and assigning them to variables and function parameters, but what about Dart's type system? How do you know that the `combineIngredients()` function takes another function as its first parameter? Fortunately, Dart allows strong function typing and provides a new keyword, `typedef`, which I'll discuss next.

4.2.2 *Defining strong function types*

So far, you've been storing your function objects in dynamically typed variables and passing the functions' objects into other functions as dynamic parameters. This approach presents a problem in that Dart's optional typing allows you to specify the type of a variable or a function parameter: what happens when you want to specify that the type is a function? You've already seen that a function "is-an" `Object` and a function "is-a" `Function`, so you can use these types as shown in the following listing.

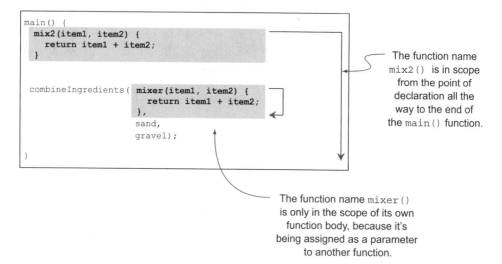

```
main() {
    mix2(item1, item2) {
        return item1 + item2;
    }

    combineIngredients( mixer(item1, item2) {
                            return item1 + item2;
                        },
                        sand,
                        gravel);

}
```

The function name `mix2()` is in scope from the point of declaration all the way to the end of the `main()` function.

The function name `mixer()` is only in the scope of its own function body, because it's being assigned as a parameter to another function.

Figure 4.9 A named function declared as an argument to another function can refer to itself by name. That name isn't available for use elsewhere.

Listing 4.7   Function type strongly types a function variable or parameter

```
Ingredient combineIngredients(Function mixFunc, item1, item2) {
  return mixFunc(item1, item2);
}

main() {
  Function mix = (item1, item2) {
    return item1 + item2;
  }

  var sand = new Sand();
  var gravel = new Gravel();
  combineIngredients(mix, sand, gravel);
}
```

> mixFunc parameter is strongly typed as a Function.

> Stores function in mix variable, which is strongly typed as a Function.

> When you pass mix into combineIngredients, type checker can validate whether you're providing a function as first parameter.

When you use a function object stored in a variable, you're using an instance of a Function class. Not all function instances are the same, however. The mix() function is different from the measureQty() function, which is different from the lay() function. You need a way to strongly type the mix() function parameter on combineIngredients() to specify that it wants a mix() function and not one of the others.

Dart provides two ways to achieve this. The first is lighter weight but slightly more verbose: provide the function signature as the function parameter definition, as shown in figure 4.10.

This approach is a verbose way of declaring that a function parameter must have a specific signature. Imagine if you had 10 functions that all accepted a mix() function; you'd need to write the function 10 times. Fortunately, Dart allows you to declare a function signature by using the typedef keyword, which lets you create a custom function type. typedef declares that you're defining a function signature, not a function or a function object. You can use typedef only in the library's top-level scope, not within another function. The following listing shows how you can use typedef to define a function signature that you can use to replace the mixFunc parameter declaration on the combineIngredients() parameter list.

Listing 4.8   Using typedef to declare a function signature

```
typedef Ingredient MixFunc(Ingredient, Ingredient);

Ingredient combineIngredients(MixFunc mixFunc, item1, item2) {
  return mixFunc(item1, item2);
}
```

> typedef declares custom function type MixFunc

> Uses new MixFunc type to strongly type parameter

With typedef, you can create shorthand for a specific function signature that you can use in variable and parameter definitions, which can let the type checker validate that the correct function objects are being passed around your application.

Now that you're familiar with the different ways to declare functions in the local scope of another function, it's time to tackle closures: when a function object refers to another variable that was declared outside of its own immediate scope. Closures are a powerful functional programming concept.

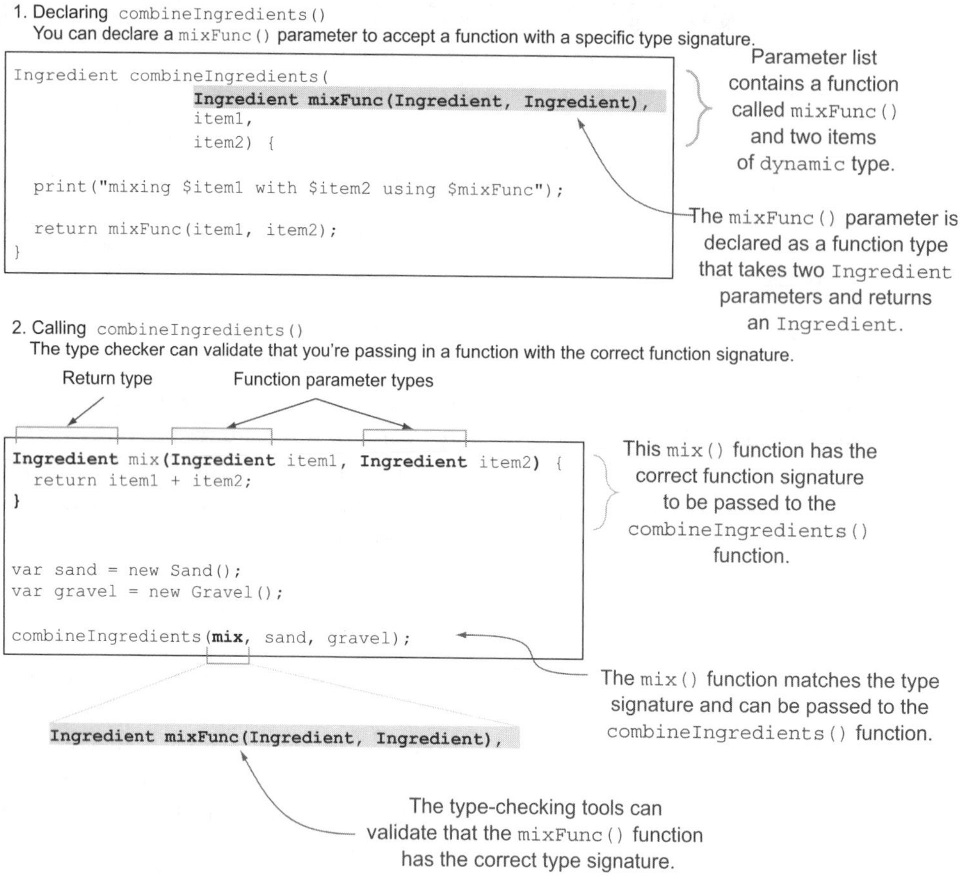

1. Declaring `combineIngredients()`
   You can declare a `mixFunc()` parameter to accept a function with a specific type signature.

```
Ingredient combineIngredients(
                Ingredient mixFunc(Ingredient, Ingredient),
                item1,
                item2) {

  print("mixing $item1 with $item2 using $mixFunc");

  return mixFunc(item1, item2);
}
```

Parameter list contains a function called `mixFunc()` and two items of `dynamic` type.

The `mixFunc()` parameter is declared as a function type that takes two `Ingredient` parameters and returns an `Ingredient`.

2. Calling `combineIngredients()`
   The type checker can validate that you're passing in a function with the correct function signature.

Return type   Function parameter types

```
Ingredient mix(Ingredient item1, Ingredient item2) {
  return item1 + item2;
}


var sand = new Sand();
var gravel = new Gravel();

combineIngredients(mix, sand, gravel);
```

This `mix()` function has the correct function signature to be passed to the `combineIngredients()` function.

The `mix()` function matches the type signature and can be passed to the `combineIngredients()` function.

```
Ingredient mixFunc(Ingredient, Ingredient),
```

The type-checking tools can validate that the `mixFunc()` function has the correct type signature.

Figure 4.10   **The parameters of a function can be defined to accept another function with a specific signature.**

Remember
- When you use a function by name, without the parameter brackets, you get a reference to its function object.
- Simple local functions declared in a similar manner to top-level, library-scoped functions are able to refer to themselves by name and can make full use of parameter and return type information to provide type information to the tools.
- Anonymous functions have no name and can't use recursion or specify strong return type information, but they do provide useful shorthand for adding functions into lists or passing to other functions as parameters.
- You can use a named function in place of an anonymous function to allow recursion and strong return type information, but its name is available only in the scope of itself.
- You can use the `typedef` keyword to declare a specific function signature so the type checker can validate function objects.

4.3 Closures

Closures are a special way of using functions. Developers often create them without realizing it when passing a function object around an application. Closures are used extensively in JavaScript to emulate various constructs found in class-based languages, such as getters, setters, and private properties, by creating functions whose sole purpose is to return another function. But Dart supports these constructs natively; you're therefore unlikely to need closures for this purpose when writing new code. A large amount of code is likely to be ported from JavaScript to Dart, though, and Dart's closure support is similar to JavaScript, which will aid this effort.

When you declare a function, it isn't executed immediately; it's stored in a variable as a function object in the same way that you might store a `String` or an `int` in a variable. Likewise, when you declare a function, you can also use other variables that you've declared before it, as in the following snippet:

```
main() {
  var cement = new Cement();         Declares cement variable
                                     in local function

  mix(item1, item2) {                Declares mix() function
    return cement + item1 + item2;   in local function
  }
}
        You can still use cement variable,
          even in a local function.
```

This code lets you create a `mix()` function that always mixes two ingredients with cement. Instead of passing in `cement` as a separate ingredient every time, you declare cement first and then use `cement` from within the function.

When you call the `mix()` function, passing in `sand` and `gravel`, you still have access to the `cement` variable that was declared outside the `mix()` function's scope. You can pass this function back to your `combineIngredients()` function, where it will happily mix the other two ingredients with the `cement` without ever knowing `cement` was involved. Figure 4.11 shows this happening.

This design is essentially a closure; it's a function that retains a reference to variables that were in its scope when it was declared.

Why "closure"?

The term *closure* derives from *close-over*, which is one way of thinking about how a closure works. It "closes over" or wraps any nonlocal variables that were valid in its scope at the time it was declared.

As you just saw with the `cement` example, one of the times a closure is useful is when you want to provide some implementation details while keeping them hidden from the function that's using that closure.

Closures are also formed when one function is returned by another function. You might have a `getShovel()` function that returns a shovel. You can use the shovel as a

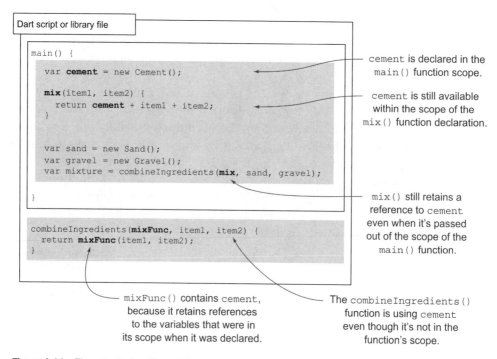

Figure 4.11   The mix() function retains a reference to the cement variable even when mix() is passed out of the scope of the main() function that declared it.

function to mix your ingredients, but—as shown in listing 4.9—the shovel also has some sticky mud on it. When the getShovel() function returns, the mix() function retains a reference to stickyMud, which is mixed with your ingredients even though the getShovel() function has exited.

Listing 4.9   Creating a closure with a function as a return type

```
getShovel() {
  var stickyMud = new Mud();          ⟵── Creates mud in shovel()

  var mix = (item1, item2) {
    return stickyMud + item1 + item2;      Declares mix() function
  }                                         that uses stickyMud

  return mix;              ⟵── Returns mix()
}
main() {
  var mixFunc = getShovel();          ⟵┐ Calls getShovel(), which
                                        │ returns mix(), still containing
  var sand = new Sand();              ⟵┘ a reference to stickyMud
  var cement = new Cement();
                                           Uses mix() to ensure that
  var muddyMortar = mixFunc(sand, cement);  cement and sand are mixed
}                                    ⟵── with more than each other
```

Closures can occur accidentally because it's perfectly valid to use variables that a function sees in its own scope and the scope of its parent. When you pass the child function out of its parent, either as a return type or as a function parameter, you'll find that you're working with a closure.

> **Remember**
> - A function that uses variables that weren't declared in its own scope has the potential to become a closure.
> - A function becomes a closure when that function is passed out of the scope from which it was declared, by either passing it into another function or returning from the function that declared it.

4.4 *Summary*

This chapter showed you how to declare functions using both shorthand and longhand syntax. When you use shorthand syntax, it also implicitly returns the value of the single-line expression that forms the shorthand function body. But when using longhand syntax, you must explicitly use the `return` keyword to return the value of an expression.

All functions return a value—`null` if no other value is specified—but you can tell the Dart tools that you aren't expecting to specify a return value by using the `void` return type.

Functions can be stored in a variable or referenced by accessing them by name without the parentheses. This approach gives you a variable containing a function object, which you can pass around your app like any other variable. You can return a function object stored in a variable or pass it into another function, where it can be called like any other declared function. Function objects share an "is-an" relationship with the `Function` class.

To strongly type a function object variable or parameter so the type checker can validate your code, use the keyword `typedef` in the library's top-level scope to define a named function signature. You can then use the name of the function signature the same way you would any other type.

We also looked at closures, which are created when a function uses variables that weren't declared within that function, and that function is passed to another part of the code. You can use closures to use implementation details that the receiving function shouldn't or can't know about.

Now that you know all about functions, in the next chapter we'll look at Dart's library and privacy mechanisms. This information is important because the names of functions and classes that you'll use in libraries have a strong bearing on privacy. The two concepts are closely linked, and it's a topic that you need to understand before you start to look at Dart's classes and interfaces.

5

Understanding libraries and privacy

This chapter covers

- Organizing your code into reusable packages
- Importing libraries into your application
- Hiding functionality with library privacy
- Using multiple source files
- Using scripts as runnable libraries

Most programming languages have a library structure that allows code to be split over multiple files and published to other developers, which promotes modularity and code reuse and improves the ability of developers to work on different parts of the same codebase by hiding the internal implementation of a library. Dart is no exception; but in Dart, the library mechanism also has a big impact on privacy, especially class and function privacy. In languages such as Java and C#, privacy is centered around the class; but in Dart, this privacy exists at the library level rather than the class level. That's why we're discussing libraries and privacy this early in this book.

In this chapter, you'll learn how to create and use libraries of code in Dart and how these libraries relate to Dart's privacy model, which you can use to hide the internal workings of a library. The library is the smallest unit of deployable code and can be as small as a single class or function or as large as an entire application. In the real world, all but the most trivial application should have its code split into multiple libraries, because this design promotes a good, loosely coupled architecture, reusability, and testability. By building a simple logger framework that you can import into your own code, you'll explore these features as you go through this chapter.

When you're building a package of code for reuse, there are often internal workings that you don't want third-party users to be able to access except via a published and agreed-on interface—for example, the internal state of some class data. In Dart, you can publish a library of code to your team members or web users with only the parts that you want to make visible available to those end users. This setup allows the internals of the library to change without affecting end users. It's different from that in Java and C#, which have a different, class-centric privacy model. In these languages, the class internals can change without affecting end users.

> ### Why doesn't Dart have a class-centric privacy model?
>
> This is one of the areas of Dart that's particularly influenced by JavaScript and web development. In JavaScript, there is no notion of privacy, except by following certain conventions such as returning closures from other functions. For this reason, the Dart privacy model should be thought of as an improvement to JavaScript, as opposed to comparing it to more traditional class-based languages such as Java and C#.

Dart's optional typing allows you to provide documentary type information in the code at the point where users interact with your library, such as on function parameters and return types, or class properties, while letting you use only as much type information in the library as you feel is necessary. As noted earlier in the book, type information doesn't change how your application runs, but it does provide documentation to tools and other developers.

In chapter 3, you were already importing the built-in `dart:html` library using the `import` keyword, and it turns out that it's just as easy to import your own library.

5.1 *Defining and importing libraries in your code*

In this section, you'll create a logger library called `loglib`. It will provide a simple debug/warn/info logger that allows you to output log messages to the web browser's debug console. A logger library with varying levels of log output is available for most languages: for example, `nLog` for .NET and `log4j` for Java. The simplest way to log in Dart is to use the `print()` function; the `loglib` example will wrap this function.

In order to properly experiment with libraries, you need some third-party code to call your library, such as the PackList application from chapter 3, a simple Dart app

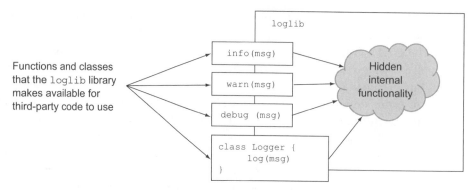

Figure 5.1 `loglib` **functions and classes made available for external code**

containing only a `main()` function. Because the PackList app already has some basic functionality that can be logged, it's an ideal third-party app to use your new `loglib` library. It has the following functionality, which provides useful items to log:

- Build UI (debug level)
- User adds an item (info level)
- User adds an item with no title (warn level)
- User marks item as packed or no longer packed (info level)

This use case gives you a set of functions that your library should make available, shown in figure 5.1.

`loglib` will contain three top-level functions—`info()`, `warn()`, `debug()`—and a single class, `Logger`. A *top-level* function is a function that exists outside a class (just like the `main()` function). Libraries can be built of functions as well as classes, and a function doesn't need to be wrapped in a class (as it does in C# or Java). Thus it's perfectly valid for a library to consist entirely of functions. (It's equally valid to have a library with no top-level functions that consists only of classes.)

You structure your code into libraries in order to let third-party code use packaged, abstracted functionality. When you use existing libraries, such as the `dart:html` library in chapter 3, you don't need to know *how* it creates HTML elements and triggers browser events—only that it *does*. By building code into sensible libraries, you're able to package and version them for others to use, providing a published interface to your library's functionality.

5.1.1   Defining a library with the library keyword

A Dart library is a .dart file that has a `library library_name;` declaration at the start of the file. The `library` declaration announces to Dart that this file represents the root file of a library and must be the first statement (before other code such as class declarations and functions), as shown in figure 5.2.

The library name's purpose is to identify the reusable block of code. The library name must be in lowercase, with multiple words separated by underscores. The library

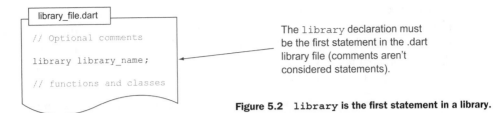

Figure 5.2 `library` **is the first statement in a library.**

name doesn't need to be the same as the filename, although by convention Dart files are also all lowercase, with multiple words separated by underscores. Unlike in Java, there's no relationship between filename and folder structure in Dart. Figure 5.3 shows some of the values you can and can't use as library names.

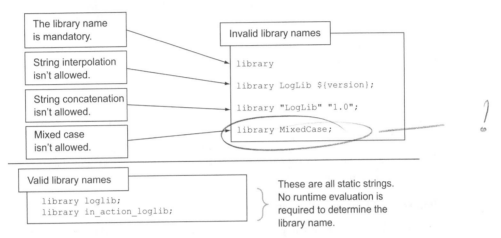

Figure 5.3   Valid and invalid library names

In addition to being able to call a library by any string, it's also possible to create a library in any folder, with no restriction placed on the number of libraries in a folder. To define the `loglib` library, you need a single file, loglib.dart, containing this single line:

```
library loglib;
```
⟵ **library definition defines this file as a library.**

The Dart Editor helpfully identifies library .dart files (as opposed to nonlibrary .dart files) by making them bold in the Editor's Files view, as shown in figure 5.4.

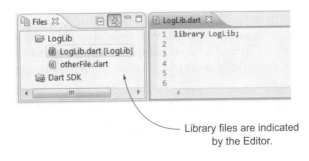

Library files are indicated by the Editor.

Figure 5.4   The Dart Editor indicates library files in bold.

Now that you have a library file defined, you can start to populate it with code. Your top-level logger functions at present will call the built-in `print("")` function to output the log message to the browser console and use the Dart shorthand function syntax discussed in chapter 4. The `Logger` class will have a function that can do the same, as shown in the following listing.

Listing 5.1   loglib.dart functions and classes

```
library loglib;

debug(msg) => print("DEBUG: $msg");          Top-level functions (which don't
warn(msg) => print("WARN: $msg");            need to be wrapped in a class)
info(msg) => print("INFO: $msg");

class Logger {
  log(msg) => print("LOG: $msg");            Logger class, which
}                                            contains a log() function
```

The `loglib` library at present doesn't add much value over the built-in `print()` function; you'll expand on it as you progress through the chapter.

> **TIP** The built-in `print()` function sends its output either to `stdout` when it's running as a server-side script or to the browser's debug console (accessible through Tools > JavaScript console in Chrome/Dartium or Web Developer > Web Console in Firefox).

Now that you have a library with some usable functions and classes, it's time to use them. You can let third-party code use your library.

5.1.2   Importing libraries with import

Import the `loglib` library using the `import "loglib.dart";` statement if the loglib.dart file is in the same folder. This `import` statement is deceptively powerful: it allows you to reference a library filename by URI, either directly from the filesystem or via HTTP over the web. The following `import` statements are all valid but offer different degrees of flexibility:

```
                                               Relative file path
import "./libs/loglib/loglib.dart";
import "http://www.mysite.com/loglib.dart";            Website URL
import "file:///c:/loglib/loglib.dart";
import "package:/loglib/loglib.dart";          Absolute file path

                                               Package (discussed
                                               later in the chapter)
```

> **WARNING** Using an absolute file path to a specific folder on a specific drive doesn't promote great reuse; it means that another developer who wants to use your app's code needs to have the same filesystem structure (and the same drive letters if they're running Windows). It's better to use relative paths or package management.

The PackList app from chapter 3 can import the `loglib` library. In the following examples, you'll use the directory structure shown in figure 5.5, which will allow for a relative `import` statement.

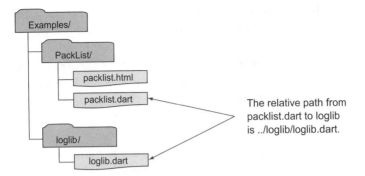

The relative path from
packlist.dart to loglib
is ../loglib/loglib.dart.

**Figure 5.5   The folder
structure for the `loglib`
and PackList example**

By using the relative path from the packlist.dart file to the loglib.dart file, PackList can import the `loglib` library with the following statement:

```
import "../loglib/loglib.dart";
```

Listing 5.2 shows the `import` statement that packlist.dart will use, in addition to the existing `dart:html` library import from chapter 3. The order of the imports isn't important, because all the imports are loaded before code starts executing, but they must appear before any code statements.

Listing 5.2   packlist.dart importing the loglib.dart library

```
import "../loglib/loglib.dart";
import "dart:html";

main() {
  // todo: output debug message
  // ...snip rest of file...
```

**Imports loglib
into PackList app**

**Imports built-in dart:html library
(import order isn't important)**

LIBRARIES IMPORTING OTHER LIBRARIES

A library can import many other libraries, too. Your `loglib` library could import a number of other libraries (if it needed to), but the `import` statement must appear after the `library` declaration and before any code statements, as shown in figure 5.6.

If `loglib` were to import the `dart:html` library, then the `dart:html` library would become available only to the `loglib` library. If the rest of your application also wanted

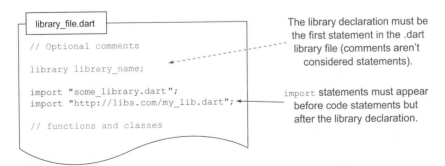

Figure 5.6   The `import` statement must appear before code statements.

to use the dart:html library, then you'd also need to specify another import statement elsewhere in your application file. Imports are local to the library that declares the import statement.

Circular references between library imports are also allowed. For example, Library A can import Library B, and Library B can also import Library A, because the Dart libraries are fully loaded before the application starts running, so the Dart tools can understand this type of dependency.

USING THE TOP-LEVEL IMPORTED FUNCTIONS

The first use case for using loglib in your PackList app was to output a debug message when you started building the UI. The ideal place to put this code is at the beginning of the main() function where you have the todo marked, as shown in figure 5.7. Running the PackList app will now put a message onto the browser console. Figure 5.7 also shows the relationship between the PackList debug() method call and the loglib library.

Dart is designed to be converted to JavaScript so it can run in browsers that don't natively support Dart. JavaScript doesn't natively support libraries: a multilibrary Dart application becomes a single JavaScript file on conversion, with each imported library in its own annotated section, commented with the library name, as in listing 5.3. Note in the JavaScript output that only the debug(msg) function exists in the loglib section—this is because you aren't yet using the other functions or classes, so it knows not to convert them.

Listing 5.3   Generated JavaScript extract of the PackList app and loglib library

```
...snip...
//   ********** Library loglib **************
//   ********** Code for top level **************
function debug(msg) {                           debug() function exists
  return print$(("DEBUG: " + msg));             in loglib section.
}
//   ********** Library C:\DartInAction\PackList **************
//   ********** Code for PackItem **************
//   ********** Code for top level **************
function main() {                    But debug() only exists because
  debug("Starting building UI");     it's called elsewhere in the code.
...snip...
```

Figure 5.7   PackList calls the top-level function in the loglib library.

You can now flesh out the logging use cases in your PackList app. The remaining ones are as follows:

- User adds an item (info level)
- User adds an item with no title (warn level)
- User marks item as packed or no-longer packed (info level)

You can achieve this by adding the following lines to your existing `PackItem` class. First, check the `itemText` length in the constructor and output either an `info` or a warning message; second, add another event handler to listen to the UI item being clicked by the user, which adds an `info` message.

Listing 5.4 Adding logging method calls to the PackList application

```
class PackItem {
    // ...snip...

  PackItem(this.itemText) {
    if (itemText.length == 0) {
      warn("User added an empty item");
    }
    else {
      info("User added an item $itemText");
    }
  }

  DivElement get uiElement {
    if (_uiElement == null) {
      _uiElement = new Element.tag("div");
      _uiElement.classes.add("item");
      _uiElement.text = this.itemText;
      _uiElement.on.click.add( (event) => isPacked = !isPacked);
      _uiElement.on.click.add( (event) => info("Item updated"));
    }
    return _uiElement;
  }
  // ...snip...
}
```

- Adds logging to PackItem constructor
- Existing event listener function
- Adds second click event listener, which logs "item updated" message

---

USING TOP-LEVEL IMPORTED CLASSES

Your PackList app is now using the publicly exposed functions. You also have a `Logger` class in `loglib`, which you've ignored so far. You can add another log message when you've finished building the UI, but this time (for the sake of example) use the `Logger` class. Create an instance of the class using the `new` keyword just as if you'd declared it in the same PackList file, as shown next.

Listing 5.5 packlist.dart using the `Logger` class imported from `loglib`

```
import "../loglib/loglib.dart";

main() {
  debug("Started building UI");
  // ...snip building the UI
  var logger = new Logger();
  logger.log("Finished building UI");
  // ...snip...
}
```

- Creates new instance of Logger class that's imported from loglib
- Calls log() method on Logger class

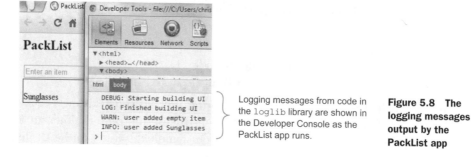

Logging messages from code in the `loglib` library are shown in the Developer Console as the PackList app runs.

Figure 5.8 The logging messages output by the PackList app

You've now wired in the `loglib` library with the PackList app. The PackList app now logs a variety of messages as it starts up and the user interacts with it. Figure 5.8 shows some of the logging that appears in the developer console.

USING LIBRARY PREFIXES TO PREVENT NAME CLASHES

Now that you have a working library, you can let other developers use it—they have a well-defined interface into your library. Unfortunately, there's nothing to stop another developer from also using a different library that also contains a `Logger` class and a top-level `info()` method. This is where `import` prefixes are used.

An `import` prefix allows you to import multiple libraries that may contain top-level functions and classes with the same names. Imagine a scenario in which a developer wants to use another (hypothetical) `Logger` library called `WebLogger`, which is able to send log messages to a server somewhere and also contains the `info()` function.

Dart wouldn't know which of the `info()` functions you intended to call, as demonstrated in figure 5.9.

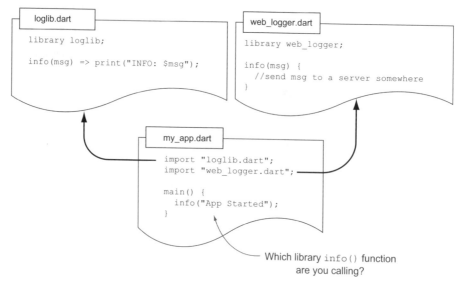

Figure 5.9 Multiple imported libraries can sometimes contain the same function names, so you need a mechanism to deal with these clashes.

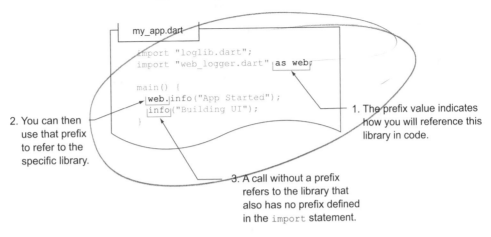

Figure 5.10   You can declare a library prefix for use when referring to the code in an imported library.

Fortunately, Dart provides an as statement, which forms part of the import declaration. This feature allows you to deal with namespace clashes by giving all the code in a specific library a name that you can reference. The as statement is followed by a prefix name that becomes your reference when you refer to any code in that specific library elsewhere in code, as shown in figure 5.10.

Once you use the prefix defined by the as statement, you must always refer to any class or function in that library with the prefix. Although it's possible to always use a prefix with every import declaration, doing so could cause your code to become cluttered because every reference to every class and method in the imported library would need to use the prefix. The pragmatic approach is best: add library prefixes only when doing so aids readability and/or prevents naming clashes, rather than using library prefixes everywhere.

Currently, your loglib logging library has all its functions and classes available to users of the library. Nothing is hidden from any app that imports the library—all your functionality is publicly available. In the next section, you'll make some items private so they aren't accessible from outside the library.

> **Remember**
> - The library *library_name*; statement must be the first statement in a library.
> - Libraries can use the import "uri/to/lib.dart"; statement to import other libraries.
> - library and import statements must appear before other code.
> - You can use library prefixes to avoid naming clashes between different libraries.

5.2   *Hiding functionality with library privacy*

When you're building a library of functionality, it's likely that there will be some internal implementation details that you won't want to expose to end users of that library. The Logger library currently contains a basic function of outputting data to the browser console. Suppose you want to add a feature to your Logger library that sends the log messages to a server somewhere. You don't want external users of your library to call this server logging code directly; it needs to be called internally by your entry-point functions. If you just declare classes and functions in your library, they will be accessible to end users; but fortunately Dart lets you declare items as private by prefixing their names with an underscore (_).

> **NOTE** *Privacy* in the context of this chapter refers to the object-oriented notion of privacy, which through language structures hides the internals of one system from another system. Making your library private so your code can't be read by prying eyes is a different concept and may be addressed by code obfuscation and minification, both of which are under development by the Dart team. In addition, privacy isn't related to security—all imported library code runs as part of a single codebase. In chapter 15, you'll see how you can create separate isolates, which provide a degree of security.

As shown in figure 5.11, privacy exists at a library level rather than a class level. Anything declared to be private is accessible from within its own library but can't be referenced by name from outside that library.

Privacy in a library can be applied to top-level functions and classes and in classes to their properties and methods by adding the underscore prefix to the name. Calling

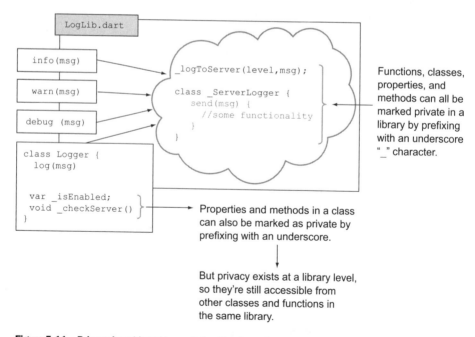

Figure 5.11   Privacy is achieved by prefixing the class, function, property, or method name with an underscore, which allows access only from other code in the same library.

code also needs to include the underscore prefix when using these private elements, as in

```
info(msg) {
  print("INFO: $msg);
  _logToServer("INFO",msg);
}
```

Calls private
_logToServer() function
from loglib info method

Building a language feature around a naming convention?

The underscore prefix is a common (but not necessarily universal) naming convention to indicate privacy, especially in languages that don't have privacy built in (such as JavaScript and Python). Dart takes this naming convention further by making it a language feature.

This feature has been the subject of some debate in the Dart community—it's perhaps one of the biggest points of contention. On the one hand, you get privacy with little developer overhead; and at the call site you can see where something being called is private, which is useful when you're exploring the internals of new libraries because you don't need to seek out the declaration. On the other hand, it does affect readability, and it's possible to have code that looks like this:

```
var someValue = new _MyClass()._getValue()._doAction(_withProperty);
```

Another argument against using the underscore prefix is that if you need to change something from public to private (or vice versa), it must be renamed everywhere that it's used. The other side to this argument is that if you're renaming from private to public, then the renaming will happen only in your library (if it's currently private in your library, then no external user will be using it). If you're changing from public to private, then there are more fundamental issues (such as breaking your library users' code by removing a function) than just renaming.

The two rules to remember are as follows:

- Code in a library can access any other code in the same library.
- Code outside a library can access only nonprivate code in that library.

These rules are particularly important for classes, which have a mixture of public and private properties and methods.

5.2.1 *Using privacy in classes*

Privacy in classes is different than in C# and Java. The first rule about Dart privacy means that two different classes both have access to each other's private methods and properties (similar to Java's package-private feature).

In the `loglib` library, you currently have a `Logger` class. Perhaps you want to determine whether the logger is enabled or disabled by storing an internal `_isEnabled` property: its internal state. Other classes using the `Logger` class that are in the same library can access the internal state directly, but users of your library can't access that

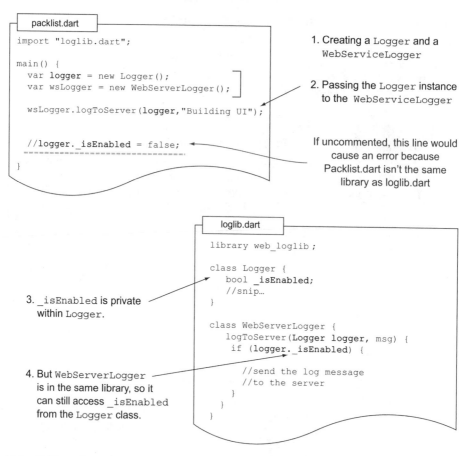

Figure 5.12 `WebServerLogger` **can access private properties of the** `Logger` **class because they're in the same library.**

internal state. Other parts of the app should have no knowledge about the workings of Logger class, only that it *does* work. Figure 5.12 illustrates this relationship.

By using the underscore prefix, you can build rich functionality into your library and ensure that only the functionality that users of your library need is exposed through a well-defined and consistent interface of classes, methods, and top-level functions.

ACCESSING PRIVATE FIELDS WITH GETTERS AND SETTERS

As discussed in chapter 3, getters and setters provide a way to access fields. They too can be made public or private through the use of the underscore. If you want to allow external users read-only access to the _isEnabled property, you can add a public getter to your class. Likewise, when you add a public setter, the value becomes writable. It's interesting to note that it's perfectly valid to have read-only or write-only values by providing only a getter or a setter. Figure 5.13 shows how your library can show and hide a class's properties through getters and setters.

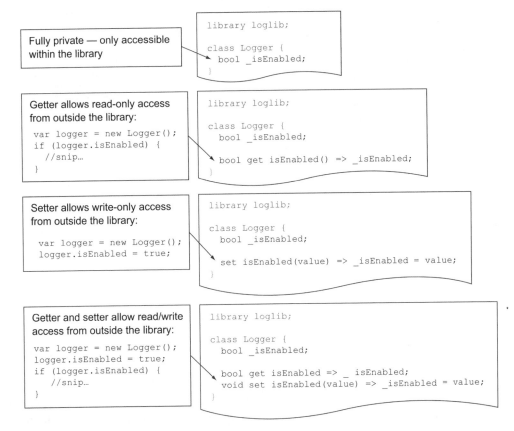

Figure 5.13 **Using getters and setters to provide varying levels of field access to external users of a class**

USING PRIVATE METHODS

In addition to private fields wrapped with getters and setters, private methods in classes can also be defined, again, by prefixing the method name with an underscore. A useful effect of this is that it makes refactoring of long methods possible, because the extracted methods, when marked private, can't be called from outside the library.

Figure 5.14 takes a typically long method, extracts a block of code, and refactors it into a private method called _sendToServer(). The _sendToServer() method can't be called from outside the library, but the original log() function still works exactly the same way, with external users of the library being unaware of the change.

A PUZZLER WITH PRIVATE CLASSES

In the same way that you can have private methods and private properties in a class, it's also possible to create private classes in a library by prefixing the class name with an underscore, as shown with the _ServerLogger class in listing 5.6. Private classes can be useful in that they can be created only in your library. You can't use the new keyword to create a new instance of a private class from outside your library.

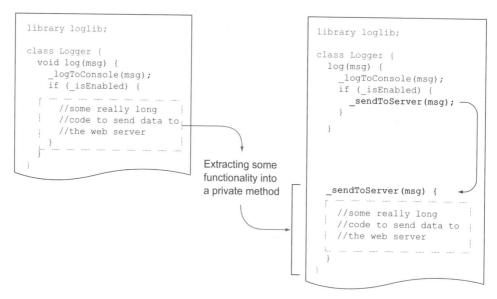

Figure 5.14   To keep your code readable and maintainable, you can extract a block of code into a private method of the same class that isn't visible from outside the library.

Private classes can have public methods and properties. The _ServerLogger class has a private property called _serverIp and a public property called serverName.

An interesting puzzler is why a private class (which is accessible only in a library) can have public methods and properties. When you're in the same library, it makes no difference whether a property is public or private; and if the class is private, how can it be referenced from outside the library? The following listing shows how this can happen, in the getServerLogger() function, which returns a new instance of the private _ServerLogger class.

Listing 5.6   mixed_loglib.dart: library containing both public and private classes

```
library mixed_loglib;

class Logger {

  _ServerLogger getServerLogger() {
    return new _ServerLogger();
  }
}

class _ServerLogger {
  var serverName;
  var _serverIp;
}
```

Logger class is public and can be directly referenced in calling code.

Method on public Logger class can still return a private _ServerLogger instance, which can be used by calling code but not directly referenced.

Private _ServerLogger class contains both public and private properties; this has no effect in the library because the whole class is private.

Although you can directly access private classes outside of a library, a public method or function in that library may return an instance of a private class. This pattern should be avoided, but Dart still handles it through optional typing.

TIP It's valid to return a public class from a library, but such a class is generally referred to by a public, implicit interface, rather than its implementation class name. I discuss this idea in the next chapter.

The calling code in a separate library can see (and instantiate) the `Logger` class, but it has no knowledge of the `_ServerLogger` private class. It can call the `getServerLogger()` function and use the private `_ServerLogger` returned, as long as it doesn't use the class name directly—storing the `_ServerLogger` instance in an untyped variable, as in the following snippet, which stores the returned `_ServerLogger` in the variable named `privateInstance`:

```
Logger logger = new Logger();
var privateInstance = logger.getServerLogger();
```
← **You can store the result only in a dynamic optionally typed variable.**

Even though you can't refer to the `_ServerLogger` class by name, once you have an instance of it you can access its public properties on that private instance with no complaint from the tools. You won't get autocomplete help, though, because you're unable to provide the type information to the tools. If you tried to access the `privateInstance._serverIp` property, you'd get a `noSuchMethod` error, because you're trying to access a private property from outside the library. Accessing `privateInstance.serverName`, though, will work fine, because that isn't marked private. Writing libraries with the intention of their being used this way should be considered bad practice unless used in conjunction with public interfaces, because there's no way for end users of your library to find out how your private classes should be used (other than looking at the source).

5.2.2 Using private functions in libraries

Functions in the top level of a library can also be public and private in the same way as classes. Prefixing a private function with an underscore makes it private to a library, meaning it can be accessed from anywhere in the library. This can be useful when you want to provide private utility functions in a library but there's no associated data, so they don't warrant becoming methods in a class.

You can see this by adding a private function to the `loglib` library, as shown in the following listing, which is called by the public-facing `info()`, `warn()`, and `debug()` functions and your `Logger` class.

Listing 5.7 loglib.dart with a private function

```
library loglib;

_logMsg(msg) {
  _ServerLogger serverLogger = new _ServerLogger();
  serverLogger.send(msg);
}

info(msg) => _logMsg("INFO $msg");
warn(msg) => _logMsg("DEBUG $msg");
debug(msg) => _logMsg("WARN $msg");
```

← **New private _logMsg function is accessible only from within same library**

← **Creates new instance every time a message is logged, for example only**

Existing public functions now call _logMsg

```
class _ServerLogger {
  // ...snip...
}
class Logger {
  log(msg) => _logMsg(msg);
}
```

Existing Logger class
now calls _logMsg

The private _logMsg() top-level function is accessible only from within the loglib library—external users of the library can't access this function. In the example, an instance of the private class _ServerLogger is created for each call for the purposes of example only—a print() function would suffice.

> **Remember**
> - The private _ prefix can be applied to functions, classes, methods, and properties.
> - Code marked as private can be accessed only from within the same library.
> - Code not marked as private can be accessed by external users of that library.

Building reusable libraries with hidden internal functionality is standard practice in most applications, and Dart enables this feature by taking the underscore convention and baking it into the language.

Although you can now split your application into reusable libraries, a library can still consist of many thousands of lines of code. Keeping track of all that code in a single library file can be awkward. Fortunately, Dart provides a way to divide libraries even further: into collections of source files.

5.3   *Organizing library source code*

The loglib library now contains a mix of public and private classes and functions. If you were to add even more functionality, it wouldn't be long before the library file would become hard to navigate, even with the tools. Even more of an issue when developing in teams is that any major refactoring to the file can easily cause issues for other developers on the team if you're working on the same library simultaneously.

Fortunately, Dart allows you to split a library into multiple source files. External users of your library have no knowledge of this, and it makes no difference to users of your library whether it's constructed of a single file, 100 files containing a class or function each, or any combination of classes and functions.

In this section, you'll take the loglib.dart file, which currently contains two classes and four functions, as shown in figure 5.15, and split it into separate source files.

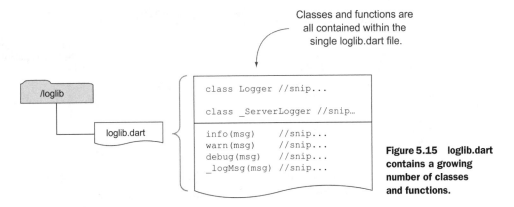

Figure 5.15 loglib.dart contains a growing number of classes and functions.

These functions and classes will be split into two separate source files, with the loglib.dart library file linking them together. The goal is to end up with three files in total, as demonstrated in figure 5.16.

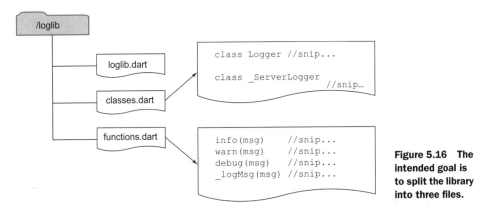

Figure 5.16 The intended goal is to split the library into three files.

This is just one way to split the library. You could split each class and function into its own file or split all the public functions and classes into one file and all the private functions and classes into another.

> **TIP** In libraries, there are likely to be multiple units of functionality, each of which may consist of a few classes. As a best practice, it's these units of functionality that you should wrap into a single source file.

5.3.1 *Using the part and part of keywords*

Dart provides the part keyword to allow you to split code into separate files in a library. It's used in the same file as the library keyword and needs to provide a relative path to the other source files that make up the library: for example, part "functions.dart";. You can create new, empty text files for classes.dart and functions.dart and cut and paste the classes and functions into them. They need no extra keyword. The following listing shows the complete functions.dart file.

Listing 5.8   Complete functions.dart source file

```
part of loglib;

_logMsg(msg) {
  print(msg);
  _ServerLogger serverLogger = new _ServerLogger();
  serverLogger.send(msg);
}

info(msg) => _logMsg("INFO $msg");
warn(msg) => _logMsg("DEBUG $msg");
debug(msg) => _logMsg("WARN $msg");
```

◁ **Indicates that this
file is part of loglib
library**

We call this a *part* file. You can only use it in the context of a library—it achieves nothing on its own. It's important to note that a source file is an extract of code that *could* have remained in the original library file but has been extracted into a separate file for developer convenience. It has no bearing on how the code is used in terms of either public and private visibility of classes and functions or conversion to JavaScript.

After extracting your functions and classes into their respective files, import them as demonstrated in figure 5.17.

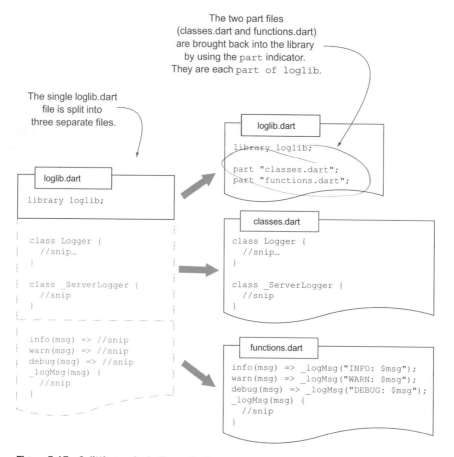

Figure 5.17   Splitting a single library file into separate source files

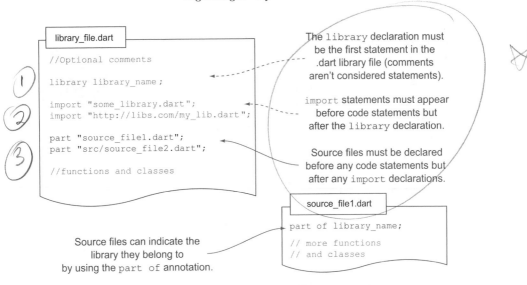

Figure 5.18 **part statements must come before any other source code.**

The `part "classes.dart";` keyword takes a filename as its parameter, which should be a filename that's relative to the `library` file; for example, you could put all the linked source files into a subfolder from the main loglib.dart `library` file:

```
part "sourceFiles/classes.dart";
```

The loglib.dart file now contains only a series of `library`, `import`, and `part` statements. This setup is perfectly valid and is a pattern you'll see around the built-in Dart source libraries. Remember that in section 5.1 we noted that a library can import other libraries. If your `loglib` library needed to import other libraries, the `import` statements also appear in this file:

```
library loglib;

import "other_library.dart";

part "classes.dart";
part "functions.dart";
```

Imports external library into loglib library

The order of the statements is important, as shown in figure 5.18.

Any classes and functions imported from external libraries such as `import "dart:html";` become available to all part files that belong to `loglib`. Thus the relationship between each class and function in the library remains unchanged, although they're organized in source files.

Source-file restrictions

You should be aware of the following restrictions when using the `part` keyword:

- Files imported into a library with the `part` command need to be treated as though they're part of the original library file. That is, they can't contain any statements of their own. If they did, they'd potentially break the strict ordering of the `library`, `import`, and `part` keywords.

(continued)

- Source files can belong to only a single library in an application. `loglib` and `webloglib` couldn't both use `part "classes.dart";`.
- A class or function must exist in a single file. There is no way to make a class or a function span multiple files (there are no partial classes as in C#).

If you think of part files as being part of the same logical library file, then these restrictions make sense. You couldn't have one part of a file also be part of a different file, and you couldn't have a library file contain another `library` statement halfway down. It would also be impossible to split a class or function into two separate parts in the same file.

It's important to remember that having classes and functions in different part files has no effect on privacy. They're all considered to be in the same library, and privacy exists at the library level.

Remember

- A single library file can be split into many part files.
- External users of the library have no knowledge that the library has been split.
- Dart treats a library file split into multiple physical part files as though it were a single library file.

In addition to encapsulating functionality into your library and making that available for third-party code to use, it's also possible to run a library directly, like a script.

5.4 *Packaging your libraries*

In Dart, a package is a standalone application or one or more libraries put together into a single unit with a version number. Packages serve two purposes: they allow your application to easily import other people's packages, and they let you format your own file structure in such a way as to allow your code to be packaged and imported by third parties.

The pub tool, which is built into the Dart Editor and is also available from the command line, lets you import packages that your code depends on. These packages may be hosted on a web server, in GitHub (or other Git repository), and in the pub.dart-lang.org repository. If you've used other package managers, such as Java's Maven or Node.js's npm, pub performs a similar function: it automatically downloads your application's dependencies and any nested dependencies. Pub also manages versioning conflicts, including highlighting conflicts in nested dependencies.

A file called pubspec.yaml, which is found in the root of your source's file structure, contains all the important information to enable pub to find and download dependencies. It uses a YAML file format: a human-readable markup language that uses indentation to define sections and subsections. Listing 5.9 shows an example pubspec.yaml file. The `name` field is mandatory, and the `version` and `description` fields are also mandatory if you want your package hosted on pub.dartlang.org. The other fields are optional, but the important one is `dependencies`, which tells pub about your dependencies (if you have no dependencies outside the core Dart SDK, then you can omit the `dependencies` field).

Listing 5.9   Example pubspec.yaml for `loglib`

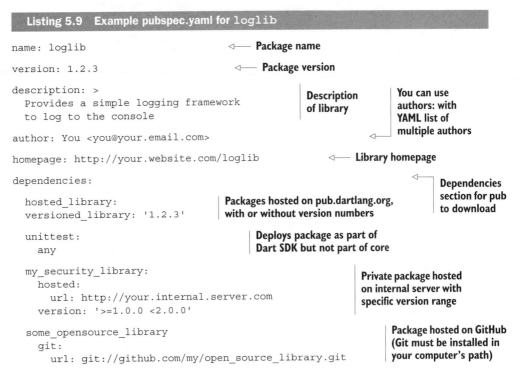

```
name: loglib                          ⟵── Package name

version: 1.2.3                         ⟵── Package version

description: >
  Provides a simple logging framework
  to log to the console
author: You <you@your.email.com>

homepage: http://your.website.com/loglib

dependencies:

  hosted_library:
  versioned_library: '1.2.3'

  unittest:
    any

my_security_library:
  hosted:
    url: http://your.internal.server.com
    version: '>=1.0.0 <2.0.0'

some_opensource_library
  git:
    url: git://github.com/my/open_source_library.git
```

- Description of library
- You can use authors: with YAML list of multiple authors
- Library homepage
- Dependencies section for pub to download
- Packages hosted on pub.dartlang.org, with or without version numbers
- Deploys package as part of Dart SDK but not part of core
- Private package hosted on internal server with specific version range
- Package hosted on GitHub (Git must be installed in your computer's path)

Pub works by using convention over configuration, and it expects a specific layout for your application. The key files and folders are shown in figure 5.19; fortunately, the Dart Editor creates this structure for you when you create a new project.

To pull the various dependencies into your project, you need to use the `pub install` and `pub update` commands, which both exist in the Dart Editor menus. These commands install or pull newer versions of the dependencies into your application's structure and create a pubspec.lock file. Packages are downloaded into a cache, normally the .pub-cache/ folder in your home directory. The pubspec.lock file contains the actual versions of the different dependencies that pub installed (useful when you've specified a version range). This file can be committed into source control, which ensures that other developers on your team use the same version of any dependencies.

Once the dependencies are installed, you can refer to them using the `import` keyword in your library code. For example, the PackList app can use the `loglib` package, as shown in this snippet:

```
import "package:loglib/loglib.dart";
```

- Maps to loglib package's /lib/ folder

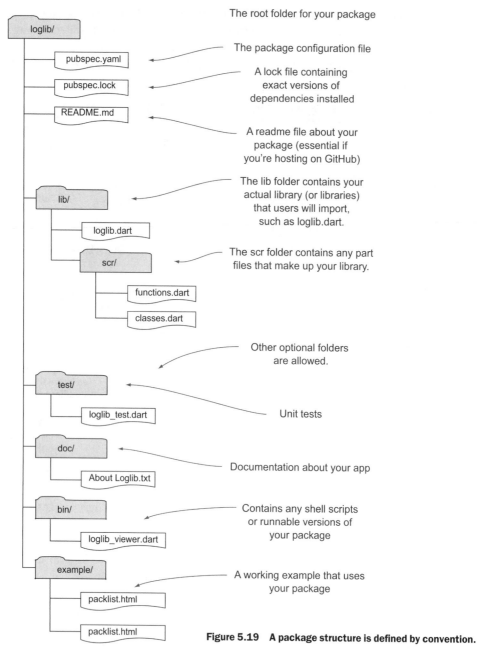

Figure 5.19   A package structure is defined by convention.

5.5   *Scripts are runnable libraries*

The loglib library provides logging functions to external users by providing a number of classes and functions that external code can use. It's also possible to run the library directly—remember that a Dart script is no more than a .dart file containing a top-level main() function.

An example using the `loglib` library is to allow it to replay a series of log messages loaded from a web server back into the developer console. You can provide a publicly accessible function such as `replay(url)` that calls a server and sends each of the returned log messages to the existing private `_logMsg()` function.

One way of running this new replay functionality is to write a separate app that imports the `loglib` library and then calls `replay()`. This seems like a lot of work in order to call a single function. Fortunately, Dart provides another alternative. A library can also contain a `main()` function, and a `main()` function is all Dart needs in order to let the library become runnable (a `main()` function is the entry-point function for all Dart scripts). The following listing shows `main()` added to the `loglib` library.

Listing 5.10 Library containing a `main()` method

```
library loglib;

import "dart:html";

part "classes.dart";
part "functions.dart";                          ◁─── main() appears
                                                       in library
main() {
  replay("http://www.someserver.com/logMessages");  ◁─── main() now calls
}                                                          replay() function

replay(url) {
  //snip... load msgsFromUrl list

  for (msg in msgsFromUrl) {              ◁─── replay() calls private
    _logMsg(msg);                                 _logMsg() function
  }
}
```

You can now use this functionality from within an HTML file by including a `script` tag in the associated HTML, such as

```
<script type="application/dart" src="loglib.dart"></script>
```

This calls the `main()` function once the code is fully loaded and ready to run.

Although it's best practice to keep `main()` in the library file (that is, the file containing the `library` statement), you can put `main()` in a different part file. Remember, a function or class in a part file performs exactly the same as if it were in the main library file, and the `main()` function is just the same.

The implication is that every Dart app that you create can also become a library by the addition of a `library` declaration at the top. In this way, it becomes trivial to take an existing Dart app and turn it into a library that can be embedded in some other application by making the existing Dart app also function as a library. By adding a `library` statement to your PackList app, you can include it in a mashup of other applications, each of which provides independent functionality, brought together by a common theme (see figure 5.20).

Dart comes with modularity and flexibility built in, and regardless of whether you start by building a library or an app, it's incredibly easy to switch between one and the other.

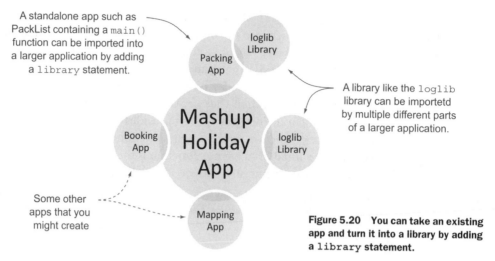

A standalone app such as PackList containing a `main()` function can be imported into a larger application by adding a `library` statement.

A library like the `loglib` library can be importetd by multiple different parts of a larger application.

Some other apps that you might create

Figure 5.20   You can take an existing app and turn it into a library by adding a `library` statement.

5.6   Summary

Dart provides a library structure for organizing and reusing your source code. With library and part files, you can structure your code in a way that makes sense for team development and third-party reuse.

The `import` statement allows apps and libraries to import other libraries in a simple fashion while avoiding naming clashes through the use of library prefixes. Library-based privacy allows you to share libraries of code and functions and classes in that library that are private from code that uses your library. Libraries can also become standalone applications through the addition of a `main()` function, which is the entry point for any Dart script.

> **Remember**
> - Libraries can import other libraries.
> - A library can also be used as a runnable script.
> - A library's source code can be split across multiple part files.
> - Any code declared as private in a library is accessible from within any other part of that library.
> - Any code not declared as private can also be used by code that uses the library.

Now that you know enough Dart to build a structured app consisting of multiple libraries and files and you understand how Dart's privacy mechanism relates to libraries rather than classes, it's time to take a deeper look at Dart's class, interface, and inheritance mechanisms and how they fit into the dynamic world of optional typing.

Constructing classes and interfaces

This chapter covers

- Defining classes
- Dart's implied interfaces
- Constructing classes

Dart is a single-inheritance, class-based, object-oriented language. It has many similarities to Java and C# in terms of its class and interface mechanisms. In this chapter, we'll look at the features of Dart's classes that enable you to design flexible libraries of classes and interfaces that promote best practices, such as coding against interfaces and providing named constructors for different, specific purposes.

We'll deal with the different ways to construct classes, including what *appears* to be the ability to construct an instance of an abstract class, rather than a specific implementation class, and why you might get the same instance of an object back when calling a constructor. In the discussion of factory constructors, we'll also look at static properties and methods, which share their state across all instances of a class. When we get to constant constructors, you'll see that you must use them in conjunction with final, read-only properties to provide a simple way to create fixed, unchanging class instances.

We'll also look at interfaces, which are also used extensively in Java and C# but don't appear in JavaScript. By following some of the lessons learned from using interfaces in Java and C#, the Dart designers have created a number of pleasing ways to make coding against interfaces easier—for example, the fact that every class is also an implied interface. In this chapter, you'll see how you can follow the maxim to "code against interfaces instead of classes." By designing your library to use interfaces, you provide the ability for users of your library to easily unit-test functions and switch implementations of classes in your library.

> **NOTE** If you're already familiar with Java or C# you might want to skim this chapter, but keep an eye out for implicit interfaces, where a class definition is also an implied interface. Dart's class and interface structure shares most of its logical concepts with those found in Java and C#. Remember to look at the appendix for a quick syntax reference.

First, let's look at how to define a simple class and see what Dart has to offer.

6.1   Defining a simple class

A class in Dart can contain simple fields, getter and setter accessors for those fields, and methods. Generically, these are known as a class's *members*. In an example user-profile scenario, you may define a User class to have firstname and lastname fields and a method to return a full name, which is a concatenation of the firstname and lastname fields (see the following listing). In use, you would use the new keyword to create an instance of this class, also shown in the main() method.

Listing 6.1   A simple User class

```
class User {                          ◄── Class name          Private field, denoted
  String _forename;                                           by underscore

  String get forename => _forename;                   Public getter and setter, accessing
  set forename(value) => _forename = value;           private _forename field

  String surname;                                             Public field,
                                                              defined as String
  String getFullName() {
    return "$forename $surname";      Method returning forename
  }                                   and surname as String
}
main() {
  User user = new User();             Creates instance
  user.forename = "Alice";            of User class
  user.surname = "Smith";
  var fullName = user.getFullName();  Sets value of fields
}
                                      Calls method on
                                      user instance
```

This is a very simple class. The important observation is that the class's members, in the form of the getFullName() method and the forename and surname fields, imply an interface. Dart uses this implied interface to allow the best practice of programming against interfaces rather than specific class implementations. At any point, you can switch your `User` implementation with a different class that implements the same interface. This is an important distinction between Dart and Java or C#, which require explicit interface definitions to be used. Let's see an example of this in practice.

6.1.1 Coding against a class's interface

Imagine a `login` library that uses your `User` class. The implementation details of both the `User` class and the authentication service class are contained in an external library, provided by another development team in a library called `LogonLibrary`. You write your own code to use the `AuthService` class and the `User` class, as shown in the following listing, without needing to be aware of the specific implementation details.

> **Listing 6.2 logon.dart: using an example `AuthService`**

Imports LogonLibrary library with implementation details hidden using library privacy

Passes into function an instance of a class that looks like AuthService

auth function forms interface point that AuthService implements

Prints "true" or "false" depending on whether service has authenticated user

Example click handler that calls doLogon()

```
import "logon_library.dart";

User doLogon(AuthService authSvc, String username, String password) {

  User user = authSvc.auth(username, password);

  print("User is authenticated:${user==null}");
  return user;
}
buttonClickHandler(event) {
  AuthService authSvc = new AuthService();
  User user = doLogon(authSvc,
                    query("#username").value,
                    query("#password").value);
}
```

As long as the `AuthService` instance has an `auth()` method that returns a `User` instance, your `doLogon()` function will run just fine.

Dependency injection or inversion of control?

The `doLogon()` function takes an `authSvc` object as one of its parameters. This is an example of dependency injection, which allows you to switch implementations. For example, when testing the `doLogon()` function, you could provide a mock object for the `authSvc` parameter. When testing locally, you can use a simple `authSvc` object, and when deploying your production system, you can provide an enterprise `authSvc` object.

If you wrote the `doLogon()` function without the `authSvc` parameter, you'd have to create a concrete instance in the function. This would mean that you couldn't switch implementations of the `AuthService`, making it harder to unit-test and harder to provide different deployment scenarios.

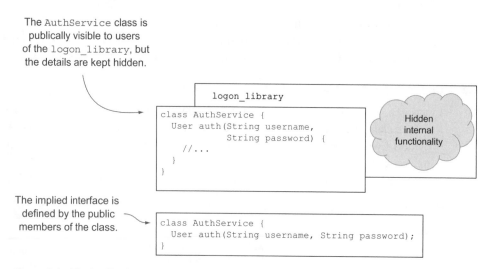

The `AuthService` class is publically visible to users of the `logon_library`, but the details are kept hidden.

The implied interface is defined by the public members of the class.

Figure 6.1   The implied interface is defined by the public members of the class.

Let's say you want to test your `doLogon()` function. By using dependency injection, you can decide which implementation of `AuthService` is used. Instead of using the `AuthService` that hits some real servers to provide authentication, you can provide a mock implementation that implements `AuthService`'s implied interface, which is shown in figure 6.1.

The public interface of `AuthService` contains a single method that takes two string parameters and returns an instance of a class called `User`. Using the `implements` keyword, you can make a mock version, called `MockAuthService`, which you'll use to test `doLogon()`. The following listing shows the mock class and the simple test, which is wrapped in the `main()` function.

Listing 6.3   Using a mock authentication service

```
import "logon_library.dart";

class MockAuthService implements AuthService {          Mock class implements another
                                                        class's implied interface
  User auth(String username, String password) {
    var user = new User();
    user.forename = "testForename";                     Mock class's
    user.surname = "testSurname";                       implementation of auth()
    return user;
  }
}
                                                        Existing doLogon()
                                                        function
User doLogon(AuthService authSvc, String username, String password) {
  User user = authSvc.auth(username, password);
  print("User is authenticated:${user==null}");
                                                        Uses mock
  return user;                                          implementation
}
```

```
main() {
    AuthService authService = new MockAuthService();
    var user = doLogon(authService, "Alice", "password");
    print(user.forename);
    print(user.surname);
}
```

Uses mock implementation in doLogon() call

Creates instance of MockAuthService

When a class explicitly implements an interface, the Dart tools can validate that if the interface changes, anything that implements the interface has also changed. If the AuthService class changed its auth() method to include a third parameter, the Dart Editor tools would indicate that the EnterpriseLogonService class also needed to change, whereas the MockLogonService, which doesn't use the implements keyword, wouldn't fail until runtime.

> **TIP** Although it's valid Dart code to write a class definition with no type information explicitly specified for the class's members (by using dynamic typing), it's good practice to specify explicit type information on your class's public interface. Doing so allows you to get the most benefit from the tools and provides documentation about the intention of your code.

6.1.2 *Formalizing interfaces with explicit interface definitions*

An interface defines the contract that a class will fulfill or the requirements that a class must meet to properly implement that interface. So far, you've been using an interface implied by the class definition. Dart allows you to define an interface explicitly, independent of the class that actually provides the implementation. Defining an interface explicitly is similar to defining a class—you define the public class members without an implementation (known as an *abstract* class). Let's change AuthService into an interface and create an implementation of it called EnterpriseAuthService, as shown next. Your MockAuthService class remains unchanged.

Listing 6.4   Defining an explicit interface

```
abstract class AuthService {                          ◁─── Defines abstract AuthService class
    User auth(String username, String password);
}                                                           An auth() method
                                                            definition without
class EnterpriseAuthService implements AuthService {  ◁─    an implementation
    User auth(String username, String password) {
        // some enterprise implementation                  Implements AuthService
    }
}                                                      Implemented
                                                       version of auth()
```

The abstract keyword is important because it lets Dart know that this is a class with methods that have no implementation. This makes it impossible to create an instance of AuthService directly, because there is no implementation of AuthService to use. Thus the following would be considered an error:

Creating an instance of the abstract AuthService is impossible.

```
var authService = new AuthService();
```

But you'll see in a later section how to use factory constructors to allow this syntax, even on an abstract class, by providing a default implementation.

> **NOTE** In Dart, when we talk about an interface, we're actually referring to a class's *implied* interface. Whether that interface is on an abstract class or an actual class containing method implementations doesn't matter. Throughout the rest of the book, the term *interface* will be used in this way.

6.1.3 Using multiple interfaces

One of the benefits of using coding against an interface is that Dart allows multiple interfaces. This means a single class can implement more than one interface. For example, you might define an abstract `RolesService` class, which provides a `getUserRoles()` method for retrieving role information about a user. `EnterpriseAuthService` can then implement `RolesService`, in addition to `AuthService`, by providing the public `getRoles()` method, as shown in the next listing.

Listing 6.5 Implementing multiple interfaces

```
abstract class RolesService {
  List getRoles(User user);              New RolesService class
}

abstract class AuthService {
  User auth(String username, String password);      Implements AuthService
}                                                    and RolesService

class EnterpriseAuthService implements AuthService, RolesService {
  User auth(String username, String password) {
    // some enterprise implementation
  }

  List getRoles(User user) {
    // some enterprise implementation      Provides implementation
  }                                        of getRoles()
}
```

You can now use `EnterpriseAuthService` anywhere a `RolesService` instance needs to be used. The simple way to remember this relationship is that a class shares an "is-an" relationship with any interface classes it implements. You can say that `EnterpriseAuthService` "is-a" `RolesService`, and `EnterpriseAuthService` "is-an" `AuthService`. Thus the code in the following listing, which passes an instance of `EnterpriseAuthService` into different functions that are expecting to receive an instance of `AuthService` or `RolesService`, is valid.

Listing 6.6 Using `EnterpriseAuthService` with multiple interfaces

```
User doLogon(AuthService authService, String username, String password) {
  return authService.auth(username, password);
}                                              Expects instance of AuthService

showRoles(RolesService rolesService, User user) {      Expects instance of RolesService
```

```
    List roles = rolesService.getRoles(user);
    print(roles);
}
main() {
    var entService = new EnterpriseAuthService();

    var user = doLogon(entService,"Alice","password");

    showRoles(entService, user);

}
```

Creates instance of **EnterpriseAuthService**

EnterpriseAuthService has "is-an" relationship with AuthService

EnterpriseAuthService has "is-a" relationship with RolesService

In this example, all the interfaces have a single method each. It's important to note that there's no restriction on the number of methods or properties that may appear on an interface definition, just as you can have any number of methods and properties on a class definition.

> **TIP** As a best practice, design your interfaces in such a way that they group similar functionality. When you design your interfaces this way, users of your code can create either a single class, which implements multiple interfaces, or multiple classes, as required. If you create a single big interface, then users of your code don't get that choice.

6.1.4 Declaring property getters and setters

So far, interfaces and classes have had only methods declared on them. Many classes also have fields defined on them. Your `AuthService` interface might define an `isConnected` field that defines whether the authentication service is connected to its back-end data store.

Back in chapter 3, you saw that a property defined with a getter and a setter is accessed by calling code in the same way as a simple field:

Are you calling a setter or writing to a field? Dart syntax is the same, so for the caller, this doesn't matter.

```
authService.isConnected = true;
```

Fortunately, because a calling class uses property getters and setters the same way as fields, you can also declare this in an interface either way. Add an `isConnected` property getter and setter (which use the `get` and `set` keywords) to the `AuthService` interface and a simple `isConnected` field to your `RoleService` interface, as shown in the following listing.

> **Listing 6.7   logon_library.dart: getters, setters, and properties in interfaces**

```
library logonlib;

abstract class AuthService {
    User auth(String username, String password);
    bool get isConnected;
    void set isConnected(bool value);
}
```

Defines property getter using get

Defines property setter using set

```
abstract class RoleService {
  List getRoles(User user);
  bool isConnected;                          <─── Defines field
}

class EnterpriseAuthService implements AuthService, RoleService {
  bool _isConnected;
  bool get isConnected => _isConnected;
  void set isConnected(bool value) => _isConnected = value;

  // snip auth() and getRoles()                 Implementation of getter and
}                                               setter fulfills both AuthService
                                                and RolesService interfaces
```

Because the syntax for reading and writing to a property is identical whether you're using a getter and setter or a property, you can implement an interface definition of a property using either method. They both meet the requirement of the interface definition, which, as you might remember, is that you can call code that looks like this:

```
authService.isConnected = true;
```

As long as you can use the implementing class in this way, it meets the requirements of the interface, whether it's using a getter and setter pair or a field.

> **Remember**
> - A class definition is also implicitly an interface definition.
> - The `abstract` keyword is used to declare a class without implemented methods and can be used for explicit interface definitions.
> - The `implements` keyword indicates that a class is providing the implementations of specific methods
> - Classes have an "is-an" relationship with interfaces.

When you define an interface, you're providing a mechanism that allows your own code to be extended and reused, and this is how the Dart libraries are built. The core "classes" in Dart, such as `String`, `int`, and `List`, are actually interfaces. Earlier in this chapter, we noted that although you need to create a new instance of a class, sometimes the Dart code looks as though you're creating a new interface. A great example of this is

```
var myList = new List();
```

This code seems as though it shouldn't work, because you can't create an instance of an interface—only a class. This is true, but the next section will show how code like this can work and how you can use a number of different ways to create new instances of your classes.

6.2   *Constructing classes and interfaces*

When you design a library, whether for your own app or for publishing to third parties, you need to make it flexible enough to meet the use cases for that library. It's good practice to deploy interfaces wherever possible to allow users of your class to swap your implementation with other implementations.

You should also allow users of your library to create instances of your classes in ways that make sense for specific use cases, as you did in chapter 3 when working with the `Element` class. In that instance, you created an element by using either an HTML snippet or a tag name, but you still got an element back. The use case differed, but the `Element` class is designed to allow this.

There's also a case in which you might want to reuse instances of your class: when there's an expensive operation (such as connecting to the enterprise authentication server). You might want to reuse that connection rather than create a new one every time.

Finally, you might want users to be able to create a single constant version of your class in a specific state. For example, an instance of a specific error message class will never change once you've created it, and all instances of a specific error message will be identical. Dart allows this functionality through constant constructors.

In this section, we'll look at a number of ways to create instances of classes. The new keyword—which in JavaScript, Java, and C# is used to create a new instance of an object—*nearly* always has the same effect in Dart. You'll see why it's *nearly*, and not *always*, when you get to factory constructors to provide object caching. You'll also learn about the `const` keyword, which is another way to create a new, unchanging instance of a class.

Let's explore a class constructor method, which we first looked at in chapter 3. You'll see how to extend the constructor's functionality to allow field initialization and how to add multiple named constructors.

6.2.1 *Constructing class instances*

When you use the `new` keyword to create an instance of a class, such as in `new EnterpriseAuthService();`, you're actually calling the class's constructor method. If no explicit constructor is defined, then a default constructor is used, which has no implementation. A class's constructor shares its name with the specific instance of the class. For example, the following constructor provides an implementation identical to that of a default (undefined) constructor, with the addition of a `print()` command:

```
class EnterpriseAuthService {
  String connection;                                  ⟵── Initializes to null

  EnterpriseAuthService() {
    print("in the constructor");                      Constructor method
  }
}
main() {
  var entSvc = new EnterpriseAuthService();           Causes "in the
}                                                      constructor" to be output
```

Just like other methods and functions, you can pass in parameters to the constructor. For example, you could modify the `EnterpriseAuthService` constructor to take a `connection` parameter, and use that parameter to initialize the `connection` field:

```
class EnterpriseAuthService {
  String connection;
  EnterpriseAuthService(String connection) {        Adds parameter
    this.connection = connection;                    to constructor
  }
}                                                    Sets connection
                                                     field using this
```

> **NOTE**   The this keyword in Dart behaves the same as in Java and C#, in that it refers specifically to the instance of the class using it. This is different than in JavaScript, where the value of this changes during execution.

All the syntax options available to functions, including optional and default parameters, are available for constructors, but constructors also have one more feature. One of the lessons learned from Java is that constructors are mostly used to initialize internal properties, as in the previous snippet. Dart introduces a shorthand by using the this keyword in the constructor's parameter list to implicitly initialize a parameter. For example, the following snippet has exactly the same effect as the previous one:

```
class EnterpriseAuthService {                     Constructor takes a
  String connection;                              connection parameter that
  EnterpriseAuthService(this.connection) { }      initializes connection field
}
```

6.2.2   *Designing and using classes with multiple constructors*

Dart, unlike Java or C#, doesn't support function, method, or constructor overloading (in which you can have the same function name but different parameter definitions). How do you have multiple constructors that allow you to create instances of the class in different ways?

In Java and C#, you'd reuse the same constructor name and provide different parameters, but Dart provides a different mechanism that's similar to the library prefixes seen in chapter 5. Dart takes the class name as the constructor prefix and allows you to use named constructors, each of which has a different name (and parameters if required). Figure 6.2 shows the equivalent constructor syntax in Java and Dart.

Back in chapter 3, you built user interface elements using Element.tag() and Element.html(). You used named constructors to create instances of Element but in two different ways. Now that EnterpriseAuthService has named constructors, you can use these, too:

```
var authSvc1 = new EnterpriseAuthService();         Default constructor
var authSvc1 = new EnterpriseAuthService
        .withConn("connection string");             Named withConn constructor
var authSvc2 = new EnterpriseAuthService
          .usingServer("localhost",8080);           Named usingServer constructor
```

Named constructors are useful because of their ability to specify their intention in the constructor name. By choosing appropriate constructor names, you can provide documentation for future users of your code, letting them know what you intended a specific named constructor to be used for.

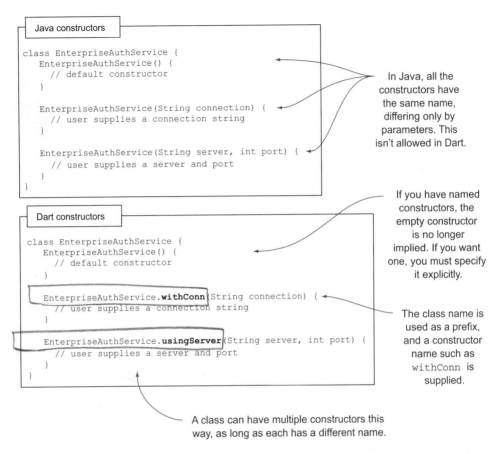

Figure 6.2 A comparison of constructor syntax between Java and Dart. Dart must provide named constructors prefixed with the class name.

6.2.3 *Using factory constructors to create instances of abstract classes*

Earlier in this chapter, you saw that it was an error to try to create an instance of an abstract class that you were using as an interface:

Creates warning about instantiating abstract class

```
AuthService authService = new AuthService();
```

When you're building an application, it's good practice to use interface type names rather than specific implementation class type names. Doing so allows you to switch implementations during development, which is great for unit-testing with mock implementations. The corollary of this practice is that when you're designing a library, it's good practice to provide interfaces in type definitions to allow the most flexibility to users of your library.

Often, though, you intend the users of your library to use a specific class in most circumstances. The AuthService abstract class, which defines the interface, is a good example. Most of the time, users use the AuthService interface type in conjunction

[handwritten: You need to know about t and t abstract the concrete]

with the `EnterpriseAuthService` class that's part of the same external library definition. Thus many users write code such as the following:

```
AuthService authSvc = new EnterpriseAuthService();
```

This approach adds complexity for the users of your library, because they now need to
know about two types and know that one is an interface and the other is its implementation class. This sort of code is prevalent in the Java world, where huge libraries exist
as chains of interfaces, and tracking down the correct class implementation to use can
be a chore.

   Fortunately, Dart allows you, the library designer, to use factory constructors on an
abstract class, which return a specific default implementation class. When you use the
factory keyword with a constructor, you're specifying that the constructor method is
responsible for creating and returning a valid object, as shown in the next listing.

Listing 6.8   Using factory constructors for default implementations

```
abstract class AuthService {
    User auth(String username, String password);

    factory AuthService() {          ◁── Defines factory
        return new EnterpriseAuthService();      constructor
    }                                ◁── It must return an
}                                         instance of an object.
```

[handwritten: Now we can construct an abstract class]

This approach validly lets users of your interface write code such as this:

```
AuthService authSvc = new AuthService();    ◁── Same as before, but factory
                                                 constructors allow this to happen.
```

This code lets the user treat the abstract class as though it were an implementation
class but still follow good practice by coding against an interface. When you use the
Dart `String`, `List`, and `int` types, you're actually using interfaces that have an underlying default implementation defined.

   Factory constructors benefit from the ability to use multiple names in the same way
as normal constructors. As you'll see in the next section, the ability of factory constructors to return an instance of a class can also be used on standard implementation
classes to provide a caching mechanism.

6.2.4   *Reusing objects with factory constructors*

Some operations in computing should be kept to a minimum. They're either expensive
in terms of processing, such as building up a large number of nested objects, or expensive in terms of time, such as connecting to another server. For example, when Alice logs
on to the enterprise system, closely followed by Bob, you shouldn't have the code wait
a second or two to connect to the enterprise system every time; that connection should
be cached in your app. In these cases, it's desirable to be able to cache objects such as
connections in a reusable pool of objects and return one of them to a user of your class
rather than create a new instance of the object every time. This is another use for factory
constructors, which can exist on any class, not just abstract classes.

You can use this behavior with `EnterpriseAuthService` by converting the `using-Server()` named constructor that you saw earlier into a factory constructor (by adding the `factory` prefix). The simplest implementation of this is

factory keyword indicates it's a factory constructor.

```
class EnterpriseAuthService {
  factory EnterpriseAuthService.usingServer(String server, int port) {
    return new EnterpriseAuthService();
  }
}
// elsewhere in your code
var authSvc = new EnterpriseAuthService.usingServer("localhost",8080);
```

It's responsible for returning an instance of EnterpriseAuthService (a new instance or an existing instance).

Syntax for calling factory constructor is unchanged.

In your simple implementation of the factory constructor, you gain nothing by using the factory. It becomes more powerful, though, when you cache the objects you're creating in the factory constructor. One way to do this is to use class static properties, which you'll see in a couple of pages. But for the moment, assume that a list of `EnterpriseAuthService` objects exists elsewhere in your application. The following listing shows how you can either get an existing object or return a new object. The interface definition remains unchanged.

Listing 6.9   Using a factory constructor to return an existing object from cache

factory keyword identifies constructor as factory constructor

```
class EnterpriseAuthService {

  factory EnterpriseAuthService.usingServer(String server, int port) {
    var authService = getFromCache(server,port);
    if (authService == null) {
      authService = new EnterpriseAuthService();
      // snip: set values on authService and connect

      addToCache(authService,server,port);
    }

    return authService;
  }
  // snip other methods and properties
}
```

Tries to get existing object from cache

If no matching object is returned from the cache, creates a new one and adds it to cache for later reuse

Returns object. Caller has no knowledge of whether it's been returned from cache or newly created.

TIP   When users of your library use the `new` keyword, they're expecting a new object. As a best practice, use caching factory constructors only if you need to provide preprocessing on new objects or when you can guarantee that reusing an existing object won't surprise a user of your class.

Factory constructors can be powerful when used with a mechanism to store instances of a specific class, but where do you store those instances? It turns out that a good place is in a static property of a class, which we'll look at next.

6.2.5   *Using static methods and properties with factory constructors*

The factory constructor example used two functions—getFromCache() and addToCache()—but didn't explain how this design might work in practice. You need a way to access a central store containing instances of EnterpriseAuthService. Fortunately, Dart, in common with Java and C#, provides static methods and properties as part of a class definition. A *static* member is one that is shared across all instances of a class; it's denoted by the static keyword, which can be applied to methods and properties. Therefore, you can create a static map (which stores a list of key/value pairs) that's shared across all instances of the EnterpriseAuthService class in the application. You need only look into that map and see whether there's an existing matching key based on the server and port values. If there is, you can retrieve the existing instance of EnterpriseAuthService in your factory constructor. Figure 6.3 demonstrates how this works.

When accessing static methods or properties, you can refer to them only by class name, not by a variable name (such as authSvc2): static members are shared across all instances of the class, so accessing them via a specific instance isn't allowed. Listing 6.10

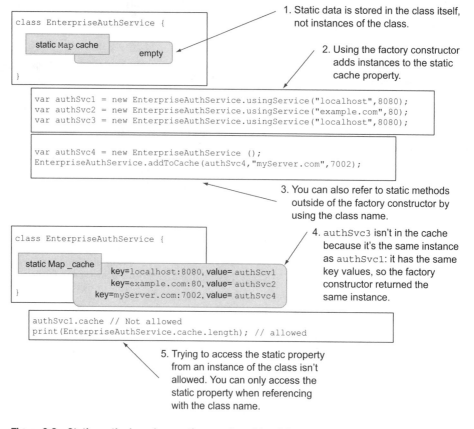

Figure 6.3   Static methods and properties are shared by all instances of a class.

shows the static cache property and a getter that initializes it on first access. The
getFromCache() and addToCache() methods are also static (which means they can't be
accessed with a specific instance of the class) and use the cache to add an instance to
and retrieve an instance from the cache.

Listing 6.10   Implementing a cache with static members

```
class EnterpriseAuthService {
  //... snip other methods and properties            Uses private static
                                                     map as cache
  static Map _cache;

  static Map get cache {                             Public static getter initializes
    if (_cache == null) {                            cache if required and returns it
      _cache = new Map();
    }
    return _cache;                                   getFromCache() returns instance if it
  }                                                  exists in cache (or null if it doesn't)

  static EnterpriseAuthService getFromCache(String server, int port) {
    var key = "$server:$port";
    return cache[key];
  }

  static addToCache(EnterpriseAuthService authService,
                             String server, int port) {
    var key = "$server:$port";                       addToCache() adds
    cache[key] = authService;                        instance to cache
  }

  factory EnterpriseAuthService.usingServer(String server, int port) {
    var authService = getFromCache(server,port);
    if (authService == null) {
      authService = new EnterpriseAuthService();
      // snip: set values on authService and connect

      addToCache(authService,server,port);
    }

    return authService;
  }
}
```

Static properties and methods are useful when you want to store a value across all
instances of a class. One of the concerns with static values in Java and C# is when multiple threads might be accessing a static value, but because Dart is single-threaded, this
isn't possible. It makes all operations thread-safe. We'll look at how to achieve concurrency without threading in chapter 15, when we discuss isolates.

Now that we've covered normal and factory constructors, we need to look at the
final way to create an instance of a class. This task uses a different keyword, const,
which is deployed to define constant constructors much like the factory keyword is
used when defining factory constructors. The const keyword also has a second meaning: it's used in place of new to create constant, unchanging classes.

> **Remember**
> - Abstract classes can use `factory` constructors to instantiate a default implementation class, which allows users to maintain good application design by working exclusively with higher-level interfaces.
> - Classes can have multiple named constructors, which are prefixed with the class name.
> - The `factory` keyword lets you create classes that can appear to return a new object but instead get the object instance from elsewhere.

6.3   Creating constant classes with final, unchanging variables

`EnterpriseAuthService` could return an error object, indicating a problem authenticating a user. If there were lots of requests and the server wasn't responding, many hundreds of identical error objects could be created and returned, which would all use memory on the client system. But if you create `const` objects, you get a single error object, which is reused each time. There are two parts to defining a constant object: the values must be `final`, and you must use the `const` keyword to define the constructor and create the instance.

6.3.1   Final values and properties

A constant class can be useful when you know that the user should never change any properties. The values are known at compile time, such as defining status codes or error messages.

To achieve this functionality, Dart places another restriction on the class: all properties on the class must be `final`. `final` is another new keyword that indicates that a variable can't change instance; it's used in place of `var` or in conjunction with a strong type:

Uses final keyword in place of var

Uses final keyword in conjunction with strong type name

```
final myObject = new Object();
final Object anotherObject = new Object();

myObject = new Object();
anotherObject = new Object();
```

Modifying contents of final variable once it's defined is an error. This won't work.

It's impossible to define a final variable without providing it with a value, because the compiler needs to be able to evaluate that value at compile time. But properties in a class *can* be declared as final without your needing to initialize the value beforehand. Instead, you can initialize them in the constructor initialization block.

6.3.2   The constructor initialization block

A class constructor allows initialization of `final` properties before the constructor code begins executing. The constructor initialization block appears between the constructor parameter list and the constructor body; it's a comma-separated list of commands that the constructor must perform in order to initialize a class properly. An initialization block is used in conjunction with the constructor body, which may

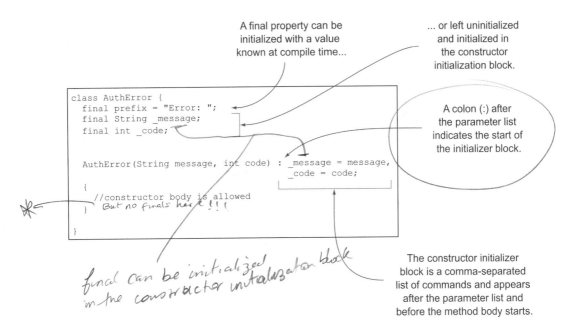

A final property can be initialized with a value known at compile time...

... or left uninitialized and initialized in the constructor initialization block.

A colon (:) after the parameter list indicates the start of the initializer block.

//constructor body is allowed

But no finals here !!!

final can be initialized in the constructor initialization block

The constructor initializer block is a comma-separated list of commands and appears after the parameter list and before the method body starts.

Figure 6.4   The constructor initializer section appears after the list of constructor parameters and can be used to initialize final properties.

also provide some initialization of nonfinal properties. A key difference between the initialization block and the main constructor body is that you can only use the `this` keyword in the main constructor body. Figure 6.4 shows the constructor initialization block.

Once you've initialized the `final` properties in their initialization block, you can't change their values. You must also ensure that you initialize all `final` properties before the start of the constructor body, because Dart will report an error otherwise. You can create instances of the `AuthError` class with the following code:

```
AuthError error001 = new AuthError("Server not available",1);
```

6.3.3   Using the const keyword to create a const constructor

You can't change any properties on the `AuthError` class because they're all marked as `final`. If you were to instantiate a second variable with the same values passed in the constructor, the second instance would effectively be identical, except that it would be a second, physical object created in memory. You can prevent this by changing the constructor into a constant constructor using the `const` keyword, as shown in the next listing.

Listing 6.11   Creating a `const` constructor

```
class AuthError {
  final prefix = "Error: ";
  final String _message;
```

```
   final int _code;                                          const keyword prefixes AuthError
   const AuthError(String message, int code) : _message = message,
                                               _code = code;
   String get errorMessage => "$prefix [$code] $message";
}
                                                       Constructor body isn't allowed
                                                          with const constructor
```

Now that you have the const constructor, you can use it by creating instances of the class. Dart knows that each instance is unchanging and allows you to compare two instances for equality in a quick and efficient manner. When you're creating an instance with a const constructor, also use the const keyword to create the instance, instead of the new keyword:

Identical parameters
passed to constructor

```
AuthError errorA = const AuthError("Server not responding",1);
AuthError errorB = const AuthError("Server not responding",1");
print(errorA === errorB);
```

Objects are the same instance in
memory, so this prints "true."

NOTE   String interpolation isn't allowed in constant constructors. The string values must be compile-time constants and not created dynamically at runtime.

Using the new keyword instead of the const keyword is still allowed. But Dart will treat two different instances as unequal, so this should be avoided.

Well done! Those are the four ways to create classes and interfaces with the new and const keywords. Good library design takes skill and practice, but Dart provides flexibility where needed in its constructor syntax.

> **Remember**
> - The final keyword declares that variables and properties can't change once initialized.
> - A constructor initialization block is required to initialize final properties.
> - The const keyword allows you to define a constant constructor and create an instance of a class that can't change.

6.4   Summary

In this chapter, we started by demonstrating how to use interfaces to enforce a contract that classes can fulfill using the implements keyword. When you code against interfaces rather than classes, you make it easy to swap implementations at runtime, which is especially useful for unit-testing with mock versions of real classes. Dart embraces this concept by allowing you to create instances of an interface while using an underlying default class and by building into the language the ability for all classes to also be interfaces, so you can still code against interfaces even when one hasn't been explicitly defined.

To use your classes and interfaces, Dart lets you create instances using the new and const keywords with the following types of constructors:

- Named constructors for providing constructors for different uses
- Factory constructors, which you can use to find existing instances of a class from a cache, a static map, or another mechanism
- Constant constructors for creating single-instance, unchanging constant classes

In the next chapter, we'll look at class and interface inheritance. Dart is an object-oriented language and provides inheritance mechanisms similar to those in Java and C#. It doesn't have the prototypical inheritance of JavaScript. By using inheritance, you can reuse code that others have written and tested, adding the extra functionality that your use cases require.

Extending
classes and interfaces

This chapter covers

- Building class and interface inheritance hierarchies
- Introducing the `Object` base class
- Understanding the `dynamic` type annotation

Object-oriented programming allows for more than just encapsulating data and behavior in a class. It allows you to extend existing behavior defined elsewhere, which promotes great code reuse. Reusing existing code lets you write less new code in your apps and has the added benefit that existing code should also be tested code.

In this chapter, we'll examine class and interface inheritance in Dart, including how to provide new functionality by overriding existing methods and properties and how to write abstract classes that you can use only as parents in an inheritance hierarchy. If you have written in Java or C#, this will be familiar. But those from a JavaScript background should note the absence of JavaScript's prototypical inheritance mechanism.

The `User` type is returned
by the call to `auth()`.

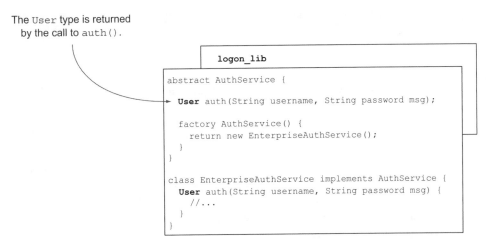

```
                           logon_lib

abstract AuthService {

  User auth(String username, String password msg);

  factory AuthService() {
    return new EnterpriseAuthService();
  }
}

class EnterpriseAuthService implements AuthService {
  User auth(String username, String password msg) {
    //...
  }
}
```

Figure 7.1   The `AuthService` definition from the `logon_lib` example

We'll explore the base `Object` class from which all other classes and types inherit, including strings, numbers, Boolean values, `null`, and your own custom classes. `Object` provides some standard methods and properties that you can override in your own classes, such as the `toString()` method. We'll also look at the `dynamic` type, which Dart uses to enable optional typing.

In chapter 6, you declared a number of classes based around an imaginary `Auth-Service` example, which was used to provide authentication and authorization functionality to your enterprise app. When Alice provides her username and password to your app, the `auth()` function authorizes her details and returns a `User` type that the application uses. You'll continue to use that example in this chapter by building on the `User` type to create a hierarchy of classes and interfaces for use with a simple `AuthService`. To recap, the abstract `AuthService` and the `EnterpriseAuthService` classes are defined in a library called `logon_lib`, as shown in figure 7.1.

You'll use inheritance to extend the `User` type so the enterprise service can return an enterprise user with the functionality defined elsewhere.

NOTE   If you're already familiar with Java or C#, you might want to skim this chapter, because Dart's class inheritance mechanism is the same. Dart allows single-class inheritance with multiple interfaces. Check the "Remember" sections in each summary for the important concepts, and keep an eye out for `noSuchMethod`.

7.1   *Extending classes with inheritance*

Let's start by defining a base class for the `User` type, which follows the same model as the one in the `AuthService` that we discussed in chapter 6. The following listing shows the `User` type.

Listing 7.1   A new `User` class

```
class User {
  User (String this._username) { }

  String _username;                          Private
  String _existingPasswordHash;              properties

  String get username => _username;

  String emailAddress;

  bool isPasswordValid(String newPassword) {
    //... some validation code ...
  }
}
```

Constructor matching that defined on the interface, initializing _username property

Getter method to return private username

Property to read and write email address

Method to check new password against existing password

`AuthService` uses this class by returning an instance of the `User` class. For example, you can write `User aUser = new User("Alice");`, which creates an instance of the `User` class, initialized with the username `"Alice"`. Your app can now use this variable to check new password validity and update the email address.

But your enterprise service needs more functionality in a `User`: for example, marking an account as expired and providing more robust password checking, such as confirming that the same password hasn't been reused for the last five password changes. You can do this by using inheritance. Inheritance allows you to take an existing type, such as a `User`, and add more functionality to it by *subclassing* using the `extends` keyword. When inheriting a class, you can also specify new behavior for existing methods and properties by overriding them.

7.1.1   Class inheritance

When classes inherit each other, the subclass gains the functionality of the methods and properties of the parent class, known as the *superclass*. The subclass also shares an "is-an" relationship with all the parent classes going up the hierarchy.

Dart allows single inheritance, which means a class can extend from a single parent. But a single parent can have multiple children, and each child can have its own children, building up a hierarchy many classes deep.

In the example app, the user Alice will log on to the system and be represented by an instance of the `EnterpriseUser` class, returned from the enterprise authentication service's `auth()` function. This class, which inherits from `User`, gains all the members of `User` by using the `extends` keyword. The representation of Alice as either a `User` or an `EnterpriseUser` will have the same functionality at the moment, provided by inheritance. This functionality works in an `EnterpriseUser` "is-a" `User` relationship. You can test the "is-an" relationship in Dart by using the `is` keyword. The `is` keyword allows you to examine the type of an object and get a Boolean value back in return, as shown in figure 7.2.

This feature provides a lot of flexibility for properties, types, and method parameters. If you know that your method will use only the features of the `User` base type, then you can specify the parameter type `User` but still pass in an `EnterpriseUser`. This

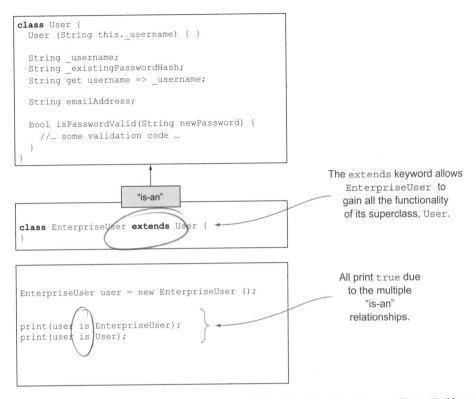

Figure 7.2 `EnterpriseUser` **shares an "is-an" relationship with all the classes going up the hierarchy.**

approach allows others to reuse your code by passing in their own inherited version of User, safe in the knowledge that the method will still function correctly.

The following snippet shows that you can use an EnterpriseUser in the same way as a User object:

```
var user = new User("Alice");
print(user.username);
var enterpriseUser = new EnterpriseUser("Alice");
print(enterpriseUser.username);
```

Uses instance of User

Uses instance of EnterpriseUser the same way as User

> **NOTE** EnterpriseUser's implicit interface is also inherited from the super-class. The public interface of any object is the aggregate of all the public interfaces of inherited classes.

You can now add functionality that's specific to EnterpriseUser, as shown in the next listing. This lets EnterpriseUser use all the existing functionality from User but also provide new functionality.

Listing 7.2 `EnterpriseUser` **with additional functionality**

```
class EnterpriseUser extends User {
  EnterpriseUser() { }          ⟵── Default, empty constructor
```

```
    void markExpired() {
      // some new implementation
    }
  }
```

Additional method specific
to EnterpriseUser

7.1.2   *Inheriting constructors*

Although inheritance allows a child class to gain the existing functionality from the superclass's methods and properties, the child class doesn't inherit any constructors from the superclass. Figure 7.3 demonstrates some of the logical members of EnterpriseUser, which inherits the methods and properties from the User class.

This means if you wanted to use the constructor in the superclass, you'd need to write your own constructor in EnterpriseUser and use the super keyword to refer to the superclass's constructor. You can do this in a special section of the constructor called the *constructor initializer block*, which appears between the constructor parameter list and the constructor body:

You can call a constructor in
the parent class by using the
super keyword in the
constructor initializer block.

```
class EnterpriseUser extends User {
  EnterpriseUser(String uname) : super(uname) {
    // empty constructor body
  }
}
```

The constructor initializer is a block of code that Dart executes before the instance of the class has been created. This is the only place you can call super constructors; calling them in the constructor body isn't allowed. You can also call any super constructor, including named constructors—the parameter list in your class doesn't need to match the parameter list of the superclass. If the base class provides named super

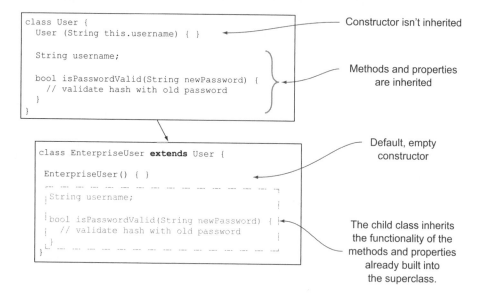

```
class User {
  User (String this.username) { }

  String username;

  bool isPasswordValid(String newPassword) {
    // validate hash with old password
  }
}
```
Constructor isn't inherited

Methods and properties
are inherited

```
class EnterpriseUser extends User {

  EnterpriseUser() { }

  String username;

  bool isPasswordValid(String newPassword) {
    // validate hash with old password
  }
}
```
Default, empty
constructor

The child class inherits
the functionality of the
methods and properties
already built into
the superclass.

Figure 7.3   A child class inherits all the existing functionality from the superclass except constructors.

constructors, you can call any of them by using the superclass as the constructor name prefix. Likewise, a named constructor in the child class can call a superclass's constructors at will:

```
class EnterpriseUser extends User {
  EnterpriseUser (String uname, String email) : super.byEmail(email) {
    // empty constructor body
  }

  EnterpriseUser.byUsername(String username) :  super(uname) {

  }
}
```

Calls named constructor on parent class

Calls parent class constructor from base class

The constructor initialization block is a comma-separated list of commands that can also be used to initialize final properties (as discussed in chapter 6), but any call to the super constructor must always come first.

7.1.3 Overriding methods and properties

When you inherit a parent class, you gain all the functionality of the members of the parent class. But sometimes you need to provide your own version of that functionality, such as when you want to be able to provide password validation in the EnterpriseUser class. The superclass User already has an isPasswordValid() method, and you get the functionality of that method when you inherit the class. But when Alice wants to change her password in your enterprise system, the requirements for changing a password are stricter than just comparing the new password with the old password. Alice can't reuse the same password for five password changes, which means that in the EnterpriseUser class, you need to *override* the functionality provided by the parent User class: for example, to remember the last five password hashes. Fortunately, this is easy to do by providing a new method implementation with the same name and parameters, as shown in the following listing. It's still possible to reuse the inherited functionality of the underlying isPasswordValid() method provided in the parent User class by using the super keyword again to refer to the same function in the base class, also in this listing.

Listing 7.3 EnterpriseUser overriding functionality from parent User class

```
class EnterpriseUser extends User {
  bool isPasswordValid(String newPassword) {
    // snip... compare against last 5 passwords

    return super.isPasswordValid(newPassword);
  }
}
```

Overrides functionality from parent class by providing new version of method

Calls underlying version in parent class by referring to parent class with super keyword

You can override properties in a similar manner. A property is just shorthand for a getter or setter method, and the same principle applies. The User class provides a username property, but when Alice logs on to your enterprise system you want to validate the username to ensure that it's longer than four characters. You can override the setter and getter by providing a new implementation of the getter and setter to perform this validation, as shown in the following listing.

```
class EnterpriseUser extends User {
  String get username => super.username;

  void set username(String value) {
    if (value.length < 4) {
      throw new ArgumentError("Error: username is < 5 chars");
    }

    super.username = value;
  }
}
```

Passes functionality straight through to parent implementation

Performs additional validation

Passes value to parent property

So far, you've seen how Dart allows classes to inherit from a parent class, optionally reusing existing functionality from that parent class. But sometimes you'll want to design a class and interface inheritance hierarchy in such a way that a user of your code *must* provide their own functionality, by using abstract classes.

7.1.4   *Including abstract classes in a class hierarchy*

You saw the abstract keyword in chapter 6, where you used it to define a class containing only method bodies, which you used as interface definitions. You can also use abstract classes to force users of your class to provide their own implementation methods, while still providing implementation methods of your own.

In the example system, you currently have two classes that form a hierarchy. When Alice logs on to the system on the developer's system, she's represented by the User class. When she logs on to the production system with the enterprise servers, she's represented by the EnterpriseUser class, which shares an "is-an" relationship with its parent. This hierarchy is captured in figure 7.4.

The system can create instances of the User class and the EnterpriseUser class because they're both complete classes that fully define the functionality required by the interfaces they implement. Developers can use the User class independently of any of its child classes. But often when designing a library, you'll want to force a developer using one of your classes to provide some of their own functionality, because you don't know at design time what the functionality needs to be.

In the example User interface, you could add a checkPasswordHistory() function. This function allows implementing classes to check the password history as part of the isPasswordValid() function. Unfortunately, when designing the User class, you wouldn't know *how* to check the password history. You can force users of the User class to provide that functionality by ensuring that they inherit the User class and override the checkPasswordHistory() function to provide their own functionality. To achieve this, use the abstract keyword when defining the User class, as shown in the next listing. The abstract keyword indicates that you can't create a

```
class User {
  User (String this.username) { }

  String username;

  bool isPasswordValid(String newPassword) {
    // validate hash with old password
  }
}
```

extends

```
class EnterpriseUser extends User {
  EnterpriseUser(username) : super(username);

  void markExpired() {
    // some implementation
  }
}
```

Inherited properties and methods
from the parent are also available.
Don't specifically declare them
unless you're overriding functionality.

Figure 7.4   The current inheritance hierarchy between your interfaces and classes

new instance of this class; instead, it allows child classes that inherit it to fully meet those requirements.

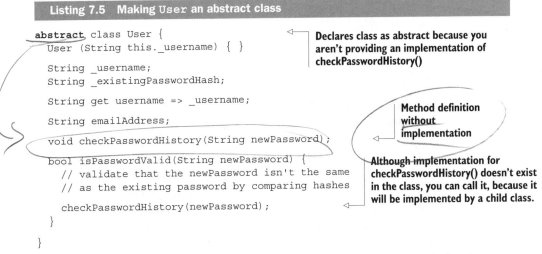

Listing 7.5   Making User an abstract class

```
abstract class User {
  User (String this._username) { }

  String _username;
  String _existingPasswordHash;

  String get username => _username;

  String emailAddress;

  void checkPasswordHistory(String newPassword);

  bool isPasswordValid(String newPassword) {
    // validate that the newPassword isn't the same
    // as the existing password by comparing hashes

    checkPasswordHistory(newPassword);
  }
}
```

Declares class as abstract because you
aren't providing an implementation of
checkPasswordHistory()

Method definition
without
implementation

Although implementation for
checkPasswordHistory() doesn't exist
in the class, you can call it, because it
will be implemented by a child class.

One of the benefits of using an abstract class is that you can call methods that have yet to have their functionality defined, which passes the responsibility down to the user of your class. Now that you've made the User class abstract, EnterpriseUser needs to provide the functionality for checkPasswordHistory(). EnterpriseUser, which has an "is-a" relationship with the User class, also needs to either declare itself as abstract or fulfill the requirements defined by the User class. Figure 7.5 shows how the implementation is used when you call the isPasswordValid() method on an instance of the EnterpriseUser class.

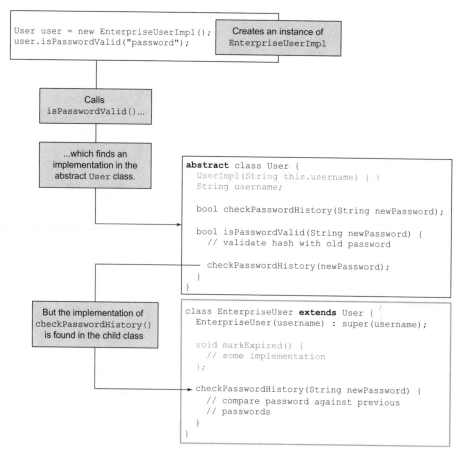

Figure 7.5   Methods declared in interfaces can be implemented by child classes if the parent class is declared as abstract.

Abstract classes are great when you want to leave the implementation decisions to a user of your library but you also want to dictate the order in which something happens. In the `isPasswordValid()` example, you first validate the password hash and then call `checkPasswordHistory()`, because the call to the enterprise system might involve an external call and you can save resources by performing that step only if you've first validated the password.

There was a lot in this section, and you've learned how Dart provides inheritance with classes and interfaces. Object-oriented programming—and inheritance in particular—is a complex topic, and the best way to understand it is to experiment with the code and try to use some of the features in your own libraries. The built-in libraries from the Dart SDK are full of interfaces and inheritance; they're open source and readily available in the Dart Editor. You can find a tour of some of the libraries in the appendix.

Now that we've covered inheritance, it's time to examine the `Object` class, which is the parent for all classes in Dart regardless of whether your class explicitly extends it.

> **Remember**
> - The extends keyword denotes that a class is inheriting (subclassing) another class.
> - The abstract keyword indicates that a class isn't providing its own implementation of a method. Classes that inherit an abstract class should provide that functionality.
> - Subclasses don't inherit a superclass's constructor. You can call constructors in the parent class by using the super prefix to refer to them in the constructor initializer block.
> - You can also call specific methods and properties of the parent class by using the super prefix anywhere in normal code.

7.2 *Everything is an object*

Everything in Dart is an object, which differs from Java and C#, where you have primitive types such as int and boolean (and have object equivalents, such as java.lang.Integer). The Object class is built into the Dart language and is the ultimate parent class of every class other than itself.

When you create an instance of a variable in your app, whether it's a String, an int, or your own class such as EnterpriseAuthService, you're creating an instance of an Object. You can look at this in two ways. First, in object-oriented programming, you create instances of objects, and from a computer science point of view, objects are the areas of computer memory that are allocated to store actual data in a running app. This isn't the same as in a class, which is the representation in a source code file that Dart uses to construct objects.

Second, Dart has an Object class from which every other class inherits automatically. This happens regardless of whether you use the extends keyword in your class definition. All the built-in classes and types such as String, int, null, and functions share an "is-an" relationship with Object.

7.2.1 *Testing the "is-an" relationship with Object*

Object inheritance creates an "is-an" relationship going up the hierarchy, and this "is-an" relationship can be tested in code, using the is keyword, which returns a Boolean true or false value. The following statements all return true:

```
print(Object is Object);
print(1 is Object);
print(false is Object);
print(null is Object);
print("Hello" is Object);
var someFunction = () => "";
print(someFunction is Object);
```

All print the word "true"

You can use the "is-an" relationship with your own classes. When you create a new class, such as EnterpriseAuthService, you're automatically inheriting from the base Object class. To create an "is-an" relationship with inheritance, use the extends keyword to

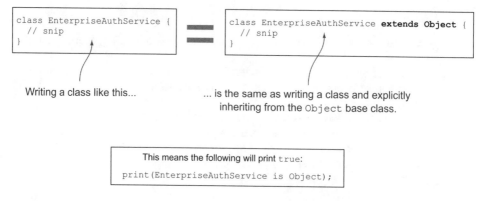

Figure 7.6   **Classes automatically extend the `Object` base class.**

define the parent of the class you're inheriting. But this isn't required with `Object`; you get the inheritance automatically without needing to use the `extends` keyword, as shown in figure 7.6.

This inheritance works all the way down the inheritance hierarchy. When your `EnterpriseUser` inherits from `User`, it too inherits from the base `Object` class but via the `User` class. This inheritance happens because inheritance provides an "is-an" relationship up the class hierarchy, meaning that each child has an "is-an" relationship with every parent going up the hierarchy, as shown in figure 7.7.

The "is-an" relationship can be also be tested with your own classes by using the `is` keyword to return a `true` or `false` value. The following statements always return `true`:

```
print(User is Object);
print(EnterpriseUser is Object);
print(EnterpriseUser is User);
```

All print the word "true"

NOTE   The "is-an" relationship works only one way (up the hierarchy, from the child to the parent), so calling `print(Object is User);` returns `false` because an `Object` isn't a `User`.

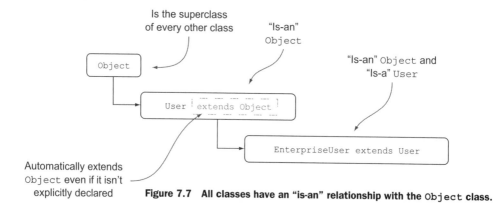

Figure 7.7   **All classes have an "is-an" relationship with the `Object` class.**

You can observe two points when you have a single base class:

- Every class has an "is-an" relationship with `Object`, meaning you can refer to everything as an object in variable and parameter declarations.
- Every class inherits some basic functionality provided by the base `Object` class.

We'll look at each of these in turn.

7.2.2 Using the "is-an" Object relationship

By having every type inherit from `Object` automatically, you can pass any type where an object is expected, including `null`, functions, and Boolean values; for example, the function `doLogon(AuthService authService, String username, String password);` from chapter 6 could be rewritten to explicitly check the type of the input parameters as follows:

```
doLogon(Object authService, String username, String password) {
  if (authService is AuthService) {                          ← Explicitly checks type
    return authService.auth(username,password);       ←        of input parameter
  }
  else {                              Uses authService if object
    // throw exception          passed in "is-an" AuthService
  }
}
```

Writing code like this removes the ability for the type checker to validate that the variables you're passing in to your function are correct. The `as` keyword lets you tell the type checker that you're expecting to treat a variable as a specific type. For example, you could rewrite the return line in the `doLogon()` function from the previous snippet as follows:

```
if (authService is AuthService) {                               Uses as
  return (authService as AuthService).auth(username, password);   ← keyword
}
```

But it can be useful when you have a function that wants to take different types that don't share another common interface or other common parent class. In this instance, it's valid to declare the parameter as an `Object` and check the type in the function:

```
processValue(Object someObject) {
  if (someObject is String) {        ←
    // snip                              Checks type of input
  }                                      parameter using is keyword
  else if (someObject is int) {     ←
    // snip
  }
  // etc...
}
```

> **WARNING** You should try to avoid using this pattern in your external-facing code, because it provides no useful documentation to users or tools. If you find yourself using this pattern, be sure to provide appropriate comments in the code to explain why.

Later in this chapter, we'll look at the `dynamic` type annotation, which is the type that all variables and parameters have when you supply no type information—and which is subtly different from using `Object`. When you use `Object`, you explicitly state that you're expecting that callers of your function *can use* any type. Specifying no type information (using dynamic typing), on the other hand, means you haven't explicitly indicated which type can be used. By using `Object` in a parameter list, you document that you're expecting users to be able to provide *any* type to the function or method.

7.2.3 Using toString() functionality inherited from the base Object class

The `Object` type provides a small number of methods and properties that all classes can use. The most commonly used one is the `toString()` method, which provides a string representation of the instance.

When you try to use an instance of any class as a string—for example, by passing it into Dart's top-level `print()` function—the `toString()` method of `Object` gets called. The example in the following listing explicitly calls the `toString()` function, but if you don't explicitly call `toString()`, Dart will call it implicitly.

Listing 7.6   Calling `toString()` outputs a textual representation of the object

```
print(1.toString());            ⟵── I
print("dart".toString());       ⟵── dart
print(true.toString());         ⟵── true
print(null.toString());         ⟵── null      Instance of    toString() is implied. You
print(new Object().toString()); ⟵───────────  "Object"       don't need to specifically
print(1);                       ⟵───────────                 call toString().
```

Calling `toString()` on an `Object` is interesting. It outputs the text `Instance of 'Object'`, which is as descriptive as it can be at that point. If you were to call `toString()` on an instance of `User`, you'd get the message `Instance of 'User'` because your class is using the functionality built into the `Object` class. If you called `toString()` on a different class, such as a list of numbers, the list of numbers would be printed rather than the text `Instance of 'List'` because the `List` class provides its own `toString()` method, which overrides the functionality provided by `Object`.

You can override this functionality in your own classes, too, by adding a `toString()` function to your class definition. For example, you can make your `User` class output the name of the user rather than use the default functionality provided by `Object.toString()`. Doing so provides a benefit if you add logging functionality, because you can pass the user instance into your logging function or the top-level `print()` function and get back a descriptive message. The next listing shows an example implementation that also uses the original functionality found in `Object` by explicitly calling `super.toString()`.

Listing 7.7   Overriding the `toString()` functionality from `Object`

```
class User {
    String username;

    String toString() {
```
Declares
implementation
of toString()

```
        var myType = super.toString();
        return "$myType: $username";
    }
}
```

Returns "Instance of 'User': Alice"

Invokes parent class's toString()

Subclasses of User, such as EnterpriseUser, also inherit this functionality if they don't override it themselves. Calling toString() on an instance of the EnterpriseUser class will result in the output Instance of 'EnterpriseUser': Alice, which is far more informative than the default. Of course, you could always override toString() again in the EnterpriseUser class definition.

7.2.4 *Intercepting noSuchMethod() calls*

The Object class also exposes another useful method: noSuchMethod(). Unlike in Java and C# (but as in many other dynamic languages such as Ruby and Python), you aren't restricted to using properties and methods that have been explicitly declared on a class you're using.

When you call a method or access a property that doesn't exist on a class definition, Dart first checks to see whether the method or property exists on any parent classes going up the hierarchy. If it doesn't, Dart then tries to find a method called noSuchMethod() declared in the hierarchy. If that method hasn't been explicitly defined, Dart calls the base Object.noSuchMethod() function, which throws a NoSuchMethodError.

You can use this feature with the User class hierarchy. When Alice logs on, you can't always trust the data that comes back from EnterpriseService because of data inconsistencies in the source system. The agreement with the EnterpriseService team is that they will return as much data as they can, and you'll validate that it meets your requirements. For this reason, no validate() method is exposed on any of the User or EnterpriseUser implementation classes, but you might sometimes want to call it nonetheless. Figure 7.8 shows how Dart handles this call.

When you call validate(), Dart—being optimistic and expecting that you, as a developer, know what you're doing—will try to run it. In the end, Dart will find the default noSuchMethod() implementation in the base Object class and will throw an error, which can be caught with a try/catch handler, as shown in the following snippet:

```
try {
    user.validate("Alice");
} on NoSuchMethodError catch (err) {
    // handle or ignore the error
}
```

You can prevent the NoSuchMethodError being thrown by implementing your own version of noSuchMethod(). This approach allows you to intercept the missing method call and execute some arbitrary code, such as validating the data.

noSuchMethod() takes two parameters: a String representing the name of the method you tried to access and a List containing a list of the parameters you passed

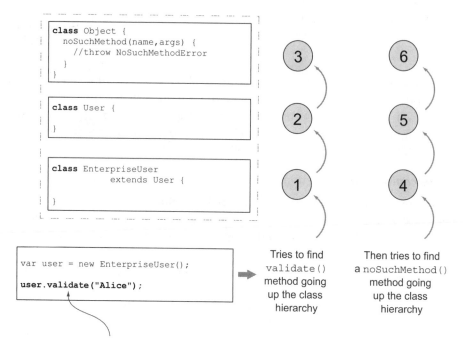

Figure 7.8   **Dart checks up the hierarchy for the method, which doesn't exist. Then it checks up the hierarchy for a noSuchMethod() implementation until it finds the one declared in the base Object class.**

The validate() method isn't defined in the class hierarchy, but Dart is optimistic, so it will attempt to run this code anyway.

into the method. We'll discuss lists in more depth in the next chapter, but for now you need to know that lists are zero-based and that you can access a list's elements by using the square bracket syntax familiar from many other languages. The following listing shows an example implementation of noSuchMethod(String name, List args). This example code prints out the method name and the number of arguments passed to the method.

Listing 7.8   Implementing noSuchMethod()

```
class User {
  noSuchMethod(String name, List args) {        <--- Declares noSuchMethod()
    print("$name, ${args.length}");        <---
  }                                         Prints name of method called and
}                                           the number of arguments passed in
```

When you call user.validate("Alice");, it results in the string "validate, 1" being output to the console. Figure 7.9 demonstrates the new flow.

It's possible to check explicitly for method names and continue to throw the noSuchMethodError from the base class, if that's required, by checking the value of the name parameter and calling super.noSuchMethod(name,args) to pass the call up the class hierarchy. This approach allows you to capture specific missing methods while ignoring others.

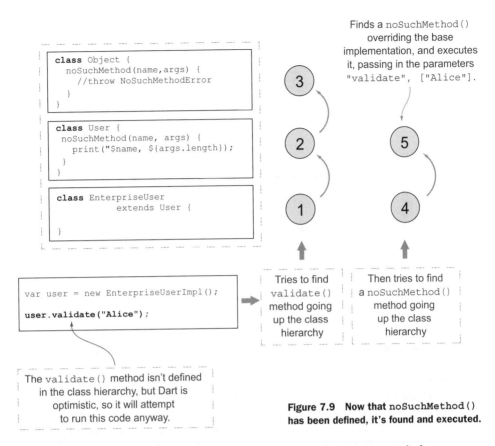

Finds a noSuchMethod()
overriding the base
implementation, and executes
it, passing in the parameters
"validate", ["Alice"].

```
class Object {
  noSuchMethod(name,args) {
    //throw NoSuchMethodError
  }
}
```

```
class User {
  noSuchMethod(name, args) {
    print("$name, ${args.length});
  }
}
```

```
class EnterpriseUser
        extends User {

}
```

```
var user = new EnterpriseUserImpl();

user.validate("Alice");
```

Tries to find
validate()
method going
up the class
hierarchy

Then tries to find
a noSuchMethod()
method going
up the class
hierarchy

The validate() method isn't defined
in the class hierarchy, but Dart is
optimistic, so it will attempt
to run this code anyway.

**Figure 7.9 Now that noSuchMethod()
has been defined, it's found and executed.**

noSuchMethod() can also intercept a property access. Suppose you tried to access on the User a password field that didn't exist. You might want to ignore the set and return a string of asterisks for the get. When noSuchMethod() receives a call for a property access, it prefixes the name field with either get: or set:, which lets you determine whether the getter or setter is being accessed. Thus calling print(user.password); can be handled by the following noSuchMethod() implementation:

```
noSuchMethod(name,args) {
  if (name == "get:password") {
    return "*********";
  }
  else if (name != "set:password") {
    super.noSuchMethod(name,args);
  }
}
```

**If it's the getter for password,
return a string of asterisks.**

**If it isn't the getter
or the setter for the
password field ...**

**... pass noSuchMethod()
call up to the parent class.**

7.2.5 *Other default functionality of the Object class*

The Object class also provides some behavior that other classes get by default, most notably the equals operator ==. In the next chapter we'll discuss how to use this and other operators by overloading them in your own classes, but the default functionality is unsurprising.

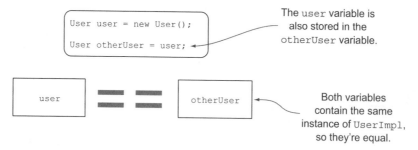

Figure 7.10   **The equals operator from the** `Object` **class allows comparison of two instances of an object.**

The equals operator defined in the `Object` class returns a `true`/`false` value when you compare an instance of an object to another instance of an object. That is, when you compare two variables for equality, they return `true` if they're the same instance, as shown in figure 7.10.

In the next chapter, we'll look at how you override the default functionality of the equals and other operators, but first we need to examine the `dynamic` type. `dynamic` is the type Dart uses when you don't specify any type information. Every instance of a variable has one, and it's accessible explicitly from the `Object` class's `dynamic` property.

> **Remember**
> - Everything "is-an" object.
> - `Object` defines the `toString()` and `noSuchMethod(name, args)` methods, which you can override in your own classes.
> - `noSuchMethod()` can capture unknown method calls and property access.

7.3   *Introducing the dynamic type*

The final type we'll look at in this section is `dynamic`. When you build your libraries, such as the `logon_lib` library that provides authentication services, it's good practice to provide type information to other developers and to the tools. Doing so allows the developers and the tools to infer meaning from the type information you choose. In your library, or when prototyping, it's perfectly valid to not specify any type information. When you don't explicitly give any type information, such as when you use the `var` keyword to declare a variable, Dart uses a special type annotation called `dynamic`.

The `dynamic` type is similar in concept to the `Object` type, in that every type "is-a" `dynamic` type. As such, you can use the `dynamic` type annotation in variable and parameter declarations and as function return types. In terms of the language, specifying the `dynamic` type is the same as providing no type information; but when you do specify the `dynamic` type, you let other developers know that you made a decision for the `dynamic` type to be used rather than just not specifying it. We'll look at this in

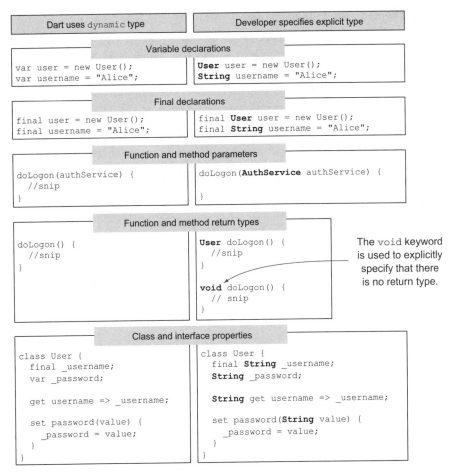

Figure 7.11 Illustration of where Dart implies the `dynamic` type, compared with the equivalent strong typing

more detail later in the chapter. First, figure 7.11 shows how dynamic is used automatically when you don't provide other type information: the dynamic type is used on the left, and an explicit type, such as String, is used on the right.

How does the "is-an" relationship with dynamic work?

Every type in Dart is an object, but every class also has an "is-an" relationship with dynamic, including Object. This is because dynamic is the base interface that every other class, including the Object class, implements. The dynamic interface provides no methods and properties, is hardcoded into the virtual machine, and, unlike Object, can't be extended or inherited from.

7.3.1   *Using the dynamic type annotation*

You can use the dynamic keyword, which identifies the dynamic type, explicitly in place of other type information; it's typically used where you want to indicate that you have explicitly decided to not provide any type information. This usage is subtly different from that of Object, which is used when you've explicitly decided to allow any object. When reading other people's code, you can make the interpretations shown in table 7.1 based on their choice of Object or dynamic.

Table 7.1 How to interpret different uses of the Object and dynamic types

Example function declaration	What you can infer
doLogon(Object user);	Developer made an active decision to allow any instance of an object to be passed into this function
doLogon(dynamic user);	Developer made an active decision that they don't yet know what type of object should be passed into this function
doLogon(username);	Developer hasn't yet declared what type of object should be passed into this function (implicitly dynamic)
doLogon(User user);	Developer actively declared that a User should be passed into this function

In practice, though, avoid using the dynamic keyword explicitly, unless you provide adequate code comments explaining your decision to use dynamic. As with all rules, there's an exception, which we'll look at in more depth when we start to use generics in chapter 8.

7.4   *Summary*

In this chapter, we looked at Dart's inheritance, which allows you to build inheritance hierarchies of classes. Object is the parent class of every other class and type, including the built-in ones such as String, int, and null. The dynamic type, on the other hand, is the type Dart uses at runtime to allow code to run without type annotations affecting the executing code.

Remember
- Use the extends keyword to declare that a class inherits a parent class.
- The super keyword lets you call members (methods and properties) on a parent class.
- You can override specific members by providing your own implementations.
- Object provides the toString() method, which you can use to provide extra information when outputting log messages.
- noSuchMethod() from the base Object class can be used to intercept missing methods and properties.
- The dynamic type annotation represents the untyped version of variables and parameters in Dart.

We aren't quite finished with classes! The next chapter introduces generics with a dis cussion of Dart's collection classes such as `Collection`, `List`, and `Map`. You'll also learn how to create flexible, general-purpose classes by implementing generics yourself. You'll also discover operator overloading, which helps you create truly self-documenting code by customizing the meaning built into the standard operators.

Collections of richer classes

This chapter covers

- Working with collections
- Building type-safe, general-purpose classes with generics
- Overloading class operators

In the previous two chapters, we discussed how you can use classes and interfaces in your Dart applications and libraries. In this final chapter on classes, we'll look at how to make classes richer and even more flexible and descriptive by using some of their advanced features.

We'll start by using the built-in collection classes, such as List and Map, which allow you to manipulate lists of data. By using generic types, you can help make accessing your collections type-safe and benefit from additional validations from the type checker. You'll use the indexer syntax to access elements directly in lists and maps and discover how to build literal maps and lists from known, preexisting values. We'll also look at the JavaScript Object Notation (JSON) methods to convert maps into strings and back to maps.

Next, we'll examine how you can make your own classes available for developers to use in a generic fashion, so that rather than creating two nearly identical classes, you'll be able to create a single class that can be used, strongly typed, in two ways.

Finally, we'll cover operator overloading. Overloading happens when you provide a new implementation, customized to your particular class, which allows you to overload the common operators such as > (greater than) and < (less than). This function provides your classes with greater readability when they're in use. We also revisit `Map` and look at overloading the `[]` and `[]=` indexer operators, which let your own classes implement the `Map` interface and be converted to JSON by the built-in JSON library.

8.1 Working with collections of data

Much of software development is concerned with moving and processing collections of data in a type-safe manner. In the example authentication service from chapter 7, the user Alice provided her logon details to an instance of an `AuthService`, which returned a `User` object. In this section, you'll expand on this example by retrieving user permissions for two roles: Reader and Administrator. When Alice logs on to the company blogging application to write a news item, the system needs to be able to identify that, as an Administrator, she can create and edit posts. Other users are Readers and can only read, comment on, and share blog posts. You'll use the class hierarchy shown in figure 8.1 to achieve this.

When Alice logs on, the system will retrieve a list of `Permissions`, which will contain a mixture of `ReaderPermission` instances and `AdminPermission` instances that the running application assigns to Alice's `User` object. The company blog app can use these permissions to allow access to part of the system, as shown in figure 8.2.

The permissions will be constant instances of the `ReaderPermission` and `AdminPermission` classes. We discussed `const` classes in chapter 5; to recap, they have a `const` constructor that must fully initialize all fields at compile time. When you create an instance of a `const` class by using the `const` keyword (instead of the `new` keyword), you can be sure that when you compare two instances that have the same field values, they're considered identical. You can use this feature to determine whether a user has a specific permission.

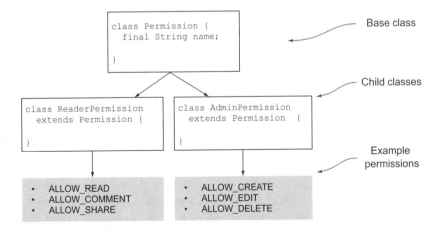

Figure 8.1 Class hierarchy for example roles and permissions

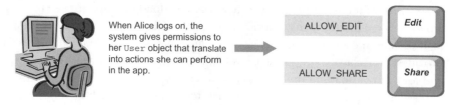

Figure 8.2 Alice's `User` object is assigned permissions by the system.

You need to create each of the permissions and assign it to a static variable in each class so you can refer to these variables throughout the application (static variables were also discussed in chapter 5). The following listing shows the boilerplate code to get your permissions working.

Listing 8.1 Permissions boilerplate code

```
class Permission {                    ← Base Permission class    Field to store
  final String name;                                             permission name
  const Permission(this.name);        ← Constant constructor
}

class ReaderPermission extends Permission {    ← Child ReaderPermission class

  const ReaderPermission(String name) : super(name);    Creates Reader permissions and
                                                         assigns them to static variables
  static final ReaderPermission ALLOW_READ =
                        const ReaderPermission("ALLOW_READ");
  static final ReaderPermission ALLOW_COMMENT =
                        const ReaderPermission("ALLOW_COMMENT");
  static final ReaderPermission ALLOW_SHARE =
                        const ReaderPermission("ALLOW_SHARE");
}

class AdminPermission extends Permission {    ← Child AdminPermission class

  const AdminPermission(String name) : super(name);    Creates Admin permissions and
                                                        assigns them to static variables
  static final AdminPermission ALLOW_EDIT =
                        const AdminPermission("ALLOW_EDIT");
  static final AdminPermission ALLOW_DELETE =
                        const AdminPermission("ALLOW_DELETE");
  static final AdminPermission ALLOW_CREATE =
                        const AdminPermission("ALLOW_CREATE");
}
```

Now that you have the boilerplate code containing two types of permissions (Admin and Reader), it's time to look at how you can use it.

8.1.1 Collections of objects

Alice is an instance of a `User` object, and generally a `User` has many permissions. In other words, you want Alice to have a list of permissions associated with her. Other programming languages include the concept of an `Array`, which is used to store lists of items. Dart, on the other hand, doesn't have a specific `Array` type; instead, it has

Collection and List interfaces. The List interface extends the Collection interface. It has a default implementation, so you can use the new keyword with it, such as to create a specific instance of a list:

```
Collection permissionsCollection = new List();
List permissionsList = new List();
```

Using the as keyword

In some instances you want to treat a specific variable as an instance of another type. A classic case of this is where you have a Collection variable, but you're instantiating it as a list. This is valid, but no add() method is defined on the base Collection interface.

In order to use the Collection typed variable as a list, you need to use the as keyword. This lets the type checker know that you intend for the Collection variable to contain a List instance, which lets you use the variable as a list:

```
(permissionsCollection as List).add(... some permission ...);
```

We'll discuss the specific differences between the Collection and List interfaces a little later in the chapter. For now, add an extra field to your User from chapter 7 that will contain a collection of permissions, as shown in figure 8.3. When Alice logs on, her permissions are added to the collection.

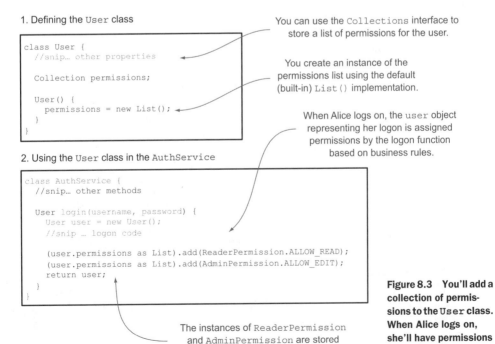

1. Defining the User class

```
class User {
  //snip… other properties

  Collection permissions;

  User() {
    permissions = new List();
  }
}
```

You can use the Collections interface to store a list of permissions for the user.

You create an instance of the permissions list using the default (built-in) List() implementation.

2. Using the User class in the AuthService

```
class AuthService {
  //snip… other methods

  User login(username, password) {
    User user = new User();
    //snip … logon code

    (user.permissions as List).add(ReaderPermission.ALLOW_READ);
    (user.permissions as List).add(AdminPermission.ALLOW_EDIT);
    return user;
  }
}
```

When Alice logs on, the user object representing her logon is assigned permissions by the logon function based on business rules.

The instances of ReaderPermission and AdminPermission are stored in Alice's permissions property.

Figure 8.3 You'll add a collection of permissions to the User class. When Alice logs on, she'll have permissions added to that collection.

METHODS ON THE COLLECTION INTERFACE

The Collection interface provides a number of generalized methods and properties that you might want to use with any collection of objects, such as retrieving the length of the collection, determining whether it's empty, and returning a subset of elements in the collection that match some condition. This ability can be useful, for example, to return a list of Admin permissions.

Listing 8.2 provides a function that returns a subset of Admin permissions from a collection by using the is keyword against each item in the collection to determine whether that item is an instance of AdminPermission. The filter() function of the Collection interface takes another anonymous function as a parameter, which is called for each permission in the collection. If the anonymous function returns true, then that permission is added to the result.

TIP   An anonymous function that's called for each element in the collection and returns true or false is known as a *predicate.*

Listing 8.2   Returning a list of AdminPermissions

```
Collection extractAdminPermissions(User user) {               Returns collection
  return user.permissions.filter( (currentPermission) {       that's a list of
    return currentPermission is AdminPermission;              AdminPermissions
  });
}
```

Predicate returns true if currentPermission is an
instance of AdminPermission. This causes
currentPermission to be added to result collection.

When you pass a User object containing Alice's user into this extractAdminPermissions() function, you get back a new Collection object containing all the AdminPermission instances.

Another useful function of the Collection interface is the some() function, which you can use to determine whether a specific permission is contained in the collection. The some() function takes a predicate and returns true if the predicate returns true for an item in the collection. For example, to determine whether Alice has the ALLOW_CREATE permission, you can call some() and store the result in a containsAllowCreate variable:

Shorthand predicate called for each
element in collection. some() returns true
when first call to predicate returns true.

```
bool containsAllowCreate = user.permissions.some(
  (currentPerm) => currentPerm == AdminPermission.ALLOW_CREATE;
);
```

ITERATING A COLLECTION

The Collection interface implements the Iterable interface, which allows you to use the Dart for(in) keywords. Similar to foreach(in) in C# and for(:) in Java, Dart shares this syntax with JavaScript. This language construct allows you to iterate through the collection, assigning each item to a variable in turn, as shown in figure 8.4.

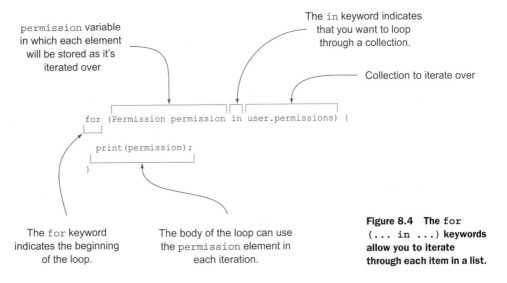

permission variable
in which each element
will be stored as it's
iterated over

The in keyword indicates
that you want to loop
through a collection.

Collection to iterate over

```
for (Permission permission in user.permissions) {

    print(permission);

}
```

The for keyword
indicates the beginning
of the loop.

The body of the loop can use
the permission element in
each iteration.

Figure 8.4 The for
(... in ...) keywords
allow you to iterate
through each item in a list.

The for (in) pair of keywords constitute a powerful way to visit every item in the list. If you need to break out of the loop, perhaps because you're looking for the first matching permission, you can use the keyword break, which exits the loop at that point, as shown in the following snippet:

```
for (Permission permission in user.permissions) {
    if (permission is AdminPermission) {
        break;
    }
}
```

**Finds first
AdminPermission in list**

**Exits for loop
immediately**

MANUALLY ITERATING THROUGH A COLLECTION

The Iterable interface also returns an Iterator interface. The Iterator interface is used internally by the for (...in...) keywords, but you can use its hasNext and next() methods explicitly in your code to control when you move through a collection of items outside of an explicit loop. hasNext returns true if there's another item to move to; next() returns the next item and moves the iterator pointer past the next item. If it has already returned the last item, it throws a StateError. The example in the following listing extracts the first two items from the collection by explicitly moving through it. Whenever you call the iterator() function on a collection, you get a new iterator that has the iterator's pointer positioned before the first item.

Listing 8.3　Extracting the first two items from a collection using an iterator

```
Iterator iterator = user.permissions.iterator();

var perm1 = null;
var perm2 = null;

if (iterator.hasNext) {
```

**Gets new iterator positioned
before first item**

**Creates variables to
store permissions**

**Checks whether there's a
next item to return**

```
    perm1 = iterator.next();
}
```
             ◁────┐ **Returns next item and moves**
                 │ **iterator pointer forward**

```
if (iterator.hasNext) {
    perm2 = iterator.next();
}
```
    │ **Checks for and**
    │ **gets second item**

8.1.2 *Using the concrete implementations of the Collection interface*

The Collection interface, combined with the Iterable and Iterator interfaces, is a powerful construct, but you can't create an instance of a Collection. An interface, remember, is a way of describing the methods and properties that should appear on a class that implements that interface. The core Dart libraries provide a number of implementation classes for the Collection interface: List, Queue, and Set. These classes provide different specializations of the Collection interface. Figure 8.5 shows the Collection interface and how it's related to its children (List, Queue, and Set) and its parent (Iterable).

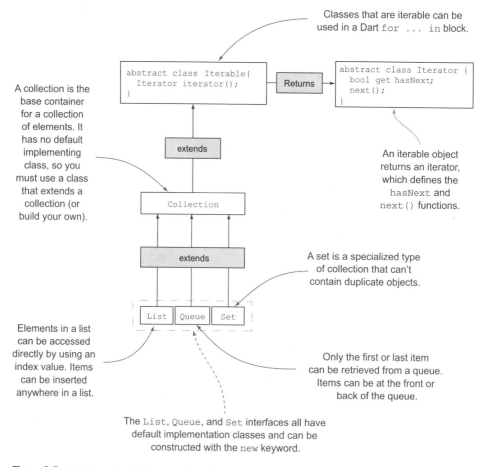

Figure 8.5 Collection **is the core interface in Dart for dealing with collections of objects, but you need to use a concrete instance of** List, Queue, **or** Set.

Dart doesn't have an `Array` type, but as mentioned earlier, it does have `List`. Lists are dual purpose, being either fixed-size or extendable. If a list is fixed-size, you can insert elements only into predefined slots by using the square bracket index `[]` operator. An extendable list, on the other hand, can also have items added to and removed from it, effectively adding and removing slots in the list.

CREATING LISTS

There are four ways to create a list, shown in listing 8.4. The simplest way is to create a literal list with the square bracket operator, which produces a prepopulated, extendable list. The second approach uses the `List()` constructor. If you don't pass in a value, you get an empty, extendable list. If you do pass in a value, you get a fixed-size list containing the number of elements you specify, each of which is null. You must access each element using a numeric indexer that's zero-based.

Finally, `List` defines another `List.from(...)` constructor that allows you to create a new extendable list from any class that implements `Iterable`. This feature is useful for converting an existing fixed-size list into an extendable list.

Listing 8.4   Different ways to create a list

```
List literal =[ReaderPermission.ALLOW_READ,ReaderPermission.ALLOW_SHARE];   ←┐

literal.add(ReaderPermission.ALLOW_COMMENT);   ←── Adds new items to list

print(literal.length);                          ←── Prints: 3                  Creates literal
                                                                                extendable list
List growable = new List();    ←── Creates new, empty, growable list          from known values

print(growable.length);                         ←── Prints: 0

growable.add(ReaderPermission.ALLOW_READ);      | Adds new
growable.add(ReaderPermission.ALLOW_SHARE);     | items to list     Creates new,
                                                                    fixed-size list
List fixedSize = new List(2);
print(fixedSize.length);                         ←── Prints: 2

fixedSize[0] = ReaderPermission.ALLOW_READ;      | Uses indexer to populate
fixedSize[1] = ReaderPermission.ALLOW_SHARE;     | empty slots in list

// fixedSize.add(ReaderPermission.ALLOW_COMMENT);   ←─┐ Would throw
                                                       UnsupportedError if it were
List fromOther = new List.from(fixedSize);             uncommented, because list
                                                       isn't extendable
fromOther.add(ReaderPermission.ALLOW_COMMENT);
```

Creates extendable list from another list ⌐→

Now you can add new items.

All elements in a list can be read from and written to by using the index operators `[]` and `[]=`. The `[]` operator lets you read a value out of a list at a specific (zero-based) index, such as `var permission = growable[2];` the `[]=` operator allows you to modify the value at a specific index, as in `growable[2] = permission`. These index operators are important; they crop up again when we look at maps, and you'll use them in your own classes later in the chapter when we examine operator overloading. They also allow you one final way to iterate through a list, in addition to the two methods defined on the Collection interface (a List "is-a" Collection, after all). You can use the indexer to access each item in turn in a for loop. The for loop syntax is identical to the for loop in all C-based languages, such as Java, JavaScript, and C#:

```
for (int i = 0; i < fixedSize.length; i++) {
  Permission permission = fixedSize[i];
}
```

The other two built in types of collection, Queue and Set, don't provide direct access to elements, but they can be converted into lists by using the List.from() constructor.

CREATING SETS

A set is a specific type of collection that doesn't allow duplicates. It has some specific methods, such as isSubsetOf(collection) and contains(value), and it has a Set.from() constructor, which means you can create an instance of a Set from any other Iterable class. The following snippet creates a set containing only one item:

```
Set set = new Set();
set.add(ReaderPermission.ALLOW_READ);
set.add(ReaderPermission.ALLOW_READ);
set.add(ReaderPermission.ALLOW_SHARE);
print(set.length);
```

Adding two of the same item to a set has the same effect as adding one item.

⟵ Set contains only two distinct items.

CREATING QUEUES

Queues, on the other hand, are useful when you want to build a first-in, first-out collection, such as when one part of a process adds items onto a list and another part of the process wants to take an item off the list, preserving the order in which they were added. The methods addLast() and removeFirst() let you add an item to the back of the queue and remove an item from the front of the queue. The following snippet creates a queue, adds one item to the back of the queue, and removes it from the front of the queue:

```
Queue queue = new Queue();
queue.addLast(ReaderPermission.ALLOW_READ);
queue.addLast(ReaderPermission.ALLOW_SHARE);
var permission = queue.removeFirst();
print(queue.length);
```

Adds two items to back of queue in order

First item **ALLOW_READ** is removed from queue.

Only one item is left in the queue.

You can't access elements in sets and queues directly by an index, as you can with lists. Instead, you can access elements only by iterating through the queue using the methods provided on the Collection interface or, in the case of a queue, with the additional addLast() and removeFirst() methods.

8.1.3 *Making collections specific with generics*

One of the problems with using the Collection interface the way you're currently using it is that you can add any instance of an object to it. Thus it's possible for you to end up with a list that contains a mixture of ReaderPermission and String, or int, for instance, by writing code such as this:

```
List permissions = new List();
permissions.add(ReaderPermission.ALLOW_READ);
permissions.add("ALLOW_WRITE");
permissions.add(123456789);
```

Correctly adds permission to list ◁

Incorrectly adds string ◁

Incorrectly adds integer ◁

You can see that code like this is wrong or that the list should be a list of `Permissions` rather than just a list of anything. One way to fix this might be for you to inherit `List`, create a `PermissionList`, and provide methods such as `add(Permission item)` that take only a `Permission` object. But a typical application has lots of lists containing many different types that don't share a common base class other than `Object`. It would be impractical (and a waste of code) to write a different list implementation for each list you might use.

Fortunately, Dart has generics built into the type system. A generic type is a way of defining a class in a general, or generic, way but allowing the user of the class to use it in a specific way, even though there's no shared type hierarchy such as a list of `Permissions`, a list of `Strings`, and a list of `ints`.

All the types in the `Collection` hierarchy have been written using generics, which allows you to use them specifically for your `Permission` class. In other words, you *can* create a list of `Permissions`, and Dart's type checker can then flag errors such as accidentally adding a `String` into your list.

Classes built using generics take the form *Name<T>*, where *Name* is the name of the class or interface and *T* is a comma-separated list of type placeholders. The collection classes that you've seen so far have generic signatures, as shown in figure 8.6, where `E` represents a placeholder for the `Element` type.

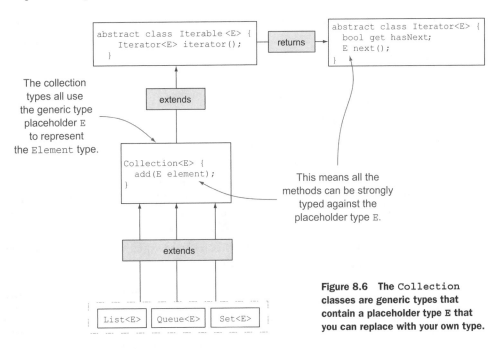

Figure 8.6 The `Collection` classes are generic types that contain a placeholder type `E` that you can replace with your own type.

REPLACING THE PLACEHOLDER TYPES

To use this generic type placeholder, specify the type you want to use in the type declaration and the constructor. For example, when Alice logs on, you know you're getting a list of permissions, which is now declared as follows:

> **Specifying Permission type replaces placeholder in class**

```
List<Permission> permissions = new List<Permission>();
permissions.add(ReaderPermission.ALLOW_READ);
```

In use, all the methods on the list now work as though you had written a custom `PermissionList` that could hold only instances of `Permission` objects. The collection methods' signatures all expect to receive a `Permission`, receive a list of `Permissions`, or return a `Permission`. Table 8.1 lists some of the method signatures defined on the `List` and shows what the Dart type checker expects when you use the `Permission` class in the constructor definition.

Table 8.1   A comparison of actual method signatures and how the Dart type checker interprets them

Actual method signature	What Dart expects in use
`void add(E value);`	`void add(Permission value);`
`E next();`	`Permission next();`

`Collection<E> filter(`
`            bool f(E element)`
`        );`
	`Collection<Permission> filter (`
	`            bool f(Permission element)`
	`        );`

This behavior is equally valid for any other class. For example, you can create a list of `Strings` or a queue of `ints` by using the type to replace the generic placeholder in the constructor:

```
List<String> stringList = new List<String>();
stringList.add("I am a string");
Queue<int> intQueue = new Queue<int>();
intQueue.addLast(12345);
```

In use, if you tried to add an `int` into a `String` list, the type system would warn you in the same way as if you tried to pass an `int` into a function that expected a `String`, because the `List` `add()` method is now expecting a `String` to be passed in.

There's another positive side effect of using generic types: they allow you to perform type checking on method signatures that you define yourself. You may have a function called `extractAdminPermissions()` that takes a list of `Permissions` and returns a list of `AdminPermissions`. This method functions identically regardless of whether it's using generic type placeholders:

```
Collection extractAdminPermissions(Collection permissions) {
  // snip method body
}
```

> **Version of method using untyped collections**

```
Collection<AdminPermission> extractAdminPermissions(
                        Collection<Permission> permissions) {
    // snip method body
}
```

Using collections provides additional validation by the type checker.

With the first version of extractAdminPermissions(), you can pass in any collection, including a collection of String or a collection of int, and the type checker won't know to warn you of a possible error. The second version of extractAdminPermissions() knows that you expect to receive a collection of Permission, and your calling code knows that it's expecting a list of AdminPermissions to be returned. The calling code can be safe in the knowledge that the resulting collection from extractAdminPermissions() won't contain any ReaderPermission instances.

SO WHAT "IS-A" LIST?

In the previous two chapters, you've been using the is keyword to determine whether a variable "is-an" instance of a specific type. For example, AdminPermission, which extends Permission, "is-a" Permission, but AdminPermission isn't a Reader-Permission. The following snippet returns the results you expect:

```
var p = AdminPermission.ALLOW_EDIT;
print(p is Permission);
print(p is AdminPermission);
print(p is ReaderPermission);
```

True

False: AdminPermission doesn't inherit from ReaderPermission.

When you're using generics, it turns out the same principle applies. A list of Admin-Permissions "is-a" list of Permissions, because every item in the list "is-a" Permission. It isn't a list of ReaderPermissions, which correctly follows the same logic:

```
var adminList = new List<AdminPermission>();
print(adminList is List);
print(adminList is List<Permission>);
print(adminList is List<AdminPermission>);
print(adminList is List<ReaderPermission>);
```

True

False: AdminPermission doesn't inherit from ReaderPermission.

This code works as expected, but a good question would be why the type checker returns true for adminList is List. Logically, any list of anything "is-a" List, but how does Dart achieve this when no type is specified? Behind the scenes, using an untyped generic is the same as using the dynamic type. The dynamic type, which we discussed in chapter 7, represents the untyped version of every class, and every instance of a class "is-a" dynamic.

Thus, all lists of any type or no type are also always lists of dynamic:

```
var dynamicList = new List<dynamic>();
print(dynamicList is List);
```

List<dynamic> is just a List.

```
var notSpecifiedList = new List();
print(notSpecifiedList is List<dynamic>);
print(listOfAdmin is List<dynamic>);
```

List of anything is also a List<dynamic>.

One final question arises, specifically with literal lists, because they have a specific syntax that Dart can use to create a list of known values (as you've seen). How do you define a list of known values to be a strongly typed list? Fortunately, you can do this using the generic syntax, providing `<type name>[element, element, ...]`, as in

```
var permissions =
    <Permission>[AdminPermission.ALLOW_CREATE, AdminPermission.ALLOW_EDIT];
```

8.1.4   *Storing lists of key/value pairs with generic maps*

The final built-in generic type that we'll look at in this chapter is `Map<K,V>`. You can use it to store lists of key/value pairs; you access the values using a key as an indexer. This is similar to the way you access values in a list by using a numeric indexer, such as `myList[1]`, except that you can specify a nonnumeric indexer (typically a `String`). The generic type placeholders `K` and `V` represent the `Key` type and the `Value` type, respectively—they don't need to be the same, and as with the other generic types we've looked at previously, they can be ignored (in which case you get a `Map<dynamic, dynamic>`).

When Alice logs on to the system, you can retrieve her `User` object. You can do the same for Bob and Charlie, but perhaps retrieving the `User` object from an enterprise system is a time-consuming exercise. You can implement a simple cache by storing a list of username strings and their associated user objects in a map. Because the `Map` interface has a default implementation class, you can create and manipulate the map as shown in the following listing.

> **Listing 8.5   Creating and using a map of `String` and `User`**

```
Map<String, User> userMap = new Map<String, User>();          Creates new
                                                              map of String
userMap["aliceKey"] = new User("Alice");     Inserts items into map    keys and User
userMap["bobKey"] = new User("Bob");         by using key indexer       values

User aliceUser = userMap["aliceKey"];        Reads items back out of
User bobUser = userMap["bobKey"];            map by using key indexer

User charlieUser = userMap["charlieKey"];
                                             Charlie doesn't exist in map,
                                             so charlieUser contains null.
```

Accessing a nonexistent key such as `charlieKey` doesn't throw an exception, as it does in other languages. Instead, it returns `null`.

CREATING PREDEFINED MAP LITERALS

You can create maps just like lists, with a predefined list of known keys and values. The map literal uses `{}` to define the map, and it contains a comma-separated list of keys and values, as shown in figure 8.7.

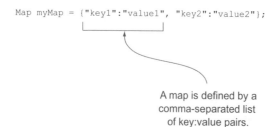

```
Map myMap = {"key1":"value1", "key2":"value2"};
```

A map is defined by a comma-separated list of key:value pairs.

Figure 8.7   A map can be defined in Dart as a list of key/value pairs.

A typical use when dealing with JavaScript Object Notation (JSON) data is a list of key/ value pairs defined in this format. The `dart:json` library provides two methods for converting a string into a map and a map into a string. The code in the following listing converts a string of usernames and their last logon date into a map and back to a string.

Listing 8.6 Using the `dart:json` library to convert between maps and strings

```
import "dart:json";

main() {                                                      Creates JSON string
  var jsonString ="{'charlieKey':'2012-07-23','aliceKey':'2012-08-16'}";
  Map lastLogonMap = JSON.parse(jsonString);
  print(lastLogonMap["charlieKey"]);                Parses JSON into a Map object
  jsonString = JSON.stringify(lastLogonMap);
}                                                    Accesses value in map by key
           Converts map back into string
```

> **TIP**   Converting JSON strings into maps and maps into JSON strings is common in web apps when you're sending and receiving data between a client app and a server-side web service. We'll deal with this in chapter 11 in more depth.

ACCESSING THE KEY AND VALUE COLLECTIONS

This raises another question. Suppose that you've stored `charlieKey` but the value is indeed `null`. You can't use this information to determine whether `charlieKey` is a valid key or perhaps a typo.

Fortunately, the `Map` interface provides `containsKey(K key)` and `containsValue(V value)` methods that you can use to confirm whether a key or value exists in the map. You can also access a collection of keys and iterate through them to access the values, as in the following snippet:

```
for (String key in userMap.keys) {          Iterates through key collection
  User value = userMap[key];          Extracts each value for current key
  print(value);
}                                     Prints current value.toString
```

INSERTING NEW ITEMS INTO THE MAP

Using the indexer `[ ] =` operator, you can insert items into the map (as you've done in the previous example), but this has the effect of overwriting an existing value with the same key. Sometimes it's useful to only insert new items into the map rather than replace existing items; for example, you could store a list of logon dates for each user, such as `Map<String, List<Date>>`, specifying that for each `Username` string, you'll access a list of `Date` objects.

When Bob logs on (and he has already logged on in the past), you want to add the logon date to the existing list of dates. When Charlie logs on, you want to create a new list of dates. Figure 8.8 demonstrates this.

The problem with using the indexer in the form `userLogons["bobKey"] = new DateList();` is that doing so will always create a new, empty list for Bob, wiping out his

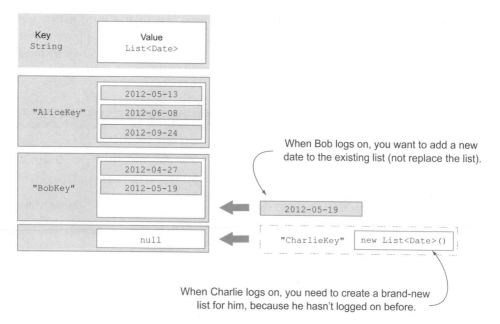

Figure 8.8   **You want to create a new value only if the key doesn't already exist.**

existing logons. Likewise, using userLogons["charlieKey"].add(new Date.now()); for Charlie will cause a null-pointer exception, because there's no List<Date> to add() a new date to.

Although you could use the containsKey("bob") check, the Map interface provides an alternative in the form of the putIfAbsent() method. This method adds a new item into the list only if the key doesn't already exist. It takes a key and a function as its parameters, and the return value from the function is inserted into the map as a value if the key doesn't yet exist in the list of keys. The following listing shows how this method works.

Listing 8.7   **Using the Map putIfAbsent() method**

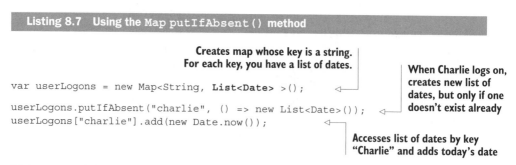

This approach lets you access the properties on the object that represents the value in the map without replacing the object.

That was a long section, but generics and collections are powerful features of Dart and (like superheroes) become even more powerful when combined. Generics aren't

> **Remember**
>
> - Collections can be created using the concrete instances of `List`, `Queue`, and `Set`.
> - Dart has no `Array` type, but you can use `List` in its place. A list can be fixed or dynamically expandable.
> - All the collection types are generic, and you can specify the type of a collection by using the `<T>` syntax with the type constructor, such as `new List<String>()` to create a list of `Strings`.
> - Lists can be accessed using zero-based indexers such as `myList[2];`, which accesses the third item in the list.
> - Maps contain a list of key/value pairs and also use the indexer syntax, but they take the key as the indexer. For example, putting a `Date` into a `Map<String,Date>` could look like this:
>
> ```
> myMap["aliceKey"] = new Date.now();
> ```

restricted to being used with collections, though. In the next section, we'll look at how to create your own "generic" classes that let you use type placeholders in your class but let users of your class create their own strongly typed versions.

8.2 *Building your own generic classes*

You've seen that generics can be useful to provide strong typing for classes where there's no shared base class. This is good news, because your bosses have seen your `User` classes and code and decided that they want it ported over to a different system for managing timesheets that uses a preexisting `Role` class rather than the `Permission` class for each user. Ideally, when Alice logs on to the blog post system, her `User` object will contain a list of `Permissions`, but when she logs onto the timesheet system, her `User` object will contain a list of `Roles`.

It turns out that roles and permissions are synonymous, but the classes are different. You rename the `User.permissions` list to be `User.credentials` and then start to think about how you could use strong typing to tell the difference between a list of `Roles` and a list of `Permissions`.

The first thought is to subclass `User` and have `RolesUser` and `PermissionsUser`, each with its own `add()` method and so on, as shown in figure 8.9. Fortunately, before going down this route, you remember generics and decide that this situation would be a perfect fit for the creation of a generic user class.

8.2.1 *Defining a generic class*

Defining a class as a generic class involves using a generic type placeholder in the class declaration, such as `class User<C> { ... }`. It's good practice to use a single letter as the type placeholder, because this convention is easily identifiable as a generic type placeholder, but you can use any value. You could use `class User<Credential> { ... }`, but this looks less like a placeholder and more like a real type. Common generic type placeholder letters that are used by convention are shown in table 8.2.

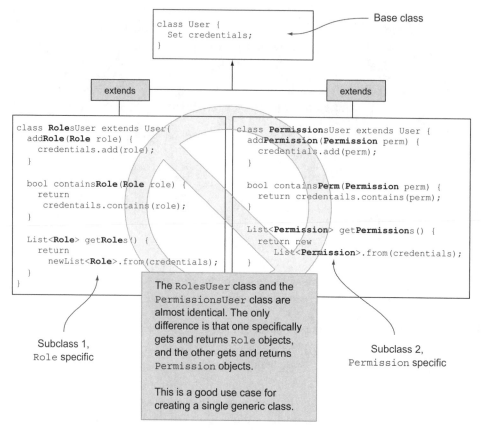

Figure 8.9   If you find yourself creating several similar classes that use slightly different objects but in the same way, then you could have a case for using generics.

You don't have to use these letters, and you could use them to mean something else, but please make sure you have a very good reason to do so, such as when the problem domain contains specific jargon. For example, the letter *E*, which typically refers to an Element, might instead logically refer to an edge in a graph structure.

Once you've defined your class name and the generic type placeholder <C>, you can reference that generic type placeholder throughout your class in method property definitions, method parameter lists, and return types.

Table 8.2   Some type placeholder letters are used by convention.

Generic type placeholder	Common meaning
<T>	Type
<E>	Element
<K>	Key
<V>	Value

The following listing shows how the User class might look now that you have a generic type placeholder rather than specific RolesUser and PermissionsUser classes.

Listing 8.8 User class that uses generic credentials

```
class User<C> {                        ◄─────  Defines class name as generic class
                                               with type placeholder <C>
  List<C> credentials;         ◄──┐
                                  └──  Declares List containing C
  User() {
    credentials = new List<C>();  ◄──  Constructor creates new
  }                                    instance of List of C.

  addCredential(C credential) {
    this.credentials.add(credential);                        Ensures that
  }                                                          only types of
                                                             C are passed
  bool containsCredential(C credential) {                    into methods
    return this.credentials.some((item) => item == credential);
  }

  List<C> getCredentialsList() {
    return new List<C>.from(credentials);        Returns classes
  }                                              that contain type C
}
```

8.2.2 Using your custom generic class

Now that you have a generic class, you can use it in the same way as any other generic type. You can be sure the type checker will catch type errors (such as if you missed some code when porting to the timesheet system and are still trying to retrieve a Permission when you really mean a Role).

You've also opened the possibility of reusing the User class in different scenarios that you might not have first envisaged. You can now reuse User when the credentials are supplied as string or integer values. The following listing shows some ways you can use your new class in a type-safe manner.

Listing 8.9 Using your generic User class in a type-safe manner

```
User<Permission> permissionUser = new User<Permission>();    ◄──┐  Creates
                                                                │  User with
User<Role> roleUser = new User<Role>();         Creates User with Role,   Permission
roleUser.addCredential(const Role("ADMIN"));    and accesses methods
print( roleUser.contains(const Role("ADMIN")) );  in type-safe manner

User<String> stringUser = new User<String>();      You can also use
stringUser.addCredential("ACCESS_ALL_AREAS");      it with String ...

User<int> intUser = new User<int>();          ... and int, or
intUser.addCredential(999);                   any other class.
```

8.2.3 Restricting the types that can be used as placeholders

Unfortunately, other developers think your new generic User class is great, and they're using it all the time in scenarios where you weren't expecting it to be used, such as storing the types of soft drinks users get from a vending machine: `User<SoftDrink>`. Your boss has started to notice and thinks people are using it as a shortcut to writing their own code that would better fit their solution. Your boss would like you to tighten it up and has given you permission to add a `validate()` method to the `Role` and `Permission` classes and have them both implement a `CredentialsValidator` interface.

The new rule is that developers can use your generic `User` class with any type, as long as that type implements the `CredentialsValidator` interface. Fortunately, generic typing allows you to implement this rule using the `extends` keyword in the generic definition. Change your class definition so that it reads

```
class User<C extends CredentialsValidator> { ... }
```

Now, wherever you try to use the `User` class, it must be used in conjunction with a class that implements or extends `CredentialsValidator` (which rules out `String`, `int`, and `SoftDrink`). It also means you can call the `validate()` method in the `addCredential()` function, as shown in the following example, without needing to check whether the class has a `validate()` method (as you'd do if you were still accepting `String`s and `SoftDrink`s):

```
class User<C extends CredentialsValidator> {        ⊲┐  Adds CredentialsValidator
  // snip other methods                                 to generic type placeholder

  addCredentials(C credential) {
    credential.validate();                          ⊲┐  You can now call validate() on
    this.credentials.add(credential);                   instance because you know it
  }                                                      "is-a" CredentialsValidator.
}
```

Well done! You've made it through the section on generics, which is an advanced topic in any language. Generics are a powerful feature of many modern class-based languages, and the principles here are very similar to those of Java and C#.

> **Remember**
> - If you find yourself making a number of nearly identical classes, then you might want to think about using generics.
> - The generic type placeholder is used throughout the class to represent the generic type that will be specified by the class's user.
> - You can restrict generic type placeholders by using the `extends` keyword.

In the next section, we'll look at operator loading, such as providing your own `equals` `==` implementation and adding custom indexers to your classes so that users of those classes can access values by using Dart's indexer syntax, `[]` and `[]=`.

8.3   *Operator overloading*

When Alice logs on to the timesheet example app discussed in the previous section, the system retrieves the `Role`s that represent the way Alice might use the timesheet

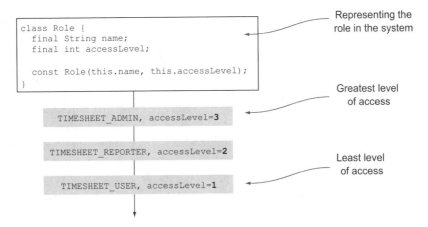

```
class Role {
  final String name;
  final int accessLevel;

  const Role(this.name, this.accessLevel);
}
```
Representing the role in the system

`TIMESHEET_ADMIN, accessLevel=3` — Greatest level of access

`TIMESHEET_REPORTER, accessLevel=2`

`TIMESHEET_USER, accessLevel=1` — Least level of access

Figure 8.10 **Example of the levels of access that Alice could have in the timesheet app**

system. For example, Alice might be a timesheet user, meaning she enters her own time into the system. She might also be a timesheet reporter, meaning she can produce reports based on other people's timesheets. Finally, she could be a timesheet administrator, meaning she can also edit any timesheet in the system.

Each of these three roles encompasses all the abilities of the previous role, such that the timesheet app needs to know only the role with the greatest access level in order to function correctly. If Alice has the TIMESHEET_ADMIN role, then she also has the abilities of the TIMESHEET_REPORTER and TIMESHEET_USER roles. You can order these roles by access-level value, as shown in figure 8.10.

8.3.1 *Overloading comparison operators*

There's a natural ordering to these roles: one is greater or lesser than the other. To test two roles' relation to each other, you can write code that compares each role's accessLevel value, which works adequately. But it would aid readability if you could compare the role instances with each other directly, using the greater-than (>) and less-than (<) operators, as shown in the following listing.

Listing 8.10 Ways to compare roles

```
var adminRole = new Role("TIMESHEET_ADMIN",3);
var reporterRole = new Role("TIMESHEET_REPORTER", 2);
var userRole = new Role("TIMESHEET_USER", 1);

if (adminRole.accessLevel > reporterRole.accessLevel) {
  print("Admin role is greater than Reporter role");
}

if (userRole.accessLevel < adminRole.accessLevel) {
  print("User role is less than Admin role");
}
```

Creates three role instances

You can use the .accessLevel property to compare each role using < and > …

```
if (adminRole > reporterRole) {
  print("Admin role is greater than Reporter role");
}

if (userRole < adminRole) {
  print("User role is less than Admin role");
}
```

... but you
get better
readability
when you can
compare roles
directly.

Fortunately, Dart allows this functionality with operator overloading, which means you can take the standard operators and let your own classes provide meaning for them. In this instance, you want to provide meaning for the greater-than and less-than operators in the context of the Role class. Dart lets you do this in the same way you created a new version of the toString() method in chapter 7, by providing your own version of the operators' implementation. The operator keyword lets Dart know that your class is defining an operator implementation, as shown in the next listing.

Listing 8.11   Providing implementations of < and > with the operator keyword

```
class Role {
  final String name;
  final int _accessLevel;

  const Role(this.name, this._accessLevel);

  bool operator >(Role other) {
    return this._accessLevel > other._accessLevel;
  }

  bool operator <(Role other) {
    return this._accessLevel < other._accessLevel;
  }
}
```

You can now hide _accessLevel
by making it private.

Pairs operator
keyword with
operator you
want to
overload, to
provide a new
function

When you overload an operator, provide a method containing your implementation of the operator. The operator's method usually takes a single parameter containing another instance of the same class. Table 8.3 shows some common comparison operators that you can overload.

Table 8.3   Some common comparison operators

Operator method	Description
bool operator >(var other) {...}	This instance is greater than the other.
bool operator <(var other) {...}	This instance is less than the other.
bool operator >=(var other) {...}	This instance is greater than or equal to the other.
bool operator <=(var other) {...}	This instance is less than or equal to the other.
bool operator equals(var other) {...} bool operator ==(var other) {...}	This instance is equal to the other. Note that there are two different versions of this method. At the time of writing, the language spec defines the word equals as the operator, but the implementations are currently using a double equal sign == to represent the equals operator.

8.3.2 Surprising use for operator overloading

When you're overloading operators, the other value *should* be the same class, but there's no requirement that it *must be* the same class. This situation provides for some interesting, if slightly unorthodox, syntax. For example, to add a role to a user, you *could* overload the Users + operator, allowing you to write the code shown in the following listing.

Listing 8.12 Overloading the addition operator to add Roles to a User

```
class User {
  List roles;

  User() {
    roles = new List();
  }

  operator +(Role newRole) {            Overrides + operator
    this.roles.add(newRole);
  }
}
main() {
  User alice = new User();
  Role adminUser = new Role("TIMESHEET_ADMIN", 3);

  alice + adminUser;              ⟵── Uses + operator       Role has been
  print(alice.roles.length);                            ⟵   "added" to User
}
```

WARNING It's good practice to overload operators only when it would be unsurprising to the reader to do so. The previous example would be more readable if it provided an add(Role) method instead. Developers don't like surprises.

8.3.3 Overloading indexer operators

When you were dealing with lists and maps earlier in the chapter, you used the indexer operators to write [] = and read [] a value in an instance of a class, such as

```
myList[1] = "Some value";      ⟵┐  Uses []= operator to
var myValue = myList[1];       ⟵   write value by index
                               ⟵
                                  Reads value with
                                  [] operator
```

The [] operator allows you to read a value by index. [] = allows you to write a value by index. And you can overload these in your classes to provide indexer access to underlying values. The [] operator method takes a single index parameter and returns a value, and [] = takes both an index parameter and a value parameter that should be applied to that index item. Imagine a User class that could only have exactly two roles. You could use an indexer to allow reading and writing to those two roles. The following listing uses indexers to access the underlying _role1 and _role2 properties.

Listing 8.13   Overloading the indexer operators

```
class User {
  Role _role1;
  Role _role2

  User() {
    roles = new List();
  }
  operator []=(int index, Role role) {
    if (index == 1) {
      _role1 = role;
    }
    else if (index == 2) {
      _role2 = role;
    }
    else throw new RangeError();
  }
  Role operator [](int index) {
    if (index == 1) {
      return _role1;
    }
    else if (index == 2) {
      return _role2;
    }
    else throw new RangeError();
  }
}
main() {
  User alice = new User();
  alice[1] = new Role("TIMESHEET_ADMIN", 3);
  alice[2] = new Role("TIMESHEET_USER", 1);
  var roleIndex1 = alice[1];
}
```

Overrides []=
write indexer

Overrides []
read indexer

Uses write indexer
to set roles by index

Uses read indexer to
read a role by index

A common reason to use indexers is to have a class implement a Map interface so that properties on the class can be read as though they were part of a map, when they actually form real properties. This method allows tools such as the JSON parser, which understands maps and lists, to convert your class into a JSON representation. When data is in a JSON format, it can be sent back and forth over the web. You can make your Role class implement a Map and convert it to JSON using the code shown in listing 8.14. Although the code has snipped some of the boilerplate methods required by the Map interface, you must provide all of them. Listing 8.14 also uses some of the other patterns you've seen in this chapter, such as returning list literals and returning typed and untyped generic collections.

Listing 8.14   Letting a class implement Map so it can be converted to JSON

```
class Role implements Map {
  String name;
  int _accessLevel;
```

Implements
Map interface

```
Role(this.name, this._accessLevel) {}

//Map methods
bool containsKey(String key) {
  return key == "name" || key == "accessLevel";
}
```
Returns true if key is
name or accessLevel

```
operator[](String key) {
  if (key == "name") return this.name;
  if (key == "accessLevel") return this._accessLevel;
  return null;
}
```
Overloads [] operator to
allow reading properties

```
void operator[]=(String key, var value) {
  if (key == "name") this.name = key;
  if (key == "accessLevel") this._accessLevel = value;
}
```
Overloads []= operator to
allow writing properties

```
Collection<String> get keys {
  return ["name","accessLevel"];
}
```
Returns typed collection of String
key names created as literal list

```
Collection get values {
  return [this.name, this._accessLevel];
}
```
Returns untyped collection of
values created as literal list

```
//...snip other map methods...

}
```

Now that you've implemented Map in your Role class, you can use the JSON.stringify()
method (defined in the dart:json library) to convert an instance of a role into a string,
as in the following snippet:

```
Role adminRole = new Role("TIMESHEET_ADMIN",3);
var roleString = JSON.stringify(adminRole);
```

You can use this serialized string to send the Role data over the web (which we'll
explore in part 3, later in the book).

Remember
- Use the operator keyword in conjunction with the operator symbol to provide a new method in your class to overload the operator.
- Ensure that you overload operators only where doing so will aid readability of the code.
- You can overload indexer operators to allow map-like access to properties of your class.
- The dart:json library can convert classes that implement the Map interface into JSON strings.

8.4   *Summary*

In this chapter, we've taken a long look at manipulating collections of data and shown you the relationship between the `Collection` interface; some concrete implementations of collections in the form of `List`, `Queue`, and `Set`; and some of the methods exposed on the collection, such as `forEach()` and `filter()`.

We also looked at the `Map` interface, which you can use to store key/value pairs of data, and you saw that the built-in JSON library can be used to convert strings into maps and back again.

By using your classes in place of a type placeholder, the generic collection classes can work in a type-safe manner, effectively giving you a "list of" your own class—for example, a list of `Strings` or a list of `Users`. You've seen how to create your own generic classes; you should try to create a generic class if you find yourself making a number of nearly identical classes that differ only by the method parameters and return types.

Finally, we looked at operator overloading, which allows you to aid readability when using your classes by providing your own versions of common operator symbols such as > (greater than) and < (less than). The culmination of operator overloading was to use the indexer operators [] and []= to provide your own implementation of the `Map` interface, which allows your class to be converted to JSON by the built-in JSON library.

In the next chapter, we'll examine functions in depth. You'll see how to use function callbacks and future values to achieve readable and performing asynchronous code.

Asynchronous programming
with callbacks and futures

This chapter covers

- The nonblocking async programming model
- Callbacks for asynchronous APIs
- Improving asynchronous readability with futures and completers
- Unit-testing asynchronous code

In web programming, you can't rely on events outside your application's control happening in a specific order. In the browser, retrieving data from a server might take longer than you expect, and instead of waiting for the data, a user might click another button. A Dart server application will likely need to handle a new request for data before a previous request has finished reading data from the file system. This type of programming is known as an *asynchronous model* (async), and its counterpart is the *synchronous model*. In a synchronous model, everything happens in order, waiting for the previous step to fully complete. This is fine for some environments, but in a web application environment, you can't block all execution while you wait for the previous task to complete.

This is a powerful but nontrivial programming model that's also used in JavaScript. We'll spend some time in this chapter getting to grips with async programming and exploring the nonblocking aspect of Dart's event loop. In JavaScript, you use callback functions with the async programming model, and you can do the same in Dart. We looked at callback functions back in chapter 4, because they're a common pattern in async programming, and we'll revisit them in this chapter. Callbacks don't come without problems for readability, maintainability, and sequencing, as you'll discover, but Dart introduces a new pair of types to address these problems: `Future` and `Completer`. A `Future` represents a future value—a value you know you'll have at some point in the future—and is perfect for async programming, so we'll also spend some time looking at this pair of types.

Finally, you'll use your new knowledge of async programming to write some unit tests that are specifically able to cope with async code. Unit tests normally run sequentially, with the unit-test app exiting once the last test has run, but this pattern doesn't work when your code is still expecting a response from some external influence. Fortunately, Dart's unit-test library allows you to wait for async calls to complete before exiting, as you'll see in action at the end of the chapter.

First, though, we should look at what happens in a synchronous, blocking web app. Many countries have a regular lottery in which numbered balls pulled from a machine represent the winning numbers for that week. Players check their tickets against the winning numbers. In order to build suspense and excitement, the numbered balls appear from the machine at random intervals. You'll build this first as a synchronous app, which will cause the browser to freeze until all the winning numbers are generated, and then you'll fix it to use correct async APIs, allowing the browser to remain responsive. Figure 9.1 shows the problem you'll experience with the synchronous version of the app.

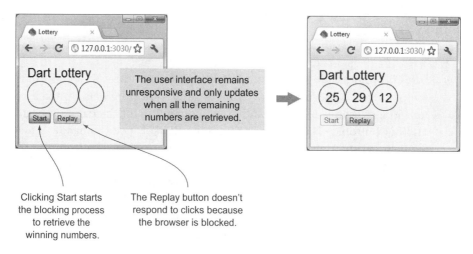

Clicking Start starts the blocking process to retrieve the winning numbers.

The Replay button doesn't respond to clicks because the browser is blocked.

Figure 9.1 The synchronous version of your Dart Lottery app will block until your code finishes executing.

9.1 Why web apps should be asynchronous

You're going to build a lottery web app to simulate a lottery game. In the app, when you click the Start button, three winning numbers are generated, each after a random delay of up to two seconds. This delay will cause the browser to lock up until it responds. The code to implement this delay gets the current time and waits in a `while` loop until it has waited the correct amount of time. Each winning number is displayed on the UI. Listing 9.1 shows the complete app's code.

> **WARNING** The code in listing 9.1 is bad in a web programming environment. It's included here only to demonstrate the impact of a blocking web app. In the next section, you'll see the correct technique to wait a given period of time using async APIs.

Listing 9.1 lottery_app.dart written in a synchronous, blocking style

```dart
import "dart:html";
import "dart:math";

int getWinningNumber() {                                    // Determines current
  int millisecsToWait = new Random().nextInt(2000);         // time, and time you
  var currentMs = new Date.now().millisecondsSinceEpoch;    // should stop processing
  var endMs = currentMs + millisecsToWait;
  while (currentMs < endMs) {                               // Loops (blocking) until
    currentMs = new Date.now().millisecondsSinceEpoch;     // you've waited long enough
  }

  return new Random().nextInt(59) + 1;       // Returns winning number from 1–60
}

startLottery() {
  int num1 = getWinningNumber();
  query("#ball1").innerHTML = "$num1";
  int num2 = getWinningNumber();             // Each getWinningNumber() call
  query("#ball2").innerHTML = "$num2";       // is blocked until the previous
  int num3 = getWinningNumber();             // one has completed.
  query("#ball3").innerHTML = "$num3";
}

resetLottery() {
  query("#ball1").innerHTML = "";
  query("#ball2").innerHTML = "";
  query("#ball3").innerHTML = "";
}

main() {
  var startButton = new Element.html("<button>Start</button>");
  document.body.children.add(startButton);
  startButton.on.click.add((e) {
    startButton.disabled = true;             // Starts lottery
    startLottery();                          // running
  });

  var resetButton = new Element.html("<button>Replay</button>");
  document.body.children.add(resetButton);
```

```
resetButton.on.click.add((e) {
  startButton.disabled = false;                    Resets
  resetLottery();                                  lottery UI
});
}
```

This code is straightforward: you read down the startLottery() function to see that it retrieves each winning number in turn and updates a specific `<div>` in the UI with that winning number. Unfortunately, this isn't what happens in practice: the browser has an event loop that processes tasks that are waiting on a queue, and because your code blocks the execution flow, your UI updates aren't acted on by the browser event loop until the code has finished executing. The longer you spend in each of your getWinningNumber() functions, the longer the browser has to wait until it regains control and can start processing the event loop again. Figure 9.2 demonstrates the flow that the browser takes when processing your code and its event loop.

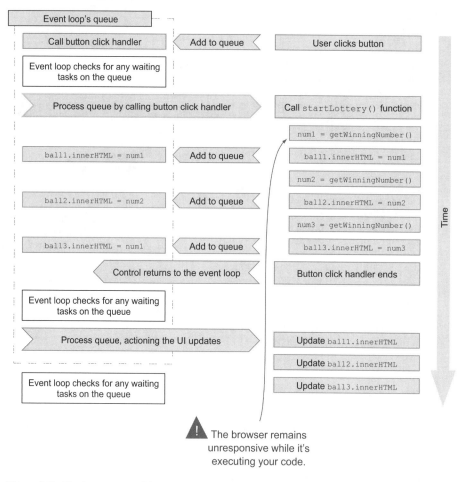

Figure 9.2   The browser event loop processes events only when your Dart code isn't executing.

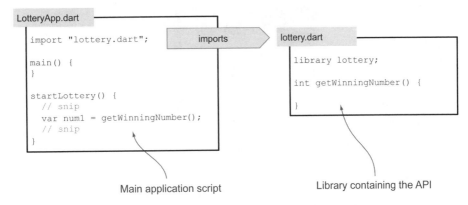

Figure 9.3   **The relationship between the lottery app and the** `lottery` **library**

In practice, many of the tasks a browser needs to perform, such as interacting with a server, are carried out on different threads internally in the browser, so the event loop only needs to start the task and be notified (again, via the event loop) that a task has finished. But it can't do this while your code is blocking, so you need to change the code to ensure that it executes and exits as quickly as possible—a task made possible by the asynchronous APIs.

As you convert this app to be asynchronous, you'll build up a set of APIs for running the lottery app in an async manner. To properly separate the UI from the API, make sure to properly organize the code into separate files. The lottery_app.dart file will contain your app, which interacts with the UI, and the lottery library will contain your API. Figure 9.3 shows this relationship.

This split will help you later when you provide async unit tests for the lottery.dart API functions.

9.1.1   *Modifying your app to be asynchronous*

Now that you have an app structure, you can start to modify it to become asynchronous. An ideal way for the Dart lottery app to work is to provide some suspense and drama by creating winning numbers in any order and displaying each number on the UI as it appears. Thus the second number could appear first, followed by the third and first, with each dependent on the random time taken for each number to appear.

Figure 9.4 shows the UI you'll build and the browser console with some of the logging. As you can see, although the winning numbered balls are requested in order, they're generated out of order.

You might have noticed that the Dart Lottery pulls only three numbered balls, so it's significantly easier to win than most lotteries.

REAL-WORLD DELAYS
The time delay from when the app starts until the numbered balls appear represents a nice async flow that you need to cope with in a client-side app. In the real world, this async flow might come from requesting data from three different server requests or

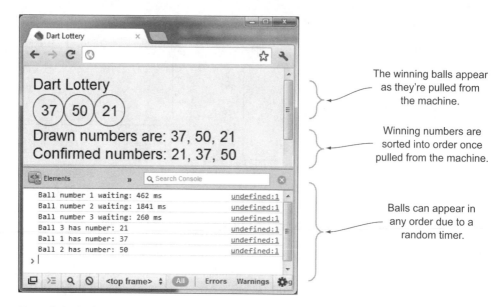

Figure 9.4   The Dart Lottery app pulls numbers after a random amount of time.

waiting for three different inputs from a user. In the Dart Lottery example, the data you're waiting for is the number pulled from the machine for each ball, and a random timer provides the I/O delay.

In the synchronous version of Dart Lottery, you wait a random amount of time before each ball is pulled from the machine, and no other ball can be drawn until the previous one has completed. But the async lottery allows multiple balls to be pulled from the machine in any order. It's possible for the third ball to appear from the machine first. The async pseudocode flow is as follows:

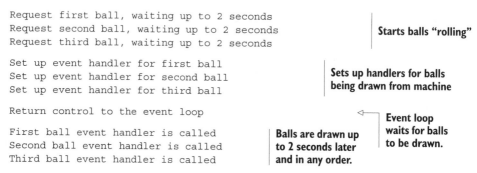

BEGINNING ASYNC PROGRAMMING WITH WINDOW.SETTIMEOUT()

The core of the lottery app is the lottery library. This library provides the code to return a random number after a certain amount of time. The lottery library uses an async API built into the web browser called window.setTimeout(callback, duration), which executes a callback function after a certain number of milliseconds. A trivial usage of it is shown in the following snippet, with the callback event handler in bold italic:

```
getWinningNumber() {
  Random r = new Random();
  int millisecsToWait = r.nextInt(2000);

  window.setTimeout((() {
    // generate our winning number
    // and update the UI
  }, millisecsToWait);
);
```

Creates random number of milliseconds, up to 2 seconds in duration

Calls setTimeout(), which executes anonymous callback function when timer finishes

The Dart app calls `window.setTimeout()` and then continues executing, finally returning control to the event loop. The event loop calls the `setTimeout()` function's callback event-handler function only when the specified milliseconds have elapsed. This is the principle of the event loop and asynchronous programming: the code starts a task and returns control to the event loop, which notifies the code when that task has completed.

Figure 9.5 shows how `window.setTimeout()` interacts with the event loop in an asynchronous manner.

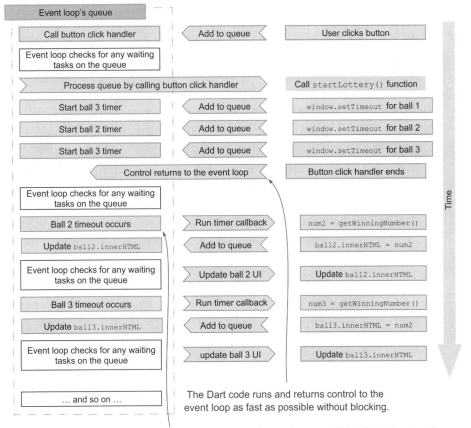

Once the timeouts occur, they trigger callbacks to Dart code, which executes and returns control to the event loop. This lets the browser remain responsive

Figure 9.5 Async calls mean that control returns to the event loop as quickly as possible.

This asynchronous handling of events in the order in which they occur also happens in other APIs, such as requesting data from a server using `HttpRequest`. Your app requests data from the server and returns control to the event loop. The event loop calls the anonymous event-handler function once the server has responded with data. An example is shown in the following code snippet; the anonymous callback function is shown in bold italic:

```
HttpRequest.get("http://example.com", (data) {
    // handle data being returned
});
```

In the next section, you'll use the async `setTimeout()` function as you start to use callback functions to interact with the async APIs provided with the browser. We first looked at callback functions in chapter 4, and now that you know the look and feel of the lottery app, it's time to revisit them in the context of async programming.

> **Remember**
> - Synchronous code executes in sequence, waiting for each blocking operation to complete in turn.
> - Asynchronous (async) code doesn't block. Instead, the event loop is responsible for notifying the app when an I/O task completes.

9.2   *Using callbacks with async programming*

Your app is split into two files: the `lottery` library, which represents the async API and provides the useful functions to generate numbers and eventually sort them into order, and the lottery_app.dart file, which contains your app's `main()` function and imports the `lottery` library. The `main()` function is the first function that executes when a Dart app starts, and splitting the key functions into a separate lottery.dart file will help later when you refactor and test your async code.

The first async version of Dart Lottery uses callback functions to retrieve numbered balls. This programming model is common in JavaScript development, both on the client and the server side, and is possible because functions can be passed as parameters to other functions.

> **NOTE**   Callbacks are a common pattern, and you should get used to reading code that uses callbacks, but they do have their drawbacks, as you'll discover. In the next section, you'll see how you can improve existing APIs that use callbacks by using the `Future` and `Completer` pair of values.

The basic callback code, which is still running in a synchronous fashion but without the delay, is shown in figure 9.6. This is a simplified version that outputs a single winning number to the browser console.

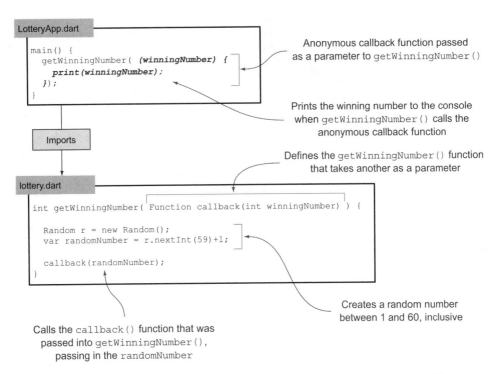

Figure 9.6 The lottery.dart file defines a `getWinningNumber()` function that takes a callback parameter. The app passes a callback to `getWinningNumber()`, which is called when a number is retrieved.

Nothing in the code shown in figure 9.6 represents async programming; instead, the code is entirely synchronous. The `main()` function is called, followed by the call to `getWinningNumber()`, which accepts a callback function as a parameter. `getWinning-Number()` creates a random number and passes it back into the callback function, which outputs the winning number to the console. Only after these steps have occurred does control return to the event loop. This is fine, because there is also no blocking code yet. The lottery app can call `getWinningNumber()` three times, and three winning numbers will be printed to the console.

To improve the app's UI slightly, you'll add a utility function `updateResult(int ball, int winningNumber)` that will populate a `<div>` element in the browser representing a ball with the winning number. lottery_app.dart now contains the code shown in the next listing, which uses both shorthand and longhand function syntax to call `updateResult()` with each winning number.

Listing 9.2 lottery_app.dart: using callbacks

```
import "lottery.dart";
import "dart:html";

main() {
```

```
    getWinningNumber( (int result1) => updateResult(1, result1) );
    getWinningNumber( (int result2) => updateResult(2, result2) );
    getWinningNumber( (int result3) {
      updateResult(3, result3);
    });
}
updateResult(int ball, int winningNumber) {
  var ballDiv = query("#ball$ball");
  ballDiv.innerHTML = "$winningNumber";
}
```

Passes anonymous callback functions to getWinningNumber()

Longhand syntax is also valid for anonymous functions.

Utility function to update correct <div> on UI

The associated API library `lottery` contains the single `getWinningNumber()` function, which accepts a callback function and generates a random number, as you saw in figure 9.6. In a moment, you'll modify this function to use the async API call `window.setTimeout()` and add some suspense and drama to the lottery app.

9.2.1 Adding async callbacks to Dart Lottery

Now the async Dart Lottery can begin. You can generate random numbers and display them on the UI. Because the code is synchronous, executing one statement after another, it will create `result1` first, `result2` second, and `result3` third.

But there's no suspense (and no async code), because you're pulling the numbers out of the machine as fast as the code will execute. Fortunately, it's easy to introduce suspense without changing lottery_app.dart: modify the `getWinningNumber()` function in the `lottery` library to use the `window.setTimeout()` function to ensure that the callback is called only after some random amount of time, which will cause the results to be generated in any order. Perhaps `result3` will appear first, closely followed by `result1` and, after a final delay, `result2`. The next listing modifies `getWinningNumber()` to call the callback function after a random amount of time of up to two seconds.

Listing 9.3 lottery.dart: adding a timer to `getWinningNumber()`

```
library lottery;

import "dart:html";
import "dart:math";

getWinningNumber(Function callback(int winningNumber)) {

  Random r = new Random();
  var randomNumber = r.nextInt(59) + 1;

  int millisecs = r.nextInt(2000);

  window.setTimeout( () {
    callback(randomNumber);
  }, millisecs);
}
```

Included for window.setTimeout()

Included for Random class

Random number, up to 2 seconds

Calls window.setTimeout() and passes anonymous function

Calls callback when timeout occurs

Passes number of milliseconds to wait as second parameter

1. The code executes in order, as fast as the machine will allow.

2. Timers start, with flow returning to the event loop until the timers complete.

```
main() {
  getWinningNumber((int result1) => updateResult(1,result1));

  getWinningNumber((int result2) => updateResult(2,result2));

  getWinningNumber((int result3) => updateResult(3,result3));
}
```

Timer 1 waits 700ms

Timer 2 waits 910ms

Timer 3 waits 200ms

3. When each timer completes, the event loop calls the timer's callback function, which executes the callback passed to getWinningNumber().

```
Executes: (int result3) => updateResult(3,result3)
```

```
Executes: (int result1) => updateResult(1,result1)
```

```
Executes: (int result2) => updateResult(2,result2)
```

Figure 9.7   The code runs as fast as possible until the `main()` function finishes executing. At that point, the event loop waits for the timers to time out, calling back into the Dart code.

TIP   For animation, the HTML5 browser function `requestAnimationFrame()` is a better choice for updating the screen periodically. This is because its refresh frequency is determined by the capabilities of the browser and hardware, and it runs only when the browser tab is visible.

The three calls from `main()` to `getWinningNumber()` happen in turn as fast as the code will execute. But because they took place before you added the `setTimeout()` call, the actual results will be generated at some unknown point in the future. Once all three calls to `getWinningNumber()` have been made, flow returns to the event loop, which responds again only when the `setTimeout` handlers need to be called after each of their timeouts expires, as shown in figure 9.7.

This is exactly how you can expect code in the real world to work. When you request data from a server, you don't know how long the server will take to respond. The user may have clicked another button in the meantime, triggering a different request to a server. The app could receive the server callback events in any order.

9.2.2   *Ensuring that all async callbacks are complete before continuing*

Dart Lottery needs to do more than just show the numbers on the screen as they're pulled from the machine. Once all three balls have been pulled, you need to display them neatly. To do this, you'll introduce a new utility function called `getResultsString`

(List<int> winningNumbers, String message). It will return a string containing the message and the list of comma-separated winning numbers.

There's now a requirement for some sequencing in your app. You can get the three numbers and display them onscreen in any order, but only after all three numbers have appeared do you want to execute the next part of the app that displays the results string.

This approach creates some complexity in async code, because each of the callbacks has no knowledge of the other callbacks. Thus you need to introduce some check or another mechanism. There are at least a couple of ways of doing this. The first is to store a flag in the main() method outside each callback and have each callback check whether all the values have been retrieved. The second is to nest the callbacks, in which case you'll look at each in turn.

Listing 9.4 shows a modified lottery_app.dart in which the callback functions call an addAndDisplay() function that's declared in main() to add each result to a result list defined in main(). Only when that list contains three items does addAndDisplay() call getResultsString() and display the list's contents in a browser <div>. The addAndDisplay() function also becomes a closure because it's passed into each callback, retaining access to the results list variable, even when it's called in the scope of getWinningNumber(). Please refer to chapter 4 for a recap on closures.

Listing 9.4 lottery_app.dart: introducing sequencing into an async callback

```
main() {
  List<int> results = new List<int>();              ⟵── Results list

  void addAndDisplay(int result) {
    results.add(result);

    if (results.length == 3) {
      var resultString = getResultsString(results, "Winning numbers: ");
      var winningNumbersDiv = query("#winningNumbers");
      winningNumbersDiv.innerHTML = resultString;        addAndDisplay() becomes
    }                                                    a closure when it's passed
  }                                                      into each callback.

  getWinningNumber( (int result1) {
    updateResult(1, result1);
    addAndDisplay(result1);
  });

  getWinningNumber( (int result2) {
    updateResult(2, result2);                        Callback functions also call
    addAndDisplay(result2);                          addAndDisplay(), passing in
  });                                                their own result.

  getWinningNumber( (int result3) {
    updateResult(3, result3);
    addAndDisplay(result3);
  });
}
```

Although this code works fine, it dramatically increases the app's complexity. As you read the code from top to bottom, it's no longer possible to see the exact order in which things occur. You can only tell by the logic in the addAndDisplay() function that the winningNumbers <div> will be populated after all three callbacks have occurred.

Fortunately, a second approach—nesting callbacks—can provide a limited amount of readability benefit and ordering, at the expense of allowing all three functions to execute simultaneously. This approach is often beneficial, though; many times you'll want to simulate a synchronous flow even when you're dealing with an async API. For example, you might need to be sure that you've retrieved data from server 1 before you retrieve data from server 2 or that you've connected to the database before you query it.

9.2.3 *Nesting callbacks to enforce async execution order*

Nesting callbacks is a technique that allows you to simulate synchronous code when you have only an asynchronous API, such as with getWinningNumbers(). This technique is used often in JavaScript, especially with server-side Node.js or a Dart VM to execute async code in the correct, logical order, such as open a file, read the file, close the file. All of these are async tasks, but they must be performed in the correct order. There's a big downside to this technique, though. Once you get more than three or four nested callbacks, readability again becomes a problem, as you'll see.

When nesting callbacks, you need to ensure that the first callback calls the second getWinningNumber() function and the second callback calls the third getWinning-Number() function, and so on. The last callback can then execute the final step in the chain, such as displaying the list of results on the UI.

Listing 9.5 modifies lottery_app.dart using nested callbacks to ensure that the winning numbers are drawn in order and that the list of winning numbers is updated only after the third number is drawn.

Listing 9.5 lottery_app.dart: using nested callbacks

```
main() {
  getWinningNumber( (int result1) {          ◄── Passes first callback into getWinningNumber()    First callback calls getWinningNumber(), passing in second callback.
    updateResult(1, result1);

    getWinningNumber( (int result2) {          ◄── Second callback calls getWinningNumber(), passing in third callback.
      updateResult(2, result2);

      getWinningNumber( (int result3 ) {       ◄──
        updateResult(3, result3);
                                                   Third callback displays winning number results.
        List results = new List();
        results.add(result1);
        results.add(result2);
        results.add(result3);
        var resultString = getResultsString(results, "Winning numbers: ");
        var winningNumbersDiv = query("#winningNumbers");
        winningNumbersDiv.innerHTML = resultString;   ◄──
```

```
        });
      });
    });
}
```

As you can see, with three levels of nesting, things are starting to get complicated. The next requirement for the app is to sort the balls into order, also using an async API, which means another nested callback in the third callback.

Unfortunately, this requirement is all too common in the real world, where you only have async APIs to work with but you need to either enforce a specific order or wait for a number of async calls to complete. A real-world example on the client side is a button-click handler to retrieve data from a server call, manipulate that data, and send the data back to the server, alerting the user when complete; a dive into many JavaScript applications will show code that contains nested async calls many levels deep, which is popularly known as *callback hell*. The following snippet shows how it might look if you had six balls instead of three:

```
getWinningNumber( (int result1) {
  updateResult(1, result1);
  getWinningNumber( (int result2) {
    updateResult(2, result2);
    getWinningNumber( (int result3) {
      updateResult(3, result3);
      getWinningNumber( (int result4) {
        updateResult(4, result4);
        getWinningNumber( (int result5) {
          updateResult(5, result5);
          getWinningNumber( (int result6) {
            updateResult(6, result6);
            //snip getResultsString()
          });
        });
      });
    });
  });
});
```

Many frameworks in the JavaScript world have been created to try to deal with this callback-nesting problem, but Dart brings its own solution to the table in the form of the `Future` and `Completer` types. These provide neat mechanisms to let async code execute in a specific order without nesting and to allow code to continue executing only after all the async operations are complete.

Remember
- Callbacks provide the standard async pattern of operation.
- A callback function that's passed to an async API will be called when the async operation is completed.

(continued)

- To ensure that all async operations are completed before the next block of code executes, you can maintain a count or other flags to indicate that all the async operations have completed.
- To enforce a specific sequence of code execution with async APIs, you can nest API callbacks.

9.3 *Introducing the Future and Completer pair*

You saw in the previous section how to run async code using callback functions. When you request a winning number from the Dart Lottery machine's getWinningNumber() function, you're making an async request that returns a winning number after a random amount of time. Once all three of the winning numbers have been returned, you perform the next step in the app's flow: formatting the numbers for use on the UI.

The code to check whether all three numbers have been returned became more complex, and you lost the ability to easily navigate the code. Fortunately, Dart provides a neat pair of types, Future and Completer, that will help you write more maintainable and readable async code.

These two types work closely together to return a *future value*, which is a value that will exist at some point in the future. A Completer object is used to return an object of type Future, which represents a future value. This future value is populated when the completer.complete(value) function is called, passing in the real value for the future. You can wrap your existing async API call to getWinningNumber(callback) to instead return a future value. Figure 9.8 shows how to achieve this; we'll then look at how to use a future value.

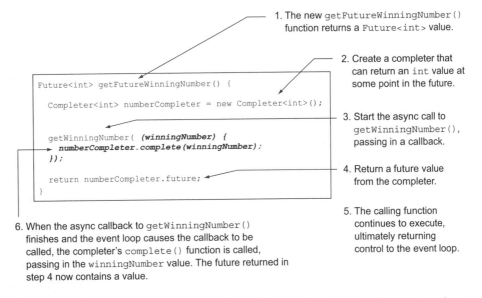

1. The new getFutureWinningNumber() function returns a Future<int> value.

2. Create a completer that can return an int value at some point in the future.

3. Start the async call to getWinningNumber(), passing in a callback.

4. Return a future value from the completer.

5. The calling function continues to execute, ultimately returning control to the event loop.

6. When the async callback to getWinningNumber() finishes and the event loop causes the callback to be called, the completer's complete() function is called, passing in the winningNumber value. The future returned in step 4 now contains a value.

Figure 9.8 It's possible to wrap an async callback API to use the Future and Completer types.

When you call getFutureWinningNumber(), you get back a result immediately in the form of a Future<int> returned from a completer. The code continues to execute, using that future value in place of a real value. In getFutureWinningNumber(), you've made a call to the async getWinningNumber() function, which itself is requesting data from an async API. At some point, when the completer's complete() function is passed the real value, the future value will finally contain a value. How do you access that future value? Once again, via a callback, which is passed into the future's then() function.

Let's see this in action by replicating the first simple callback example to display three numbers. The next listing shows the new lottery_app.dart file, which uses getFutureWinningNumber(), and the original version with callbacks for comparison.

Listing 9.6 lottery_app.dart using Future values and then() callbacks

```
main() {

    Future<int> f1 = getFutureWinningNumber();        Request for winning number
    Future<int> f2 = getFutureWinningNumber();        returns future value
    Future<int> f3 = getFutureWinningNumber();

    f1.then((int result1) => updateResult(1, result1));     Callback in future's then()
    f2.then((int result2) => updateResult(2, result2));     function executes when
    f3.then((int result3) => updateResult(3, result3));     future value has a value.
// getWinningNumber( (int result1) => updateResult(1, result1) );
// getWinningNumber( (int result2) => updateResult(2, result2) );
// getWinningNumber( (int result3) => updateResult(3, result3) );
}

                                                       Original callback
                                                       code for comparison
```

A more concise way of writing this code is to chain the then() function onto the original function call:

```
getFutureWinningNumber().then((int result1) => updateResult(1, result1));
```

In terms of functionality, it appears you've gained little. You still provide a callback into the then() function, and each callback is executed when the future value has a value (with the future value being passed on the callback parameter). What "extra value" does a future value give you?

9.3.1 *Passing around future values*

The first thing you can do with a future value is pass it around the application. With the callback version, you need to decide what you want to do with the winning number when you call getWinningNumber()—in this example, by passing the winning number into the updateResult() function.

With the future version, you can put off that decision and allow another part of the code, such as an updateUserInterface() function, to decide what happens to the future value by passing in the futures as parameters. This approach has the twin benefits of reducing callback nesting and allowing you to pass all three future values into another function, even though the async result that they represent hasn't yet been

returned. You can refactor the lottery_app.dart file again to pass the future values into
updateUserInterface(), as shown next.

Listing 9.7   lottery_app.dart: passing future values into a function

```
main() {

    Future<int> f1 = getFutureWinningNumber();
    Future<int> f2 = getFutureWinningNumber();
    Future<int> f3 = getFutureWinningNumber();                     Passes future values
                                                                   to another function
    updateUserInterface(f1,f2,f3);
}

void updateUserInterface(Future first, Future second, Future third)
    first.then((int result1) => updateResult(1, result1));
    second.then((int result2) => updateResult(2, result2));       Other function can
    third.then((int result3) => updateResult(3, result3));        decide to use future
}                                                                  value via future value's
                                                                   then() method.
```

This is a powerful feature of futures. Real-world scenarios include passing a number of
future data values retrieved from the server into a UI component and handling a
user's "future" button click by passing it to a function in the app. Because the future
values are variables that know they'll have a value in the future (via the then() function), it's easy to store them in other classes such as lists. This brings us to a second
powerful feature of futures: performing async calls in sequence.

9.3.2   *Ordering async calls by chaining futures*

Back in the callback discussion, async callbacks were nested in each other to ensure
that they were executed in order. When you get a few callbacks deep, you can end up
in nested callback hell, in which you're nesting so deep that readability and indenting
start to be a problem. This nesting effect can be achieved with futures by embedding
each future in the previous one's then() function, as shown in the following snippet:

```
getFutureWinningNumber().then( (result1) {
  updateResult(1, result1);
  getFutureWinningNumber().then( (result2) {
    updateResult(2, result2);
    getFutureWinningNumber().then( (result3) {
      updateResult(3, result3);
    });
  });
});
```

This way is no better than using nested callbacks, so although it's possible to nest
futures, doing so is clearly a suboptimal solution. Fortunately, Dart's futures provide a
mechanism to chain futures together so the next one is executed only when the previous one finishes, without nesting. This mechanism is achieved via the
future.chain(callback) function, which is used in place of future.then(). The

chain() function allows you to return another future, providing a mechanism to chain futures together, as shown in the following listing.

```
main() {
    getFutureWinningNumber().chain( (result1) {      ←┘  Uses chain() function of returned
        updateResult(1, result1);                         future instead of then()
        return getFutureWinningNumber();             ←——  In chain(), return next future ...
    }).chain( (result2) {
        updateResult(1, result2);                         ... and so on, until you've
        return getFutureWinningNumber();             ←┘  chained all futures together.
    }).then( (result3) {                             ←┐  Last call uses then() because
        updateResult(1, result3);                       it doesn't return a future.
    });
}
```

As you can see, you can continue to chain many futures together without nesting or affecting readability. Each call to getFutureWinningNumber() is made only when the previous call has completed.

9.3.3 *Waiting for all futures to complete*

In the discussion on callbacks, results were to be displayed as a formatted string using the getResultsString() function, but only after all three winning numbers had been retrieved. You achieved this by retrieving each value asynchronously and having each callback call an addAndDisplay() function that added the value to a list and performed the display action only when there were exactly three items in the list (one for each async value). This solution, although it works, introduces complexity in what should be a straightforward piece of code. You want to make three calls to getWinningNumber(), and only when all three calls have completed will you execute the next step.

This is one area in which future values shine. Dart provides a Futures.wait(futures) function that takes a list of future values and returns a single future. The single future contains a list of all the values returned from the futures passed in. Although this sounds complex, it's simple to use in practice, as shown in figure 9.9. The function waits for three real values to be returned from three future values and then passes the three real values—the three winning numbers—to be formatted on the display.

By passing all the future values into the wait() function, you can be sure all the futures have completed and returned real values before you continue to the next step. Because wait() also returns a future value, you can use its chain() function to chain it to other futures. This is helpful if, for example, you want to wait for the three numbers to complete and then request a fourth "bonus ball" number, as shown in the next listing. In this listing, you also add the future value results from getFutureWinningNumber() directly into a list.

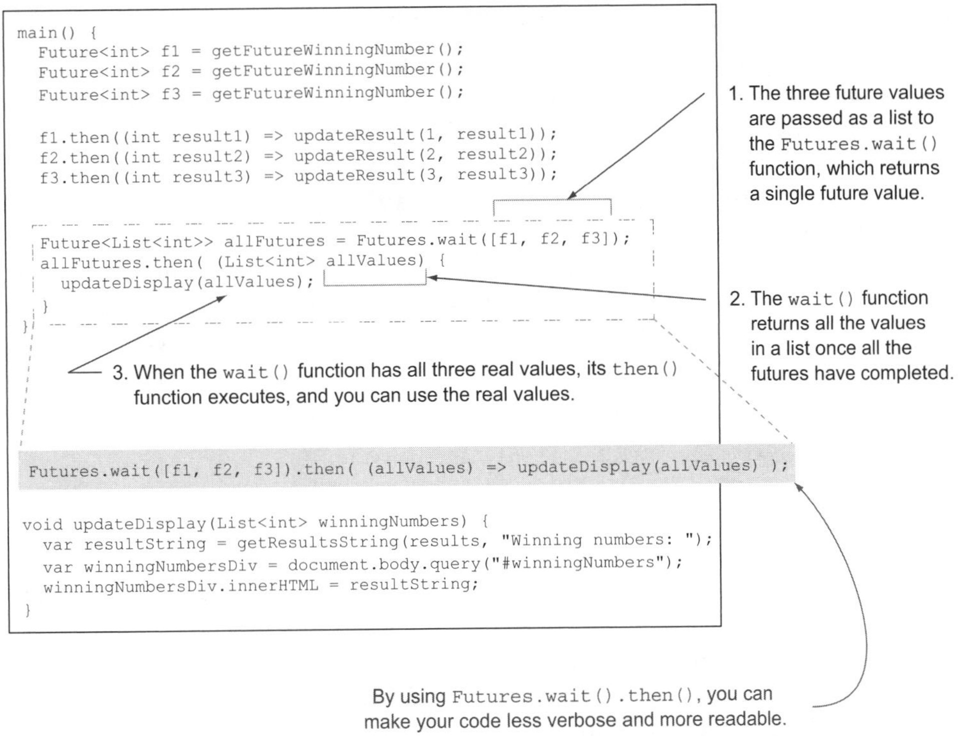

```
main() {
  Future<int> f1 = getFutureWinningNumber();
  Future<int> f2 = getFutureWinningNumber();
  Future<int> f3 = getFutureWinningNumber();

  f1.then((int result1) => updateResult(1, result1));
  f2.then((int result2) => updateResult(2, result2));
  f3.then((int result3) => updateResult(3, result3));

  Future<List<int>> allFutures = Futures.wait([f1, f2, f3]);
  allFutures.then( (List<int> allValues) {
    updateDisplay(allValues);
  }
}

Futures.wait([f1, f2, f3]).then( (allValues) => updateDisplay(allValues) );

void updateDisplay(List<int> winningNumbers) {
  var resultString = getResultsString(results, "Winning numbers: ");
  var winningNumbersDiv = document.body.query("#winningNumbers");
  winningNumbersDiv.innerHTML = resultString;
}
```

1. The three future values are passed as a list to the `Futures.wait()` function, which returns a single future value.

2. The `wait()` function returns all the values in a list once all the futures have completed.

3. When the `wait()` function has all three real values, its `then()` function executes, and you can use the real values.

By using `Futures.wait().then()`, you can make your code less verbose and more readable.

Figure 9.9 Futures.wait() allows you to wait for many futures to complete before continuing execution.

Listing 9.9 lottery_app.dart: waiting for futures and chaining

```
main {
  List futureValues = new List();
  futureValues.add(getFutureWinningNumber());          Adds three future       Waits for
  futureValues.add(getFutureWinningNumber());          values to list          future values
  futureValues.add(getFutureWinningNumber());                                  to complete
                                                                               with chain()
  Futures.wait(futureValues).chain( (List firstThreeNumbers) {

    getResultsString(firstThreeNumbers, "Winning numbers");          Displays
      // ... snip display code ...                                   three winning
                                                                     numbers
      return getFutureWinningNumber();

  }).then( (int bonusBall) {                                         Returns future
    getResultsString([bonusBall], "Bonus ball");                    from chain() to
      // ... snip display code ...                                  get bonus ball

  });                        In bonus ball's then()
}                            method, displays number
```

By using the `then()` and `chain()` methods of the Future class and the `wait()` static method of the Futures class, it's possible to write readable async code that avoids multiple levels of nesting and preserves order. There's still one more method of the Future class to look at: `transform()`.

9.3.4 *Transforming nonfuture values into futures*

You saw earlier how to take future values and pass them around your application. This approach is fine when it's the future values you need, but sometimes the future values are just a means to an end. In the Dart Lottery app, you're interested in the results string, which is generated by the getResultsString() function. It's the string value returned from getResultsString() that you want to pass around your app. Because a number of async calls need to complete before you can get the results string, you can't just call getResultsString() and pass its value to another function. Instead, you can call getResultsString() in the final then() handler of the final future, but sometimes you also need to use another future value. The result can be nested futures, which is what you're trying to avoid with futures in the first place. The following snippet shows the problem:

```
Future.wait([f1, f2, f3).then((List results) {          Gets result
  String resultString = getResultsString(results);       string

    formatResultString(resultString).then(( formattedResultString ) {
      // do something with the formatted result string
    });                                                  Passes resultString to
});                            Result: nested futures     another function that
                                                          returns a future
```

At this point, the transform(callback) function comes in. It's similar to the chain() function in that it returns a future. The difference is that chain() expects its callback function to return a future, and transform() wraps any value in a future, allowing you to return a future value as part of a sequence of async method calls—even when some of those method calls aren't async.

Listing 9.10 shows transform() in action: it waits for all three winning numbers to be drawn, passes them to getResultsString(), and automatically wraps the return value from getResultsString() into another future that you can use to chain to the next call to formatResultString(), which is used by the updateWinningNumbersDiv() function. This avoids nesting the call to formatResultString() in the wait().then() callback function.

Listing 9.10   lottery_app.dart: transforming a nonfuture value into a future value

```
main() {
  List futureValues = new List();
  futureValues.add(getFutureWinningNumber());          Async calls to get
  futureValues.add(getFutureWinningNumber());          winning numbers
  futureValues.add(getFutureWinningNumber());

  Futures.wait(futureValues).transform( (List winningNums) {    Returns
    String result = getResultsString(winningNums, "Winning numbers");   a future
    return result;
                                             ... but the string
  }).chain((resultString) {                  is wrapped into
    return formatResultString(resultString);  a future by      Passes
                                             transform().      future result
  }).then((formattedResultString) {                            to another
    var winningNumbersDiv = query("#winningNumbers");          function
```

Returns a
string, not
a future ...

```
        winningNumbersDiv.innerHTML = resultString;
    });
}

Future<String> formatResultString(String resultString) {
    // snip some async implementation
}
```

When the future
resultString completes,
it's displayed.

Future values, supported by their completers, provide a powerful mechanism for writing code that uses async APIs in a readable and maintainable manner. By chaining async calls with `chain()` and nonasync calls with `transform()`, you can mix asynchronous and synchronous code while maintaining a coherent flow.

Many Dart async APIs return future values rather than using callbacks, but some still do use callbacks. In this section, you've seen how to wrap callback APIs such as `getWinningNumber(callback)` to return future values by hiding the callback functionality in a wrapper function, instead returning a future value that's completed when the callback itself is called.

Remember
- You can wrap async callback API functions to return future values.
- The future value's `then(callback)` callback function is called when the future has finally received a value.
- `transform(callback)` wraps its callback's returned value in a new future.
- `chain(callback)` expects its callback's returned value to be a future.
- The `chain()` and `transform()` callback functions are called when the future receives its value but also let you return another future. You can use these to build a sequence of multiple async and synchronous calls.

In the final section, we'll look again at unit testing, which we last discussed in chapter 3, and you'll see how to unit-test the async library functions.

9.4 *Unit-testing async APIs*

Dart's unit-testing framework allows you to test your functions in a separate script with its own `main()` function. This script imports the library APIs and tests the various pieces of functionality you've built. When you write unit tests, you expect each test to run some code, complete, and report whether that test passed or failed, depending on your expectations. The following listing shows an example unit test to test the `getResultsString()` function from the `lottery` library. This code is similar to the testing code we looked at earlier in the book.

Listing 9.11 lottery_test.dart: unit-testing `getResultsString()`

```
import "lottery.dart";
import "dart:html";
import "lib/unittest/unittest.dart";
import "lib/unittest/html_config.dart";
```

Boilerplate to import
test and HTML libraries

Imports library
under test()

```
main() {
  useHtmlConfiguration();              ◁── Boilerplate code to register HTML test library

  test('Results String', () {
    var result = getResultsString([23,44,57], "Winning numbers: ");   ◁─┐ Performs
                                                                         │ call under
    expect(result, equals("Winning numbers: 23, 44, 57"));   ◁─────────┘ │ test()
  });                                                                    │
}                                                      Checks expectations ┘
```

This is a standard, synchronous unit test. The flow follows the expected execution sequence:

1 Start the main() function.
2 Start the test() function.
3 Call getResultsString() with sample parameters.
4 Check the expectations on the return value.
5 The test() function exits.
6 The main() function exits.

You can test async APIs such as getWinningNumber(callback), which uses callbacks, or getFutureWinningNumber(), which uses futures and requires a slightly different approach.

Because of their asynchronous nature, the test() and main() functions will have exited before the callback or future value is returned, as in the following sequence:

1 Start the main() function.
2 Start the test() function.
3 Call getFutureWinningNumber() with sample parameters.
4 The test() function exits.
5 The main() function exits.
6 The future value is returned.

This sequence presents a problem because it's the future value that you need to check against your expectations, and test() and main() have already exited. Fortunately, the Dart unit-test framework contains a number of expectAsync functions in the form of expectAsync0(), expectAsync1(), and expectAsync2(), which wrap the callback that you'd pass into the async API functions or the future value's then() function. The numerical suffix on the expectAsync functions represents the number of arguments the callback function expects. Because future callbacks only ever have a single argument (representing the real value used to populate the future) passed to them, this is perfect for our example. Likewise, the callback version of your API also returns a single value, so you can use expectAsync1() in both cases. Let's test the callback version of your API function with getWinningNumber() first and then test the getFutureWinningNumber() function.

9.4.1 Testing async callback functions

The expectAsync function wraps the callback function passed to getWinningNumber(). The following snippet is a reminder of the call to getWinningNumber() and its callback function:

```
getWinningNumber( (int result) {
  // ...snip ... do something with result value
} );
```
The callback takes a single argument: an int.

Calling this code is fine in the context of a web browser, because once you call getWinningNumber(), control returns back to the event loop. But in the context of a unit test, you need to ensure that the unit test waits for the result value to be returned before it exits. This is where the expectAsync() function comes in: it wraps the callback, which forces the unit-test framework to wait until the async call has completed before exiting. This gives you the ability to check your expectations of the result value and is shown in the following snippet, with the expectAsync1() function highlighted in bold italic:

```
getWinningNumber( expectAsync1( (int result) {
  // ...snip ... test the result value
}));
```

In the simple test shown in the following listing, a real unit test verifies that the number returned is in the range 1–60 inclusive.

Listing 9.12 lottery_test.dart: testing async callback functions with expectAsync()

```
import "lottery.dart";
import "dart:html";
import "lib/unittest/unittest.dart";
import "lib/unittest/html_config.dart";

main() {
  useHtmlConfiguration();

  test('Winning Number Callback', () {
    getWinningNumber( expectAsync1( (int result) {
      expect(result, greaterThanOrEqualTo(1));
      expect(result, lessThanOrEqualTo(60));
    }));
  );

}
```
Wrapping the callback in expectAsync() lets you properly test the result.

Now that you've seen how to test async callback functions, let's apply the same knowledge to async functions that return future values.

9.4.2 Testing future values

The final step in async testing is to test the result of getFutureWinningNumber(). A future value's then() function takes a callback function to receive the final value. It's this callback function that you wrap in the expectAsync1() function, which lets you check your expectations on the future value returned. The following snippet shows the test code for testing the future value, with expectAsync1() highlighted in bold italic:

```
test("Future winning number", () {
  getFutureWinningNumber().then( expectAsync1( (int result) {
    expect(result, greaterThanOrEqualTo(1));
    expect(result, lessThanOrEqualTo(60));
  }));
);
```

You can even test multiple futures by using the Futures.wait() function and wrapping its then() function in an expectAsync1() function, as shown in the next listing, which expects three values to be returned in the list.

Listing 9.13   lottery_test.dart: testing multiple futures with wait() and expectAsync()

```
import "lottery.dart";
import "dart:html";
import "lib/unittest/unittest.dart";
import "lib/unittest/html_config.dart";

main() {
  useHtmlConfiguration();

  test('Winning Number Callback', () {
    Future f1 = getFutureWinningNumber();
    Future f2 = getFutureWinningNumber();        Waits, then expects async
    Future f3 = getFutureWinningNumber();         values to be returned

    Futures.wait([f1,f2,f3]).then( expectAsync1( (List<int> results) {
      expect(results.length, equals(3));
    }));                                   Checks that three values
  );                                       are in returned list
}
```

When checking futures, the future value's then() function callback needs to be wrapped by expectAsync1(). This also means you can use .chain() and .transform() to link futures together in a specific order. Finally, you wrap the last future's then() function callback in expectAsync1() in a manner similar to that of the previous listing.

> **Remember**
> - Testing async APIs requires special treatment; otherwise, the unit test will exit before the returned value has been checked.
> - The callback function passed either to the async API function or into a future's then() function needs to be wrapped by an expectAsync() function, which forces the test framework to wait for the async call to complete.

9.5 *Summary*

There's no doubt about it: asynchronous programming is harder than synchronous programming. But nonblocking async APIs provide your app with the means to stay responsive, even when multiple requests are running that would otherwise block execution. On the server side, this could be file system access and network socket access; on the client side, it could be requesting data from a server or waiting for a user to enter some input. Dart's async APIs allow your code to execute and return control to the event loop, which will call back into the code again only when something happens, such as a file read completing or a server returning data.

Callback functions will be familiar to JavaScript developers, but many nested callbacks, which are often needed to enforce execution sequence, can create a callback hell. Dart allows callback functions but also provides the Future and Completer pair of types that work together to provide a future value that can be passed around your app. Only when the async call completes does the future value get a real value.

Multiple async requests can be chained together using the chain() function, which lets you avoid many nested callbacks. The future's transform() function also lets you use synchronous APIs interspersed with async APIs. The wait() function lets you wait until all futures have received real values before you continue processing.

Finally, unit-testing async code uses the expectAsync functions, which let the unit-testing framework know that it should wait for the callback or future value to be returned before the test is complete. These functions let you test your own async APIs in the same way you test standard, synchronous code.

Now you know about nearly all the concepts in the Dart language, and you're ready to start building apps. In the next section, you'll see more interaction with the browser, and we'll look at how to build a single-page web application with multiple views, offline data storage, and interaction with servers.

Part 3

Client-side Dart apps

In the third part of the book, you'll see how to build the client s̶ ̶̶ ̶̶ ̶̶ng browser-based, single-page Dart apps using the latest HTML5 tech̶

Chapter 10 introduces the Dart event loop and explains h̶ ̶̶ ̶̶ a user interface using Dart's browser DOM manipulation libraries a̶ ̶̶ your app to listen for browser-based events.

In chapter 11, you'll learn how to interact with the browser, letting your single-page app react to browser navigation events. You'll use in-browser cookies and offline storage to persist state and data across sessions and learn how to serialize your objects into a JSON form.

By chapter 12, you'll be ready to look beyond the Dart ecosystem and let your app interact with external systems such as external JavaScript functions and communicate with external servers. You'll use HTML5 AppCache technology to let your app run without a server, and go further by turning your app into a Chrome packaged app.

This part is focused on the client side. By the end of part 3, you'll be ready to investigate Dart on the server, building a back-end for your client-side app.

Building a Dart web app

This chapter covers

- The structure of a single-page web app
- Building dynamic views with `dart:html` elements
- Handling browser events with Dart

Dart's primary use is building complex web apps. A web app typically comprises a single web page that loads in the browser and provides a host for the application's code. This application source code is responsible for building the user interface, providing methods for navigating around the application, and storing the user's data by either sending it to the server or storing it locally.

When building a web app in Dart, it's good practice to build it working offline first. Working offline has a number of benefits, both for you as the developer and for the end user. When you build a web app offline first, you provide some mock injected data that will ultimately be replaced by a combination of local, client-side storage (supported by HTML5 APIs) and server-side data persistence. This setup lets you write the client-side app in Dart without needing a server component or database up and running, thereby reducing debug times and aiding the ability to unit-test your app.

211

The end user of your app will be able to use your app in disconnected situations, such as on a flight or in areas of limited network coverage. This setup allows you to write mobile, browser-based apps in Dart that function even when the device isn't connected. Another benefit to the end user is that apps designed to work offline also work much faster when online: the data that they use tends to be stored locally, so the app can start up much faster without needing to first load a large amount from the server.

This chapter shows that by using HTML elements, you can build a multiscreen UI from a single set of source code files. At the time of writing, there's no UI widget library in the Dart SDK, but you can build compelling UIs using the dart:html library Element and Event classes with relatively little code. Once you're familiar with the Element classes, we'll examine the browser event model and show you how the browser can trigger Dart event handlers to react to the user. While exploring the dart:html library, you'll discover how to build a reusable grid from scratch that you can use in your own applications.

10.1 *A single-page web app design*

Single-page application design is different from traditional web application design. In a traditional website built with Java or C# (or even PHP, Ruby, or Python), you typically use a server-side controller to compose the UI by merging an HTML view with some data classes (the models), and this information is then sent to the client. Navigating to another page (perhaps to perform an edit) triggers a new request to the server for another view and data.

But in recent years, frameworks have appeared that first let you send the view to the client and then use AJAX requests to get the data from the server and bind it to the view. In effect, the view, data model, and controller classes have moved onto the client, where they can take advantage of the power of the user's computer and leave the server free to serve more requests, as shown in figure 10.1.

This is the model that Google's GWT product uses; it's a model you can also achieve with a number of JavaScript frameworks. Dart apps also follow this model, with the Dart environment and tools working best when you design your Dart app to function this way. By combining the view with the data on the client, you also get the ability to provide mock data in the client, which can be used for development and testing.

10.1.1 *Introducing DartExpense*

In this chapter, you'll create an example expense application called DartExpense that lets you store a list of your work expenses. Your finance department has decided to rid themselves of spreadsheets that employees send by email; instead, they want a web app. The current spreadsheet system works regardless of whether the users are online; typically, they submit the spreadsheet only once a month. The sales team has a habit of using flying time to complete their expenses, and the finance department wants to ensure that they don't do so.

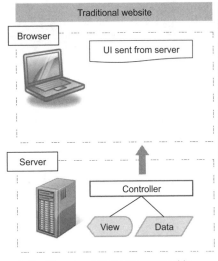
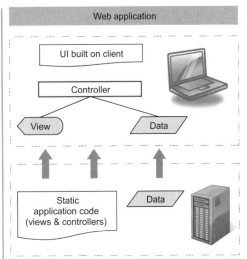

1. Traditional websites use server-side code to bind the view to the data on the server.
2. The server sends the result to the browser for rendering.
3. The server uses more resources building client user interfaces.

1. Single-page web apps send the application code as a set of static files to the browser.
2. The browser runs that code to request data and render the user interface.
3. The server is free to serve more requests.

Figure 10.1 **Modern web apps use the capabilities of the client to build a UI from views and data, rather than performing that processing on the server.**

The existing spreadsheet app contains only five fields of data for each expense claim:

- The date of the expense
- The type of expense
- The amount
- Some detail text
- Whether it has been claimed already

Your task is to implement this model in Dart.

The app, although simplified for the purposes of example, represents a real-life application design containing model and view classes. At the time of writing, Dart doesn't have a separate UI abstraction library such as ExtJS or jQuery UI; but the Dart development team has stated that they want Dart to be a fully featured solution and that a UI library will appear. This means UIs need to be constructed using HTML snippets and elements and bound with the data as required. We'll explore ways to achieve this using the `dart:html` library, which we first looked at back in chapter 3. The `dart:html` library is analogous to the jQuery core library for JavaScript, which standardizes HTML and browser DOM manipulation.

The DartExpense app will have two screens that users can navigate: the list of expenses and the Add/Edit screen to modify expenses. The screens are shown in figure 10.2.

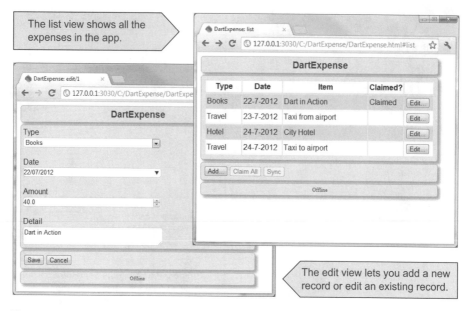

Figure 10.2   The DartExpense example application has list and edit views.

For this chapter, the app works entirely offline using mock data, which allows you to run it directly using the Dart Editor and Dartium. You can find the source code on the book's website at www.manning.com/DartinAction. In the next chapter, you'll add HTML5 client-side storage, and in chapter 14, you'll add a server component. But for now, the data access classes are hardcoded mocks.

Dart to JavaScript tree-shaking

In JavaScript, if you want to use mock data, you need a mechanism to prevent the mock data code from being deployed to the client browser (wasting bandwidth). In Dart, only code that will actually be executed ends up in the resulting JavaScript, via a mechanism called *tree-shaking*. You can safely create mock data in your app while developing; once you remove references to the mock data-access functions, you can be sure that no mock data is sent to the end user, even though the original mock functions remain in the project.

Two model classes, `Expense` and `ExpenseType`, store the data from the user and the standard reference data. There are also two views: `ListView`, which shows the list of expenses, and `EditView`, which allows you to add and edit expenses. Each view contains two top-level elements: the view itself, stored in the `viewElement` property, and the actions container, which holds the menu buttons such as Save and Cancel. A single controller class, `AppController`, is responsible for bringing together the views and the data. The public methods and properties on these classes are shown in figure 10.3.

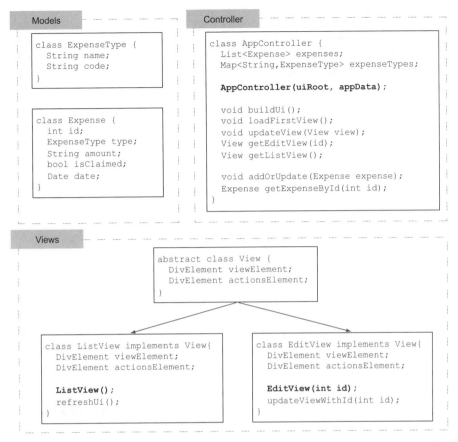

Figure 10.3 The main classes in the application are the models, the views, and the controller, with the constructors marked in bold.

In addition to these model, view, and controller classes, additional classes represent your data-access functions. The `DataAccess` interface specifies properties and methods to retrieve a list of expenses and add a new expense. For the purposes of this chapter, and for building your app in an offline fashion, a `MockData` class implements the `DataAccess` interface:

```
abstract class DataAccess {
  Map<String, ExpenseType> expenseTypes;
  Map<int, Expense> _expenses;
  List<Expense> get expenses;
  bool addOrUpdate(Expense expense);
}
```

The `MockData` implementation prepopulates the expenses and expense types and is passed into the constructor of the `AppController` class. Calling `addOrUpdate()` adds or updates the expenses list by adding a new item to the list or updating an existing item. In the following chapters, you'll replace the `MockData` class with locally persisted data, and later with server-persisted data.

10.1.2 *Dart application structure*

When you navigate to the Dart app, either on a real web server or by running it from the Dart Editor, the browser requests the HTML file that contains a link to the application code. The DartExpense app's HTML file, shown in listing 10.1, is minimal. There are two script tags in the standard editor-created HTML file. The first specifies a script type of `application/dart` that references your app's entry-point source file. The second script tag links to a JavaScript file, which uses a snippet of JavaScript to detect whether Dart is supported natively by the browser. If not, it modifies all `application/dart` script tags in the HTML page to use the JavaScript version.

Listing 10.1   DartExpense.html

```
<!DOCTYPE html>                                    ◁── HTML5
                                                        doctype
<html>
  <head>
    <title>DartExpense</title>
    <link rel="stylesheet" type="text/css                  Attaches CSS
                     href="dartexpense.css" />              stylesheet
  </head>
  <body>
                                                       DartExpense app
                                                       goes in this <div>
    <div id="dartexpense"></div>                    ◁──

    <script type="application/dart" src="DartExpense.dart">  ◁──   App's <script>
    ➥ </script>                                                   tag loads entire
    <script src="http://dart.google...snip.../client/dart.js"> ◁──  application code
    ➥ </script>
  </body>                                           Dart detection script
</html>
```

> **TIP** In JavaScript, you can use detection to determine whether the browser supports native Dart by checking to see if the function `navigator.webkit-StartDart()` exists.

The `application/dart` tag loads the initial .dart script, which in turn loads all other files required by `part` and noncore `import` statements. Once the entire app is loaded and parsed by the Dart VM, the `main()` function is called. This ability to parse the entire application when it's loaded provides a large performance gain over JavaScript applications. This gain doesn't come without cost, however. Unlike JavaScript, you can't modify Dart code dynamically at runtime—a practice known as *monkey-patching*.

You can write a Dart application in a single, monolithic file—or better, as you saw in chapter 5, as a library split into multiple `part` files. Dart treats `part` files as though they were part of the same physical library file, which means the application behaves identically regardless of whether you split it into multiple files. This is a feature to help developers organize their code.

> **TIP** Start building your app in a single file and then move classes and functions into #part files as you begin to find logically grouped functionality.

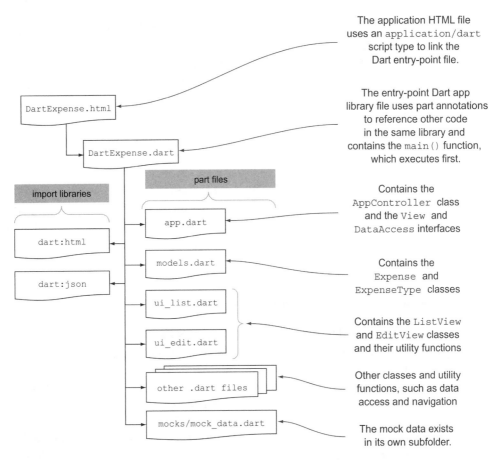

Figure 10.4 The structure of the DartExpense app is split across multiple files referenced with the #part tag.

DartExpense consists of a single library. It imports two core libraries—dart:html and dart:json—and has its own major classes and functions in separate part files, as shown in figure 10.4.

As you build a Dart app, you may find other logical units of code. This might be a reason to structure the app in a different fashion, such as putting the model classes in one library and the data-access functions in a different library, especially if you plan to reuse them in other applications.

10.1.3 Dart app execution flow

All Dart applications start with a main() function, which executes automatically once all the code has been loaded—and DartExpense is no exception. When a Dart app starts running, it uses the code started by main() to build a UI and wire up event handlers, such as button on-click events. Once that code finishes executing, the app is still running, but in a passive state, waiting for the browser to trigger events in the app.

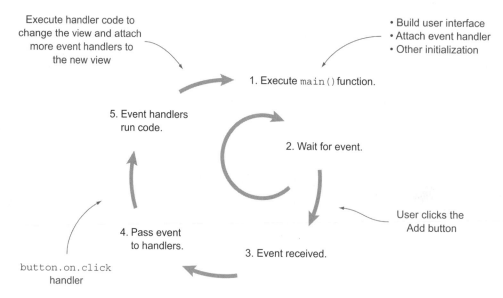

Figure 10.5   The app remains running and waiting for events.

These events could be internal, such as an `HttpRequest` completing, or external, such as a user interacting with the UI or clicking the back button in the browser. The app continues waiting for events until the app is unloaded from the browser by either closing the browser tab or navigating to a different URL. Figure 10.5 shows this flow.

Dart is single-threaded, just like JavaScript. This design feature was built into the language: one of the core requirements of Dart is that tools can convert it to JavaScript. This means events are each processed in turn as the app receives them from the browser.

As you can see, `main()` is particularly important. If it built up a UI without attaching any event handlers, the browser UI would render but never respond to any events. Likewise, if the app started a number of calls to retrieve data but didn't build a UI, although the data would be loaded into the app, the user would never see it.

The DartExpense app, therefore, has the following flow in the `main()` function:

1 Get the `dartexpense <div>` from the HTML in which the app will be placed.
2 Create a `datasource` that the app will use to access data. This is your mock data source at present.
3 Create an instance of `AppController`, passing in the `<div>` and the data source.
4 Call the `AppController`'s `buildUI()` function, which builds the basic UI elements, such as the header and footer, and the container `<div>`s for each view and actions panel. This doesn't wire up any event handlers yet.
5 Call the `AppController`'s `loadFirstView()` function, which takes the window location as a parameter. This is responsible for setting up the initial application view, which to start with is the `ListView`, showing the list of expenses and attaching event handlers to the buttons shown in the view.

The instance of `AppController` is stored in a library-level private variable accessed by a getter called `app()`. This lets you reference the `AppController` instance elsewhere in the application.

Of course, it's better to see this in code, so the following listing shows the DartExpense.dart entry point file with the `main()` function.

Listing 10.2 DartExpense.dart `main()` function

```
library "dartexpense";            ◁── Declares app as library

import "dart:html" ;              │ Imports built-in
import "dart:json";               │ libraries

part "models.dart";               │
// …snip other part files…        │ Adds source
part "app.dart";                  │ files to library

part "mocks/mock_data.dart";      ◁── Adds mock data

AppController _app;                │ Library-scoped private property and
AppController get app => _app;     │ getter return instance of AppController.

void main() {                     ◁── main() is executed first.

  var uiContainer = query("#dartexpense");        │ Gets container <div>
  var dataSource = new MockData();                │ and data; uses them to
  _app = new AppController(uiContainer, dataSource);  │ create AppController

  app.buildUI();                  │ Builds core UI; attaches
  app.loadFirstView();            │ first view to it
}
```

Once the UI is built and the first view is attached, `main()` finishes. The application goes into its wait-event loop phase, during which the user can begin to interact with the application by clicking the Add button to create a new expense or the Edit button to edit existing expenses.

Remember

- Dart's primary use case is complex web applications.
- Single-page web apps bind the view code to the data on the client side rather than on the server.
- Offline-first design provides benefits such as availability and speed to developers and users of the application.
- A Dart app can be made up of many `part` files linked to the main entry-point Dart script.
- The `main()` function is the first function to execute and should call code to build the UI and hook up event handlers.

Now that you know how a Dart app fits together, the next step is to build a UI with the `dart:html` library, which lets you create UI elements with code and HTML.

10.2   Building a UI with dart:html

This section concentrates on building a UI with a combination of HTML and dart classes defined in the `dart:html` library. We'll look at what happens in the Dart-Expense `buildUI()` and `loadFirstView()` methods.

The `dart:html` library provides a set of APIs and classes for working with the browser DOM elements. In this way, it's similar to the core jQuery library for JavaScript, and it provides ways to query the browser DOM for specific elements and Dart lists, sets, and maps for accessing attributes, child elements, and event handlers.

No widget libraries?

At the time of writing, there's no built-in UI library, although a number of open source third-party libraries are appearing on the web. Instead of working with library abstractions such as `LayoutPanel` and `MenuBar` (found in the GWT widget library), you deal with lower-level Dart classes such as `DivElement` and `ButtonElement`. This way of working gives you fine-grained control over the HTML that's built, especially because in many cases you're dealing with the HTML directly. This should provide you with a good understanding of how to use Dart to manipulate the browser DOM, which will still be of use when higher-level widget libraries appear.

Looking forward, Dart will use web component technology, allowing components to be built using Shadow DOM templates. You will be able to insert and manipulate these components like native HTML elements. For more information, search online for "Dart web components."

10.2.1   Understanding the Element interface

The primary class in the `dart:html` library is the `Element` interface. It provides two named constructors—`Element.html()` and `Element.tag()`—which you saw back in chapter 3 and which both construct an HTML element, but in slightly different ways.

`Element.tag(String tag)` creates an empty HTML tag from the name given; for example, if you provide `"div"` as the tag parameter, you get back an element object that creates this HTML: `<div></div>`. You can then use properties and methods on that object to add attributes, child elements, and event handlers.

`Element.html(String html)`, on the other hand, can be used to create a nested hierarchy of HTML tags, with the restriction that any child tags must be wrapped in a single HTML element. For example, using Dart's multiple-line string syntax, which starts and terminates strings with three quotes (for example, `"""text"""`), you can define a block of HTML that lives in a single `<div>` element:

```
var actionDiv = new Element.html("""
  <div id="actions">Select:
    <button id="saveButton" class="primary, selected">Save</button>
    <button id="cancelButton" name="cancel">Cancel</button>
  </div>""");
```

You can use the `Element.tag` constructor only to create a single element, but you can use the `Element.html` constructor to create either a single element or multiple nested elements. Once you've created an element, you can use two key methods to access child elements:

- `query(String selector)`
- `queryAll(String selector)`

These methods let you find a single child element or multiple matching child elements. For example, the following snippet lets you access the `saveButton` and then all the buttons from the previously declared `actionDiv` element:

```
var saveButton = actionDiv.query(".primary")

var cancelButton = actionDiv.query("#cancelButton");

var buttonList = actionDiv.queryAll("button");

var primaryButtons = actionDiv.queryAll(".primary .selected");

var cancelButtons = actionDiv.queryAll("[name='cancel']");
```

First element with "primary" class

First element with id=cancelButton

All button elements

All elements with "primary" and "selected" classes

All elements for which name = cancel

These methods take CSS selectors as their parameters, just like the jQuery `$()` function. CSS selectors provide a mechanism to identify a tag or groups of tags based on their properties, such as their ID (which should be unique to the page) or class (which can be shared by multiple tags).

The `Element` interface provides a host of properties and methods you can use to manipulate elements programmatically. These start from the browser's `document` and `window` objects, which are both top-level properties in the `dart:html` library, and both of which implement the `Element` interface.

Emulating jQuery's $() function

`$` is a valid function name in Dart, so if you like the jQuery `$()` function, you can simulate it in Dart by providing a function in your library that redirects to the `document.query()` function:

```
$(String selectors) => query(selectors);
```

This code has the effect of providing a `$` function in your library that you can use in the same manner as jQuery:

```
$("#actionDiv").innerHTML = "No Actions";
```

All other HTML elements implement the `Element` interface; some commonly used properties and methods are shown in table 10.1.

Specific HTML elements also have their own `Element` interfaces with additional properties and methods; for example, `InputElement` also has a `value` property to

Table 10.1   Key properties and methods of the `Element` interface

Property of method signature	Purpose
`Element.tag(String tagName)`	Constructor to create an element by tag name.
`Element.html(String html)`	Constructor to create an element from a block of HTML.
`String id`	Get/set the element ID.
`String innerHTML`	Read and write the element's inner HTML.
`List<Element> children`	Access the child element's collection.
`List<Element> queryAll(String selectors)`	Select a group of matching child elements. For example, `myDiv.queryAll("button")` returns all the buttons in the `<myDiv>` element.
`Element query(String selectors)`	Select a single child element.
`ElementEvents on`	Access the element's events to attach event handlers.
`AttributeMap attributes`	Access the attributes of the element.
`Collection classes`	Access the collection element classes.

access the value that has been entered. When using the element constructors, if you know you're creating a <div>, <input>, <button>, or some other specific element, you can strongly type the variable with a specific element type that inherits from the `Element` interface. This approach allows the tools to validate your code by providing specific attribute properties on the element:

```
InputElement textbox = new Element.tag("input");          value property exists on
textbox.value = "Some text";                              InputElement interface
```

Currently, approximately 70 subinterfaces inherit the `Element` interface; some of the more common ones are listed in table 10.2. You can find more on the Dart API reference website: http://api.dartlang.org.

Table 10.2   Common subinterfaces that inherit the `Element` interface

`BodyElement`	`ButtonElement`	`CanvasElement`
`DivElement`	`EmbedElement`	`FormElement`
`HeadingElement`	`ImageElement`	`InputElement`
`LabelElement`	`LinkElement`	`OptionElement`
`ParagraphElement`	`ScriptElement`	`SelectElement`
`SpanElement`	`StyleElement`	`TableElement`

Most of the common HTML tags have specific element interfaces defined, but you can still use the base element class `attributes` property to access any attribute that doesn't explicitly appear on an element implementation. Here's an example:

```
textbox.attributes["value"] = "Some text";
```

10.2.2 *Element constructors in action*

To see the element constructors in action, look at the `AppController.buildUI()` method, which is called by the `main()` function and produces a skeleton UI such as that shown in figure 10.6. The skeleton contains only the header and footer and empty `view` and `action` `<div>` elements.

> **NOTE** The dartexpense.css stylesheet attached by the entry-point DartExpense.HTML file provides the styling that produces the UI look and feel. Detaching the content from the specifics of the design is good practice because it allows you to provide different skins for your app, which makes it easier to specify alternative stylesheets for the desktop and mobile browsers, for example. And although specific CSS usage is out of scope for this book, there are many good books and internet resources on CSS design.

When the user starts the DartExpense app, the `buildUI()` method builds the UI skeleton, which contains header and footer sections and the `content` and `action` `<div>` elements that will contain your views. These are all added to the root `<div>` that was passed into the `AppController` constructor. The `buildUI()` method and the HTML it creates are shown in figure 10.7.

Once the skeleton UI is built and you have a handle on the two important `<div>` elements, to which the `AppController` has stored a reference in the private `_actionsContainer` and `_viewContainer` properties, DartExpense's `main()` function calls the method `app.loadFirstView()`. This has the effect of loading a specific view into the relevant `content` and `action` `<div>` elements by removing any other view and adding the new view. Views implement the `View` interface, which contains two `DivElement` properties: `viewElement` and `actionsElement`. When a new view such as `ListView` is created, it's responsible for building the relevant HTML

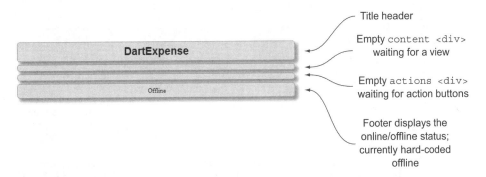

Figure 10.6 The skeleton DartExpense UI, waiting for views and actions to be added

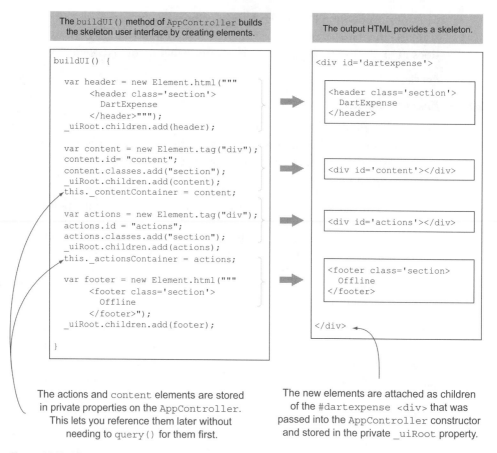

Figure 10.7   **The buildUI() function uses Dart Element constructors to build the skeleton UI.**

structures into these elements (which you'll soon see). The AppController.update-
View() function first clears any existing view from the _viewContainer and
_actionsContainer properties; then the elements from the new view are attached.
The next listing shows relevant code from AppController to populate the content
and actions <div>s in the UI from a view.

Listing 10.3   Populating the content and actions <div>s with a view

```
class AppController {
  ...snip other methods and properties...

  DivElement _viewContainer;
  DivElement _actionsContainer;

  List<Expenses> get expense => ...snip...

  loadFirstView() {
    var view = new ListView(this.expenses);
    updateView(view);
  }
```

Containers for view
and its actions

Property to retrieve list of
expenses from underlying
source

Creates new ListView,
passing in list of expenses

```
updateView(View view) {
  _viewContainer.children.clear();
  _viewContainer.children.add(view.viewElement);
  _actionsContainer.children.clear();
  _actionsContainer.children.add(view.actionsElement);
}
}
```

Inserts ListView's viewElement and actions <div>s into skeleton layout

The elements.clear() function that's used to remove the child elements from the _viewContainer and _actionsContainer properties is part of the standard Dart List interface and has the effect of removing those items from the browser DOM. When you use the elements.add() method, you're adding new elements into the browser DOM, and at this point, your application begins waiting for events.

NOTE The types used in the DartExpense app, such as the View interface and the ListView and EditView classes, are specific to DartExpense, not part of a built-in Dart model-view framework. At the time of writing, such a framework doesn't come with Dart, but it's the intention of the Dart team for these features to ultimately be available.

10.2.3 *Building interaction with views and elements*

The DartExpense application's ListView uses an HTML table to display the list of expenses. When users access DartExpense, the first view they see is the list of expenses, as shown in figure 10.8.

There are two views in the application. A class called ViewType, which looks like the following snippet, uses a private constant constructor to create two types of view, ViewType.LIST and ViewType.EDIT:

```
class ViewType {
  final String name;

  const ViewType._withName(this.name);

  static final ViewType LIST = const ViewType._withName("list");
  static final ViewType EDIT = const ViewType._withName("edit");
}
```

Private constructor

Initializes LIST and EDIT constants

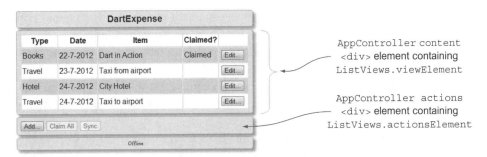

Figure 10.8 The ListView content and actions rendered with the mock data

---

No enums in Dart

Unlike C# and Java, Dart doesn't have enums built into the language. Enums let you define a fixed number of constant values for a special type of class. Defining a class with a private constant constructor and a fixed list of static final values is a neat alternative.

SWITCHING BETWEEN VIEWS

These `ViewType` instances are used by a top-level library function called `navigate()`, which provides a central point of navigation for the app. The `navigate()` function, which is called when the user clicks the Edit button, allows transitioning between UI elements and has a simple implementation. It creates a new view based upon the `ViewType` and passes it into the `AppController`'s `updateView()` function, which, as you saw earlier, removes the existing view and populates `contentContainer` and `actionsContainer` with the new view:

```
void navigate(ViewType view, int id) {
  if (view == ViewType.LIST) {
    app.updateView(new ListView(app.expenses));      ◁──┐  Passes list of
  }                                                        expenses to a
  else if (view == ViewType.EDIT) {                        new ListView
    app.updateView(new EditView(app.getExpenseById(id)));  ◁──┐  Passes new or
  }                                                              existing expense
}                                                                to a new EditView
```

This is a trivial implementation for the purpose of example. It would be more efficient to cache these views in the `AppController` so that you don't need to re-create them every time.

BUILDING THE LISTVIEW

The `AppController.loadFirstView()` method, which is called as part of `main()`, calls the `ListView(List<Expense> expenses)` constructor, passing in the list of expenses to render. The `ListView` then passes the list of expenses to the `refreshUI()` function, which builds up the HTML table from `Element` instances, storing the result in the view's `viewElement` property, as shown in listing 10.4. This is a long code listing because there's a lot going on, but essentially it creates a table element and adds a table header and rows to that table. Each row in the table is built by calling the private `_getRowElement(Expense ex)` function in a loop over the list of elements, passing in the current element. A `TableRowElement` is built for each row and added into the `table.children` list. The `_getRowElement(ex)` function is also the first place an event handler is added: an `on.click` event handler for the Edit button appears next to each row.

We'll look at event handlers in more detail in the next major section, but for now you need to know that the event handler calls a top-level library `navigate(ViewType, int id)` function. The interesting part is that the anonymous event-handler function (shown in italic in listing 10.4) that calls `navigate()` forms a closure around the specific expense object passed to _getRowElement(ex). This is because although the method exits, the event handler retains a reference to the ex.id value (see chapter 4 for more discussion on closures). The ex.id value is an autogenerated number on the Expense class that's required by the navigate() function along with the name of the view to which you currently want to navigate.

Listing 10.4 `ListView` **class, which builds the HTML table of expenses**

```
class ListView implements View {
  DivElement viewElement;                          ←  Properties to implement
  DivElement actionsElement;                           View interface

  ListView(List<Expense> expenses) {               ←  Constructor updates
    refreshUI(expenses);                               content and actions
    _buildActions();
  }

  refreshUI(List<Expense> expenses) {                    Creates new, empty
    viewElement = new Element.tag("table");        ←    table element

    var head = new Element.html("""                ←  Creates new <thead>
          <thead>                                       table header
            <td class="type">Type</td>
            <td class="date">Date</td>
            <td class="detail">Item</td>
            <td class="amount">Amount</td>
            <td class="claimed">Claimed?</td>
            <td class="edit"> </td>
          </thead>""");                                  Adds head
                                                         to table
    viewElement.children.add(head);                ←

    for (Expense ex in expenses) {
      var rowElement = _getRowElement(ex);           Loops for each expense, adding
      viewElement.children.add(rowElement);          new TableRowElement
    }
  }

  TableRowElement _getRowElement(Expense ex) {
                                                       Creates
    TableRowElement row = new Element.tag("tr");   ←  TableRowElement

    row.children.add(new Element.html('<td>${ex.type.name}</td>'));
    ... snip other columns ...
    row.children.add(new Element.html('<td>${ex.detail}</td>'));

    var editCol = new Element.html("""                 Adds columns
          <td>                                         containing
              <button>Edit...</button>     Adds Edit   data to row
          </td>""");                       button
    row.children.add(editCol);             column

    editCol.query("button").on.click.add((event) {     Click event handler forms a
      navigate(ViewType.EDIT, ex.id);                  closure over the ex.id value
    });

    return row;
```

```
  }
  _buildActions() {
    ...snip...
  }
}
```

The code in the `ListView.refreshUI()` function iterates through each row and builds up the expense properties into an HTML table. In a real-world application for which you might use this functionality in multiple places, it would be better to write a generic function to return a table that dynamically builds rows and columns based on the data passed into it, rather than being tightly bound to the `Expense` class.

10.2.4 *Building a simple generic grid*

A generic list should be able to create a table dynamically based on the list of objects passed in and some configuration that determines which columns are shown. For example, for your `Expense` objects, you want to display the following values on each row:

```
expense.type.name, expense.date, expense.detail, expense.amount
```

Unlike with JavaScript, you can't dynamically access these properties as attributes of the object. In JavaScript, because objects are also maps of key/value pairs, you could pass in a list of column names and a list of objects and, for each object, access the property. A trivial implementation is shown in the following JavaScript snippet:

```javascript
// JavaScript
function getDynamicTable(objects, columnList) {        // JavaScript function
  var table = "<table>";                               // to dynamically
                                                        // build a <table>
  for(item in objects) {                               // Outer loop; each
    table += "<tr>";                                   // object is a row.

    for (propertyName in columnList)  {                // Inner loop;
      var cellText = item[propertyName];               // each column
      table += "<td>" + cellText + "</td>";            // is a property.
    }                                                  // Extracts value of each
    table += "</tr>";                                  // property dynamically
  }

  table += "</table>";
  return table;
}
```

But Dart doesn't allow this type of property access. You could create a similar function in Dart that accepted a `List<Map>` instead of a `List<Object>` (or `List<Expense>`), but doing so would require the calling function to iterate through each `Expense` object in the list, converting each expense to a map and passing in that list of maps. A better implementation would be to provide a way for the `getDynamicTable()` function to extract the value of each property only when it's required. Using this approach would be especially important for performance if you implemented paging in the list—for example, if the table loop processed only 10 items at a time.

Fortunately, by using first-class functions stored in a list as part of the column config, you can let the calling code define how each value is retrieved in an anonymous function and pass that list of anonymous functions to the getDynamicTable() function. Instead of passing in a column list, pass in a map, keyed on the column (or property) name and setting the value to a function that extracts the relevant property as the value. This function type, called GetValueFunc(), has the following definition; it's expected to take an item as its parameter and return a string from that item:

```
typedef String GetValueFunc(dynamic item);
```

Now that you have a function type, you can rewrite refreshUI(List<Expense>) as follows to define a column configuration that's passed into the getDynamicTable() function:

```
refreshUi(List<Expense> expenses) {
  var columnConfig = new Map<String, GetValueFunc>();
  columnConfig["detail"] = (expense) => expense.detail;
  columnConfig["type"] = (expense) => expense.type.name;
  columnConfig["date"] = (expense) => expense.date.toString();
  columnConfig["amount"] = (expense) => expense.amount.toString();

  viewElement = getDynamicTable(expenses, columnConfig);
}
```

- Declares columnConfig as map of String and Function
- For "detail" column, returns expense.detail
- Passes list of expenses and columnConfig

By storing a function in a map, keyed on the column name, the getDynamicTable() function can later extract the property for each item by using the function associated with that property stored in the map:

```
var getValueFunc = columnConfig["detail"];
var detailText = getValueFunc(expense);
```

- Extracts detail function from map
- Uses detail function to extract text of detail property

You now have a way to dynamically extract values from an object based on arbitrary text such as "detail". The full getDynamicTable() function is shown in the following listing.

Listing 10.5 `getDynamicTable()` to dynamically build an HTML table

```
typedef String GetValueFunc(dynamic item);

TableElement getDynamicTable(List items,
                Map<String, GetValueFunc> columnConfig) {

  var table = new Element.tag("table");

  var header = new Element.tag("thead");
  for (String colName in columnConfig.keys) {
    header.children.add(new Element.html("<td>$colName</td>"));
  }
  table.children.add(header);
```

- getValueFunc() type definition
- Creates empty table element
- Iterates through each columnConfig key to create header row

```
for (var item in items) {
  var row = new Element.tag("tr");
  table.children.add(row);

  for (String colName in columnConfig.keys) {

    var getValueFunc = columnConfig[colName];

    var textValue = getValueFunc(item);

    row.children.add(new Element.html("<td>$textValue</td>"));
  }

}

return table;
```
}

Outer loop: for each item, create a row

Inner loop: for each column ...

... uses getValueFunc() to get value from current item

... accesses getValueFunc() for this column and ...

Adds new column element to row

This is an effective solution to providing a generic way to access properties. Instead of accessing the item property directly, you can pass the item into the getValueFunc() implementation specific to the current column, which the caller defined. In this way, you can dynamically access property values without knowing the property names in advance. The table created by using the getDynamicTable() function rather than your original ListView code is shown in figure 10.9.

getDynamicTable() is fairly simplistic in its current design, for the sake of example, but with a couple more development iterations, you could add extra features. Examples that shall be left as an exercise for you include better header row descriptions (instead of using the columnConfig key), passing in a list of actions that should be performed for each row (such as edit and delete), and CSS class information so rows and columns can be attached to CSS styles.

Let's continue with the original ListView code, because it also provides an Edit button that you'll use in the next section when you start to navigate around the application UI.

Earlier in this section, you saw the Edit button get an event handler attached to it. In the next section, we'll look in more detail at event handlers as you add a second view, Edit, to the DartExpense app.

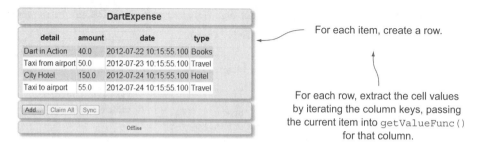

For each item, create a row.

For each row, extract the cell values by iterating the column keys, passing the current item into getValueFunc() for that column.

Figure 10.9   The table created by the new generic table-generation function

> **Remember**
>
> - The `Element` interface is a key class in the `dart:html` library, implemented by the top-level document and window `dart:html` properties and all other HTML elements.
> - Many HTML elements also have their own subinterface that inherits from the `Element` interface, such as `ButtonElement` and `InputElement`.
> - `Element` defines two constructors: `Element.tag()` for creating a single, empty element that you can attach children to in code, and `Element.html()` for creating a single HTML element that can contain many predefined child elements.
> - Dart SDK doesn't currently provide a widget library, so you need to build your own elements such as grids and lists, either specifically for your use case or in a more general fashion so they can be reused.

10.3 Handling browser events with dart:html

In the previous section, you saw how to build a view and attach it to the browser. That's only half of the story before you get to a working web app, though. The code executed from the `main()` function needs to build a UI and attach event handlers to that interface. This section deals with the event handlers.

Event handlers are functions that you attach to HTML elements, which react when a specific event occurs. The most common example is clicking a button on a web page, such as when the user clicks the Add button from the DartExpense app's list view. Browser events all live in a property of the `Element` interface called on, which is an implementation of the `ElementEvents` interface. It provides a list of events by name (useful for autocomplete in the Dart Editor) and overrides the [] operator so you can attach event handlers to unlisted events (maybe to support some experimental browser technology) or events that you want to declare dynamically. Each event is an implementation of `EventListenerList`, which lets you attach multiple events handlers to an event. Listing 10.6 shows the two ways you can attach an event handler to the Add button, which is created in the DartExpense `ListView` class's `_buildActions()` method. The private `_buildActions()` method is used to populate the `actionsElement` <div> containing the action buttons associated with the view. The event-handler functions are highlighted in bold.

Listing 10.6   Attaching an event handler to the Add button

```
class ListView {
  DivElement viewElement;
  DivElement actionsElement;                    ListView constructor
                                                from previous section
  ListView(List<Expense> expenses) {
    refreshUI(expenses);
    _buildActions();
  }

  _buildActions() {
    actionsElement = new Element.tag("div");

    ButtonElement button = new Element.tag("button");     Creates new, empty
                                                          button element
```

```
    button.text = "Add...";
    actionsElement.children.add(button);

    button.on.click.add( (event) {
      navigate(ViewType.EDIT, null);
    });

    button.on["mouseOver"].add( (event) {
      print("button mouseOver")
    });
  }

  ...snip other methods...
}
```

Adds it to
actionsElement <div>

Adds event handler
by property name

Adds event handler
with string "click"

The function that's added to the EventListenerList for the specified event, such as click or mouseOver, is executed when the browser triggers the event on that element. You can add many events to a specific event on a single element; likewise, a single element can have listeners for many different types of event. It's also possible to intercept events that are intended for child elements, as you'll see in the next section.

Approximately 50 named event properties are available on the Element's ElementEvents on property. Table 10.3 shows some of the common events.

Table 10.3   Some of the named event properties available on the ElementEvents on property

Events	Purpose
click, doubleClick	Fired when user clicks the mouse on an element
focus, blur	Fired when an element receives or loses focus
keypress, keyDown, keyUp	Fired when a key is pressed on a focused element
mouseOver, mouseMove, mouseUp	Fired when the mouse pointer is moved over an element
mouseDown, mouseUp	Fired when the mouse button is pressed or released
touchStart, touchMove, touchEnd	Fired when a touch-sensitive device detects a touch

These are just a few of the events the browser can fire. Many more are listed on the dartlang API website under the ElementEvents interface documentation at http://api.dartlang.org.

10.3.1 *Managing browser event flow*

When a user clicks the Add button in the DartExpense app, the web browser creates an event that propagates from the top-level document element down through each child element until it reaches the innermost child. At that point, the event begins to rise back up the element hierarchy (also known as *bubbling*), calling any event handlers on each element that's listening for that event. Thus, under normal circumstances, parent elements can listen and respond to events targeted at their child elements, but only after the child has responded to the event. In DartExpense, the Add button is the innermost

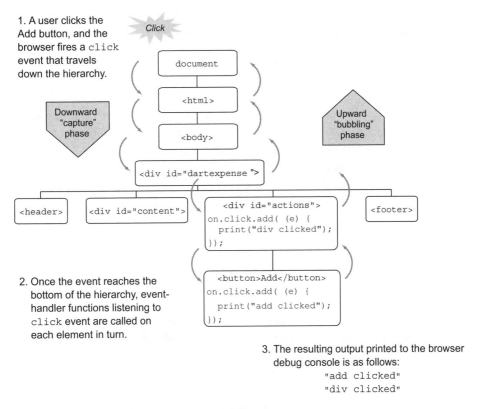

1. A user clicks the Add button, and the browser fires a `click` event that travels down the hierarchy.

2. Once the event reaches the bottom of the hierarchy, event-handler functions listening to `click` event are called on each element in turn.

3. The resulting output printed to the browser debug console is as follows:
```
"add clicked"
"div clicked"
```

Figure 10.10   The default browser event flow finds the innermost child element of the hierarchy and begins calling event-handler functions, going back up the hierarchy.

child in the hierarchy shown in figure 10.10. The `actions <div>` and the Add button both have `click` event handlers registered, but the Add button event handlers execute first, followed by the `actions <div>` event handlers.

This is the default flow; the downward event flow is called the *capture phase*, and the upward flow is the *bubbling phase*. There are exceptions to every rule: some specific event types, such as `focus`, don't bubble. You can find a comprehensive list on the `DOM_events` Wikipedia page, but there are also a number of things you can do in your own code to modify this default flow.

MODIFYING THE BUBBLING PHASE

The first thing you can do to stop the upward flow is call the `stopPropagation()` method on the event parameter, which is passed into the event-handler function:

```
button.on.click.add( (event) {
  print("add clicked");
  event.stopPropagation();
});
```

Prevents event from rising up hierarchy

This code will stop the click event from calling the on.click handler functions of any other elements, but it doesn't stop the event from being raised on other handler functions of the same element. You can add a second handler to the button:

```
button.on.click.add( (event) => print("second event handler"));
```

Although the event-handler function on the actions <div> won't be called, both event handlers on the button *will* be called. Fortunately, there's a way to stop this, too: calling the event's stopImmediatePropagation() method, which stops the event from calling any further event handlers on any element.

MODIFYING THE CAPTURE PHASE

You might at some point want the parent elements to handle an event before the child event. Fortunately, there's an optional parameter on the event-handler method signature:

```
add(eventHandler, [bool useCapture=false])
```

The useCapture parameter, when passed true, causes the event handler to be fired on the downward capture phase, before any child elements have had a chance to respond. Figure 10.11 shows how you can modify the actions <div> click event handler to handle the click event on the downward flow.

Event handlers that are called in the downward capture flow can also use the event parameter's stopPropagation() and stopImmediatePropagation() methods to prevent the event from going any further.

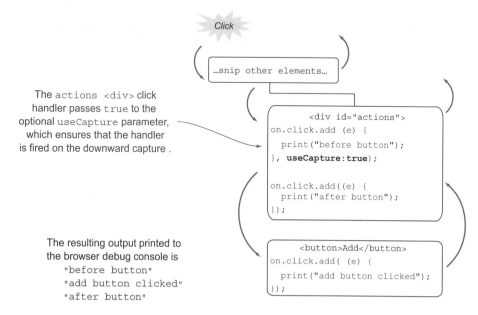

Figure 10.11 Event handlers can intercept the event on the downward capture flow instead of waiting for the default upward flow to be called.

In the last section of this chapter, we'll examine the `Event` interface. You've already seen the `stopPropagation()` and `stopImmediatePropagation()` methods that are available on the base `Event` interface, and as with the base `Element` interface, there are a number of specialized subtypes.

10.3.2 Common event types

When the browser calls an event-handler function, it passes data about that event into that function via the `event` parameter. This is a generic event interface that contains a number of properties and methods that are common to all events, such as `stopPropagation()`, `timestamp`, and `type`. Some events contain more information about the specific event, and approximately 25 event types inherit from the base `Event` interface. Many of these support newer technologies, such as `SpeechRecognitionEvent` and `DeviceOrientationEvent`; but other event types support more mundane uses, such as `MouseEvent`, which provides mouse coordinates of the event, and `KeyboardEvent`, which provides the key code of the key that was pressed on the keyboard. Table 10.4 lists some of these common event properties.

Table 10.4 Common `MouseEvent` properties

Property	Purpose
`int button`	The button number that was pressed. Zero is the left button.
`int clientX, int clientY`	The X and Y coordinates of the event in the browser client.
`int screenX, int screenY`	The X and Y coordinates of the event in the whole screen.
`bool altKey, bool ctrlKey, bool metaKey, bool shiftKey`	True if one of these keys was also pressed at the time of the event.

You can use these specific event types by accessing the property on the event parameter passed into the event handler. If you also specify the event type, you get the benefit of type-checking support from the tools. The next listing shows how you can add the screen coordinates to your button `click` event.

Listing 10.7 Using the specific `MouseEvent` type to extract more event details

```
button.on.click.add( (MouseEvent event) {        ← Uses event
  var x = event.clientX;                            type on
  var y = event.clientY;                            handler
  print("add button clicked, co-ordinates: $x, $y");  parameter
});                                                  list
```
Extracts coordinates from event

The browser event flow isn't something specific to Dart; instead, it's built into the browser, and unfortunately, there are differences in browser-specific implementations. Dart is designed to work primarily with modern web browsers, which means when it's converted to JavaScript, IE6 is unlikely to work well with much of the code shown here.

HINT   If this lack of backward compatibility troubles you, please visit the Microsoft-run website www.ie6countdown.com, which states that "it's time to say goodbye" to IE6.

> **Remember**
> - Event-handler functions can be added to the `Element.on` property either by name, such as `on.click.add(...)`, or by value, such as `on["click"].add(...)`.
> - Elements can call multiple event-handler functions that have been added to a specific event.
> - Elements can have handlers listening to multiple events.
> - When an event is raised, the browser sends the event from the `document` element downward through the hierarchy of elements. This is the capture phase; event handlers aren't fired by default.
> - After the capture phase, the bubble phase begins, as event-handler functions are called in turn going back up the hierarchy.
> - This default capture and bubble event flow can be modified in Dart code.

This was a long section, but a good understanding of browser events can help you build interesting and reactive UIs. We'll look at some of the more interesting events relating to browser storage and touch in later chapters, but you should now have a good handle on how events flow around the web browser. For more information about the general principles of browser events, the Mozilla Developer Network (https://developer.mozilla.org/en-US/docs/DOM/DOM_event_reference) and w3.org (www.w3.org/TR/DOM-Level-3-Events/#event-flow) websites are both useful references.

10.4   Summary

This was a pretty lengthy chapter, in which we looked at the design of a single-page web app that works offline in order to aid development and provide an enhanced user experience. Then you saw how the `main()` function is key to starting a Dart app; it should be responsible for building the UI and attaching event handlers.

We discussed building a UI with the `dart:HTML` library, which is like Dart's version of the core jQuery library for browser manipulation. At the time of writing, there's no widget library in the Dart SDK, so you need to deal with HTML elements via Dart's various `Element` classes. As part of building your UI, you saw how it's possible to build from scratch a generic grid that accepts a list of arbitrary objects and lays them out in an HTML table.

Finally, we looked at the browser event model, and you saw how Dart uses event handlers to react to browser events and how to modify the default browser event flow of downward capture and upward bubble.

In the next chapter, you'll learn how to store real data in the browser using JSON and client-side storage, and you'll explore the navigation between views, including reacting to the browser forward and back button events by manipulating the browser history.

Navigating offline data

This chapter covers

- Handling browser navigation in a single-page app
- Storing cookies to remember user settings
- Serializing objects to JSON
- Storing offline data in the browser

Users are accustomed to using built-in browser navigation tools, such as the browser's forward and back buttons and bookmarks, to navigate web apps in the same way they have been doing for years with normal websites. Users also expect apps to have fast response times, which apps achieve by persisting data offline.

Modern browser technology makes it possible to meet your users' expectations. In this chapter you'll add these features to the DartExpense example application you started in the previous chapter.

In a single-page web app, when the user switches between two views, such as from list view to edit view, they expect to be able to use the browser's back button to navigate back to the prior view. Your app, therefore, needs be able to notify the web browser that a view change has occurred. We'll look at how you can manipulate the browser's history to make it possible to use back-button navigation and to bookmark specific views.

After exploring a mechanism for navigating using the standard browser navigation tools, we'll examine how you can store user settings in cookies. This will allow the app to return to the same view the user was visiting when they closed the browser.

In the last chapter, the DartExpense app was restricted to using mock offline data that was hardcoded in the app. In this chapter, you'll replace the mock data with an in-browser persistence mechanism by using HTML5 Web Storage APIs.

As a reminder, the DartExpense app currently has a list view and an edit view. A function called navigate() is called when the user clicks a button, as shown in figure 11.1.

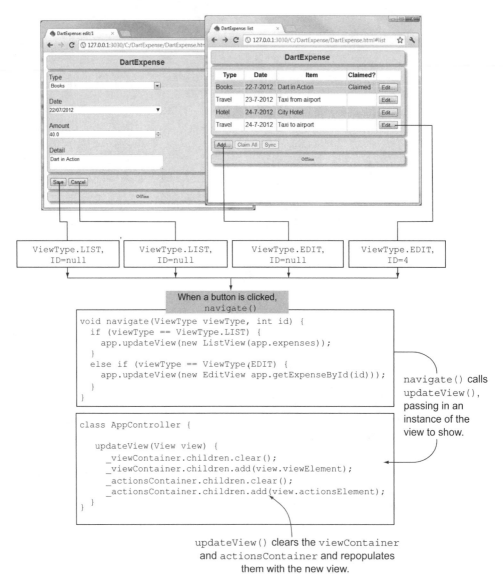

Figure 11.1   Figure 11.1 When the user clicks a button, the existing view is replaced with a new view passed from the navigate() function.

If a `null` ID is passed to the `getExpenseById()` function, it returns a new expense object rather than an existing expense object. This way, the app reuses the edit view between the *add* and *edit* functionality.

The `updateView()` function that you saw in the previous chapter clears the `AppController`'s `_viewContainer` and `_actionContainer` `<div>` elements and repopulates them with the element object from the view.

The problem with this approach is that it's transparent to the web browser. When the user navigates to the page DartExpense.html, the app starts running; but no matter how many times the user changes views by clicking buttons on the page, the browser remains at DartExpense.html without any record of the navigation between views. This means the browser's forward and back buttons don't remember the user's navigation history as the user moves around the app. It's time to change that.

11.1 *Integrating navigation with the browser*

When the user clicks the Edit button on DartExpense's list view, all the browser knows is that it's executing some arbitrary code. You need to tell the browser that the page location has been updated, so the browser can add the new page location to its history. Fortunately, this is easy to achieve by using a new HTML5 API, the browser's `pushState()` function, which you can use to add information to the browser's navigation history.

The DartExpense application, when run from the Dart Editor in Dartium, loads with the URL shown in figure 11.2.

You need to let the browser know that this URL has changed, but without navigating anywhere.

Figure 11.2 **A typical URL, made up of the protocol, domain and port, and location**

11.1.1 *Using pushState() to add items to the browser history*

When the user navigates to a different web page and the URL changes, the web browser pushes the new URL onto its history list. With the `pushState()` function, you can simulate this without navigating anywhere, such as when the user clicks the Edit button. The `pushState()` function takes three parameters: some state data, which represents the state of your application; a title (currently unused by most browsers); and a new location to appear on the URL. You can't change the protocol or domain and port, but the location part of the URL will change to whatever value you pass in. For example, the call to `pushState()` in figure 11.3 changes the browser's URL location to `"/edit/1"`.

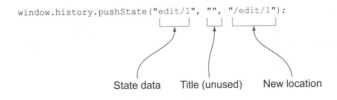

Figure 11.3 **Calling the browser's `pushState()` function**

This call stores the data passed in the first parameter `"edit/1"` as state information in the browser's history. For the DartExpense app, this represents `viewName/idValue`, but it can be any text data to represent the current state of the app. DartExpense understands that `"edit/1"` means you're in the edit view, editing an `Expense` with ID 1. When the user clicks the Save or Cancel button, you call `pushState()` again, storing the state data `"list"` without any ID.

The second parameter, the title, is currently unused by most browsers. If you want to modify the browser title, you need to set the `document.title` property, for example:

```
document.title = "DartExpense: Editing expense with ID:1";
```

The final parameter, which represents the new location, is particularly interesting. The new location you specify in `pushState()` updates the location part of the URL shown in the browser to produce a fake URL, such as changing the location from

```
http://127.0.0.1:3030/DartExpense/DartExpense.html
```

to

```
http://127.0.0.1:3030/edit/1
```

without navigating anywhere. Only the location part of the URL changes; you can't modify the domain name. You can't navigate with this fake URL as it currently is, though. If you tried to navigate to http://127.0.0.1:3030/edit/1, you'd likely get a "404 page not found" error. But fortunately, the location parameter respects the standard browser URL location conventions. Table 11.1 shows location strings and the URL locations they generate.

Table 11.1 Common ways to modify the browser's URL location with `pushState()`

Location	Resulting URL	Type
`/edit/1`	http://127.0.0.1:3030/edit/1	Absolute path
`edit/1`	http://127.0.0.1:3030/DartExpense/DartExpense.html/edit/1	Relative path
`?edit/1`	http://127.0.0.1:3030/DartExpense/DartExpense.html?edit/1	Query string
`#edit/1`	http://127.0.0.1:3030/DartExpense/DartExpense.html#edit/1	Location hash

The purpose of the browser URL information at this stage is primarily to provide feedback to the user; the application doesn't need this information to perform any navigation. In the next section, you'll use the data stored in the actual URL to allow the user to bookmark the application at specific views, so DartExpense will use the location hash method to represent the current location in the application.

In the DartExpense app, rather than tightly coupling the `pushState()` call to each button click, the best place to add the call is in the existing `navigate()` function, which is the central point of navigation around the app. The following listing shows the updated `navigate()` function, which converts the view type and any ID value into state data and a URL location hash.

Listing 11.1 Updated `navigate()` function that integrates with browser history

```
void navigate(ViewType viewType, int id) {

  String state = id == null ?                          Gets view name
                      "${viewType.name}" :             and value not null
                      "${viewType.name}/${id.toString()}";

  window.history.pushState(state, "", "#$state");  ←── pushState() to store
                                                       state and location hash
  document.title = "DartExpense: $state";

  if (viewType == ViewType.LIST) {
    app.updateView(new ListView(app.expenses));       Existing code
  } else if (viewType == ViewType.EDIT) {
    app.updateView(new EditView(app.getExpenseById(id)));
  }
}
```

Updates browser title →

If you call this function with the parameters `navigate(ViewType.EDIT, 1);` it performs as follows:

1 Populates the state variable with "edit/1".
2 Calls `pushState("edit/1","","#edit/1");` resulting in a URL of http://127.0.0.1:3030/DartExpense/DartExpense.html#edit/1.
3 Sets the document title to "DartExpense: edit/1".
4 Calls the existing navigation code to show the edit with Expense ID=1.

This results in a new item appearing as the URL. The user interface shows the Edit screen, and the previous URL is pushed onto the browser history, as shown in figure 11.4.

Being able to push state information onto the browser history is only half the story. The next step is for the browser to alert DartExpense when the user clicks the browser's back or forward button.

11.1.2 Listening for popState events

Although DartExpense uses `pushState()` to tell the browser that your app is changing its navigation, you need a mechanism for the browser to tell DartExpense that the user has clicked the browser's built-in navigation buttons. When the user clicks the back or forward button or navigates to a specific page in the navigation history, the browser

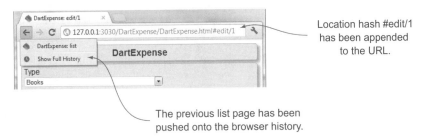

Location hash #edit/1 has been appended to the URL.

The previous list page has been pushed onto the browser history.

Figure 11.4 Calling `pushState()` when navigating now pushes the previous location to the browser's history.

triggers the popState event. DartExpense needs an event-handler function to be called when the popState event is triggered, so it can perform the correct navigation.

When the user clicks the back button, the browser passes you the state data that you previously passed by the pushState() call. You can use that information to update your app to get back to the correct state. For example, if the state data passed to the popState handler contains "edit/1", you need to convert that to ViewType.EDIT and id=1, which you can pass to your navigate() function. The navigate() function is then responsible for updating the user interface so you visit the edit screen for the Expense with ID 1. When you call the navigate() function from a popState call, you must ensure that you don't add the state data back onto the browser history (using pushState()), because the browser has just removed it! To achieve this, you'll add an optional isFromPopState parameter to the navigate() function so you can perform a check before the call to pushState():

```
navigate(ViewType viewType, int id, [bool isFromPopState=false])
```

Figure 11.5 shows the sequence of pushState() and popState calls you expect to encounter.

To ensure that DartExpense responds to the browser-triggering popState events, you need to add the onPopState() function to the browser's popState event as part of

1. The user clicks the Edit button to edit Expense 1.

```
navigate(ViewType.EDIT,1) {
  pushState("edit/1","",#edit/1")
  app.updateView(...);
}
```

Previous view state data: "list"
Current view state data: "edit/1"

2. The user clicks the Save button that navigates to the list view.

```
navigate(ViewType.LIST,null) {
  pushState("list","",#list")
  app.updateView(...);
}
```

Previous view state data: "list"
Previous view state data: "edit/1"
Current view state data: "list"

3. The user clicks the browser's back button to return to the previous view, edit/1.

```
onPopState(PopStateEvent event) {
  var currentState = event.state;
  // ...snip convert state to
  // viewType and id
  navigate(viewType, id);
}
```

The PopStateEvent object's event.state property contains the current state data, edit/1.

Previous view state data: "list"
Current view state data: "edit/1"

```
navigate(ViewType.EDIT, 1) {
  // do not pushState this time
  app.updateView(...);
}
```

Figure 11.5 Calling pushState() adds the state to the browser history. The browser triggers popState events when the user clicks the back and forward buttons.

the application startup. In the previous chapter, we discussed how the main() function should call any relevant code to build a user interface and hook up event handlers; the following listing shows the onPopState() function, which properly extracts the ViewType and ID from the state information, and an updated main() function that adds the onPopState() event handler.

> **Listing 11.2   Updated `main()` function to listen for `popState` events**

```
void main() {
  var uiContainer = query("#dartexpense");
  var dataSource = new MockData();

  _app = new AppController(uiContainer, dataSource);
  app.buildUI();                                         Adds onPopState()
  app.loadFirstView();                                   to browser event
                                                         listener list
  window.on.popState.add(onPopState);
}

void onPopState(PopStateEvent event) {    ⟵── Defines onPopState()       event.state
  if (event.state != null) {                                              contains "edit/I"
    List<String> stateData = event.state.split("/");                      or "list"

    var viewName = stateData[0];                          Creates viewType
    var viewType = new ViewType(viewName);                from name part

    var id = stateData.length == 2 ? int.parse (stateData[1]) : null;    ⟵

    navigate(viewType, id, isFromPopState:true);    ⟵┐        ID is an int
  }                                                           or null.
}                              Calls navigate(), passing true
}                              to isFromPopState parameter
```

Now your user can navigate around the app using the Add, Edit, and Save buttons supplied by your user interface or the browser's back, forward, and history navigation functions.

> **Remember**
> - The `window.history.pushState(data,title,url)` function adds items to the browser history.
> - The event handler `window.on.popState.add( ... );` is called when the user clicks the browser's back and forward buttons.

There's another thing you can do to make the user experience even better. As well as storing the user's current view in the browser history with pushState(), you can store their current view state information in a browser cookie so that when they return to your app, it will load the view they were last using.

11.2 *Using browser cookies to enhance user experience*

Browser cookies are small text files of data associated with a website that a web browser stores on the user's computer. Applications such as DartExpense can store around 4,096 KB of data per cookie and can store between 80 and 140 cookies per site; but the size and number restrictions vary among browsers, so it's generally better to store smaller amounts of data. The data in the cookie is stored in plain text and consists of a key/value pair and an expiry date or age after which the cookie is no longer valid. Cookies exist for a specific domain, so the cookies your app creates aren't readily accessible by other websites.

> **WARNING**   Cookies are stored in plain text, and you must not use them to store any sensitive data such as passwords. Users can also disable cookies, so you should only use cookies to enhance the user experience, rather than relying on them being available.

When a user navigates to the DartExpense app, they use the entry-point HTML file DartExpense.html. Instead of always loading the list view first, you can enhance the user's experience to return them to the last view they used when they last visited the app.

> **NOTE**   Cookies are browser-specific. For example, the cookies stored by DartExpense in Chrome aren't available to DartExpense when run on the same machine in Firefox.

As with `pushState()` and `popState`, there are two parts to using cookies. The first is to store the state information in the cookie when you navigate, and the second is to retrieve the information from the cookie (if it exists) when you start the app.

11.2.1   *Storing data in a cookie*

Just like the `pushState()` call, the ideal place to store the current view in a cookie is in the `navigate()` function. You set a cookie by storing a key/value pair in the `document.cookie` property, as in

```
document.cookie = "stateData=edit/1";
```

The `cookie` property is somewhat unlike other properties. Instead of setting the value on a property, it adds or edits an underlying set of data. If the `stateData` cookie already exists, the `cookie` property overwrites it. If it doesn't already exist, the `cookie` property creates a new one. If you set a different cookie key, such as the last `ExpenseType` used, the browser adds another cookie. For example, writing to `document.cookie` twice like this

```
document.cookie = "stateData=edit/1";
document.cookie = "expenseType=books";
```

will result in two cookies being stored. Calling `print(document.cookie)` will return the string `"stateData=edit/1; expenseType=books"`.

Setting cookies this way won't achieve the desired effect, because as they're currently defined, they'll only last for the current session. This is fine if the user opens the app in a second browser tab, but the cookies will be lost when the user closes their browser: without an expiry date or `max-age`, they're considered to be session cookies.

To ensure that they're persistent cookies that last across browser sessions, you need to specify either the `expires` property or `max-age` property when setting the cookie.

Expiry dates need to be in a specific format. In JavaScript, this is the JavaScript `toGMTString()` format, `"Wdy, DD Mon YYYY HH:MM:SS GMT"`, which looks like this:

```
document.cookie="stateData=edit/1;expires=Fri, 3 Aug 2012 20:47:11 GMT";
```

Unfortunately, there isn't an equivalent function in Dart that outputs the date and time in this exact format. For the moment, you'll need to roll your own or use the much simpler `max-age` property.

The `max-age` cookie property specifies the number of seconds until the cookie expires. For example, you can specify a cookie to last a week by using the following statement:

```
document.cookie="stateData=edit/1;max-age=${60*60*24*7}";
```
    One week in seconds

You can view the cookies that are set in Chrome or Dartium by viewing the Cookies section of the Elements tab in the Developer Tools console built into the browser, as shown in figure 11.6.

You need to update your `navigate()` function to add the line

```
document.cookie="stateData=$state;max-age=${60*60*24*7*4}";
```

at around the same point you update `document.title`. Every time you navigate, it will overwrite the previous setting, storing the value of the `state` variable for four weeks.

11.2.2 Reading data from a cookie

Now that you have some data stored in a cookie, you need to modify the app to retrieve the data and, just like the `onPopState()` function, extract the view name and ID from the cookie and pass them to the `navigate()` function. Unfortunately, the

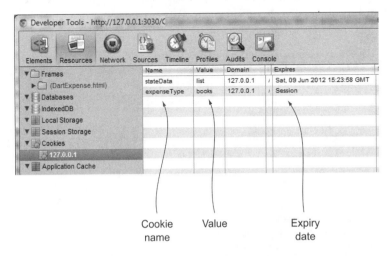

Figure 11.6   You can use the Cookies view of the Chrome and Dartium developer tools to see the cookies your application has set.

`document.cookie` property returns a string of a semicolon-separated list of values, such as

`"stateData=edit/1; expenseType=books"`

You need a utility function to extract the relevant value for a given key, if it exists. Listing 11.3 uses the `string.split()` function to break the cookie string into a list of key=value strings by splitting on the semicolon. Then, for each key=value string, the list splits again until the correct key is identified. If the key doesn't exist, because either the cookie has not yet been set or the cookie has expired, the function returns an empty string.

Listing 11.3   Utility function to extract a cookie value for a given cookie key

```
String getValueFromCookie(String key) {
  for (String cookieKV in document.cookie.split(";")) {    // For each cookie in document.cookie property ...
    List cookie = cookieKV.split("=");                      // ... split into key=value pairs.
    if (cookie.length > 1) {                                // If there's a value ...
      var cookieKey = cookie[0].trim();
      if (cookieKey == key && cookie.length > 1) {
        return cookie[1];                                   // ... return value if it's the requested key.
      }
    }
  }
  return "";                                                // Return empty string instead of default null return value.
}
```

Now that you have a utility function to retrieve the specific value from a specific cookie, you need to modify your app's startup. The `main()` function calls the `load-FirstView()` method of the `AppController` class, so `loadFirstView()` seems like an ideal place to check for the existence of the cookie and change the app's first view as required. You'll copy some of the code from `onPopState()` to decode the `ViewType` and ID value. It's left to you to refactor this as required. The next listing shows the updated `loadFirstView()` method.

Listing 11.4   Changing the application's first view if there's a `stateData` cookie

```
class AppController {
  // ...snip other methods and properties...

  loadFirstView() {
    var viewType = ViewType.LIST;                                    // Sets default list view
    var id = null;

    var stateCookieValue = getValueFromCookie("stateData");          // Tries to load stateData cookie value

    if (stateCookieValue != null && stateCookieValue.length > 0) {
      List<String> stateData = stateCookieValue.split("/");
      var viewName = stateData[0];
      var viewType = new ViewType(viewName);
      var id = stateData.length == 2 ? int.parse(stateData[1]) : null;
    }                                                                // If there is a value, uses same code from onPopState() to extract data
```

```
    navigate(viewType, id);
  }
}
```
←┐ **Passes either default**
  │ **or value from cookie**
  │ **to navigate()**

The app now uses data stored offline in cookies to persist information between sessions. It uses the browser's native history functionality to navigate backward and forward through the application's views.

> **Remember**
> - You can use cookies to store small amounts of data that are persisted across browser sessions.
> - Cookies are insecure and might be disabled by the user, so you should only use them to enhance the user's experience, rather than relying on their existence.

In the next section, you'll see how you can store larger amounts of data by using the HTML5 Web Storage APIs found in modern browsers. You'll finally replace your mock data with real data.

11.3 *Persisting data offline with Web Storage*

Modern browsers provide a number of offline storage mechanisms with varying degrees of support. The simplest and most widely supported is the Web Storage API, which is a list of key/value pairs, similar to cookies, but without expiration and with much larger size limits of 5 MB per domain. Next is IndexedDB, an indexed object store conceptually similar to server-side NoSQL databases such as MongoDB and CouchDB. This system allows you to query an index to retrieve matching records, which provides better performance than the Web Storage API when you want to access a specific subset of records. Finally, there's Web SQL Database, which is an embedded SQL database. This isn't widely supported, due in part to Mozilla's decision not to support it, preferring instead to drive development in the IndexedDB set of APIs. The Web SQL database specification is no longer being maintained, so browsers that do currently support it may drop support in future versions. Table 11.2 shows the browser support for these three technologies as of summer 2012.

Table 11.2   Browser support for offline storage technologies

Browser and version	Web Storage	IndexedDB	Web SQL DB
Chrome 17+	Supported	Supported	Supported
Android Browser 2.1+	Supported	Not supported	Supported
Firefox 3.6	Supported	Not supported	Not supported
Firefox 8+	Supported	Supported	Not supported
Internet Explorer 8	Supported	Not supported	Not supported

Table 11.2 Browser support for offline storage technologies *(continued)*

Browser and version	Web Storage	IndexedDB	Web SQL DB
Internet Explorer 9	Supported	Not supported	Not supported
Internet Explorer 10	Supported	Supported	Not supported
Safari 5+	Supported	Not supported[a]	Supported
iOS Safari 3.2+	Supported	Not supported	Supported
Opera 11.6+	Supported	Not supported[a]	Supported
Opera Mobile 11+	Supported	Not supported	Supported

a. Future Safari and Opera support for IndexedDB is unknown at the present time.
   Source: caniuse.com, June 2012

As you can see, all modern browsers support Web Storage, but IndexedDB isn't supported in Safari and iOS and older versions of IE and Firefox. Web SQL support was added to Chrome and Safari browsers while the specification was still active, but it's not supported at all by IE and Firefox.

> **NOTE** Data stored in local storage, just like cookies, is browser specific. This means the DartExpense data stored in Chrome's local storage isn't available to DartExpense when it's run in Firefox on the same machine.

In this section, you'll modify DartExpense to use the most widely supported Web Storage API. Web Storage key/value pairs must both be strings, which means you can't store the expense instances in them directly. Instead, you must first convert them to a string representation such as JavaScript Object Notation (JSON). Dart's JSON library contains two functions, JSON.stringify() and JSON.parse(), for converting maps and lists into strings and back to maps and lists. You need some way to expose your Expense and ExpenseType objects as a map of key/value pairs.

11.3.1 *Converting Dart objects to JSON strings*

In JavaScript, objects are maps of key/value pairs rather than instances of real classes as in Dart. The JSON data format, which is prevalent around the web, represents a JavaScript data structure that doesn't map directly to Dart's class model. Instead, it converts to Dart's Map class, which contains key/value pairs. In order to convert your Expense and ExpenseType classes to JSON, you need to convert the list of properties in each class to a map. This map can then be passed into JSON.stringify() to convert the map to a JSON string.

Figure 11.7 shows how a map of key/value pairs, which also contains a nested expenseType map, is converted to a JSON string by the JSON.stringify() function. There's also an associated JSON.parse(string) function that converts the JSON string back into a map.

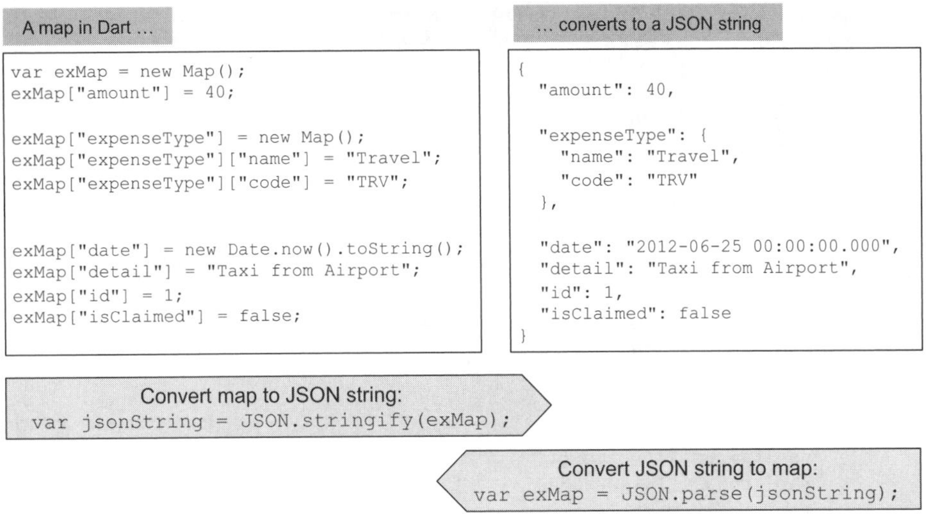

A map in Dart …	… converts to a JSON string

```
var exMap = new Map();
exMap["amount"] = 40;

exMap["expenseType"] = new Map();
exMap["expenseType"]["name"] = "Travel";
exMap["expenseType"]["code"] = "TRV";


exMap["date"] = new Date.now().toString();
exMap["detail"] = "Taxi from Airport";
exMap["id"] = 1;
exMap["isClaimed"] = false;
```

```
{
  "amount": 40,

  "expenseType": {
    "name": "Travel",
    "code": "TRV"
  },

  "date": "2012-06-25 00:00:00.000",
  "detail": "Taxi from Airport",
  "id": 1,
  "isClaimed": false
}
```

> Convert map to JSON string:
> `var jsonString = JSON.stringify(exMap);`

> Convert JSON string to map:
> `var exMap = JSON.parse(jsonString);`

Figure 11.7 Converting a map into a JSON string using `JSON.stringify()`

Because Dart's JSON functions can't convert native Dart objects to JSON and back, you manually need to add this functionality to your Expense and ExpenseType classes.

> ### Milestone 1
> Support for reflection, which should allow dynamic analysis of a class's properties at runtime, is due to be added to the language in Milestone 1. This should allow Dart's library developers to provide additional functionality in the JSON libraries to convert native Dart objects to JSON and back. Sometimes you'll only want to convert certain fields to JSON (rather than every field), so the techniques that follow will still apply.

You can use two techniques to convert a Dart object to a map of key/value pairs that's accepted by the JSON.stringify() function. The simplest is to provide a toMap() function on the class, which returns a map. A slightly more complex technique is to make your class implement the Map interface. The result is more flexible and readable.

PROVIDING A CUSTOM TOMAP () FUNCTION

Using this method, you can write code such as

```
var jsonString = JSON.stringify(expense.toMap());
```

which will work for most purposes. The following listing shows the toMap() methods of the Expense and ExpenseType classes.

Listing 11.5   Providing a `toMap()` method on the `Expense` and `ExpenseType` classes

```
class Expense {
  int _id;
  int get id => _id;
  ExpenseType type;
  Date date;
  num amount = 0;
  String detail;
  bool isClaimed = false;

  Map toMap() {                                        ←──  Expense.toMap()
    final map = new Map<String, Object>();                  function
    map["id"] = _id;
    if (date != null) {
      map["date"] = date.toString();
    }                                                       Properties such as String,
    map["amount"] = amount;                                 num, and bool in map
    map["detail"] = detail;
    map["isClaimed"] = isClaimed;

    if (type != null) {                                     Stores nested
      map["expenseType"] = type.toMap();                    expenseType map
    }

    return map;                                      ←──┐
  }                                                      │
}                                                        │
class ExpenseType {                                      │
  final String name;                                     │
  final String code;                                     │    ExpenseType.toMap()
                                                         │    function
  const ExpenseType(this.name, this.code);               │

  Map toMap() {                                          │
    final map = new Map<String,Object>();          ←──┘
    map["name"] = name;
    map["code"] = code;
    return map;
  }

  bool operator ==(other) {
    if (other == null) return false;
    return this.name == other.name && this.code == other.code;
  }
}
```

This technique ensures that every object used in the top level returns a map or string representation of itself. The JSON functions can convert the types `String`, `num`, `bool`, `List`, `Map`, and `null` into JSON strings, but no others. This means other types, such as the `Date` type, need to be converted to strings (via their `toString()` method) or converted to maps, such as with the `ExpenseType`'s custom `toMap()` function.

IMPLEMENTING THE MAP INTERFACE

The second technique is for your classes to implement the `Map` interface, which will allow them to be passed directly into the `JSON.stringify()` function. You need to write more boilerplate code (to implement the interface), and the code that does the work in your class is similar to `toMap()`. The result, though, is nicer, more readable code when converting to JSON, such as this:

```
var jsonString = JSON.stringify(expense);
```

The additional benefit of implementing the `Map` interface is that as well as passing a single instance of an expense into the `stringify()` function, you can also pass in a list of `Expense` objects. The `stringify()` function treats each item in the list as a map and converts it accordingly. This wouldn't work with the `toMap()` method, because the `stringify()` function wouldn't know it needed to call `toMap()` for each expense in the list.

When implementing the `Map` interface, the key properties and methods are as follows:

- `keys`—Returns a list of the `Expense` class's properties as a list of strings.
- Overloaded `operator[]` function—Returns the correct property value (converted to a `String`, `num`, `bool`, `List`, `Map`, or `null`) for the given key.
- `forEach()`—Takes another function as a parameter. The function parameter is called for each key in the list, passing it the key and its associated value.

Requests for a key that isn't listed in the `keys` collection return `null`. All other map functions throw an `UnimplementedError` because they aren't required for this particular use case. The next listing shows the `Expense` function with its `Map` implementation.

Listing 11.6 Implementing the `Map` interface to support `JSON.stringify()`

```
class Expense implements Map {                         Implements Map
  //...snip properties and other methods...            interface

  Collection get keys {
    return ["id","amount","expenseType","date","detail","isClaimed"];
  }

  operator [](key) {              Returns fixed list          Returns
    if (key == "id") {            of key names                value for a
      return this.id;                                         given key ...
    } else if (key == "amount") {
      return this.amount;
    } else if (key == "expenseType") {
      return this.type.toMap();
    } else if (key == "date") {
      return date == null ? null : date.toString();
    } else if (key == "detail") {
      return this.detail;
    } else if (key == "isClaimed") {
      return this.isClaimed;
    } else {                                      ... or
      return null;                                returns null
    }
  }

}
```

```
forEach(funcParam(key,value)) {
  for (var k in keys) {
    funcParam (k, this[k]);
  }
}
```
> For each key in keys
> collection, passes key and
> value into funcParam()

```
bool get isEmpty(){ throw new UnimplementedError(); }
bool containsValue(value) { throw new UnimplementedError(); }
bool containsKey(value) { throw new UnimplementedError(); }
Collection get keys { throw new UnimplementedError(); }
Collection get values { throw new UnimplementedError(); }
int get length { throw new UnimplementedError(); }
void clear() { throw new UnimplementedError(); }
void remove(key) { throw new UnimplementedError(); }
putIfAbsent(key, ifAbsent) { throw new UnimplementedError(); }
void operator[]=(key, value) { throw new UnimplementedError(); }
}
```
> Not
> implemented
> map functions

There's a lot of boilerplate code here to support the Map interface, but overall the usage is cleaner because you can now transparently convert single instances or lists of the Expense class to a JSON string using JSON.stringify().

11.3.2 Converting JSON strings to Dart objects

Now that you have a mechanism to convert your class to a string, the next step is to convert it back from a string to an object again using JSON.parse(). Unfortunately, there's no nice way to achieve this with the current JSON libraries. Even though the Expense class implements the Map interface, the JSON.parse() function returns an instance of a map rather than an instance of an expense, because it has no knowledge of your Expense class.

The typical way to achieve this in Dart is to provide a named fromMap() constructor, which populates the initial properties on the object in a manner similar to toMap(). This lets you create a new instance of an object by using the following snippet:

```
var jsonString = ...snip expense as a JSON string...
var map = JSON.parse(jsonString);
var expense = new Expense.fromMap(map);
```
> Converts JSON
> representation
> to a map

> Constructs expense
> from converted map

The fromMap() constructor shown in listing 11.7 reads each of the values from the map and uses it to populate each of the Expense object's properties, including ExpenseType, which is constructed by reading its name and code properties from an inner expenseType map. In addition to the fromMap() named constructor, the default constructor remains, so you can still create new, empty instances of an expense.

Listing 11.7 fromMap() constructor: initializes an object from a map of properties

```
class Expense implements Map {
  //... snip other methods and map implementation

  int _id;
```

```
int get id => _id;
ExpenseType type;
Date date;
num amount = 0;
String detail;
bool isClaimed = false;

Expense() {                                    ┌─ Existing default
  _id = _getNextId();                          │  constructor
};                                                        ┌─ Named fromMap
                                                          │  constructor
Expense.fromMap(Map map) {         ◄──────────┘
  _id = map["id"];
  date = new Date.fromString(map["date"]);     ┌─ Populates properties
  amount = map["amount"];                      │  with values from map
  detail = map["detail"];
  isClaimed = map["isClaimed"];

  if (map.containsKey("expenseType")) {        ┌─ Accesses expenseType
    var expenseTypeName = map["expenseType"]["name"];   │  values from inner map
    var expenseTypeCode = map["expenseType"]["code"];

    type = new ExpenseType(expenseTypeName, expenseTypeCode);   ◄──┐
  }                                                               │
}                                          ┌─ Sets type with a
}                                          │  new expense type
```

NOTE A recent addition to aid conversion of an object to JSON is that the
`dart:json` libraries now attempt to call a `toJson()` method if they can't otherwise convert your class to JSON via one of the standard JSON types. You can
use this default handling to return a string representation of your object.

You now have a mechanism to convert your expense objects to and from a string in
JSON format. With your data in the required format, the next step is to store it with
the browser Web Storage API.

11.3.3 *Storing data in browser web storage*

The browser Web Storage API has two implementations with the same syntax: session
storage and local storage. The following examples use local storage, which persists
data across browser sessions. This was chosen in preference to session storage, which
persists data for the length of the session only (until the browser is closed) and is
accessible via the `window.sessionStorage` property.

NOTE Although the syntax to access both session and local storage is identical, there's an important difference. Local storage is limited to 5 MB per
domain, whereas session storage is limited only by system resources.

The browser's local storage API is accessed using the `window.localStorage` property.
This property implements Dart's `Map` interface, allowing you to use indexers to read
data from and write data into the store:

```
window.localStorage["expense"] = JSON.stringify(expense);
var jsonString = window.localStorage["expense"];
expense = new Expense.fromJson(jsonString);
```

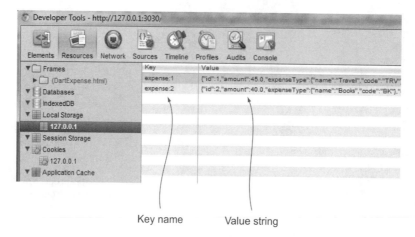

Figure 11.8   You can inspect local storage keys and values with the web browser's developer tools.

As with cookies, local storage key/value pairs exist for a specific domain, so the data the DartExpense app creates is stored separately from any other website's data. Also as with cookies, the data stored in local storage is viewable in plain text, so you shouldn't store any sensitive data such as passwords in the browser's local storage. Figure 11.8 shows the Chrome/Dartium developer tools to inspect the values stored in local storage.

> **WARNING**   Just like cookies, all local storage is insecure and can be inspected by anyone with access to the web browser. Your app should either encrypt the data or, better, only store in the browser data that isn't sensitive.

INSERTING DATA INTO LOCAL STORAGE

Because DartExpense needs to store multiple instances of `Expense` objects, it will build a key by using the string `expense:${expense.id}`, which gives key names such as `expense:1`, `expense:2,` and so on. This allows you to access and modify a single expense record. But an alternative strategy could be to store a JSON-converted list of expenses in a single property:

```
List<Expense> expensesList = ...snip building the list...
window.localStorage["expenses"] = JSON.stringify(expensesList);
```

The disadvantage of this method is that if you want to modify a single expense record, you need to update the entire list in local storage again.

When you insert a single expense into local storage by assigning a JSON string to a specific key such as `expense:1`, you either create a new value or overwrite the existing stored value. Sometimes you want to check whether you're creating or overwriting, perhaps in order to display a message such as "Expense was created" or "Expense was updated." The `Map` interface provides a `containsKey()` method you can use to check before you insert the value, for example:

```
var isNewValue = window.localStorage.containsKey("expense${expense.id}");
window.localStorage["expense${expense.id}"] = JSON.stringify(expense);
```

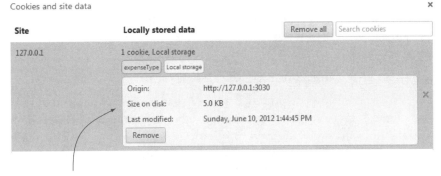

You can see the amount of cookie or local storage data for a particular website by checking the Cookies and Site Data page in Chrome's advanced settings.

Figure 11.9 Inspecting the amount of data stored for a particular site

The amount of data stored is limited to 5 MB per domain for local storage (or unlimited for session storage). You can inspect the amount of data stored in Chrome by looking at the Cookies and Site Data settings in the browser's advanced settings, as shown in figure 11.9.

Users or installed plug-ins and extensions can also disable Web Storage, so your app needs to be able to handle this. If you try to write data into local storage when storage is disabled, the browser will throw a DOMException. Best practice is to wrap your writes to local storage in a try/catch handler:

```
try {
  window.localStorage["expense:${expense.id}"] = JSON.stringify(expense);
}
on DOMException catch (ex) {
  window.alert("Local storage is not available");
}
```

You can now update the existing addOrUpdate() function to store the data in local storage, as shown in the following listing.

Listing 11.8 Adding/updating an expense in local storage

```
bool addOrUpdate(Expense expense) {
  var localStorageKey = "expense:${expense.id}";
  bool isNew = !window.localStorage.containsKey(localStorageKey);

  try {
    window.localStorage[localStorageKey] = JSON.stringify(expense);
  }
  on DOMException catch (ex) {
    window.alert("Local storage not enabled");
  }

  return isNew;
}
```

READING DATA FROM LOCAL STORAGE

Reading data from local storage is even simpler. Because the localStorage property implements Dart's Map interface, you read the value by passing the key name to the accessor:

```
var jsonString = window.localStorage["expense:1"];
```

The DartExpense app needs to load a list of all expenses. To achieve this, you need to load all the localStorage values that have a key beginning with expense:. This again is straightforward using the keys property, as shown in the next listing, where you retrieve each JSON representation of an expense and convert it back into an Expense object using the fromMap() named constructor.

Listing 11.9   Reading the list of expenses out of local storage

```
List<Expense> loadExpenses() {                          Creates new,
  var expensesList = new List<Expense>();        ◁——   empty list
                                                                  Iterates through
  for (var key in window.localStorage.keys) {           ◁——   local storage keys

    if (key.startsWith("expense:")) {          ◁——  If key starts with expense: ...
      String value = window.localStorage[key];
      var map = JSON.parse(value);                       ... converts string into a map
      var expense = new Expense.fromMap(map);            and then to an expense.
      expensesList.add(expense);
    }                                               ◁——  Adds expense
  }                                                      to result list

  return expenses;                     ◁——  Returns list
}
```

PUTTING IT ALL TOGETHER: REPLACING MOCK DATA WITH WEB STORAGE

Now that you can store data in local storage and read data out of local storage, you can replace your MockData class in DartExpense's main() function. MockData implements a DataAccess interface:

```
interface DataAccess {
  List<Expense> get expenses;
  bool addOrUpdate(Expense expense);
}
```

You need a new LocalStorageData class containing the two functions shown here in order to return a list of expenses from local storage and update a single expense in local storage. When you've completed that step, you can modify the main() function as shown next.

Listing 11.10   Replacing mock data with real data

```
void main() {
  var uiContainer = query("#dartexpense");
  var dataSource = new MockData();               Changes dataSource to
  var dataSource = new LocalStorageData();   ◁——  work with LocalStorage
```

```
  _app = new AppController(uiContainer, dataSource);
  app.buildUI();
  app.loadFirstView();

  window.on.popState.add(onPopState);
}
```

Passes dataSource to AppController

The DartExpense app now functions as a real client-side offline app that persists data between sessions using web storage.

> **Remember**
> - Web Storage is the most widely supported offline storage technology and the simplest to use.
> - `window.localStorage` provides up to 5 MB storage per domain, persisted across browser restarts.
> - `window.sessionStorage` provides unlimited storage (restricted by the system resources) but doesn't persist across browser restarts.

11.4 Summary

This chapter extended the DartExpense app to improve the user experience. You added functionality to use browser history via `pushState()` and `popState` so users can navigate views in a single-page web app using standard browser functionality. You also used browser cookies to enhance the user experience by allowing DartExpense to return to the same view after the browser was restarted.

You learned how to convert Dart objects to JSON strings and back by using the `JSON.stringify()` and `JSON.parse()` functions. These functions can only convert `Map`, `List`, `String`, `bool`, `num`, and `null` types to JSON; you need to manually provide a mechanism to convert your own classes, such as `Expense`, to a map, which you achieved by implementing the `Map` class. To convert back from a JSON map, you created a `fromMap()` named constructor to repopulate the object's properties.

Finally, you learned how to store JSON data in the browser's web storage, by using the `localStorage` key/value storage API available in all modern browsers. This functionality replaces the mock data that DartExpense was using with real data that's persisted offline across browser sessions.

In part 4 of the book, when we look at Dart on the server, you'll extend the DartExpense app to sync its data to the server. But first, in the next chapter, we'll look at ways of communicating with other JavaScript functions and discuss how to use Dart and JavaScript interaction to request JSON data from public servers.

Communicating with other systems and languages

12

This chapter covers

- Interacting with JavaScript
- Getting data from external servers with JSONP
- Running an app without a server
- Packaging an installable Chrome app

Although you can write an app entirely in Dart, that isn't the end of the story. Dart apps live in a wider ecosystem encompassing browser apps, existing JavaScript frameworks and libraries, and APIs on third-party servers. Each of these environments has its own challenges in the areas of server availability, browser security, and communication between different virtual machines.

In this chapter, you'll modify the DartExpense app to interact with external JavaScript by passing messages between the Dart and JavaScript VMs. This modification lets you call out from Dart code to JavaScript code and lets JavaScript code call back into Dart code.

You'll use this JavaScript mechanism to communicate with third-party servers, such as public Google APIs, by using JSON with padding (JSONP) callbacks. This is a mechanism to return data from a third-party server without the security restrictions around AJAX calls.

Next, you'll improve DartExpense's ability to use the offline capabilities provided by HTML5's AppCache technology, which lets the browser start an app even when the server isn't available—perfect for mobile apps when you can't always guarantee connectivity.

Finally, we'll look at how to package your app as a Chrome app that you can run purely offline and install into Google Chrome via the Chrome Web Store. Installable Chrome apps offer a method to get your app in front of a large audience via the Web Store.

You'll start by taking the existing Dart-Expense app and adding a pie chart of expense types by taking advantage of a third-party JavaScript charting library. This is the first external system you'll incorporate with Dart; see figure 12.1.

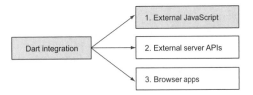

Figure 12.1 Integrating Dart with JavaScript

12.1 *Communicating with JavaScript*

Thousands of libraries have been built with JavaScript, and many developers want to incorporate some of them into their apps. As Dart's popularity increases, Dart versions of popular libraries will appear; but until that happens, you'll need to communicate across virtual machines, from the Dart VM to the JavaScript VM and back again. This applies even if Dart is converted to JavaScript, because although there's only the JavaScript VM, the Dart code isn't easily exposed to other JavaScript because of optimization processes.

> **NOTE** Be aware that calling JavaScript from Dart is different than Google Web Toolkit's (GWT) JavaScript Native Interface (JSNI) functions, which let you embed JavaScript code in Java code. In Dart, there's a distinct boundary between when the Dart code stops and the JavaScript code starts. But it's likely that this boundary will become increasingly transparent as the Dart team develops object proxies to provide greater Dart and JavaScript interoperability.

You'll modify the DartExpense app by adding a third view, a chart view, to go along with the current list and edit views. The chart view will provide an empty <div> that will be populated by the Google chart library, which is written in JavaScript. You'll communicate from the Dart app to the JavaScript, passing expense data into the chart library in order to produce a pie chart of expenses, as shown in figure 12.2.

In order to communicate between native JavaScript and Dart code, you need to pass messages, typically in the form of JSON, back and forth between the JavaScript and Dart VMs. The DartExpense code, running in the Dart VM, written in Dart, will send a message to the JavaScript charting function telling it to render a chart in a specific <div>. Your JavaScript code will receive the message and call the JavaScript chart API to render the pie chart.

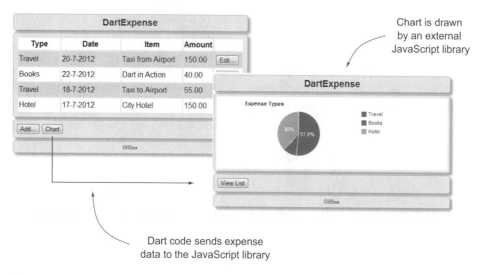

Figure 12.2   Adding a JavaScript-generated pie chart to the DartExpense app

NOTE   The text refers to the Dart VM when talking about Dart code or Dart converted to JavaScript, and it refers to the JavaScript VM when talking about native JavaScript code written in JavaScript. Dart converted to JavaScript should be treated as though it's still Dart code and separate from native JavaScript code.

The mechanism for passing data between Dart and JavaScript is via a function provided by a browser window called `postMessage()`, which is part of the `window` object in the `dart:html` library. This allows communication back and forth between Dart and JavaScript by letting the receiving side add an event listener to listen for messages posted to it. The browser takes the message sent from one VM and passes it across the boundary where another VM can receive it. Figure 12.3 shows the flow between the two VMs.

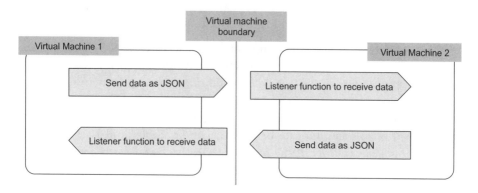

Figure 12.3   Sending data from one VM to another requires a listener function on the receiving side.

The postMessage() function sends messages out to all listeners, which may be listeners from the Dart app, listeners in your JavaScript, or listeners from third-party imported scripts. Each listener function needs to decide, based on the content of the data, whether the message is targeted at that particular listener function.

To achieve this, you'll pass your data to the postMessage() function with the data wrapped in JSON, with a type field of dart2js or js2dart so each receiving function knows the data is meant for it. You'll also add an action field so you can have multiple receiving functions. At the moment you'll only have a chart action, but later you'll add more. You pass your expense summary data using the payload field. The JSON data and the flow from Dart to JavaScript are shown in figure 12.4.

The postMessage(data, targetOrigin) function provided by the browser takes two parameters: the data, which you're sending as JSON, and targetOrigin, which is the URL from which the receiving page was served. This means if you're sending data to http://localhost:8080/DartExpense.html, the target origin is also http://localhost:8080/DartExpense.html. In most cases, you can use the value of window.location.href, because you're sending messages in the same page, but being able to change this value lets you send messages between different iframes (different, complete web pages embedded in another web page but served from a different location). To simplify this, you'll create a utility function called sendToJavaScript(), which will take an action type string and payload data.

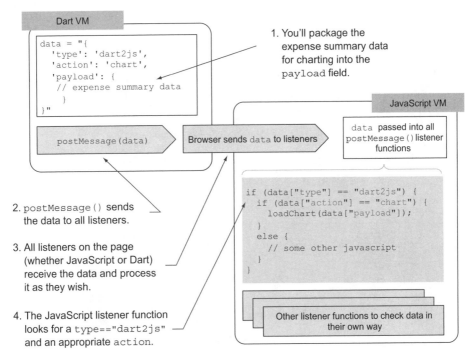

Figure 12.4 postMessage() **data is sent to all listener functions, so you need to identify that the data is meant for you.**

12.1.1 Sending data from Dart to JavaScript

In order to send data from Dart to JavaScript, your utility function sendToJavaScript(),
shown in listing 12.1, will package the dart2js postMessage type string, the action
string, and the payload (which will contain your expense summary data) and convert
them to JSON before calling the window.postMessage() function. Add this utility function to DartExpense's app.dart source file.

Listing 12.1   app.dart: sendToJavaScript() function that calls postMessage()

```
// snip other functions and classes

sendToJavaScript(String action, var payload) {
  var data = new Map<String,Object>();        Creates new map
                                               to hold data
  data["type"] = "dart2js";
  data["action"] = action;                     Assigns postMessage()
  data["payload"] = payload;                   type, action, and payload
  var jsonData = JSON.stringify(data);
  window.postMesage(jsonData, window.location.href);   Converts
}                                                       map to JSON
                   Sends JSON data to all
                   postMessage() listeners
```

Now that you've seen how you send data to JavaScript, you need to provide data from
the DartExpense app. You need an aggregate of all your expense data, showing the
total amount for each expense type. Figure 12.5 illustrates the transformation the data
makes from original data to aggregated totals to pie chart.

To provide the aggregated data you'll send to the JavaScript pie chart library,
create a boilerplate getAggregatedData() function. This function will return a
Map<ExpenseType, double> containing the total amount claimed for each expense type.
The summary data needs to be converted into a specific format for the JavaScript chart
library: a list of key/value pairs, with each key/value being an item in a child list. The
first key/value pairs represent the chart headings, shown in the following JSON snippet:

```
[                           Containing list of key/value pairs
  ['Type','Amount'],
  ['Travel',205.0],                     Header information
  ['Books',40.0],          Expense
  ['Hotel',150.0]          summary data
]
```

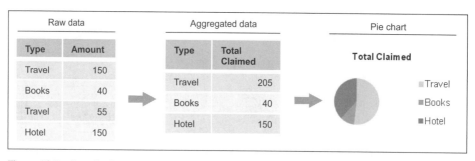

Figure 12.5   How the DartExpense data is transformed from raw data to a pie chart

When the user clicks the View Chart button, the app calls the `getAggregatedData()` function to generate the expense summary data and passes the results into the new `ChartView` class.

`ChartView`, shown in listing 12.2, implements the `View` interface, just like the existing list and edit views. It provides a `rootElement` to render the content of the view and an `actions` element that renders the view's buttons. `ChartView` creates a `<div>` with `id=chartView`, which is used by the JavaScript chart library to display the pie chart. Each expense type and total amount in the payload is added to a list, forming the payload you pass to the JavaScript chart library in order to draw the pie chart. Finally, you call the `sendToJavaScript()` utility function you created earlier, with the `chart` action, to convert the payload to JSON and send the data to all `postMessage()` listeners.

> **Listing 12.2 ui_chart.dart: `ChartView` class that calls the JavaScript chart library**

```
class ChartView implements View {
  DivElement rootElement;
  DivElement actions;

  ChartView(Map<ExpenseType, double> aggregatedData) {      The constructor takes the
    _buildView(expenseSummary);                              expenseSummary data
    _buildActions();
  }

  _buildView (var expenseSummary) {

    rootElement = new Element.html("""                  Creates <div> called
      <div id='chartView'                               chartView for JavaScript
          style='width:500px;                           to use
          height:150px'></div>""");

    List payload = new List();                          Creates new list for payload
    payload.add(["Type","Amount"]);                     data and adds header row

    for (var expenseType in expenseSummary.getKeys()) {       Adds each
      var totalAmount = expenseSummary[expenseType];          expense type and
      payload.add([expenseType.name, totalAmount]);           total amount
    }

    var action = "chart";
    sendToJavaScript(action,payload);                        Sends data to
  }                                                          JavaScript
  _buildActions() {
  // snip adding "Return to List" button
  }
}
```

This is only half the picture. Your Dart code has sent some data, but you need to write the JavaScript `postMessage()` event listener that will receive the data.

12.1.2 *Receiving data in JavaScript sent from Dart*

In order to do anything with the data sent by `postMessage()` from your Dart code, you also need some JavaScript that's waiting to receive the data. You do this by writing an event-listener function in JavaScript and attaching it to the JavaScript `window` object with the `window.addEventListener()` function. The JavaScript `addEventListener()` function takes two parameters: the type of event it's listening for (in this case, `message`) and a JavaScript callback function.

> **NOTE**   All the code in this section is JavaScript, embedded directly into `<script>` tags in the DartExpense.html file. Dart and JavaScript look similar.

The following listing shows the JavaScript required to receive the expense summary data and print the payload to the browser development console.

> **Listing 12.3   DartExpense.html: JavaScript to receive `postMessage()` data**

```
<!DOCTYPE html>

<html>
  <head>
    <!-- snip other head tags -->                          JavaScript
                                                           <script> tag
    <script type="text/javascript">
                                                           Declares JavaScript
      function receiveFromDart(event) {                    receive() function
        var data = JSON.parse(event.data);
        var type = data["type"];                           Converts data
        var action = data["action"];       Extracts values from JSON to
        var payload = data["payload"];     from JavaScript JavaScript map
                                           map
        console.log(type + ", " + action + ", " + payload);
      }                                                    Adds listener function
                                                           to window object
      window.addEventListener("message", receiveFromDart);
    </script>
  </head>
  <body>
    <div id="dartexpense"></div>
    <script type="application/dart" src="DartExpense.dart"></script>
    <script src="dart.js"></script>
  </body>                                             Standard HTML to host
</html>                                               DartExpense application
```

Outputs them to developer console

If you call the `sendToJavaScript()` function from your Dart code, this piece of JavaScript outputs your expense summary data to the browser developer console. Now that you can get data into JavaScript, it's time to bring in the Google Chart API. The Google API has two components: the API and a function to use the API. You add the API to the page by linking in the `jsapi` script hosted at Google:

```
<script type="text/javascript" src="http://www.google.com/jsapi"></script>
```

This brings in all the code required to load the specific Chart API from all the available Google APIs. To use the Chart API, you need to add another JavaScript function, `loadPieChart(chartData)`, that will take the expense summary data and use it to build a pie chart. This function loads the Google charting library and takes another JavaScript function, `drawChart()`, which draws the chart with your data when the charting library is properly loaded. Listing 12.4 shows both functions and also modifies the JavaScript `receiveFromDart()` function, which checks that the `postMessage()` data is meant for it, and passes the payload expense summary data to the `loadPieChart()` JavaScript function.

Listing 12.4 Calling Chart library code from `receiveFromDart()`

```
<!-- snip other html -->
<head>
  <script type="text/javascript" src="http://www.google.com/jsapi">
  </script>                                                              ◁──  Includes Google API

  <script type="text/javascript">

    function receiveFromDart(event) {
      var data = JSON.parse(event.data);
      if (data["type"] == "dart2js") {                    ┐   Extracts payload
        if (data["action"] == "chart") {                  ├── expense data
          var chartData = data["payload"];
          loadPieChart(payload);          ◁──  Passes data to
        }                                       loadPieChart
      }
    }

    window.addEventListener("message", receiveFromDart);

    function loadPieChart(chartData) {
      var packageData = { packages:["corechart"], callback: drawChart};
      google.load("visualization", "1", packageData);

      function drawChart() {
        var data = google.visualization.arrayToDataTable(chartData);
        var options = {title: 'Expense Types'};

        var divElement = document.getElementById("chartView");
        var chart = new google.visualization.PieChart(divElement);

        chart.draw(data, options);       ◁──  Draws pie
      }                                         chart
    }
  </script>
</head>
<!-- snip other html -->
```

When corechart package loads, calls drawChart() callback function

Converts chartData to correct format and creates options

Creates PieChart with chartView `<div>` element

You can try a number of different options, such as `is3d:true` to make the chart 3D, or specify colors and sizes. A quick search for "Google Chart API" will bring up the full list of options and many other charts, such as bar or line graphs, on the http://developers.google.com website.

Now that you've called JavaScript code from Dart, you should reverse the route and call Dart code from JavaScript. The pattern is the same but reversed: the JavaScript code sends data via `postMessage()`, and the Dart code listens for a message event sent by the browser.

12.1.3 Sending data from JavaScript to Dart

At this point, your DartExpense app sends data to the JavaScript Chart API. You'll complete the cycle and have the JavaScript `drawChart()` function send a message

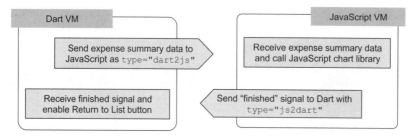

Figure 12.6   The flow from Dart to JavaScript and JavaScript to Dart

back to Dart code when the chart is drawn. You'll use this functionality to enable the Return to List button on the `ChartView` class's actions panel. The flow from Dart to JavaScript and back is shown in figure 12.6.

In exactly the same way you created a `sendToJavaScript()` function in your Dart code, you'll create a utility function in your JavaScript code called `sendToDart` `(action,payload)`. It will package up the action and payload data into a JSON string and send it to the browser via `window.postMessage()`, as shown in the following listing. You'll also modify the existing `drawChart()` function to call the new `sendToDart()` function when the chart is drawn.

Listing 12.5   JavaScript `sendToDart()` utility function

```
<script type="text/javascript">
  function loadPieChart(chartData) {
    var packageData = { packages:["corechart"], callback: drawChart};
    google.load("visualization", "1", packageData);

    function drawChart() {
      var data = google.visualization.arrayToDataTable(chartData);
      var options = {title: 'Expense Types'};

      var divElement = document.getElementById("chartView");
      var chart = new google.visualization.PieChart(divElement);

      chart.draw(data, options);
      sendToDart("chartComplete","finished");      ◁──┤ Lets Dart know chart
    }                                                  │ drawing has finished
  }

  function sendToDart(action, payload) {
    var data = {};
    data["type"] = "js2dart";                    ┐
    data["action"] = action;                      ├ Builds up data
    data["payload"] = payload;                    ┘ to send to Dart
    var jsonData = JSON.stringify(data);         ◁──┤ Converts
    window.postMessage(jsonData,window.location.href);   ◁──┤ data to JSON
  }                                                         └ Sends data back
</script>                                                     via postMessage()
```

The JavaScript code now sends the data to all `postMessage()` listeners, so the final step in the chain is to add a `postMessage()` listener to the Dart code. There's only one postMessage() queue, and all messages, whether sent from Dart code or JavaScript code, are sent to all listeners. This is why each listener needs to check that the data sent to it is meant for that specific listener. The JavaScript listener receives messages meant for the Dart listener, and the Dart listener receives messages meant for the JavaScript listener. Each listener checks the data["type"] value to see if the data is meant for it. JavaScript listeners continue processing only if the data["type"] value is dart2js, and Dart listeners continue processing only if the data["type"] value is js2dart.

NOTE All the code listings from here on are Dart code.

The following listing shows the modified ChartView class. It calls out to draw the chart and then listens for a response from the JavaScript, enabling the Return to List button when the JavaScript indicates that the chart is drawn.

Listing 12.6 ui_chart.dart: receiving data from JavaScript into Dart

```
class ChartView implements View {
  DivElement rootElement;
  DivElement actions;
  ButtonElement returnToListButton;

  // snip constructor

  _buildView (var expenseSummary) {
    // snip building payload data

    var action = "chart";
    sendToJavaScript(action,payload);

    onFinishedListener(event) {                      // Extracts postMessage() data
      var data = JSON.parse(event.data);
      if (data["type"] == "js2dart") {               // Check whether data is meant
        if (data["action"] == "chartComplete") {     // for this listener function
          window.on.message.remove(onFinishedListener);
          returnToListButton.disabled = false;       // Enables returnToListButton
        }                                            // Removes this event listener
      }                                              // so it doesn't fire again
    };

    window.on.message.add(onFinishedListener);       // Adds event-listener
  }                                                  // function to listen to
  _buildActions() {                                  // postMessage() events
    // snip adding "Return to List" button
  }
}
```

You've seen the round trip from Dart to JavaScript and JavaScript to Dart. As a result of the multiple VMs with their separate memory and browser interactions, it's more complicated than embedding JavaScript code in Dart code. The only way to communicate between the VMs is to pass messages from one to the other.

> **Remember**
> - You can pass data out of Dart code by using `window.postMessage()`.
> - JavaScript code can listen for the `message` event to receive data from Dart code by attaching a listener function with `window.addMessageListener()`.
> - Multiple listeners can receive data sent with `postMessage()`, so each listener needs to decide if the data is intended for it.

In the next section, you'll use the `sendToDart()` function to receive data from external servers via a mechanism called JSONP, which is a common JavaScript workaround for the security restrictions imposed by the browser when making `HttpRequest` calls.

12.2 *Communicating with external servers*

One of the great aspects of web development is that you can access public APIs on external servers to retrieve data required by your app. This is the next external system you'll integrate with Dart (see figure 12.7).

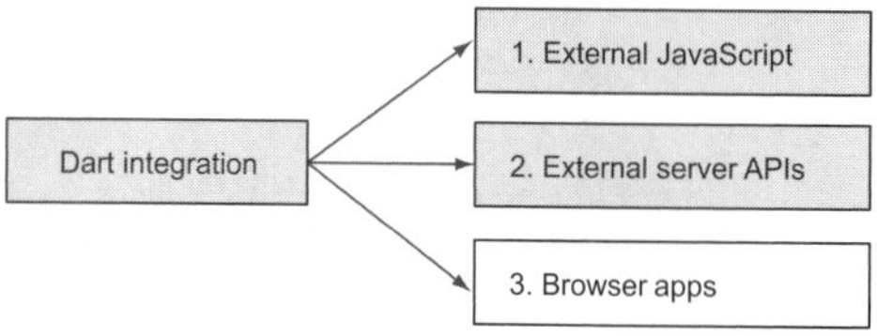

Figure 12.7   Integrating Dart with external server APIs

You'll modify the DartExpense app again to add a conversion function that will convert a US dollar expense amount into British pounds. In order to do this, you need to get the current exchange rate, which is helpfully provided by http://openExchangeRates.org, through the URL http://openexchangerates.org/api/latest.json.

Your edit screen will have an additional Convert to GBP button that will take the amount edited, grab the latest exchange rate information, and update the value with the converted amount, as shown in figure 12.8.

The exchange rate information is returned as JSON, as in the following snippet of JSON data showing only four exchange rates:

```
{
  "rates": {
      "EUR": 0.816139,
      "FJD": 1.820003,
      "FKP": 0.639819,
      "GBP": 0.639819
  }
}
```

You're interested in the GBP exchange rate.

When your code receives this information, you need to extract the exchange rate and multiply it by the dollar value using the following snippet of code:

```
var data = JSON.parse(exchangeRateData);
var conversionRate = data["rates"]["GBP"];
var gbpAmount = dollarAmount * conversionRate;
```

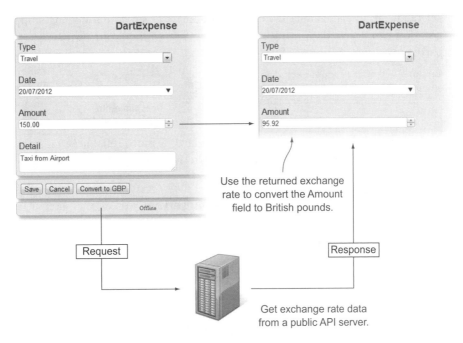

Figure 12.8 Using exchange rate information from a public API to convert the amount from USD to GBP

You'll then update the Amount text box with the new GBP amount. Unfortunately, getting your hands on this exchange rate data isn't entirely straightforward, thanks to browser security restrictions designed to prevent a page served by one site from communicating via an AJAX HttpRequest to another site.

12.2.1 *Understanding the same-origin security restrictions*

The normal way to request data from a server in an asynchronous manner is with an HttpRequest. The HttpRequest is an asynchronous API provided by the web browser, and it provides the A in AJAX. HttpRequest, also known as XHR (from the browser's DOM XMLHttpRequest() function), started appearing in popular browsers around 2005. It's used by a web page to request more data from a server, but it was soon hijacked to send user data from one server to another in cross-site scripting attacks. Browser manufacturers countered by adding a *same-origin policy*: if your web page is served from a server at http://dartexpense.com, then you can only use HttpRequest to communicate with http://dartexpense.com and not with other servers.

This is a problem because at the moment the DartExpense app isn't served by a server; it runs entirely in a browser (we'll look more at using HttpRequest when you add server-side Dart in the next chapter). Fortunately, there are a number of ways to circumvent this restriction, including the new cross-origin resource sharing (CORS) standard that's starting to be supported on servers. If a server supports CORS by adding special headers to the response, then the browser won't prevent you from using

HttpRequest to access data from the third-party server. The following snippet shows how you can access data using HttpRequest from either your own server or a third-party server that supports CORS:

```
var url = "http://openexchangerates.org/api/latest.json";        XHR request
new HttpRequest.get(url, (response) {                              to URL
    print(response.responseText);
});                                          Does something
                                             with returned data
```

Unfortunately, this is still an emerging standard. A more reliable but also more complex method of requesting data from an external server is to use JSON with padding (JSONP).

12.2.2 Using JSONP to request data from external servers

JSONP relies on the fact that you can link external scripts with a <script> tag served from any server to your page, just as you did with the Google jsapi script in the previous section. Rather than request regular JSON data, you request JSON data that's wrapped in a JavaScript function call known as a *callback*. When the page loads the script from the external server, it executes the JavaScript, passing the data into the JavaScript callback function. The name of the callback function is indicated by adding a callback=myCallbackFunctionName query string parameter to the URL, as in

```
http://openexchangerates.org/api/latest.json?callback=onDataLoaded
```

This URL is added to the src property of the first script, whereas a second script defines the onDataLoaded(data) JavaScript function that receives the data. Figure 12.9 shows this in use.

DYNAMICALLY ADDING THE SCRIPT ELEMENT

You can add the first script that requests the data from the external server dynamically in Dart by creating a ScriptElement and setting the src property to the correct URL. As soon as you add it to the DOM, the browser will request the data. You add and then remove the <script> tag to keep things tidy, as in the following Dart snippet:

```
ScriptElement scriptElement = new Element.tag("script");   ←— Creates <script> element
scriptElement.src =
 ⇨    "http://openexchangerates.org/api/latest.json?callback=onDataLoaded";
scriptElement.type = "text/javascript";
document.head.children.add(scriptElement);                    Adds it to browser DOM,
scriptElement.remove();        ←— Removes it from DOM        triggering request
```

When the browser receives the returned JavaScript containing your exchange rate data, it tries to execute a JavaScript function called onDataLoaded(). You use the sendToDart() function to send the data from the JavaScript function back to the Dart-Expense app, using this JavaScript:

```
<script type="text/javascript">
  function onDataLoaded(data) {                     Sends retrieved data
     sendToDart("exchangeRates", data);             back to Dart app
  }
</script>
```

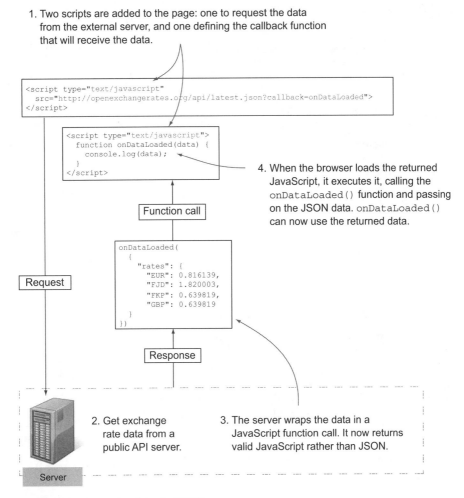

1. Two scripts are added to the page: one to request the data from the external server, and one defining the callback function that will receive the data.

```
<script type="text/javascript"
  src="http://openexchangerates.org/api/latest.json?callback=onDataLoaded">
</script>
```

```
<script type="text/javascript">
  function onDataLoaded(data) {
    console.log(data);
  }
</script>
```

4. When the browser loads the returned JavaScript, it executes it, calling the `onDataLoaded()` function and passing on the JSON data. `onDataLoaded()` can now use the returned data.

Function call

```
onDataLoaded(
  {
    "rates": {
      "EUR": 0.816139,
      "FJD": 1.820003,
      "FKP": 0.639819,
      "GBP": 0.639819
    }
  })
```

Request

Response

2. Get exchange rate data from a public API server.

3. The server wraps the data in a JavaScript function call. It now returns valid JavaScript rather than JSON.

Server

Figure 12.9 Accessing data via JSONP

The final step in the chain is to set up a message listener back in your Dart code that receives the exchangeRates action from the JavaScript onDataLoaded() function. You saw this functionality earlier in the chapter when you added a listener so you could be notified when the chart had been drawn; the exchangeRates data listener is no different. Put all the Dart code together in the Convert to GBP button click handler, shown in the following listing.

Listing 12.7 ui_edit.dart: converting from USD to GBP

```
class EditView implements View {
  DivElement rootElement;
  DivElement actions;
// snip other methods and functions
```

```
_buildActions() {
  actions = new Element.tag("div");
  actions.children.add(_getSaveButton());
  actions.children.add(_getCancelButton());
  actions.children.add(_getConvertToGBPButton());        ◁── Adds convert button
}                                                              to actions panel

_getConvertToGBPButton() {
  ButtonElement convertButton = new Element.tag("button");    │ Creates convert
  convertButton.text = "Convert to GBP";                      │ button

  convertButton.on.click.add( (event) {         ◁── In button click listener ...

    ScriptElement scriptElement = new Element.tag("script");
    scriptElement.src =
    "http://openexchangerates.org/api/latest.json?callback=onDataLoaded";
    scriptElement.type = "text/javascript";
    document.head.children.add(scriptElement);          ... add remove script to
    scriptElement.remove();                                 get exchange rates

    onRateListener(event) {                         When
      var data = JSON.parse(event.data);            you retrieve
      if (data["type"] == "js2dart" &&              exchange        ... remove
          data["action"] == "exchangeRates") {      rate data ...   postMessage()
                                                                    listener
        window.on.message.remove(onRateListener);   ◁──

        InputElement amountEl = query("#expenseAmount");
        var dollarValue = double.parse(amountEl.value);

        var payload = data["payload"];                Extracts exchange rate
        var gbpRate = payload["rates"]["GBP"];        from returned data and
        var gbpValue = dollarValue * gbpRate;         calculates GBP value
        amountEl.value = gbpValue.toStringAsFixed(2);  ◁──
      }                                                  Updates text box
    };                                                   with GBP value

    window.on.message.add(onRateListener);   ◁──
  });                                            Adds postMessage()
                                                 listener to browser
  return convertButton;
  }
}
```

Left margin annotation: **Gets current dollar value entry**

Using JSONP to get data from external servers does take more boilerplate code to
go from Dart > Script Tag > JavaScript Callback > Dart; but until more servers start
to implement the CORS header standard, browser security restrictions will continue
to block XHR AJAX requests from third-party servers. Using the technique shown,
you can make multiple calls to external servers to request more data as your
app requires.

You've seen how to integrate Dart with JavaScript and how to use that integration
to request data from external servers via the JSONP callback mechanism. In the next
section, we'll look at how to integrate Dart with another external component: the web
browser. You'll use HTML5 AppCache technology to run the app even when the server

> **Remember**
>
> - `HttpRequest` only works with servers that support CORS or the server that's hosting your app.
> - JSONP requests add a `<script>` tag to get the requested data wrapped in a JavaScript function call.
> - The data retrieved by the JavaScript function call can pass the data back to Dart by using the `postMessage()` mechanism you saw earlier in the chapter, which you wrapped in a `sendToDart()` JavaScript function.

isn't running, and install the app into the Chrome web browser as a standalone app that can be published in the Chrome Web Store.

12.3 *Building installable, server-less browser apps*

One of the technologies that HTML5 enables is offline apps that run without a server connection. The app does need to be served from a server such as http://dartexpense.com initially, but once its files are stored in the browser, your users can navigate to http://dartexpense.com and the app will load even if they have no inter-

net connection. By combining offline technology with the capability to install apps into Google Chrome, you can build apps that work just as well on an intermittently connected mobile or tablet device as they do on a desktop device. This is the third step to integrate Dart with external systems (see figure 12.10).

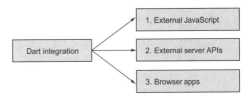

Figure 12.10   Integrating Dart with the browser

In order to create a purely offline app, the first step is to let it run even when there's no internet connection. You can achieve this in your apps with an HTML5 technology known as AppCache.

12.3.1 *Using AppCache to run applications offline*

AppCache uses a *cache manifest file*, a special file that contains a list of files such as the HTML, Dart, and JavaScript files and any images and CSS that make up your app. You specify that your app will use AppCache by adding a `manifest` attribute to the HTML tag and specifying the filename of a cache manifest file, as shown in the following snippet that forms the basis of DartExpense.html:

```
<!DOCTYPE html>                              |  HTML5 doctype
<html manifest="dartexpense.appcache">       |  dartexpense.appcache
// snip page content                         |  file referenced in
</html>                                      |  manifest attribute
```

Now, when you load the app, if the browser can connect to the server, it will read the dartexpense.appcache manifest file and attempt to store files listed in it locally. If the browser can't connect to the server, it will use the files held locally as an alias for the real files on the server.

> **NOTE** Although you aren't yet serving your app from a real server, if you use the Dart Editor, your app is served from a built-in debug server. You'll need to shut down the Editor to check that your app is working offline. Alternatively, you can serve your app, which is made up of static files, from any web server, such as Apache or IIS.

The AppCache manifest file is what lets the offline magic happen. It has three sections, shown in figure 12.11, which let you cache files offline, indicate which files will only be available when online, and provide a fallback option to a local file when the network version isn't available. Figure 12.11 shows the files you'd use with Google Chrome, rather than Dartium, and lists the file's version of your app converted from Dart to JavaScript.

Each section has a specific meaning, so we'll look at them in turn.

FILES TO CACHE LOCALLY

The CACHE section lists files the browser caches locally. Once the browser has loaded them the first time the app is accessed, the browser always loads these files from its cache without requesting data from the server. This differs from the normal browser cache, which still requires the server to be available. These files are accessed completely offline, so if you try to browse to http://127.0.0.1:8080/DartExpense.html,

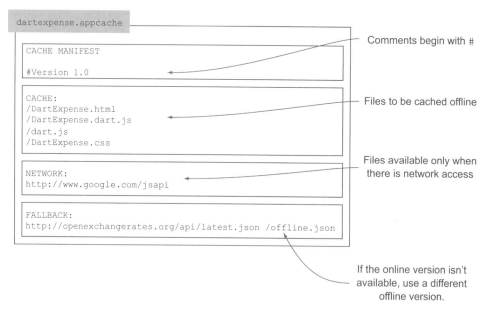

Figure 12.11 The dartexpense.appcache file lists which parts of the application are cacheable and which aren't.

even without the server running, your file will still be loaded. This is great for sporadically connected devices such as phones and tablets, or even laptops, because users can still use parts of your app when offline.

> **WARNING**   AppCache works only if it can cache *all* the files listed in your App-Cache. If even one of them isn't successfully returned from the server the first time you access your app, none of the files will be stored.

But what happens when you modify DartExpense.html or some of the application code changes if the browser never hits the server? The browser attempts to load the manifest file to see if it has changed. If it can't load the manifest file, or the manifest file hasn't changed, the browser uses the local copy. When you update your app, the simplest way to force the manifest file to change is to modify a comment line, such as the #Version 1.0 comment. Changing this to read #Version 1.1 forces the browser to re-cache the files the next time the server is available.

By loading the locally cached files rather than hitting the server, your app has fast startup times even for apps that contain a lot of code and images. Once these resources are on your local machine, repeated visits to your app don't require them to be reloaded from the server.

> **TIP**   You can view the details for all the websites that are currently storing files in the browser AppCache by entering the URL chrome://appcache-internals into Google Chrome. You might be surprised by how many are using it.

What if parts of your app rely on dynamic data or an external API to perform some processing for you? This is where the NETWORK section comes in.

FILE AVAILABLE ONLY WHEN THERE'S A NETWORK CONNECTION

Sometimes, although your app works perfectly well offline, parts of it rely on server-side dynamic data or external content. When you list files and URLs in the NETWORK section, which can be wildcards such as http://www.google.com/*, any requests made by the browser bypass the cache even if the browser is offline. In order to make this work with your app, you need to be able to tell whether the browser is offline; otherwise you'll receive an error when you try to request the URL. You can modify the Dart app to enable the View Chart button only if the app is online by checking the boolean window.navigator.onLine property as shown in the following listing.

> **Listing 12.8   ui_list.dart: enabling the View Chart button only if the app is online**

```
class ListView implements View {
  // snip other properties and methods

  _getChartButton() {
    ButtonElement chartButton = new Element.tag("button");
    chartButton.text = "Chart";
    chartButton.on.click.add( (e) {
      navigate(ViewType.CHART, null);
    });
```

```
    if (window.navigator.onLine == false) {        Disables UI features
      chartButton.disabled = true;                 if browser is offline
    }

    return chartButton;
  }
}
```

By enabling and disabling features depending on whether the browser is online and combining this method with the NETWORK section in the AppCache file, you can progressively fall back from an online state to an offline state. This is further improved with the third section in the AppCache file, FALLBACK.

FALL BACK TO AN OFFLINE FILE WHEN THE ONLINE VERSION ISN'T AVAILABLE

Whereas with files and URLs listed in the NETWORK section you need to explicitly check whether the app is online, files and URLs listed in the FALLBACK section provide an elegant solution for returning an offline version of a file only if the online version isn't available. That offline version might contain dummy data, or it might contain a state your app can use to determine that the data isn't available. In DartExpense, when you convert from USD to GBP, you call out to an external API to retrieve exchange rates as JSON. You can provide an offline fallback set of exchange rates by using the FALLBACK section to list first the real URL and then the fallback file that will be cached offline, as shown here:

```
FALLBACK:
http://openexcahngerates.org/api/latest.json /offline.json
```

This offline file could indicate exchange rates rather than the most current version. You can modify the DartExpense app accordingly to inform the user, as shown in listing 12.9. Here you modify the convertButton handler you saw earlier to request exchange rate data, but the updated version alerts the user that the data may be out of date and they should go online to get up-to-date data. This is possible because, instead of getting an error when requesting data from an external server, AppCache transparently returns the offline.json version of the exchange rates.

Listing 12.9   ui_edit.dart

```
//snip other parts of class EditView

convertButton.on.click.add( (e) {
    InputElement amountEl = document.query("#expenseAmount");
    var dollarValue = double.parse(amountEl.value);

    ScriptElement scriptElement = new Element.tag("script");
    scriptElement.src =
    "http://openexchangerates.org/api/latest.json?callback=onDataLoaded";
    scriptElement.type = "text/javascript";       Bypasses cache when
    document.head.children.add(scriptElement);     online but falls back to
    scriptElement.remove();                        cached file offline.json

    onRateListener(event) {
      var data = JSON.parse(event.data);
```

```
if (data["type"] == "js2dart" && data["action"] == "exchangeRates")
{
  window.on.message.remove(onRateListener);

  var payload = data["payload"];
  var gbpRate = payload["rates"]["GBP"];
  var gbpValue = dollarValue * gbpRate;
  amountEl.value = gbpValue.toStringAsFixed(2);
  if (window.navigator.onLine == false) {
    window.alert("Please go online to get up to date rates");
  }
}
};

window.on.message.add(onRateListener);
});
```

You can perform this check because the call for online data works even when offline.

These three parts give your app a combination of resources that are always cached offline, never cached offline, or available when online but fall back to cache when offline. By using these three sections in the AppCache, your app can maintain its usefulness to your users as they transition between online and offline states.

The last step in the process is to turn your app from a URL result in a search engine into an application your users can install in Google Chrome.

12.3.2 *Packaging your app as a Chrome web app*

Packaging your app as a Chrome app provides a number of benefits to you as an app developer by loosening browser restrictions, such as the 5 MB offline local storage restriction, and addressing the age-old problem: how to get users to use your app.

When you write an app and publish it on the web, you have to put a lot of effort into making sure users find it and return to it. Often, users will use an app a couple of times and then forget about it or forget the URL. When you provide users with an installable Chrome app, which is available via the Chrome Web Store, your app's name and icon are displayed in front of those users every time they create a new tab in Chrome, as shown in figure 12.12.

To install an app in Chrome, you need to use the JavaScript-converted version of the Dart app (until such time as mainstream Chrome supports Dart natively). In order to provide your app as an installable Chrome app, you must provide an additional file in the form of a Chrome manifest (rather than the AppCache manifest you saw earlier, but the two can work together if required) and a 128 x 128 pixel icon file.

The Chrome manifest is a JSON file called manifest.json that provides application configuration settings for Chrome. The manifest.json file contains three main sections: the application metadata, such as the name, description, and icon file; the URLs the app will access and be launched from; and a list of permissions the app requires. In the last chapter, we looked at storing data offline, and you saw that local storage is limited to 5 MB. When you create a Chrome app, one of the permissions you can request from the user is to have unlimited storage. This provides an extra benefit to the user in the form of being able to store significantly more data offline. Other permissions include

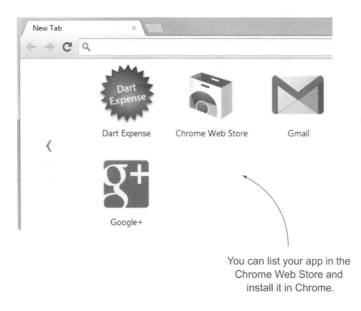

You can list your app in the
Chrome Web Store and
install it in Chrome.

**Figure 12.12   When a
user installs your app
in Chrome, the app
appears in front of the
user regularly.**

accessing browser history, the clipboard, and bookmarks. You can find the complete list
by searching for "Chrome Manifest Permissions." An example manifest.json file for
DartExpense (running locally) is shown in the following listing.

Listing 12.10   manifest.json: settings for creating an installable Chrome app

```
{
  "name": "Dart Expense",
  "description": "Track Expenses",          Application
  "version": "1",                           metadata
  "icons": {
    "128": "icon_128.png"
  },

  "app": {
    "urls": [
      "*://127.0.0.1/",
      "*://www.google.com",                 URLs the app
      "*://openexchangerates.org"           will access
    ],
    "launch": {                             URL to launch
      "web_url": "http://127.0.0.1:3030/DartExpense.html"    the app
    }
  },

  "permissions": [           Requested
    "unlimitedStorage"       permissions
  ]
}
```

Once you have your manifest.json file and your icon image, you need to place them in
the same folder as your other application files and install or package the app with
Google Chrome. An example file list could look like this:

```
c:\Projects\DartExpense\DartExpense.html
c:\Projects\DartExpense\DartExpense.dart.js
c:\Projects\DartExpense\DartExpense.css
c:\Projects\DartExpense\dart.js
c:\Projects\DartExpense\dartexpense.appcache
c:\Projects\DartExpense\manifest.json
c:\Projects\DartExpense\icon_128.png
```

Files that form your app

Optional AppCache manifest

Chrome app manifest

Chrome app icon

You now have two options. As a developer, you probably want to test that it works. Fortunately, Chrome provides a developer mode to install Chrome apps; but first you need to open the Chrome Extensions window, either from the menu or by navigating to chrome://chrome/extensions, where you'll see a Developer Mode check box (see figure 12.13). Selecting this box gives you two new options: Load Unpacked Extension and Pack Extension.

To test your app locally, click Load Unpacked Extension. This lets you add an app directly from a local folder, such as c:\Projects\DartExpense. When you're certain the app is working, you can use the Pack Extension option to convert your app folder into a Chrome crx (Chrome extension) file. This is the file you upload to the Chrome Web Store or host locally on your own servers. Each time you deploy a new version to the Web Store, you'll need to increase the version number in the manifest file—this lets apps know they need to update, perhaps because you've added a new icon or additional permissions.

Once your app is in the Web Store, Google provides tools to track and promote it, such as Google Analytics, Google Plus, and the opportunity to add screenshots and videos of your app in action. These are all designed to help users spread the word about how great your app is.

You can turn on developer mode...

...which gives you more options.

Figure 12.13 Developer mode provides more options for working with installable apps.

> **Remember**
> - AppCache lets your app run offline even when no server is available.
> - AppCache also provides a fallback option to use locally cached files when no online version is available.
> - Installable Chrome web apps ease browser restrictions and help users find and use your app.

12.4   Summary

In this chapter, you saw how Dart integrates outside of its own ecosystem by talking to JavaScript, running in a separate VM in the browser. You can communicate from Dart to JavaScript and JavaScript back to Dart by passing data from one VM to the other using the browser's `postMessage()` function.

Next, you saw how you can use JavaScript-to-Dart message passing to communicate outside of the Dart ecosystem to request data from external servers. To do so, you dynamically add a JavaScript `<script>` tag that retrieves data from a third-party API by wrapping it in a JavaScript function call. When the JavaScript receives the data, it sends that data back into the Dart app. This bypasses security restrictions imposed by the browser's `HttpRequest` for servers that don't yet support the new CORS headers.

Finally, you learned how the Dart ecosystem can be expanded from clients and servers to produce an offline, installable app that works even when the server isn't available—ideal for mobile and tablet devices. By providing an app that your users can install in their browser, you remove some of the browser permission restrictions, such as the 5 MB local storage restriction, and you also put your app in front of users every time they use the browser.

This is the last chapter in this section of the book. We've covered lots of topics, but HTML5 provides many more APIs to produce compelling business and leisure apps. Many books and examples on HTML5 are available on the web. Although many of the examples are in JavaScript rather than Dart, we hope you've gotten a sense in the last few chapters of how to access these APIs in Dart. Most examples map easily from JavaScript to Dart.

In the next section, you begin to work with Dart on the server side, looking at files and folders, serving HTTP and web sockets, and eventually hooking the DartExpense app to a database via a Dart server that both serves the DartExpense app's static files and provides a RESTful API for data transfer.

Part 4

Server-side Dart

In the last part of the book, you'll learn about building Dart on the server. Being able to use code in both the browser and the server can provide productivity boosts by reducing the amount of code you need to write and test.

Chapter 13 starts by showing how you can write simple server-side scripts that you can run from the command line. By running command-line Dart scripts, you'll learn how to use server-side APIs to access files and folders, and you'll see how to serve HTTP data to clients.

Chapter 14 picks up on serving HTTP data to serve and communicate with the client-side app from part 3 of the book. You'll learn how to use web sockets to provide two-way communication between the client and the server, sharing Dart code on both sides of the app. Chapter 14 also shows how you can use a server-side database to persist data sent from the browser client.

In the last chapter, chapter 15, you'll see how to use Dart's Isolate technology to achieve concurrency. Isolates let you use multiple processes running in the Dart virtual machine, similar to multithreading in server-side languages, but using a simpler message-passing mechanism. You'll also see how you can use Dart's Isolate architecture to load and run Dart code dynamically from a running Dart app, which is useful for developing plug-in architectures.

Server interaction
with files and HTTP

13

This chapter covers

- Running Dart scripts from the command line
- Interacting with the filesystem
- Serving content via HTTP

The Dart virtual machine is hosted in two different environments. In the previous part of the book, we looked at using Dart in the web browser, where the VM is embedded in the Dartium web browser and has access to the browser DOM via the `dart:html` library. In this chapter, we'll start to explore the server-side Dart VM, which doesn't have access to the browser DOM but instead has access to operating system I/O, such as files and network sockets via the `dart:io` library.

The Dart File Browser example project scenario for this chapter has a client-and-server solution that provides a browser-based text editor for editing Dart files, which we'll tackle in three steps starting with the server side. The server-side Dart VM is hosted in a command-line executable, available for Windows, Mac, and Linux. We'll begin by looking at how you can write a simple Dart script that interacts with the filesystem, passing command-line arguments to output a directory listing.

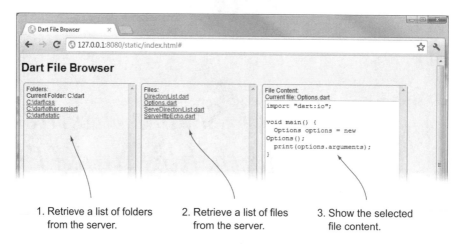

Figure 13.1   The client side of the Dart File Browser app

Next, we'll look at serving HTTP to react to HTTP requests from a web browser. We'll show you how to match URL request paths and serve static files from a server-side Dart application. This gives you the ability to develop a complete client-and-server solution in Dart.

Finally, we'll combine the HTTP server and directory-listing script to build a client-and-server application to serve the directory listing to the browser as JSON and let users browse the filesystem and read .dart files via a client-side web application.

At the end of this chapter, you'll have a client-and-server application that you can use to browse the local filesystem and load .dart files (or other text files) into the browser for viewing. Figure 13.1 shows the client-side part, which runs in the browser and communicates with a server-side Dart script.

But before you start getting fancy with the user interface, we need to look at the server part of the application and how you can interact with the computer's operating system to read files and folders from it.

13.1   *Running server-side Dart scripts*

The Dart File Browser server-side application runs as a Dart script, either from the command line or from the Dart Editor, and can output text to the console using the `print("")` command. In this section, you'll create a server-side script to output a file-and-directory listing for a given path provided as a parameter to the script. For example, the command

```
dart.exe DirectoryList.dart C:\Dart\
```

outputs the following:

```
<DIR>  c:\dart\css
<DIR>  c:\dart\other_project
<DIR>  c:\dart\static
```

```
<FILE> c:\dart\DirectoryList.dart
<FILE> c:\dart\Options.dart
... etc...
```

When you use the Dart Editor to create a new project, you get the option to create either a web application or a command-line application. Up to this point, you've been using the web-application option, which creates a .html file and a linked .dart file. But a command-line application doesn't have an HTML component, so it only requires the .dart file.

A Dart script that runs on the command line is known as a *server-side script*. It's the same as a Dart script on the client side in that it's a .dart file containing a `main()` function, which is the function that executes first. As with client-side scripts, the server-side Dart script can also be a library, can import other libraries, and has an event loop, just like browser-based scripts, as shown in figure 13.2.

Figure 13.3 shows a simple server-side script running in the Dart Editor and from the command line. The Dart Editor uses the Dart VM executable you'll find in the Dart SDK when you run a script, and the output is shown in the Dart Editor's console. When you run a script from the command line, you see the output in the command-line output.

> **TIP** The Dart Editor, available free from dartlang.org, provides you with all the tools required to run and debug server-side scripts. This chapter assumes you're using the Dart Editor, but you can equally run server-side scripts from the Dart executable file, available in the bin/ folder of the Dart SDK download.

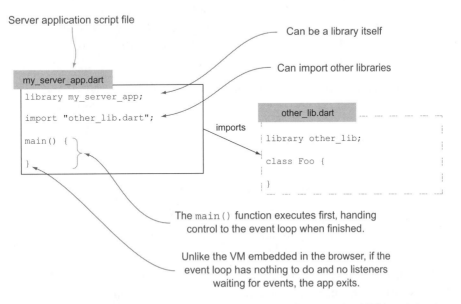

Figure 13.2 Dart scripts running from the command line have the same capabilities and structure as client-side scripts.

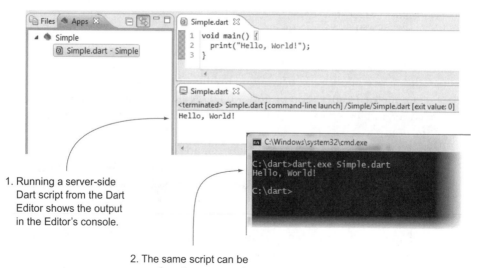

1. Running a server-side Dart script from the Dart Editor shows the output in the Editor's console.

2. The same script can be run from the command line using the Dart binary.

Figure 13.3   Running a simple server-side script

The big difference between client-side scripts and server-side scripts is the hosting environment. Client-side scripts run in a web-browser-hosted VM and have access to the browser DOM. This allows them to import the `dart:html` library. Server-side scripts don't exist in a web browser, and you'll get an error if you try to use the `dart:html` library on the server side. But server-side scripts do get access to the `dart:io` library, which provides classes and functions for accessing the filesystem, serving HTTP and web sockets, and communicating across the network with network sockets. Table 13.1 summarizes the differences.

Table 13.1   Summary of the differences between the `dart:html` and `dart:io` libraries

`dart:html`: Browser only	`dart:io`: Server only
Manipulates browser DOM elements	Accesses OS files and folders
Attaches events to the browser	Starts other executables in the OS
Accesses browser storage APIs	Makes `HttpClient` connections to other web servers
Performs AJAX requests with `HttpRequest`	Serves HTTP requests and web sockets
Renders on the browser user interface	Communicates via sockets

One other difference between client-side and server-side scripts is that server-side scripts can access the command-line arguments passed into the script. In order to let your server-side Dart directory-listing application list a specific directory, let's look at how to access those arguments.

> ### Event loop differences between client and server
>
> In previous chapters, we've looked at the Dart event loop. When a Dart script runs in the browser, you can start with the `main()` function, build a user interface, attach event handlers, and, finally, pass control to the event loop. When the event loop receives an event from an external source, such as a button click, the event loop calls back to your application's code, which lets the application respond. This continues until the application is shut down by either closing the tab or navigating away.
>
> On the server side, this is slightly different. You still have an event loop, and as you'll see a little later in the chapter, it's still possible to hook up event handlers and pass control to an event loop. The difference, though, is that Dart scripts exit when there are no event handlers listening for events to complete. This means that a simple script such as the "Hello World" example in figure 13.3 will exit immediately once it's finished running. The equivalent code in the browser would instead return control to the event loop hosted in the browser's Dart VM.

13.1.1 Accessing command-line arguments

Dart provides the `Options` type to access command-line arguments. Creating an instance of `Options` with the `new` keyword gives you a fully populated object containing the path to the current Dart executable binary, the script file containing the `main()` function, and a list containing the arguments passed on the command line. Listing 13.1, which prints the following output to the console when run with the command, shows a simple Dart script to output the command-line arguments and information about the executing script:

```
>dart.exe TryOptions.dart hello world
C:\dart-sdk\bin\dart.exe
C:\dart\TryOptions.dart
2
[hello, world]
```

Listing 13.1 Accessing command-line options

```
void main() {
  Options options = new Options();      <--- Creates new instance of Options

  print(options.executable);            Accesses Dart executable
  print(options.script);                path and script file path

  List<String> args = options.arguments;    Accesses command-
  print(args.length);                       line arguments
  print(args);
}
```

In the Dart Editor, you pass command-line arguments to the command-line script using the Run > Manage Launches dialog, shown in figure 13.4, which passes the two arguments `hello` and `world` into the script.

When you run command-line scripts from the Dart Editor, the output from `print("")` commands appears in the Dart Editor's console.

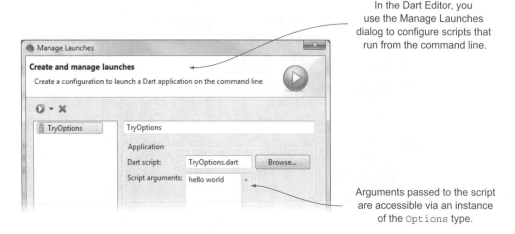

In the Dart Editor, you use the Manage Launches dialog to configure scripts that run from the command line.

Arguments passed to the script are accessible via an instance of the Options type.

Figure 13.4   Passing arguments to the command line in the Dart Editor

Now that you can access command-line arguments in your script, it's time to use them in the Dart File Browser application, which will output a list of files and folders. To do this, you also need to start using some of the types provided in the server-side dart:io library.

13.1.2 *Accessing files and folders with dart:io*

The Dart File Browser server-side application will have two features available from the command line. If you pass in the command-line argument --list option, followed by a path, you'll output to the console a list of files and folders in that path.

If, instead, you pass in the --out command followed by a filename, you'll read that file and output it to the console. Listing 13.2 shows the starting-point code for the Dart File Browser application, which outputs the two command-line options if no arguments are passed into the application. You also import the dart:io library, which contains the File and Directory types you'll be using as you add functionality to the listDir() and outputFile() functions in following listings.

Listing 13.2   Display the command-line options if none are provided

```
import "dart:io";              ⟵── Imports server-side dart:io library

void main() {
  Options options = new Options();

  if (options.arguments.length != 2) {
    printHelp();
  }
  else if (options.argments[0] == '--list') {
    listDir(options.arguments[1]);
  }
  else if (options.argments[0] == '--out') {
    outputFile(options.arguments[1]);
```

Creates options to access command-line args

If two args weren't passed, prints help message

If first arg is --list, passes second arg to listDir()

If first arg is --out, passes second arg to outputFile()

```
    }
  }
printHelp() {
  print("""
Dart Directory Lister. Usage:
  List files and directories: --list DIR
  Output file to console    : --out FILE""");
}

listDir(String folderPath) {

}

outputFile(String filePath) {

}
```

> Outputs usage text to console using multiline string syntax

> You'll implement these functions over the next few sections.

In DirectoryList.dart, you need to implement two functions: `listDir(folderPath)` outputs a list of child files and folders in the directory specified by `folderPath`, and `outputFile(filePath)` reads the file specified by the `filePath` parameter. In these functions, you'll use the `File` and `Directory` types.

LISTING FILES AND FOLDERS WITH A DIRECTORYLISTER

The first use case is to provide arguments such as `--list c:\dart` to your DirectoryList.dart script. The first argument determines that you're in list mode, and the second argument provides the `folderPath` for your script to output the contents.

The `Directory` type provides a number of methods that are also common to the `File` type, such as `exists()`, `create()`, and `delete()`. The `Directory` type also provides a `list()` function that returns a `DirectoryLister`, which you'll use to provide a file and folder listing. `DirectoryLister` provides asynchronous access to return a list of files and folders in a specific directory.

The filesystem I/O types provide both synchronous and asynchronous access to the filesystem, with a preference for async operations. Whereas the library provides both async and sync methods, the async option is the default, with the sync version of the method having a sync suffix, as in `Directory.exists()` and `Directory.existsSync()`.

Sync vs. async methods

In a script such as DirectoryList.dart, using the async or sync version of file and directory access methods has subtle differences. With the sync version of a method, such as `existsSync()`, the application will wait, blocked until the filesystem responds. When the filesystem responds, `existsSync()` returns a `true/false` value, and the application continues running.

With the async version, a `Future<bool>` value is returned, and the application continues to run without waiting for the filesystem. The future value is populated once the filesystem responds.

(continued)
The subtle difference has little impact in a script such as DirectoryList.dart, because nothing else happens in the application either way the "exists" value is determined. Despite that, the following examples use the async versions, because this difference will begin to have an impact when you start serving HTTP requests to send directory listings to the browser. If you were using blocking, synchronous method calls, a second browser request would be blocked by a first request waiting for the filesystem to respond. In order to scale to hundreds or even thousands of requests, you need to ensure that your code uses nonblocking, asynchronous I/O calls. The sync methods are great for quick, simple scripts, but for scalability, we recommend that you use the async versions.

For a recap of the difference between blocking and nonblocking, check out the discussion in chapter 9.

Async calls that expect to return a single value, such as `exists()`, return a `Future` whose value is populated in its `then()` callback function. Method calls that return multiple values, such as a list of files and folders in a directory, provide methods that are assigned a callback function that's called as each entry in the list is returned. This lets you begin outputting data to the console while the filesystem is still in the process of returning data to your application.

The `exists()` function and the `DirectoryLister` type are shown in figure 13.5, which demonstrates how to open a folder and list the files and directories in it. This provides the implementation for the `listDir(folderPath)` function in the DirectoryList.dart script.

If you start the application by passing in the arguments `--list c:\dart`, it will output a list of files and folders in the c:\dart folder, as you were expecting earlier in the chapter:

```
<DIR>  c:\dart\css
<DIR>  c:\dart\other_project
<DIR>  c:\dart\static
<FILE> c:\dart\DirectoryList.dart
<FILE> c:\dart\Options.dart
```

> **NOTE** The example paths are shown on the Windows operating system, but they're equally applicable for Mac or Linux systems. Try replacing `c:\dart` with `~/dart` to list the contents of a dart folder in your home directory.

Now that your application can return a list of files in a directory by using the `Directory` and `DirectoryLister` types, let's see how to use the `File` type to read the contents of a file in an asynchronous manner.

READING FILES WITH THE FILE TYPE
The second use case for the `DirectoryLister` script outputs the contents of the file when its name is passed as an argument along with the `--out` parameter, such as

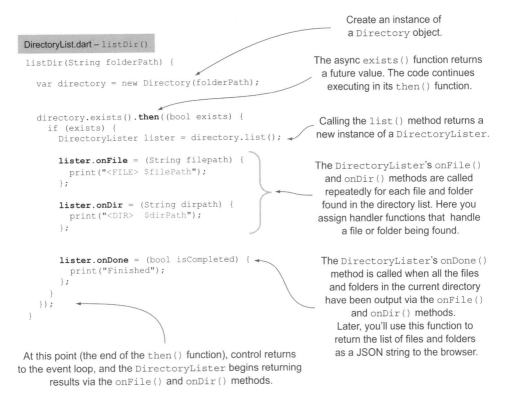

Figure 13.5　The `listDir()` function uses the async `exists()` function and a `DirectoryLister` to return the list of files and folders in a directory.

`--out c:\dart\TryOptions.dart`. This command should read the contents of the file and print it back out on the console, and for this you use the `File` type.

Like the `Directory` type, the `File` type also offers sync and async API methods, such as `readAsString()` and `readAsStringSync()`. The async version returns a `Future<String>` containing the file content and uses nonblocking I/O, whereas the sync version will block but returns a `String` value containing the file content. You can use the async `readAsString()` method, as shown in the following snippet:

```
outputFile(String filePath) {                          Creates new file
  File file = new File(filePath);                       object from path
  file.readAsString().then((content) {              Reads contents of that file
    print(content);                       Prints complete contents
  });                                     when Future completes
}
```

This asynchronously reads c:\dart\TryOptions.dart. Once all the data has been read and returned from the filesystem, the `Future` value is populated, passing the complete content of the file into the `Future`'s `then()` callback function.

Behind the `readAsString()` method, `File` uses an `InputStream` type, which returns sequential data in a buffered, nonblocking fashion. The data returned by the

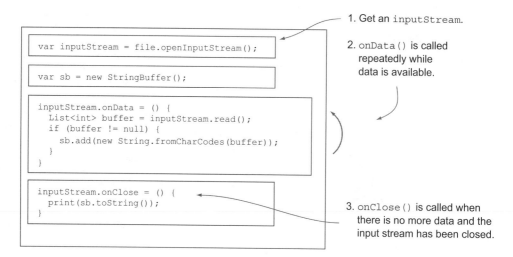

Figure 13.6 Reading data from a file's InputStream

InputStream's read() method is a List<int>, but it represents an array of bytes, each byte representing a single byte in the TryOptions.dart file.

NOTE Dart doesn't have different numeric types, such as byte, word, and long. Instead, it has a parent type of num and two child types: int and double.

The String type provides a utility constructor called String.fromCharCodes() that allows you to create a new String object from a List<int>.

Listing 13.3 uses an InputStream to implement the outputFile() function. The InputStream's onData() method is called repeatedly when data is available; you access that data by calling the InputStream's read() function, which may return data or may return null if no more data is available, as shown in figure 13.6.

When no more data is available, the onClosed() method is called, allowing you to output the complete data to the console. You use a StringBuffer type to store the multiple strings created by each call to onData(). The contents of the StringBuffer's internal list of strings is efficiently converted into a single string when you call the StringBuffer's toString() function. The following listing uses a file's InputStream in the outputFile() function and also contains the existing listDir() function you saw earlier in the chapter, for completeness.

Listing 13.3 Implementing outputFile() with an InputStream

```
//...snip other methods...

outputFile(String filePath) {                          Creates new
  File file = new File(filePath);                       instance of
  file.exists().then((exists) {                         file object
    if (exists) {
      InputStream inputStream = file.openInputStream();  Gets
                                                         InputStream
                                                         for file
```

```
        StringBuffer sb = new StringBuffer();          ◁──  Creates stringBuffer
        inputStream.onData = () {                            to hold file data
          List<int> data = inputStream.read();        ◁──  In onData handler, reads
                                                             available data from InputStream
          if (data != null) {
            sb.add(new String.fromCharCodes(data));  ◁──  Creates new string
          }                                                 from List<int>
        };

        inputStream.onClosed = () {
          print(sb.toString());                       ◁──  When InputStream is closed,
        };                                                  prints string from buffer

      }

    });
}

listDir(String folderPath) {
  var directory = new Directory(folderPath);
  directory.exists().then((bool exists) {
    DirectoryLister lister = directory.list();

    lister.onDir = (dirPath) {
      print("<DIR>  $dirPath");
    };/

    lister.onFile = (filePath) {
      print("<FILE> $filePath");
    };

    lister.onDone = (completed) {
      print("Finished");
    };
  });
}
```

USING AN OUTPUTSTREAM TO WRITE FILE DATA

You can also use the OutputStream type to easily write data to a file. Data is retrieved from an instance of File and provides write(List<int> buffer) and writeString (String string) functions to provide nonblocking writes to the underlying filesystem. Once all the data has been written (using one or more calls to one of the write() methods), you use the close() function to indicate that all the data has been sent.

Although not required for your Dart File Browser application, the following snippet shows how you can create a new file and write data to it:

```
new File("example.txt").create().then((File newFile) {     ◁──  Creates
  OutputStream stream = newFile.openOutputStream();              example.txt
                                                          ◁──  Gets OutputStream
  stream.writeString("test");                             ◁──  Writes some text

  List<int> buffer = "some more data".charCodes();        ◁──  Gets more text as a list<int>
  stream.write(buffer);                                   ◁──  Writes buffered text

  str.close();                                            ◁──  Closes input stream
});
```

Although the underlying system behind the output stream takes the data as fast as it can, the data being written is buffered internally, if required. The `write()` functions return a `bool` value indicating whether this buffering is taking place.

The `File` and `Directory` types provide all the standard mechanisms for interacting with the filesystem in an efficient, nonblocking manner by using underlying input and output streams. We've covered a lot in this section, from reading arguments from the command line to accessing files and folders and looking at async methods for nonblocking I/O.

In the next section, you'll start to send and receive HTTP data to allow communication with a web browser, which also uses input and output streams. We'll also show you how to send data directly from one `InputStream` into another `OutputStream`, known as `piping`.

> **Remember**
> - Dart scripts can access command-line arguments using an instance of `Options`.
> - The `dart:io` library can only be used on server-side command-line applications; the `dart:html` library is only available in a browser-hosted VM.
> - Methods ending with the `sync` suffix block the application flow, whereas async method calls are nonblocking and return `Future` values.
> - Input and output streams are also nonblocking and provide a buffered mechanism to read and write data.

13.2 *Serving browser HTTP requests*

Although the Dart File Browser application is great as a command-line application and can output file and folder information to the command line, it would be even better as a web application, able to send file and folder information to multiple web browsers and other HTTP clients. In the next section, you'll use Dart to build a RESTful API to send file and folder information to the web browser.

> **RESTful APIs**
>
> REST stands for Representational State Transfer, which is one model to use when designing web services. It uses HTTP verbs such as `GET` and `POST` to describe the request method and URL paths to represent functions for resource transfer.
>
> For example, performing a `GET` request to http://localhost:8080/folderList/c:/dart could be a valid API call to retrieve a folder list. The folder list is the resource being transferred. On the server this could call a function such as
>
> ```
> getFolderListAsJson("c:/dart")
> ```
> returning the folder list as a JSON-formatted object.
>
> Many good resources are available that describe the architecture of REST, and you should refer to them if you're not familiar with at least the basics.

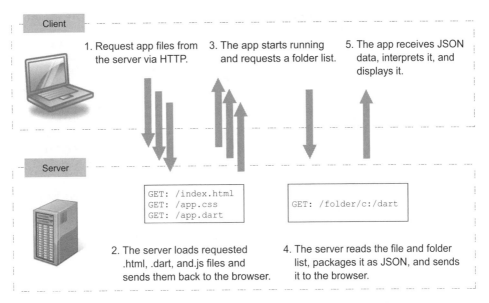

Figure 13.7 The flow of requests between the client and server parts of the application

Your Dart script is going to change, too, from a script that runs and exits to one that continues running until you forcibly kill it. This is because the HttpServer type that comes in the dart:io library reintroduces the event loop when it starts listening for HTTP requests.

You'll make your new client-and-server Dart File Browser application from two Dart applications. First, you'll create the server-side application, which is jointly responsible for serving the files that make up the client application and responding to requests from the client application. Second, you'll create the client application that, once served, makes requests back to the server to load file and folder lists. The flow is shown in figure 13.7.

This is where nonblocking I/O comes into its own. By using async APIs to ensure that the server part of the application doesn't block, control returns to the event loop as fast as possible, allowing the server to handle other requests before the first has completed.

13.2.1 *Using the Dart HttpServer*

The dart:io library provides three key classes that you'll use when serving HTTP requests: HttpServer, which provides handlers that are triggered when a request is received; HttpRequest, which represents the incoming data; and HttpResponse, which represents the outgoing data. Table 13.2 lists some of the common properties and methods for these types.

The HttpServer class receives requests, tries to match a request handler by calling all the assigned matcher functions until one is found, and finally calls the default request handler if no others match. You can try this with a small amount of code,

Table 13.2 Common methods and properties of the key classes that serve HTTP requests

Class	Method or property	Description
HttpServer		Used to serve HTTP requests.
	addRequestHandler (matcher, handler)	Takes two functions: a matcher with the signature `bool matcher(HttpRequest req)` and a handler with the signature `void handler(HttpRequest req, HttpResponse res)` If the matcher returns `true`, then the handler is called to handle the request.
	defaultRequestHandler (handler)	Takes a single handler function, which is called if no other request handler has handled the request. If no default request handler is specified, the server returns a 404 (not found) error status.
	listen(String host, int port)	Starts the server listening on a specific host and port.
HttpRequest		Contains data sent from the browser.
	String method	The request method, such as GET, POST, or PUT.
	String path	The path part of the URI, such as /file/C:/dart from a request for http://localhost/file/C:/dart.
	String queryString	The query string part of the URI, such as `key=value` from a request for `http://localhost/file?key=value`.
	Map queryParameters	A map containing a list of key/value pairs from the query string.
	InputStream inputStream	Any incoming data on the request.
HttpResponse		Contains data sent to the browser.
	HttpHeaders headers	Used to set any headers sent to the browser, such as content type.
	OutputStream outputStream	Used to send data to the browser.

shown in listing 13.4, which looks for a GET: /echo/ request and returns the method and path properties of the request to the browser. If none are found, it returns the string "Hello World." Figure 13.8 shows the browser response for two sample URLs.

Matches method=GET, and path starts with /echo/

Doesn't match, so returns Hello World

Figure 13.8 The output you expect from your server

Listing 13.4 shows the complete code to return this data. Once you call `HttpServer`'s `listen()` function, the event loop gains control and calls back into the matcher and handler functions when a browser request occurs to the correct *host:port* combination. The examples that follow use port 8080, but you can replace it with another port that's valid for your machine if 8080 is already in use.

Listing 13.4 Serving simple `HttpRequests` from Dart

```
import "dart:io";

main() {
  HttpServer server = new HttpServer();          // Creates server instance

  server.addRequestHandler(
    (HttpRequest req) => req.path.startsWith("/echo/"),    // Matcher that returns true if request starts with /echo/
    (HttpRequest req,HttpResponse res) {                    // Handler: returns a simple string
      var method = req.method;
      var path = req.path;
      res.outputStream.writeString("Echo: $method $path");  // Closes output stream when you finish adding data
      res.outputStream.close();
    }
  );

  server.defaultRequestHandler = (HttpRequest req, HttpResponse res) {   // Default handler: called if no others match
    res.outputStream.writeString("Hello World");
    res.outputStream.close();
  };

  server.listen("127.0.0.1", 8080);     // Starts server listening on specific IP host and port
  print("Listening...");
}
```

Now that you've seen how to respond to browser HTTP requests, let's look at how you use this technique to send static files to the browser.

13.2.2 Serving static files over HTTP

To form the basis of your Dart File Browser server-side application, you need to use `HttpServer` to send the files that make up the client-side application to the browser. These include the .html, .css, and .dart or .js JavaScript files containing your browser application's application code. In the previous section, we covered how to read files from the filesystem with an input stream—the `HttpResponse` object requires an output stream to send data back to the browser. Fortunately, Dart provides a function called `pipe()` that allows you to send the data read from one `InputStream` directly into another `OutputStream`, closing the output stream when all the data is transferred. You'll use this mechanism to serve files to the browser.

The server application includes the following files, which contain the client application in a client subfolder:

```
c:\DirectoryServer
                \ServerApp.dart
                \client
                        \index.html
```

```
\ClientApp.css
\ClientApp.dart
\ClientApp.dart.js
```

To send the correct files requested from the browser, you need to use the `HttpRequest.path` property. In order to achieve this, you'll create a matcher and a handler class that are responsible for handling your static file requests by checking to see if the requested file ends with one of the four file extensions you're expecting: .html, .dart, .css, or .js. Listing 13.5 shows the `StaticFileHandler` class and its use in `HttpServer`. The matcher function returns `true` if the request is for one of your four file types. The handler gets the requested filename, appends it to the ./client subfolder, and pipes the file's `InputStream` directly to the response's `OutputStream`. Note that you don't have a `close` command to close the output stream—the `pipe()` method does this for you.

Listing 13.5   Serving static files

```dart
import "dart:io";

class StaticFileHandler {
  bool matcher(HttpRequest req) {                   // Matcher function:
    return req.path.endsWith(".html") ||            // returns true if
      req.path.endsWith(".dart") ||                 // requested path
      req.path.endsWith(".css") ||                  // ends with correct
      req.path.endsWith(".js");                      // file extension
  }

  void handler(HttpRequest req, HttpResponse res) {  // Handler function called
                                                     // if matcher matches
    var requestedFile = "./client${req.path}";       // Gets relative filename
    File file = new File(requestedFile);             // for requested file in a
    file.openInputStream.pipe(res.outputStream);     // ./client subfolder
  }                                                  // Opens file
}                                  // Pipes file's input stream into
                                   // response's output stream
main() {
  var server = new HttpServer();

  var staticFiles = new StaticFileHandler();         // Creates static file-
                                                     // handler instance
  server.addRequestHandler(staticFiles.matcher, staticFiles.handler);

  server.listen("127.0.0.1",8080);                   // Passes matcher and handler
  print("Listening...");                             // methods as arguments
}
```

This is a trivial example, and any real `HttpServer` should provide extra functionality such as error-handling and security. At the moment, if you request a file that doesn't exist, the server will crash (you need to use `file.exists()`). And if you provide a request such as `http://localhost:8080/../../someOtherFolder/someFile.txt`, you can navigate to other files and folders on the same machine.

Now that the Dart File Browser server-side application can send the client-side application to the browser, you'll build a RESTful API to send your folder and file list formatted as JSON.

Remember
- Dart's `HttpServer` listens for HTTP requests on a specific host and port.
- A pair of matcher and handler functions is required to handle a specific HTTP request, added with a call to `addRequestHandler()`.
- `defaultRequestHandler()` is called if no other handlers have matched.

13.3 *Serving clients with a RESTful API*

You now have enough information to combine the HTTP server code with the directory listing code from earlier in the chapter. You want to take a GET request for a specific folder on your local disk and send a list of files and folders in the requested folder. You'll use `DirectoryLister`'s `onDir()` and `onFile()` functions to build two lists, and you'll combine these using the `dart:json` library. The `dart:json` library is a good example of code that's shared between the client and the server; it contains identical code that runs in both places.

You also want to be able to send the contents of a specific file to the browser; but instead of serving the file to the browser as a native file, this time you'll wrap the file's content as JSON data. This gives you two API calls that your application needs to support, shown in figure 13.9.

In order to achieve this, you'll have three request handlers: one to serve the static client-side application files, one to serve the folder list, and one to serve the file content. You'll use the `StaticFileHandler` class you've already seen, along with two new classes: `FolderListHandler` and `FileContentHandler`. Figure 13.10 shows the `ServerApp` outline code and how to use these classes.

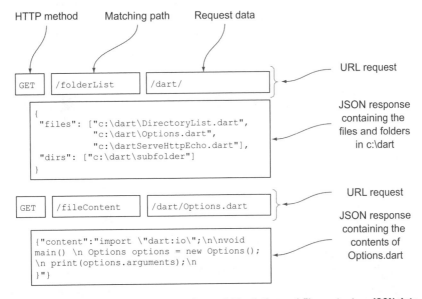

Figure 13.9   The two API calls to retrieve a folder listing and file content as JSON data

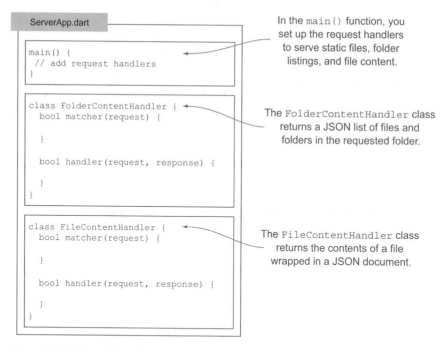

Figure 13.10 The outline of `ServerApp`

The `main()` method using these classes is shown in listing 13.6. The listing also contains a utility function called `addHeaders()`. It adds two important headers to your application, allowing you to use the Dart Editor's client-side debugger when you build the UI. Web browsers come with a security feature to prevent `HttpRequests` (AJAX requests) from accessing data on a different URL than the rendered HTML file. These two headers tell the browser that, in this instance, it's valid to accept the script from a different URL. For more information, search the web for information about cross-origin resource sharing (CORS).

Listing 13.6 Updated `main()` function using all three handler classes

```
import "dart:io";
import "dart:json";                                    Imports dart:json
                                                       library, server side
main() {
  HttpServer server = new HttpServer();

  var staticFile = new StaticFileHandler();                          Wires
  var folderList = new FolderListHandler();      Creates instances    up
  var fileContent = new FileContentHandler();    of handler classes  server
                                                                     handlers
  server.addRequestHandler(staticFile.matcher, staticFile.handler);
  server.addRequestHandler(folderList.matcher, folderList.handler);
  server.addRequestHandler(fileContent.matcher, fileContent.handler);

  server.listen("127.0.0.1",8080);          Starts server listening for requests
```

```
        print("Listening... on 127.0.0.1:8080");
}
```
Utility function: prevents browser from blocking AJAX requests
```
addHeaders(res) {
    res.headers.add("Access-Control-Allow-Origin", "http://localhost/*");
    res.headers.add("Access-Control-Allow-Credentials", true);
}
```

The `main()` function is fairly straightforward. Adding extra handlers would mean creating more handler classes. For the moment, all of these classes are in the same file, but in a large project you'd split the handlers among multiple libraries.

Next, you'll send your file and folder list as JSON data with the `FolderListHandler` class.

13.3.1 Sending a directory list as JSON data

The `FolderListHandler` class provides two methods: `matcher()` and `handler()`. The `matcher()` method returns `true` if the request is a `GET` request, and it has a `path` that starts with a `/folderList` prefix. When `matcher()` returns `true`, the associated `handler()` function is called, and you can extract the request data from the request path. The request data follows the `/folderList` prefix on the path, so you'll use the core library `subString()` function to remove the `/folderList` part from the path and extract the folder name to list.

Once you have the folder name, you'll use the `Directory` and `DirectoryLister` classes that you used earlier in the chapter. As you receive file and folder names, you'll add them to two separate lists; and in the `DirectoryLister`'s `onDone()` function, you'll put these two lists into a map and convert the map to a JSON string. You're only interested in showing .dart files in the file list, so you'll ignore any others.

Finally, you'll send that JSON string to the `HttpResponse`'s output stream and close the output stream. Let's look at the code, shown in the following listing.

Listing 13.7 Implementing the `FolderListHandler` class

```
...snip main() and other functions...

class FolderListHandler {

    bool matcher(HttpRequest req) {
        return req.path.startsWith("/folderList")                  Returns true if path and
                && req.method == "GET";                             method are correct
    }

    void handler(HttpRequest req, HttpResponse res) {              Handler function: adds
        addHeaders(res);                                           CORS headers to response

        var folder = req.path.substring('/folderList'.length);     Gets DirectoryLister
        DirectoryLister lister = new Directory(folder).list();     for requested folder

        List<String> dirList = new List<String>();                 Creates empty lists for
        List<String> fileList = new List<String>();                file and folder names

        lister.onDir = (dirName) {                                 Handles folder
            dirList.add(dirName);                                  names
```

```
    };

    lister.onFile = (fileName) {
      if (file.endsWith(".dart")) {          Handles filenames, only
        fileList.add(fileName);              adding .dart files
      }
    };

    lister.onDone = (done) {                 When all file and
      var resultMap = new Map<String,List>();  folder names have
      resultMap["files"] = fileList;         been retrieved ...
      resultMap["dirs"] = dirList;
      var jsonString = JSON.stringify(resultMap);   ... converts map of
                                                     file and folder names
      res.outputStream.writeString(jsonString);     to JSON string
      res.outputStream.close();              Sends string to browser
    };                                       and closes stream
  }

}
```

If you start running the server, you can browse to a URL such as http://local-host:8080/folderList/dart, and it will return all the files and folders formatted as JSON in the c:\dart folder, as you can see in figure 13.11.

Requested URL

JSON representation
of the file list

Figure 13.11   Returning JSON data from the server API

13.3.2 *Sending the file content as JSON data*

The file content is equally similar to the DirectoryLister command-line application that you built earlier in the chapter. You use the FileContentHandler class to match on a path prefix of /fileContent, extract the filename that follows, read the file's content as text, and return the text wrapped as a JSON string.

A URL such as http://localhost:8080/fileContent/dart/Options.dart will return the contents of the Options.dart file wrapped as JSON data. The FileContentHandler class is shown next.

Listing 13.8   Sending data to the browser with `FileContentHandler`

```
...snip main() and other functions...

class FileContentHandler {
```

```
bool matcher(HttpRequest req) {
  return req.path.startsWith("/fileContent")
➡         && req.method == "GET";
}
void handler(HttpRequest req, HttpResponse res) {
  addHeaders(res);

  var filename = req.path.substring("/file".length);

  File file = new File(filename);

  file.readAsString().then((String fileContent) {
    var result = new Map<String,String>();
    result["content"] = fileContent;

    res.outputStream.writeString(JSON.stringify(result));
    res.outputStream.close();
  });
}

}
```

Matches on correct path and method

Extracts requested filename from path

◁— **Creates file object**

Reads text of file and content to a map

Converts map to JSON and sends it to the browser

You've finished the server-side part of the application. It can respond to requests for files and folders and request specific file content. Next, you'll add a simple client-side user interface that will be served by, and interact with, your server.

13.3.3 Adding the client-side user interface

The client-side part of the Dart File Browser application loads into the browser and uses the HttpRequest that we covered in the previous section to make asynchronous requests to the server's REST API for data. When the browser receives data from the server, the user interface is updated. The key actions are shown in figure 13.12.

1. GET .html, .dart, and .css files from the server.

2. Use GET /folderList to return a list of files and folders.

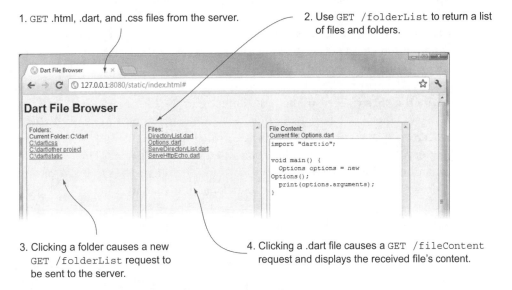

3. Clicking a folder causes a new GET /folderList request to be sent to the server.

4. Clicking a .dart file causes a GET /fileContent request and displays the received file's content.

Figure 13.12 The main actions of the client-side application request data from the server and render it in the user interface.

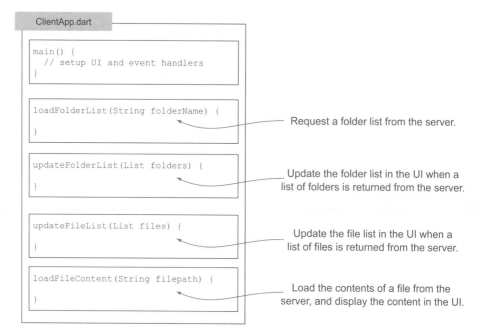

Figure 13.13 The outline of the `ClientApp` code

Because the browser is a single-page web application and doesn't transition between different physical web pages, you need to manage the browser navigation history yourself by using the pushState() and popState() functions (covered in chapter 11). Listing 13.8 shows the complete client-side application's Dart code: the navigate() function is responsible for adding browser navigation history with pushState(), and the popState() handler is declared in main() and is responsible for the browser's back button click. This is the same thing you saw in the DartExpense example earlier in the book, but the code is now served from server-side Dart and talks to your server's REST API by using GET requests. Like the outline of the server-side code shown previously, the ClientApp's outline is shown in figure 13.13.

The other key functions in the client-side code (shown in listing 13.9) are load-FolderList() and loadFileContent(), which perform the GET HttpRequests to your server API to update the user interface when the data is loaded. The loadFolderList() function is called when you navigate to a different folder. The loadFileContent() function is called when you click a specific filename to load it.

Listing 13.9 The client-side part of the Dart File Browser application

```
import "dart:html";
import "dart:json";

main() {
  window.on.popState.add((data) => loadFolderList(data.state));
  navigate("/");
```

Hooks up popState() handler
for back button navigation

◁── **Navigates to root folder**

```
  }
navigate(String folderName) {
  loadFolderList(folderName);
  window.history.pushState(folderName, folderName,"#$folderName");
}
loadFolderList(String folderName) {
  document.query("#currentFolder").innerHTML = "Current: $folderName";
  var url = "http://127.0.0.1:8080/folder$folderName";

  new HttpRequest.get(url, (response) {
    var jsonData = response.responseText;
    Map result = JSON.parse(jsonData);

    updateFolderList(result["dirs"]);
    updateFileList(result["files"]);
  });
}

updateFolderList(List folders) {
  var content = document.query("#folderList");
  content.children.clear();

  for(String dirName in folders) {
    var link = new Element.html("<div><a href='#'>$dirName</a></div>");
    link.on.click.add((e) => navigate(dirName));
    content.children.add(link);
  }
}

updateFileList(List files) {
  var content = document.query("#fileList");
  content.children.clear();

  for(String filepath in files) {
    var filename = filepath.substring(filepath.lastIndexOf('\\')+1);
    var link = new Element.html("<div><a href='#'>$filename</a></div>");
    link.on.click.add((e) => loadFileContent(filepath));
    content.children.add(link);
  }
}

loadFileContent(String filepath) {
  var filename = filepath.substring(filepath.lastIndexOf('\\')+1);
  document.query("#filename").innerHTML = "Current: $filename";

  var url = "http://127.0.0.1:8080/file$filepath";
  new HttpRequest.get(url, (response) {
    var contentText = JSON.parse(response.responseText)["content"];
    var content = document.query("#fileContent");
    content.innerHTML = contentText;
  });
}
```

Loads requested folder *(points to `loadFolderList(folderName);`)*

Adds requested folder onto browser history *(points to `window.history.pushState`)*

Updates UI and builds request URL

Loads file and folder list data from server

Uses returned file and folder lists to update UI

Gets folderList <div> and adds each folder to it

When a folder name is clicked, calls navigate()

Gets fileList <div> and adds each file to it

When a filename is clicked, calls loadFileContent()

Extracts filename and updates UI

Gets requested file data ...

... and displays it in fileContent text area

For completeness, the associated client-side HTML is shown in listing 13.10. You can add your own CSS styles to the application to lay it out as you wish or grab the CSS file from the source code website that accompanies this book. The HTML provides boilerplate

`<div>` elements to hold `folderList`, `fileList`, and `fileContent` and is served, along with the ClientApp.dart file, by the server-side part of the application.

Listing 13.10 Client HTML file hosting the client-side application

```
<!DOCTYPE html>

<html>
  <head>
    <meta charset="utf-8">
    <title>Static</title>
    <link rel="stylesheet" href="directoryList.css">
  </head>
  <body>
    <h2>Dart File Browser</h2>

    <div id="application">
      <div class="content">Folders: <br/>
        <span id="currentFolder">Current Folder:</span>        <div> for
        <div id="folderList" ></div>                           folder list
      </div>

      <div class="content">Files: <br/>                        <div> for
        <div id="fileList"></div>                              file list
      </div>

      <div class="content">File Content: <br/>
        <span id="filename"></span><br/>                       <div> for
        <textarea id="fileContent" rows="20"></textarea>       file content
      </div>
    </div>

    <script type="application/dart" src="ClientApp.dart"></script>   ⟵
  </body>                                                    Client-side Dart code script
</html>
```

You now have a fully working, fully Dart client-and-server application. The server side serves static files and dynamic data read from the filesystem, and the client side requests data via a RESTful interface and displays it in the browser. Multiple browsers can request data from your server without being blocked by previous requests.

An exercise left for you is to add a Save button to the client-side application and transmit file content back to the server via an `HttpRequest POST` method. The server can then use the file's `OutputStream` (covered earlier in the chapter) to write updated data back to a file. In this way, you'll have transformed the Dart File Browser application into a file editor.

Remember

- Single-page web applications load into the browser and request data using `HttpRequest`.
- A Dart `HttpServer` uses async APIs to efficiently serve multiple browser requests.
- You can use some libraries, such as `dart:json`, in both the client and the server.

13.4 *Summary*

You've produced a complete Dart solution in this chapter, with Dart running on both the client and the server. This Dart server application uses the `HttpServer` type provided in the `dart:io` library and uses the `File` and `Directory` types to read from the filesystem using nonblocking, server-side async APIs.

We covered how you can access command-line arguments from server-side scripts and how to read and write file data using `InputStream` and `OutputStream`. We also reviewed some of the utility wrapper functions, such as `readAsString()`, which make working with streams easier.

You used `HttpServer` to send both static files and dynamic data into a client, and you learned how to pipe the `InputStream` being read from a file into an `HttpResponse`'s `OutputStream` to send the file data to a browser. You also used the `dart:json` library on both the client and the server.

In the next chapter, we'll return to the DartExpense application you built in chapters 10 and 11, and you'll hook it up with a server-side database. You'll serve the DartExpense application from a server-side application, as you did for the one you've built in this chapter; but instead of interacting with the filesystem to return a directory listing, you'll interact with a database. You'll use `HttpServer` to send JSON data between the client-side application and a NoSQL database via HTTP.

Sending, syncing, *and storing data*

This chapter covers

- Using two-way client and server communication with web sockets
- Sharing code between the client and server
- Using `HttpClient` to communicate between servers
- Storing server-side data

Although your web application should be designed to work offline, most web applications also need to store some data on a server, whether in the filesystem, in an SQL-based solution such as MySQL, or in a NoSQL database such as CouchDB. The nature of the web is that users of your application will connect from different machines, which means even if data isn't stored on the server, you'll use a server component to provide server synchronization.

In this chapter, we'll revisit the DartExpense application from part 3 of the book and add server-side synchronization with web sockets, an HTML5 technology that provides two-way, client-server communication by maintaining a permanent connection between the client and the server. Once you have DartExpense clients in separate browsers communicating with each other via the server, we'll look at persisting data on the server using Apache CouchDB, a scalable NoSQL database server. We chose this particular database because it doesn't require any other third-party drivers or libraries—it provides a REST API that your server can access using Dart's HttpClient classes. You can use the server-side HttpClient classes to access any servers that provide an HTTP-based API—the HttpClient is not only for data storage.

But to get started, you need to take the static fileserver you built in the last chapter and use it to serve DartExpense to the client. This will be your base for adding web socket support and data storage.

14.1 Serving DartExpense from the server

In the previous chapter, we showed you how to write a server-side static fileserver that serves the client-side application files to the browser. You'll use this static fileserver again to serve part 3's DartExpense application to the browser. Figure 14.1 shows the DartExpense application and flow from the server, as a reminder.

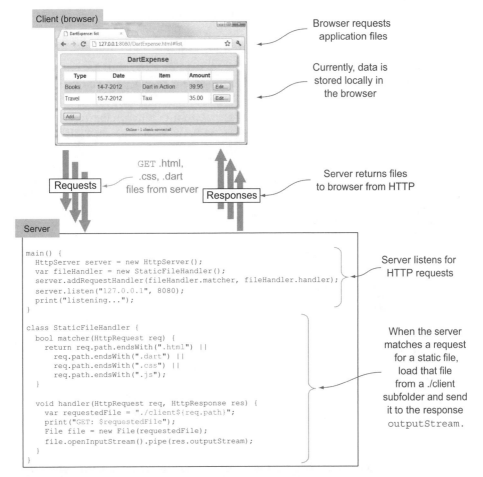

Figure 14.1 Dart HttpServer sends the application's files to the browser.

The client-side DartExpense files live in a ./client subfolder of the server part of the application, in which the server serves the client-side application files from HTTP. The application doesn't run any differently than if you load it directly from the server's filesystem; it's still only a client-side application that happens to have its files sent from a Dart server. Now that you have this, you can start to add server interactivity in the form of HTML web sockets.

14.2 Using web sockets for two-way communication

In the previous chapter, we discussed how to use a RESTful API to send data in the form of GET requests for directory listings from the client to the server. The server *requested* a list of files and folders in c:/dart, and the server *responded* with JSON data representing the files and folders. This represents the standard way that data is transmitted around the web: clients make requests, and servers respond to those requests. The connection between the client and server is maintained only for the length of each request/response.

Web sockets provide a new model of transmitting data by allowing the server to maintain a persistent connection to the client. This lets the server send data to the client without the client making a request for it. Later, you'll use this feature in DartExpense to provide synchronization between multiple DartExpense clients, allowing you to edit an expense in one browser and see the update appear in another browser. First, though, we'll look at a simpler example: you'll display the number of connected DartExpense clients that the server knows about. When a new client connects, the server will send the number of connected clients back to each connected browser, as shown in figure 14.2.

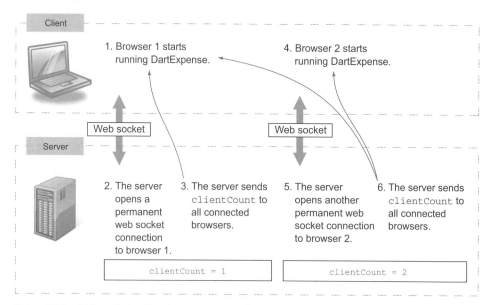

Figure 14.2   Web sockets allow two-way communication between the client and server, which lets the server send data to the client without the client requesting it first.

To use web sockets, you need to add code to both the client and server parts of the application. The client must connect to the server and respond to messages sent from the server with an event-handler callback function. The server must listen for new clients connecting, store a list of connected clients, and handle a client sending data.

> **NOTE** Web sockets and traditional `HttpRequest` `GET` and `POST` requests can coexist perfectly well. It's common to use `GET` and `POST` request methods to communicate with a server's RESTful API and also provide specific additional functionality with web sockets.

14.2.1 Connecting web sockets on the client side

The client application running in the browser needs to initially open the web socket connection with the server. To do this, you'll add a new method called `connectToWeb-socket()` in the DartExpense `AppController` class. The `AppController` class, which you built in chapter 10, is responsible for building the user interface and hooking up event handlers, so this is a perfect place to connect to a server and provide a mechanism for listening to web socket messages. Listing 14.1 shows DartExpense's `main()` function, which calls `connectToWebsocket()`. It also introduces a constant called `WEBSOCKET_URL`, which contains the URL to connect to the web socket. This uses the `ws://` protocol rather than `http://` to indicate to the browser that it's a web socket connection.

Listing 14.1 DartExpense.dart `main()` function creating a web socket connection

```
...snip imports...
final WEBSOCKET_URL = "ws://127.0.0.1:8080/websocket";        URL that browser
                                                              uses to connect to
void main() {                                                 server web socket
  var uiContainer = document.query("#dartexpense");
  var dataSource = new LocalStorage();

  _app = new AppController(uiContainer, dataSource);

  app.buildUI();
  app.loadFirstView();

  app.connectToWebsocket();                                   New call to connect
                                                              to web socket
  window.on.popState.add(onPopState);
}

AppController _app;
AppController get app => _app;
```

The new client-side `connectToWebsocket()` function needs to perform two tasks: it creates a web socket connection object using the `WEBSOCKET_URL` and then sets up an `on.message` event listener to listen to events retrieved from the server. This event listener is like other asynchronous browser event listeners, such as button clicks; in the same way that a user can click a button on the browser at any time, the server can send data to the client at any time. The message-listener function extracts the number of client connections sent from the server and displays them in the DartExpense footer area by calling refreshFooterStatus().

Listing 14.2 shows the new connectToWebsocket() and refreshFooterStatus() methods of the AppController class. The server sends the number of connected clients as JSON data containing an action type and some data, such as {"action":"CLIENT_COUNT_REFRESH","connectedClients": 3}. If the action type is CLIENT_COUNT_REFRESH, you need to extract the connectedClients value from the JSON map and display it in the footer.

Listing 14.2 Adding connectToWebsocket() to the AppController class

```
class AppController {
 // ... snip other methods and properties ...        New property to
                                                      store web socket
 WebSocket _websocket;                                connection
 int _conectedClients = 0;                            New property to store
                                                      number of connected clients
 connectToWebsocket() {
   _websocket = new WebSocket(WEBSOCKET_URL);         Creates web
                                                      socket connection
   _websocket.on.message.add( (MessageEvent message) {   with server URL
     Map data = JSON.parse(message.data);
     if (data["action"] == "CLIENT_COUNT_REFRESH" {
       _conectedClients = data["connectedClients"];   Adds event-handler function to
       refreshFooterStatus();                          respond to data sent from server
     }
   });
 }                                                    Updates footer status text to
                                                      show number of connected clients
 refreshFooterStatus() {
   var statusText = "$_conectedClients clients connected";
   document.query("#footer").innerHTML = statusText;
 }

}
```

The act of creating the new web socket connection opens the two-way connection to the server. Next, you need to get the server side to respond when this connection is opened and send an updated count back to all the connected browsers.

14.2.2 *Handling web socket connections on the server*

The server-side application already handles HTTP requests by using the HttpServer class, which is provided in the dart:io library. You've added a specific request handler to serve static files to the browser, but now you can also add a WebSocketHandler to manage web socket connection requests. WebSocketHandler is also provided in the dart:io server-side library and is responsible for creating a new WebSocketConnection object for each browser that connects. This WebSocketConnection object provides a send() function for the server to send data to the client and an onMessage() callback that's called when the browser sends data to the server. Figure 14.3 shows the client and server classes that make up the web socket story.

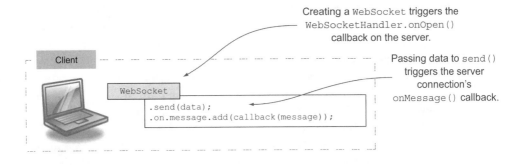

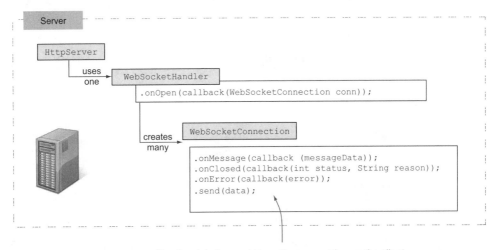

Figure 14.3 **The built-in classes you use to manage web socket connections on the client and server**

HANDLING THE WEB SOCKET REQUEST

In order for the server side to handle web sockets, it needs to use HttpServer's addRequestHandler() method, which you saw in the last chapter. You pass in the built-in WebSocketHandler's onRequest() function, as shown in the following snippet:

```
HttpServer server = new HttpServer();
var websocketHandler = new WebSocketHandler();
var matcher = (req) => req.path == "/websocket";
server.addRequestHandler(matcher, websocketHandler.onRequest);
server.listen("127.0.0.1",8080);
```
Adds WebSocketHandler to handle web socket requests

To perform actions when a browser connects, you need to also provide an implementation for the WebSocketHandler's onOpen() method. This method's callback handler gets a new connection object to allow communication between the specific browser connected and the server.

TRACKING BROWSER CONNECTIONS

The server gets a new `WebSocketConnection` object for each browser that connects, and you need to store each of these connections. Each web socket connection provides a unique identifier (in the form of the `hashCode` property), allowing you to store the connections in a `Map` so you can identify them and remove each connection from the map when it's closed. This will also be useful later, when you want to send synchronization data to all browser connections except the one that sent some original data.

When the server gets the new `WebSocketConnection` object from the `WebSocketHandler.onOpen()` method, you can send the updated count of connections back to the browser. This is performed by passing `String` or `List<int>` data to each connection's `send()` method. You send the data as a JSON string, iterating through the list of connections and calling the `send()` method on each, as shown in the following listing.

> **Listing 14.3   Sending a client count when each browser connects**

```dart
import "dart:io";
import "dart:json";

main() {
  HttpServer server = new HttpServer();                          // Creates new
  var fileHandler = new StaticFileHandler();                     // WebSocketHandler instance
  server.addRequestHandler(fileHandler.matcher, fileHandler.handler);

  var wsHandler = new WebSocketHandler();

  var matcher = (req) => req.path == "/websocket";
  server.addRequestHandler(matcher ,websocketHandler.onRequest);   // Adds matcher
                                                                   // and handler to
  var connections = new Map();                                     // HttpServer
                                         // Creates empty
  var sendUpdatedConnectionCount = () {  // map to store client
    var data = new Map();                // connections
    data["action"] = "CLIENT_COUNT_REFRESH"
    data["connectedClients"] = connections.length;
    var message = JSON.stringify(data);                   // Provides a closure
                                                          // to send size of
    for(var clientConnection in connections.values) {    // client connections
      clientConnection.send(message);                    // map to each client
    }
  };

  wsHandler.onOpen = (WebSocketConnection conn) {     // Stores new
    var key = conn.hashCode();                        // connection in map
    connections[key] = conn;

    sendUpdatedConnectionCount();        // Sends updated
  };                                     // count to all clients

  server.listen("127.0.0.1", 8080);
  print("listening...");
}
```

TRACKING BROWSER DISCONNECTIONS AND ERRORS

In addition to adding the new connection to a map and sending an updated count to
all connections, you need to provide implementations for the callback functions on
the `WebSocketConnection` object: `onMessage()` and `onClosed()`. The `onMessage()`
implementation is empty for now because the browser clients aren't sending data to
the server yet. But the `onClosed()` handler needs to remove the connection from the
map and send the updated client count to the remaining connected browsers. The
`onClosed()` callback is called when the browser explicitly closes the connection
or when there's an error. The `status` parameter, which has values defined in the
`WebSocketStatus` class, indicates whether an error condition occurred. You need to
add these handlers in the `wsHandler.onOpen` callback, shown in the following listing,
while you still have access to the `WebSocketConnection`.

Listing 14.4 Adding `onClosed()` handler to the connection

```
main() {
  // ...snip other code from earlier listing...

  wsHandler.onOpen = (WebSocketConnection conn) {
    var key = conn.hashCode();
    connections[key] = conn;

    conn.onClosed = (int status, String reason) {      Removes this
      connections.remove(conn.hashCode());             connection from list
      sendUpdatedConnectionCount();
    };                                                 Sends updated
                                                       count to all clients
    conn.onMessage = (message) {
      // do nothing                                    No implementation
    };                                                 needed yet

    sendUpdatedConnectionCount();
  };

  server.listen("127.0.0.1", 8080);
  print("listening...");
}
```

The server can now send arbitrary data to all connected client browsers. When you
run the server and start adding clients, you'll see the number of connected clients
shown in the DartExpense footer panel change in each browser as the server notifies
the browser that there has been a change, as shown in figure 14.4.

Now that you've implemented a simple client-connection scenario, let's look at a
slightly more complicated scenario: synchronizing the expenses between browsers.

14.2.3 Using web sockets for cross-browser synchronization

You have a method for the server to *push* data to multiple clients, so you can begin to
send synchronization data to multiple clients. In the simple count example, you didn't
send any data to the server with the client web socket's `send()` command. Merely connecting to the server was all you needed. You can use this `send()` command, though,

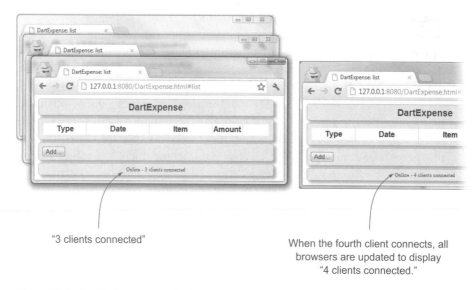

"3 clients connected"

When the fourth client connects, all
browsers are updated to display
"4 clients connected."

Figure 14.4   As clients connect, they're notified of the updated number of connected clients.

to send a JSON representation of an Expense to the server via your web socket connection. When the server receives the JSON expense, it can send that to all the other connected client browsers without the other browsers needing to explicitly request that data from the server. This will trigger the user interface to be refreshed with the updated data, as shown in figure 14.5.

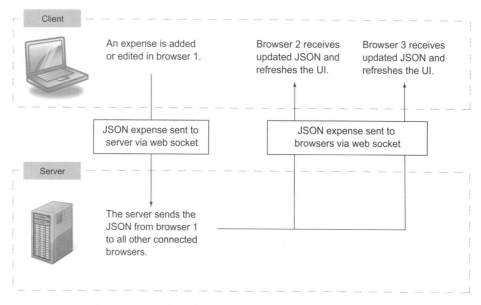

Figure 14.5   Sending synchronization data from one browser to other browsers via web socket connections

The synchronization mechanism will be simple for the purpose of example (see the sidebar "Real-world synchronization"). Currently, when you click Save when editing a record, you save a JSON expense in browser web storage via an `addOrUpdate(Expense expense)` function. You'll modify the client-side DartExpense application to also send the edited `Expense` object to a `sync(Expense expense)` function that's responsible for sending the JSON data to the server.

Real-world synchronization

In the real world, data synchronization is a more complex problem. Issues arise such as what happens if two users are editing the same data simultaneously. Typical solutions include the following:

- *Latest edit wins*—Take each edit as it comes, so the second user's edit clears the first user's edit. This is the easiest approach to implement but provides a poor user experience (for the second user).
- *First edit wins*—When the second user tries to save the record, notify the second user that it's been edited elsewhere. This keeps the first user's edit and allows the second user to make informed choices.

With web sockets, you also get the possibility of more advanced solutions. These are available because you can send data back to a client in response to changes elsewhere. Example solutions include the following:

- *Collaborative editing*—As the first user keys in an edit, the edit appears on the second user's screen at the same time, and vice versa.
- *Disabling editing*—When the first user starts to enter data, the record being edited becomes disabled in the second user's interface. When the user clicks Save, the data updates on the second user's screen and becomes enabled again. This is a more advanced version of "first edit wins," with better feedback for the second user.

These more advanced solutions are also more complex to implement and thus require careful thought regarding their design, but a user experience such as this helps make a good web application great.

SENDING WEB SOCKET DATA FROM THE BROWSER

Sending the data to the server is as simple as calling the web socket's `send()` method and passing the `String` or `List<int>` data into it. In fact, it's a mirror of the server-side `send()` function that you saw earlier. You'll implement that part first, as shown in figure 14.6.

Listing 14.5 shows the modifications to the DartExpense `AppController` class to send the JSON data to

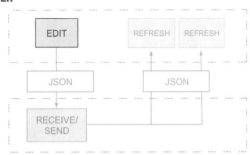

Figure 14.6   Sending the edited JSON

the server via web sockets. In order to keep the `Expense`'s ID values in sync between browsers, you also send the current value of the `Expense` class's static `nextId` value. You send the data as a new action type of `SYNC` so the data can be distinguished from the `CLIENT_COUNT_REFRESH` action.

Listing 14.5 Sending JSON data to the server with web sockets

```
class AppController {
  // ... snip other methods and properties ...

  WebSocket _websocket;                           ◁──┐ Existing web
                                                       socket connection

  addOrUpdate(Expense expense) {
    _appData.addOrUpdate(expense);                ◁──┐ Syncs expense and stores
    sync(expense);                                     it in local storage
  }

  sync(Expense expense) {
    Map data = new Map();
    data["action"] = "SYNC";
    data["expense"] = expense.toJson();           ┐ Adds JSON expense and
    data["nextId"] = Expense.currentNextIdValue;  ┘ next ID value to map

    var jsonData = JSON.stringify(data);          ◁──┐ Converts map
                                                       to JSON
    _websocket.send(jsonData);     ◁──┐ Sends data
  }                                    to server
}
```

RECEIVING WEB SOCKET DATA FROM THE BROWSER

The data has started its journey to the other browsers. Now you'll implement the server side, shown in figure 14.7.

Earlier you left the `WebSocketConnection onMessage()` callback without an implementation. Now is the time to provide that implementation. If the action type is `SYNC`, then the server should resend the edited expense data to all the other connected browsers. You can use the connection's hash code to identify the current connection (that received the data) and ensure that you don't send the edited expense data back to the same browser that initiated the edit. The server-side changes to DartExpenseServer.dart are shown in the next listing.

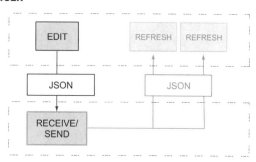

Figure 14.7 Receiving JSON expense data from a connected client

Listing 14.6 Receiving and resending data from a web socket message

```
main() {
  // ...snip other code from earlier listing...

  wsHandler.onOpen = (WebSocketConnection conn) {
```

```
    var key = conn.hashCode();
    connections[key] = conn;

    conn.onClosed = (int status, String reason) {
      //... snip implementation from earlier
    }

    conn.onMessage = (message) {
      var data = JSON.parse(message);
      if (data["action"] == "SYNC") {
        for (var clientConnection in connections.values) {

          if (clientConnection.hashCode() != conn.hashCode()) {
            clientConnection.send(message);
          }
        }
      }
    };

    sendUpdatedConnectionCount();
  };

  server.listen("127.0.0.1", 8080);
  print("listening...");
}
```

For each client connection ...

... if it's not the current connection ...

... resend the received data.

RECEIVING SYNCHRONIZATION DATA IN OTHER BROWSERS

The final part of the sequence is to return to the browser code in order to let other browsers update when they receive the updated data, shown in figure 14.8.

You already have an on.message handler that looks for the CLIENT_ COUNT_REFRESH action. You need to add another if clause to look for the SYNC action. When the browser receives a SYNC action, it will convert the JSON

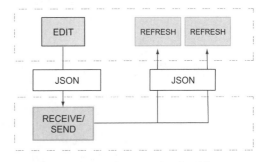

Figure 14.8 Other clients receive the JSON data and refresh.

expense data back to an Expense object and pass it into its addOrUpdate(Expense expense) method, as though it had been edited from the browser. Finally, you'll update the browser to display the list of expenses by navigating to the list view. The following listing shows this step in action.

Listing 14.7 Receiving synchronization data in the browser

```
class AppController {
  // ... snip other methods and properties ...

  WebSocket _websocket;
  int _conectedClients = 0;

  connectToWebsocket() {
    _websocket = new WebSocket(WEBSOCKET_URL);
```

```
_websocket.on.message.add( (MessageEvent message) {
  Map data = JSON.parse(message.data);
  if (data["action"] == "CLIENT_COUNT_REFRESH" {
    _conectedClients = data["connectedClients"];
    refreshFooterStatus();
  }
  else if (data["action"] == "SYNC") {
    var expenseJSON = data["expense"];                    Converts JSON expense
    var expense = new Expense.fromJson(expenseJSON);      to Expense object

    Expense.currentNextIdValue = data["nextId"];          Updates next
                                                          ID value
    _appData.addOrUpdate(expense);

    navigate(ViewType.LIST, null);      Navigates back    Adds or updates
  }                                     to list view to   expense in same
});                                     see the edit      manner as a UI edit
}
}
```

That was a long section, but now you have an application that can communicate between browsers, using a server to push data to multiple browsers. This is useful for providing push notifications such as "new mail" notifications, keeping browser-based multiplayer games in sync, and improving the user experience in line-of-business applications.

In the next section, you'll take the sync data received from a browser and use it to save data into a CouchDB NoSQL database.

> **Remember**
> - A server can handle web socket connections by using a `WebSocketHandler` to provide a request handler for the `HttpServer` class.
> - The client needs to open the web socket connection to the server by creating an instance of the `WebSocket` class pointing at a specific server URL.
> - When a client connects to the server, the `WebSocketHandler` creates a new `WebServerConnection` instance that lets the server communicate back to that browser.
> - The `send()` method on the client or server connection sends data to the recipient's `on.message` (client side) or `onMessage()` (server side) callback function.

14.3   *Storing data with HttpClient and CouchDB*

In this section, you'll use Dart's server-side `HttpClient` to store data in an Apache CouchDB database. CouchDB is a NoSQL database that stores data in a JSON format; in this respect, it functions similarly to the browser-based local storage you saw in part 3 of the book.

CouchDB has a RESTful API that serves data to client systems such as DartExpense's server using HTTP. Even if you don't plan to use CouchDB in your solution, the following examples will build on your use of the `InputStream` and `OutputStream` types you saw in the previous chapter and introduce the use of `HttpClient` to talk to HTTP-based RESTful

APIs. `HttpClient` is server-side Dart's version of the `HttpRequest` you've already used to request data in the web browser.

Interacting with other database systems

Dart's HTTP client and HTTP server are built on a lower-level `Socket` type, which is used for binary transfer of data between TCP systems. The `Socket` type lets database driver developers communicate directly with database servers that expect to communicate via a proprietary protocol. At the time of writing, open source drivers in various states of development are available for MySQL, MongoDB, Redis, and Riak.

It's also possible to interface server-side code with third-party native code via the `external` keyword, which allows native drivers written in C/C++ to be bound to Dart libraries. An open source SQLite binding is an early example, but this advanced topic is outside the scope of this book.

At the moment, the DartExpense application receives data from the application running in a browser and uses web sockets to sync that data to other browsers. Each client also stores the data offline in local storage. The problem with this at present is that if the application starts in one browser and a user enters a new expense, the expense record isn't added to the application running in a second browser that starts up later; it's only synchronized to browsers that are running at the time the edit is made. You need to pull the existing data from the server each time the application begins running in the browser. You'll add the following features to the application to enable server-side data persistence:

- Loading all existing records from the server
- Saving edited (new and existing) records to the server

At present, the client sends JSON data over web sockets with a `SYNC` action and a `CLIENT_COUNT_REFRESH` action. You'll add a `LOAD` action to request the initial data load from the server and reuse the `SYNC` action to send the data to the database as well as to other browsers. The flow of data with these new features is shown in figure 14.9.

Adding a new layer to the application's architecture will also add some complexity. At the core, you're LOADing expenses from the database and SYNCing expenses to other browsers and the database. But before you begin, let's take a quick look at how you can talk to CouchDB.

14.3.1 *A quick CouchDB primer*

Apache CouchDB is a NoSQL database. It stores data such as your expenses in JSON form, accessible via a RESTful API. Installers are available from the CouchDB website, and no configuration is required other than running the installer and starting the server (on Windows systems, a handy batch file to start the server is added to the Start menu).

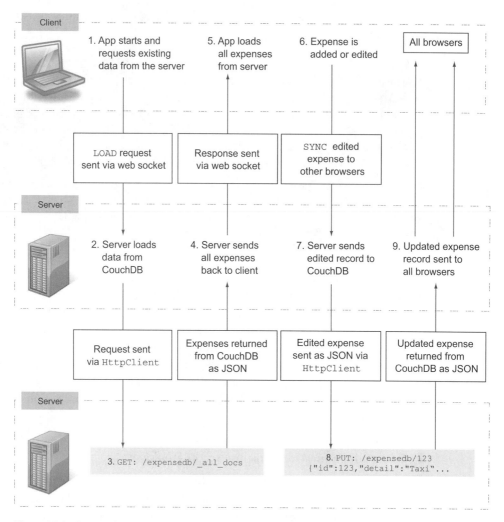

Figure 14.9   Integrating server-side persistence with CouchDB

When the server is running, you can access data using HTTP methods such as GET, PUT, and POST to interact with the server and get and store data. You can also use the Futon locally hosted web application that's built into the server to manipulate the data in a more visually friendly way. Figure 14.10 shows an expense record with ID=1 in the Futon application that was returned via a GET API call in the browser, which is possible because the CouchDB server communicates via browser-friendly HTTP.

You'll use the HTTP API, which uses HTTP methods and paths to access specific records in a database in the server-side code. Table 14.1 shows the API calls you'll use in the code. Where a specific Expense ID is used, you'll replace it with the ID the expense was given in the browser.

Figure 14.10   The CouchDB GUI web interface and the HTTP API interface

Table 14.1   API calls that you'll use in your code

HTTP method	Path	Request data	Result
PUT	/expensedb/	None	Creates a new database called expensedb
GET	/expensedb/_all_docs	None	Retrieves all records in the database
PUT	/expensedb/1	New or existing expense as JSON	Creates or updates an expense with ID = 1
GET	/expensedb/nextId	None	Retrieves the nextId record

Each JSON document is represented by an ID value, which can be any string. A single document called nextId will store the current next expense ID value that running instances of the browser application should know about. This prevents the application from assigning two different expenses the same ID value. You currently SYNC this value along with the Expense record, and you'll also store it whenever a record is updated.

One more important feature of CouchDB is that it requires you to store a unique revision number as part of the Expense JSON data. This allows CouchDB to identify whether it's a new or existing record; and if it's an existing record, this ensures that the most recent version of the record is updated.

WARNING   Adding a layer to your application in the form of a database increases the app's complexity. The listings in this chapter build on listings from this and earlier chapters, and only the relevant extracts to demonstrate the use of `HttpClient`, `InputStream`, and `OutputStream` are shown. The full code that makes up the working application is available on the book's website: www.manning.com/DartInAction.

14.3.2   Sharing the Expense model class between client and server

The `Expense` class, stored in the models.dart file, will now be used on the server as well as on the browser. Rather than writing nearly identical code twice, you can use the same source file by converting models.dart into a library in its own right. To do so, you add a `library` indicator at the start of the file. Now the client and server parts of the application can `import` the same library code.

JSON data stored in CouchDB also needs a _rev property to store the unique revision number inserted automatically by CouchDB. To achieve this, you'll modify the `Expense` class to also have a _rev property. Listing 14.8 shows models.dart converted to a library and the additional _rev property added to the `Expense` class. When you use `JSON.stringify()` on the `Expense` object, it will use `Expense`'s `Map` implementation methods to return the value of the _rev property.

Listing 14.8   models.dart: Expense class updated to include a _rev JSON property

```
library expense_models;                          models.dart is
import "dart:json";                              now a library.

class Expense implements Hashable, Map {
  // ...snip other properties
  String _rev = null;
  String get rev => _rev;                        Adds _rev property
  set rev(value) => _rev = value;                and getter/setter pair

  // ...snip other methods

  operator [](key) {
    if (key == "id") {
      return this.id;
    } else if (key == "_rev") {                  Adds JSON property to
      return this.rev;                           the Map indexer method
    } else if //...snip other JSON properties
  }
}
```

14.3.3   Adding server support for data persistence

All interaction with the CouchDB database will be via Dart's `HttpClient` class, which is also in the `dart:io` library. `HttpClient`, like other server-side APIs, is asynchronous and nonblocking. You need to make a request and return a future value that will complete when the CouchDB server returns data to you. In order to achieve this, you'll wrap all your calls to CouchDB in a class called `CouchDbHandler`.

When using `HttpClient`, you typically make a request for data to a specific URL path, such as http://localhost:5984/expensedb/1, using either `GET` or `PUT`. If you use `PUT`, then you might also supply some request data, such as the edited expense you're `PUT`ting into the database. The `HttpClient` response from CouchDB is always a `String` delivered as an `InputStream`. Because these are common patterns for all your interactions with CouchDB, you'll also create two private utility methods in the `CouchDbHandler` class. `_getStringFromInputStream()` will convert an `InputStream` to a `Future<String>`, and `_getData()` will return a `Future<String>` from a call to CouchDB.

UTILITY FUNCTIONS FOR HTTPCLIENT INTERACTION

These two utility functions are where all the interesting work happens when you talk to CouchDB. `_getStringFromInputStream()` is similar to the code we looked at in chapter 13 when you read data from a file's `InputStream`. This time, instead of reading the data from a file, you're reading the data from an `InputStream` provided by an `HttpClientResponse` object, which is created when the server responds to a request. Although data is available, you read that data into a `StringBuffer`; and when the `InputStream` is closed, you complete the `Future<String>` value with the contents of the `StringBuffer`. The following listing shows the `_getStringFromInputStream()` method.

Listing 14.9 `CouchDbHandler` class's `_getStringFromInputStream()` utility method

```
class CouchDbHandler {

  Future<String> _getStringFromInputStream(var inputStream) {

    var completer = new Completer<String>();              Creates string buffer
    StringBuffer sb = new StringBuffer();                 to hold response text

    inputStream.onData = () {
      var buffer = inputStream.read();
      if (buffer != null) {                               onData is called repeatedly
        sb.add(new String.fromCharCodes(buffer));         when data is available.
      }
    };

    inputStream.onClosed = () => completer.complete(sb.toString());

    return completer.future;         Returns              Passes string buffer's
  }                                  Future value         value to Future String

  // snip other methods

}
```

This method is used by the second utility method, `_getData()`, which you'll use as a general-purpose method to send and retrieve data from CouchDB. It uses the `Http-Client.open()` method, which returns a new connection object to create a connection to the CouchDB API. This returned connection object is important because you need to assign `handler()` functions to its `onRequest()`, `onResponse()`, and `onError()` methods. Figure 14.11 shows how these methods are used in conjunction with an `HttpClient` object.

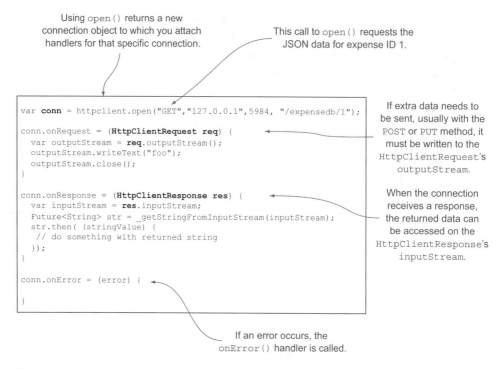

Using `open()` returns a new connection object to which you attach handlers for that specific connection.

This call to `open()` requests the JSON data for expense ID 1.

```
var conn = httpclient.open("GET","127.0.0.1",5984, "/expensedb/1");

conn.onRequest = (HttpClientRequest req) {
  var outputStream = req.outputStream();
  outputStream.writeText("foo");
  outputStream.close();
}

conn.onResponse = (HttpClientResponse res) {
  var inputStream = res.inputStream;
  Future<String> str = _getStringFromInputStream(inputStream);
  str.then( (stringValue) {
    // do something with returned string
  });
}

conn.onError = (error) {

}
```

If extra data needs to be sent, usually with the POST or PUT method, it must be written to the `HttpClientRequest`'s `outputStream`.

When the connection receives a response, the returned data can be accessed on the `HttpClientResponse`'s `inputStream`.

If an error occurs, the `onError()` handler is called.

Figure 14.11   Using `HttpClient` to read data from `HttpServer`

You can add to the `CouchDbHandler` class your specific implementation of `_getData()` that follows this pattern. As shown in listing 14.10, `_getData()` has two optional parameters, `method` and `data`, which let you change from the default GET request to a PUT or a POST, and add data such as an edited expense, as required. The `Future<String>` returned by `_getData()` represents the JSON retrieved from CouchDB.

Listing 14.10   `CouchDbHandler` class's `_getData()` utility method

```
class CouchDbHandler {

  Future<String> _getData(String path, {method:'GET',data:null}) {

    var conn = client.open(method, host, port, path);

    if (data != null) {
      conn.onRequest = (HttpClientRequest req) {
        var outputStream = req.outputStream;
        outputStream.writeString(data);
        outputStream.close();
      };
    }

    var completer = new Completer<String>();
    conn.onResponse = (HttpClientResponse response) {
      _getStringFromInputStream(response.inputStream)
        .then((responseText) {
```

Calls server, getting a new connection in return

If there is data to send, adds onRequest handler

Sends responseText from CouchDB to Future String

```
            completer.complete(responseText);
        });
    };

    conn.onError = (e) {
        print(e);
    };

    return completer.future;
  }
}
```

△ **Sends responseText from CouchDB to Future String**

If there is an error, prints it to console

ADDING DARTEXPENSE FUNCTIONALITY

Now that you have the utility functions in the `CouchDbHandler` class, you can add the rest of the functionality in the form of a constructor and three public methods. The constructor will create a new expensedb database if it doesn't already exist; and you'll add a `loadData()` method, an `addOrUpdate()` method, and a `getNextId()` method, all of which return `Future` values. The outline for these methods is shown in figure 14.12.

The `_getData()` function will be called from these methods, and you'll use the `Future<String>` returned from it to convert the returned JSON string back into `Expense` objects. Table 14.2 shows the method calls to `_getData()` that the code will use.

The following listing adds the constructor and three methods to the `CouchDbHandler` class. The method calls listed in table 14.2 are highlighted in bold; the rest of the code is straightforward and converts CouchDB JSON to and from `Expense` records.

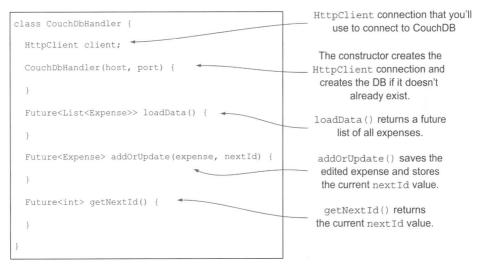

```
class CouchDbHandler {

  HttpClient client;

  CouchDbHandler(host, port) {

  }

  Future<List<Expense>> loadData() {

  }

  Future<Expense> addOrUpdate(expense, nextId) {

  }

  Future<int> getNextId() {

  }

}
```

`HttpClient` connection that you'll use to connect to CouchDB

The constructor creates the `HttpClient` connection and creates the DB if it doesn't already exist.

`loadData()` returns a future list of all expenses.

`addOrUpdate()` saves the edited expense and stores the current `nextId` value.

`getNextId()` returns the current `nextId` value.

Figure 14.12   The skeleton of the server-side `CouchDbHandler` class

Chapter 14 Sending, syncing, and storing data

Table 14.2 The calls to the `_getData()` utility function that your code will make

Method call	Action
`_getData("/expensedb/", method:"PUT");`	Creates the database
`_getData("/expensedb/` ➥ `$id?include_docs=true");`	Retrieves all expense JSON strings

`_getData("/expensedb/$id",`
                `method:"PUT",`
                `data:expense.toJson());`
	Creates or updates an expense in the database

`_getData("/expense/nextId");`	Retrieves the nextId value

Listing 14.11 `CouchDbHandler`: adding specific DartExpense functionality

```
class CouchDbHandler {

  //...snip _getStringFromInputStream()
  //...snip _getData()

  HttpClient client;
  var host;
  var port;

  CouchDbHandler(this.host, this.port) {
    this.client = new HttpClient();
    _get("/expensedb/", method:"PUT");          ← Creates database if it
  }                                               doesn't already exist

  Future<List<Expense>> loadData() {
    var completer = new Completer<List<Expense>>();

    var expenseList = new List<Expense>();

    _getData("/expensedb/_all_docs?include_docs=true")   ← Gets all records
      .then( (responseText) {                              stored in database
        Map data = JSON.parse(responseText);

        for (var rowData in data["rows"]) {
          if (rowData["id"] != "nextId") {            ← If this isn't the
            var expenseJSON = rowData["doc"];           nextId record, it's
            var expense = new Expense.fromMap(expenseJSON);  an Expense: add
            expenseList.add(expense);                   to result list
          }
        }

        completer.complete(expenseList);            ← Completes Future
    });                                               expense list

    return completer.future;
  }

  Future<Expense> addOrUpdate(Expense expense, int nextId) {
    var completer = new Completer<Expense>();

    _getData("/expensedb/${expense.id}",            ← PUTs expense JSON
    ➥            method:'PUT', data:expense.toJson() )    data into CouchDB
```

```
    .then( (responseText) {
      Map data = JSON.parse(responseText);
      expense.rev = data["rev"];                    ← Stores returned "rev" revision value
      completer.complete(expense);                      and returns completed expense
    });

  var nextIdMap = new Map();
  nextIdMap["nextId"] = nextId;                     ← Saves current nextId
  _getData("/expensedb/nextId",                        value to database
           method:"PUT", data:JSON.stringify(nextIdMap));

  return completer.future;
}

Future<int> getNextId() {
  var completer = new Completer<int>();
                                                    ┐ Gets current nextId
  _getData("/$dbName/nextId").then( (responseText) {  ← value from database
    var data = JSON.parse(responseText);
    var nextId = 1;
    if (data.containsKey("nextId")) {
      nextId = data["nextId"];
    }
                                                    ┐ Completes Future
    completer.complete(nextId);                     ← nextId value
  });

  return completer.future;
}
}
```

That's a long listing, but it provides all the functionality you need in order to save and load expense data on the server. You can integrate this class with the existing application by making calls to loadData() and addOrUpdate() from the existing web socket connection code you saw earlier in the chapter. When the browser requests a LOAD action, you send the JSON expenses to the client side; and when a browser requests a SYNC, you pass the expense to the addOrUpdate() method. The complete source code is available on the Manning website.

> **Remember**
> - HttpClient's open() method returns a connection object that provides onRequest() and onResponse() handler functions.
> - The onRequest() handler has an HttpClientRequest parameter, and you can send data by writing to its OutputStream.
> - The onResponse() handler has an HttpClientResponse parameter, and you can receive data by reading from its InputStream.

14.4 Summary

We've tackled two more server-side APIs in this chapter that will help you build exciting and functional applications in Dart. HTML5 web sockets let you maintain a permanent, two-way connection between the client and server, allowing the server to push data to connected web browser applications without the browser needing to request the data first. You can use this to provide collaborative editing and cross-browser synchronization of data.

We also looked at the `HttpClient` class, which lets your Dart server-side application talk to other `HttpServers` via a RESTful API. It's the server-side equivalent of the browser's `HttpRequest`. You also used CouchDB's HTTP server to store DartExpense objects in the form of JSON data sent to the server from the client-side application.

In the next chapter, we'll look at an advanced area of Dart: isolates. Isolates let you use modern multicore processors by providing multiple event loops with message passing between them to achieve concurrency. This can be useful when you have long-running batch processes but you still need your event loop to respond to client requests.

Concurrency with isolates

This chapter covers

- Spawning new function isolates
- Passing messages between isolates
- Loading Dart code dynamically
- Using isolates for batch processing

Modern computer hardware provides more processing power than ever before, whether it's in a server room serving thousands of requests per minute or in your pocket as a mobile phone or tablet. Rather than providing ever-increasing processor speeds, chip designers have achieved this improvement by adding more CPU cores. To take advantage of this greater processing power, web application design also needs to be able to scale out to use the additional CPU cores.

Earlier in this book, we discussed how Dart code runs in a single thread but can call out to asynchronous APIs, such as accessing the filesystem or external servers. In the browser, applications use async APIs to perform AJAX-type requests for data from the server. But your Dart code still runs in a single thread and will take advantage of only a single CPU core. This is a design constraint imposed by the goal to allow Dart to be converted to JavaScript, which is also single-threaded.

In this chapter we'll look at *isolates*, which are Dart's solution to taking single-threaded Dart code and allowing your application to make greater use of the hardware available. Isolates, as the name suggests, are isolated units of running code. The only way to send data between them is by passing messages, similar to the way you pass messages between the client and the server or from Dart to JavaScript. You'll use isolates on the server to modify the Dart File Browser application from chapter 13 to use isolates to analyze the file list in the results.

Once we've explored the basic concept of isolates, you'll see how you can use the isolate mechanism to load and run code dynamically. Loading code dynamically allows you to provide a plug-in type of mechanism, where your application can run third-party code without knowing what that code is in advance.

Finally, you'll see how isolates can be used to create a number of workers to process a list of items concurrently. This is a powerful technique for creating applications that perform well and make full use of the underlying hardware.

Let's get started with exploring isolates and starting a new isolate. Concurrent programming is an advanced topic, and although Dart's isolate concept simplifies it somewhat, you need to come to grips with two new classes: `ReceivePort` and `SendPort`.

15.1 Using isolates as units of work

Back in chapter 13, you created a server-side script to list files and folders in the current directory. When you use the `DirectoryLister()` async function to retrieve the contents of the current directory, you hand control to the underlying operating system. In the same way, you can hand control from your Dart code to another piece of Dart code running asynchronously and use this to analyze the results, counting the types of files and file sizes for each type. You'll write this code first as a straightforward single-isolate server-side script and then build on it to analyze the file list in multiple isolates. Figure 15.1 shows the structure of the Directory Analysis app, which retrieves a list of files, counts them, and totals the size.

The two key functions are `getFileTypes()` and `getFileSizes()`. In the implementation shown previously, they run sequentially; you'll use isolates to make them run at the same time.

15.1.1 Creating an isolate

You've seen isolates already. Every running Dart script or application is running in an isolate known as the *default isolate*. When a Dart application starts, the Dart VM spawns an isolate, passing in the script's `main()` function as the entry-point function. `main()` begins the flow of single-threaded code in the isolate. The `main()` function is a top-level function and must return nothing and take no parameters.

In the same way that the Dart VM spawns an isolate, your Dart code can also spawn an isolate, passing in an entry-point function to it. As with `main()`, the isolate entry-point function must also be a top-level function, return nothing, and take no parameters. The function name can be any valid function name—`main()` is restricted to the default isolate.

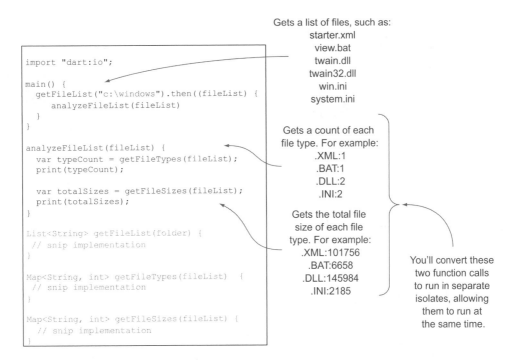

Figure 15.1 Skeleton of the Directory Analysis code

To spawn a new isolate with an entry-point function, you need to import the
dart:isolate library and use the spawnFunction() function, passing in the entry-
point function name. Listing 15.1 shows a modified version of the analyzeFileList()
function, which modifies your Directory Analysis script to get the file types and file
sizes in two new isolates (FileTypes and FileSizes) by using spawnFunction(). The
script doesn't do anything useful yet: it creates two new isolates that print a message
and exit immediately, the isolate equivalent of printing "hello world."

> **NOTE** If you run this code, you might be surprised that the FileSizes isolate
> print statement never completes. The default isolate (running the main()
> function) exits first, and program execution halts without waiting for the
> spawned isolate to complete. For the example only, a time-wasting for loop is
> included at the end of main(); you'll remove it later.

Listing 15.1 directoryAnalysis.dart

```dart
import "dart:isolate";              Imports
                                    dart:isolate library
void main() {
  // snip ...
  analyzeFileList(fileList);
}

analyzeFileList(fileList) {
```

```
    spawnFunction(getFileTypesEntryPoint);
    spawnFunction(getFileSizesEntryPoint);
    print("Default isolate");

    for (int i = 0; i < 100000; i++) { }
}
void getFileTypesEntryPoint() {
  print("FileTypes isolate");
}

void getFileSizesEntryPoint() {
  print("FileSizes isolate");
}
```

Spawns new isolate entry-point functions

Time-wasting for loop: allows spawned isolate to finish before application exits

Entry-point function: takes no parameters and returns void

spawnFunction() starts a new isolate. The underlying VM is responsible for creating a new thread for the code to run in, and as you'll see, this new thread doesn't share any state with the thread that spawned it.

It's important to understand this. Although the code exists in the same single physical source file, there are now three execution contexts, each with its own memory, objects, and state. You can prove this by adding a top-level property to the library and modifying its value in each of the three isolates, as shown in figure 15.2.

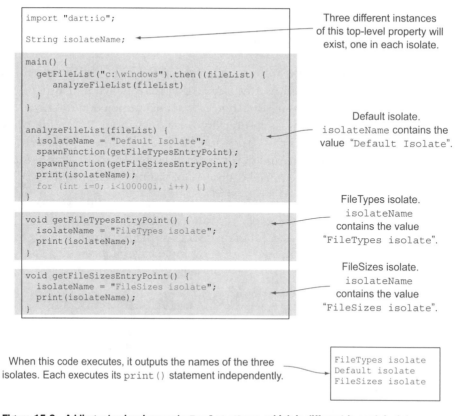

Figure 15.2   Adding a top-level property `IsolateName`, which is different in each isolate

Each of the three isolates get a new memory context, separate from the other. In this respect, it's conceptually similar to the way Dart and JavaScript code executes separately or the code on the client and server executes separately.

Now that you can start new isolates, you need to make them do some work. That means passing data into them, such as your list of files. You'll also see how to keep the default isolate running (rather than adding a temporary for loop) so the other isolates can fully complete.

15.1.2 One-way isolate communication

Each Dart isolate runs in a separate execution context. This means isolates have no shared memory. The default isolate stores the list of files in the fileList variable. In order to make that file list available to the other isolates, the default isolate must send it as a message to the other isolates, like sending a message from a client to a server or from Dart to JavaScript.

But isolates are more flexible than sending a message from client to server or Dart to JavaScript. Instead of needing to convert a message to a JSON string, you can pass any types you'd otherwise be able to convert to JSON. Table 15.1 lists the valid types you can send to another isolate.

Table 15.1 Valid types to send between isolates

Types	Classes	Notes
Primitive types	null, num, bool, double, String	Although these are object instances, they're treated as primitives for the purpose of copying between isolates.
Collection types	List, Map	Can contain any valid primitive or collection type, including other lists and maps.

SENDING MESSAGES TO ANOTHER ISOLATE

When you spawn an isolate, the spawn function returns a SendPort instance, which provides a send() function to send data to that isolate:

```
SendPort fileTypesSendPort = spawnFunction(getFileTypesEntryPoint);
var message = "Hello FileTypes Isolate from the Default isolate"
fileTypesSendPort.send(message);
```

This is simple enough so far, but the code doesn't work yet. The receiving FileTypes isolate must be able to receive data, and it could receive data from multiple other isolates.

RECEIVING DATA FROM ANOTHER ISOLATE

Each isolate receives messages via a listener callback function attached to a Receive-Port instance. Every isolate, including the default isolate, has a ReceivePort, which you access through the top-level port property. The port property, which comes from the dart:isolate library, is like the IsolateName property you created earlier in that each isolate has its own independent instance of port, separate from the other.

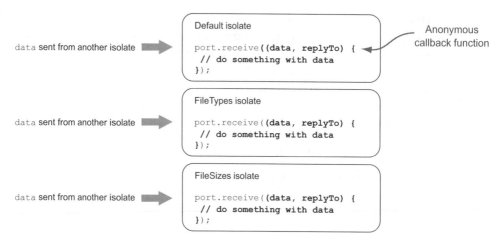

Figure 15.3 The `port.receive()` handler attaches a callback function to the current isolate.

When you access the `port` property, you're accessing *that isolate's* `ReceivePort` instance, of which there's only one in that isolate. This means you'll use the `port.receive` `(callback)` handler to handle messages being sent into the isolate from some other isolate. This works for both the default isolate and spawned isolates, such as the FileTypes isolate and the FileSizes isolate, as shown in figure 15.3. The receive callback takes two parameters: `data`, which is one of the valid inter-isolate data types, and `replyTo`, which is a `SendPort`. We'll look more at the `replyTo` parameter in a couple of pages.

When the default isolate sends data to the FileTypes isolate, the FileTypes isolate receives the message and can act on it. The following listing shows a cut-down version of the server-side script so far, with the FileTypes isolate receiving data in the form of a `"hello world"` type message from the default isolate.

Listing 15.2 FileTypes isolate receiving data from the default isolate

```
import "dart:isolate";

void main() {
  // snip ...
  analyzeFileList(fileList);
}

analyzeFileList(fileList) {
  var fileTypesSendPort = spawnFunction(getFileTypesEntryPoint);
  fileTypesSendPort("Hello from default isolate");
  print("This is the default isolate");
}

void getFileTypesEntryPoint() {
  print("This is the FileTypes isolate");
  port.receive( (data, replyTo) {
    print(data);
  });
}
```

Default isolate spawns a new FileTypes isolate

Default isolate sends message to FileTypes isolate

FileTypes isolate receives callback function

Prints "Hello from default isolate"

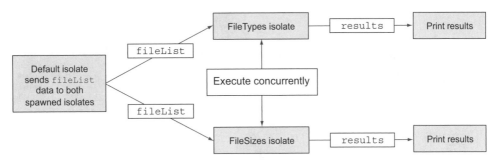

Figure 15.4   Default isolate sending data to other isolates

The sendPort.send() function lets you send data from the default isolate to the File-Types isolate. You're now in a position to modify your application to perform the analysis of a file list. You can rewrite the app to send the file list from the default isolate to the FileTypes and FileSizes isolates. The flow of execution is shown in figure 15.4.

Listing 15.3 performs the file analysis in your two separate isolates by sending the file list data to both isolates where the file analysis code runs. Each isolate is responsible for printing the output to the console.

Listing 15.3   Performing the file type and file size analyses in separate isolates

```
import "dart:io";
imoprt "dart:isolate";

void main() {
  getFileList("c:\windows").then(List<String> fileList) {
    analyzeFileLisT(fileList);
  });
}
analyzeFileList(fileList) {
  var fileTypesSendPort = spawnFunction(getFileTypesEntryPoint);
  fileTypesSendPort.send(fileList);

  var fileSizesSendPort = spawnFunction(getFileSizesEntryPoint);
  fileSizesSendPort.send(fileList);
}
void getFileTypesEntryPoint() {
  var receivePort = port;
  receivePort.receive((data, replyTo) {
    Map<String,int> typeCount = getFileTypes(data);
    print(typeCount);
  });
}
void getFileSizesEntryPoint() {
  var receivePort = port;
  receivePort.receive((data, replyTo) {
    Map<SYtring,int> totalSizes = getFileSizes(data);
    print(totalSizes);
  });
}
// snip getFileList(), getFileSizes(), getFileTypes()
```

Spawns FileTypes
isolate top-level
function

Sends fileList
data to FileTypes
isolate

Attaches receive handler
to FileTypes isolate

When fileList data is
received, analyzes it
and outputs to console

FileSizes isolate
uses same pattern
as FileTypes isolate.

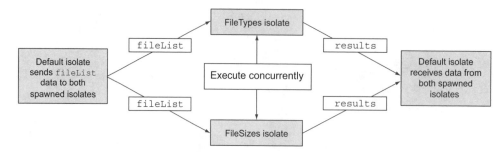

Figure 15.5   Default isolate waiting for the result data to be returned from the spawned isolates

This code still has a problem, though: the default isolate doesn't wait for the other isolates to finish. Ideally, you'd start the file analysis in the FileTypes and FileSizes isolates, and then the default isolate would wait for them to finish. You'll deal with this next and look at the `replyTo` parameter, which provides a mechanism for two-way isolate communication.

15.1.3   *Two-way isolate communication*

You've seen how to send data into an isolate, but one-way data transfer isn't as useful as sending data back and forth between isolates. The next step is to have the default isolate wait for the FileTypes and FileSizes isolates to return the processed file information back to the default isolate, as shown in figure 15.5.

In the modified script, when the default isolate receives the results, it prints them to the console. This also means that because the default isolate is waiting for results, it doesn't exit immediately.

USING A SENDPORT TO SEND DATA TO AN ISOLATE, REVISITED

In order for the FileTypes isolate to return data to the default isolate, the FileTypes isolate needs the default isolate's `SendPort`. A `SendPort`, remember, is used to `send()` data into an isolate, and this includes sending data into the default isolate. This relationship between `SendPort`, `ReceivePort`, and the isolates is shown in figure 15.6.

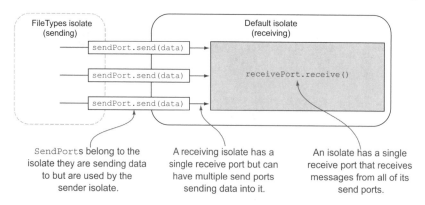

Figure 15.6   A receiving isolate has a single `ReceivePort` but multiple `SendPorts`.

One isolate can send data to another isolate with a `SendPort`. You saw that earlier when you used `spawnFunction()` to get the `SendPort` of a new FileTypes isolate. But how does the FileTypes isolate get the default isolate's `SendPort` so it can return data?

USING SENDPORT AS A REPLYTO ARGUMENT

This is where the `replyTo` argument of the receive callback function comes in. The `send()` function has an optional `replyTo` parameter, allowing the sending isolate to pass *its own* `SendPort` to the receiving isolate.

The sending isolate gets its own `SendPort` instance by using a function on its own `ReceivePort`. The sending isolate uses the top-level `port` property to call `port.toSendPort()` to get a `SendPort` it can pass to another isolate, as in the following snippet:

```
main() {
  var defaultIsolateSendPort = port.toSendPort();
}
getFileTypesEntryPoint() {
  var fileTypesIsolateSendPort = port.toSendPort();
}
```

Gets default isolate's SendPort

Gets FileTypes isolate's SendPort

Once an isolate has an instance of its own `SendPort`, it can pass it into the `send(data, replyTo)` function of the receiving `SendPort`. Figure 15.7 shows a simplified version of the Directory Analysis script in which the default isolate sends a "hello world" message to the FileTypes isolate, and the FileTypes isolate sends a "hello back" message back to the default isolate.

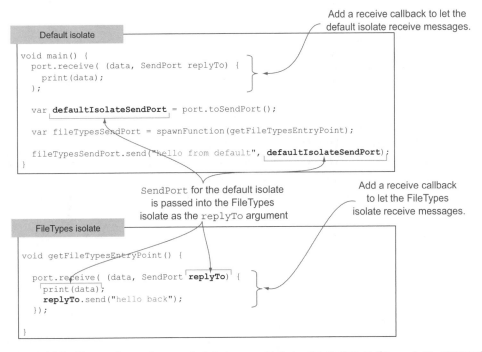

Figure 15.7 The `SendPort` from one isolate is passed into another isolate as the `replyTo` argument.

SENDING AND RECEIVING DATA BETWEEN ISOLATES

Now that you have a way to send data back to the calling isolate, you can modify your Directory Analysis application to let the default isolate wait for results from the File-Types and FileSizes isolates. The next listing shows this in action.

Listing 15.4   FileTypes and FileSizes isolates send results to the default isolate.

```
// snip other functons and imports

analyzeFileList(fileList) {
  port.receive((data, replyTo) {          Adds receive        Retrieves SendPort
    print(data);                          handler to          for default isolate
  });                                     default isolate

  var defaultIsolateSendPort = port.toSendPort();

  var fileTypesSendPort = spawnFunction(getFileTypesEntryPoint);    Sends default
  fileTypesSendPort.send(fileList, defaultIsolateSendPort);         isolate's SendPort
                                                                    to FileTypes isolate
  var fileSizesSendPort = spawnFunction(getFileSizesEntryPoint);
  fileSizesSendPort.send(fileList, defaultIsolateSendPort);         Sends
}                                                                   default isolate's
                                                                    SendPort to
void getFileTypesEntryPoint() {                                     FileSizes isolate
  var receivePort = port;
  receivePort.receive((data, replyTo) {
    Map<String,int> typeCount = getFileTypes(data);
    replyTo.send(typeCount);                          Passes results back
  });                                                 to default isolate
}

void getFileSizesEntryPoint() {
  var receivePort = port;
  receivePort.receive((data, replyTo) {
    Map<String,int> totalSizes = getFileSizes(data);
    replyTo.send(totalSizes);                         Passes results back
  });                                                 to default isolate
}
```

The default isolate is now responsible for printing the results from the FileTypes and FileSizes isolates. The default isolate no longer exits immediately; instead, it waits to receive messages from other isolates via its receive callback handler. This means you have a new problem. Instead of the application exiting too early, it waits indefinitely for messages to be passed to it from other isolates. You need a way to let the default isolate know that it has received all the data it's waiting for.

CLOSING A RECEIVEPORT

Fortunately, you can use a ReceivePort's close() function to close an isolate's communication port. When you call close() on a ReceivePort, any messages that are in the process of being sent are lost, and the ReceivePort doesn't receive any more messages. If this is the default isolate ReceivePort, the default isolate continues execution without waiting for any more messages.

Because your Directory Analysis script is waiting for two sets of results to be returned, you can add a simple counter to the default receive handler. When two sets of results have been received, you can close the `ReceivePort`, as shown in the following listing.

Listing 15.5 Closing a `ReceivePort` when all data is received

```
analyzeFileList(fileList) {
  var replyCount = 0;

  port.receive((data, replyTo) {          Increments reply
    replyCount ++;                        counter for each
    print(data);                          reply received

    if (replyCount == 2) {                If you have two replies,
      port.close();                       closes ReceivePort
    }
  });

  var defaultIsolateSendPort = port.toSendPort();

  var fileTypesSendPort = spawnFunction(getFileTypesEntryPoint);
  fileTypesSendPort.send(fileList, defaultIsolateSendPort);
  var fileSizesSendPort = spawnFunction(getFileSizesEntryPoint);
  fileSizesSendPort.send(fileList, defaultIsolateSendPort);
}
```

The Directory Analysis application now runs processes concurrently, using isolated execution units of code and passing messages back and forth between them. Each top-level isolate entry-point function shares the same function signature as the default isolate's `main()` function (returns `void` and takes no parameters). You'll use this feature in the next section when you split the Directory Analysis application into separate code files that are dynamically loaded from the default isolate.

> **Remember**
> - Every isolate has access to a top-level `port` property, which is its `ReceivePort` instance.
> - `SendPort spawnFunction(entryPointFunction)` creates a new isolate and returns a `SendPort` for sending data into the new isolate.
> - You can send data to an isolate by using the receiving isolate's `send-Port.send()` function.
> - An isolate can access its own `SendPort` by calling `port.toSendPort()`.

15.2 *Loading code dynamically*

The Directory Analysis application currently provides two analysis functions that count the file types and count the file sizes. By opening your application to let users extend it with plug-ins, the application will become useful without users having to edit any of the app's code.

You'll modify the application to dynamically load source files that are passed on the command line. Each source file will be responsible for analyzing a file list and returning the results to the main application. This is similar to the Directory Analysis application

1. A list of Dart files that will be used to analyze the c:\windows
   folder are passed as command-line arguments.

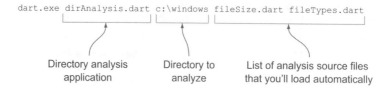

2. Each file is dynamically loaded into its
   own isolate and receives data from
   the default isolate.

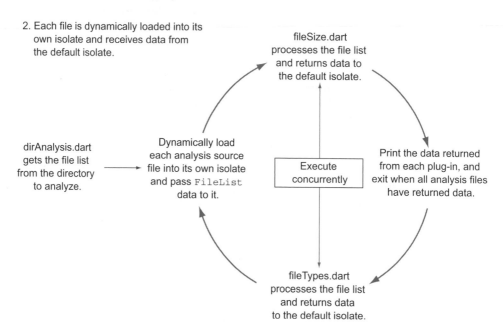

Figure 15.8   The Directory Analysis application will load a list of source files dynamically to analyze the list.

you already have, except the user will be able to provide a list of source files to analyze, rather than you specifying them up front in the source code. Figure 15.8 shows how the dynamically loading Directory Analysis application will work.

To achieve this flow, you need to modify the entry-point application file DirAnalysis .dart to read command-line parameters. You'll use the `Options` class you saw back in chapter 13, which provides the list of arguments passed to the Dart application on the command line. The first parameter will be the folder to analyze, followed by a list of source files, each of which is loaded and used to analyze the file list. The following listing shows the boilerplate `main()` function in the entry-point DirAnalysis.dart that you'll use to populate the `fileList` and `dynamicSourceFiles` list variables.

Listing 15.6   DirAnalysis.dart: reading the command-line arguments

```
import "dart:io";
import "dart:isolate";

void main() {
  var options = new Options();                          ⟵ Creates instance of
                                                          Options to retrieve
                                                          command-line arguments
  var analysisFolder = null;                            Variables to store folder you'll analyze,
  var dynamicSourceFiles = new List<String>();          and list of source files to load dynamically

  for (String argument in options.arguments) {          ⟵ For each
    if (analysisFolder == null) {                         command-line
      analysisFolder = argument            ... expect first one to   argument ...
    }                                      be analysis folder.
    else {
      dynamicSourceFiles.add(argument);    All others will be
    }                                      analysis source files.
  }
                                                        Get file list from
                                                        analysis folder
  getFileList(analysisFolder).then(List<String> fileList) {   ⟵
    analyzeFileList(fileList, dynamicSourceFiles);            ⟵
  });                          Pass file list and list of dynamic
}                              source files that will do the analyzing

analyzeFileList(List<String> fileList, List<String> dynamicSourceFiles) {
  // todo: Load each dynamic source file and pass it the file list
}

// snip getFileList() function
```

15.2.1   *Spawning an isolate from a filename*

Now you have a `fileList` variable, which, for example, could contain a list of filenames in the c:\windows folder, and a `dynamicSourceFiles` list, which could contain the filenames fileSize.dart and fileTypes.dart. Each of the dynamic source files, which the running application doesn't know about in advance, must be loaded into an isolate and have some data passed into it. This is similar to the `spawnFunction()` function, except that to dynamically load code from an external file, you use the `spawnUri()` function, passing in a URI or filename to load, such as `spawnUri("fileTypes.dart");`.

You can update the `analyzeFileList()` function to iterate through the list of dynamic source files, spawning an isolate from each one in turn and passing the `fileList` data into it. The default isolate (the DirAnalysis.dart application) will wait until it has received the same number of replies as there are source files before closing its port. The next listing shows the new `analyzeFileList()` function to perform this task.

Listing 15.7   DirAnalysis.dart: using `spawnUri()` to load a source file dynamically

```
// snip main() and getFileList functions()

analyzeFileList(List<String> fileList, List<String> dynamicSourceFiles) {
  var replyCount = 0;                                       Maintains count
  port.receive( (data, replyTo) {          ⟵ Sets up default isolate's   of replies from
                                           receive handler          spawned isolate
```

```
    print(data);                              ◁── Outputs received data

    replyCount++;
    if (replyCount == dynamicSourceFiles.length) {     Closes port when you've
      port.close();                                    received a reply from
    }                                                  each spawned isolate

  });                                                  Gets SendPort for default isolate
                                                       so spawned isolate can reply
  var defaultIsolateSendPort = port.toSendPort();  ◁──┘

  for (String sourceFileName in dynamicSourceFiles) {        ◁──   For each dynamic
    var dynamicSendPort = spawnUri(sourceFileName);     ◁──┐       source file ...
    dynamicSendPort.send(fileList, defaultIsolateSendPort);  ◁──┘
  }                                                   ... spawns new
}                           Sends new isolate the file list and    isolate from
                            default SendPort so it can reply        filename
```

You've seen how to load source files such as fileTypes.dart and fileSizes.dart dynamically and send them data. Next, let's see what these dynamic source files look like.

15.2.2 *Defining a dynamic source file*

When you load a Dart application, it has `main()`, which returns `void` and takes no parameters. This is the entry-point function for the main isolate. When you load an isolate dynamically from a source file, `main()` is also the entry-point function that begins executing in a new isolate. This means any source files that are loaded dynamically need to define a `main()` function, the same as a Dart script. This makes sense, because each Dart script runs in its own isolate, including the default isolate; internally, the default isolate and dynamically loaded isolate use the same mechanism. Figure 15.9 shows the outline of the default isolate and the dynamic source files.

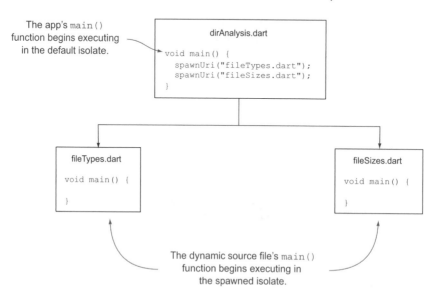

Figure 15.9 Dynamically loaded source files need a `main()` function that begins executing when loaded.

In the `main()` function of the dynamically loaded source file, you can attach a receive listener to the isolate's `ReceivePort`, accessible via the top-level `port` property, as you did when you started the isolate from a function with `spawnFunction()`. The following listing shows the `main()` function in fileTypes.dart; it receives file list data from the default isolate, analyzes it, and returns the data to the default isolate.

Listing 15.8   Adding the receive handler to the isolate

```
import "dart:isolate";

void main() {
  ReceivePort receivePort = port;                         ◁── Accesses top-level ReceivePort for this isolate

  receivePort.receive( (data, replyTo) {                  ◁── Attaches receive callback handler
    Map<String, int> typeCount = getFileTypes(data);      ◁── Analyzes passed-in file list
    replyTo.send(typeCount);                              ◁── Returns results to default isolate
  });
}
// snip getFileTypes(List<String> fileList)
```

You've provided a model for third-party users to provide their own file-analysis code, and the Directory Analysis application can use that third-party code without needing to modify the core application. The fileSizes.dart file is a second analysis source file, and users can provide their own analysis files, perhaps to return the average file size for each file type.

By using dynamic code-loading in isolates, you have a safe way to use code from a third party without needing to be concerned with shared internal state or external code directly accessing values without your application. By providing a message-passing mechanism, Dart isolates allow safe communication between different code bases with a concurrency model that's simpler than the multithreaded shared-state concurrency found in C# and Java.

> **Remember**
> - `spawnFunction()` dynamically loads a Dart source file into a new isolate.
> - Dynamically loaded Dart code needs to provide a `main()` function, which begins executing in the new isolate.

In the next section, we'll take a deeper look at isolates and explore how you can create multiple, identical isolates to distribute a single task among multiple worker isolates.

15.3   *Spawning multiple workers*

Often, a server-side process has a batch of work to perform. The Directory Analysis application currently counts the types of each file type in a single folder, one level deep. Isolates, which run concurrently, are also ideal for batch-processing tasks such as processing a list of folders. Each folder in the list is independent of the other; the default isolate is interested in getting it analyzed as fast as possible. This is where

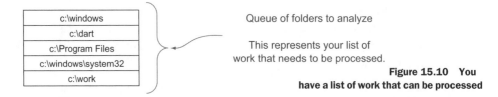

Queue of folders to analyze

This represents your list of
work that needs to be processed.

**Figure 15.10   You
have a list of work that can be processed**

worker isolates come in. By starting up a number of background worker tasks, you can
process a list of items, passing a new item into each isolate when it finishes processing
the last. Figure 15.10 shows the list of folders you'll process.

This is a small list of work, but you can imagine that you might have many hundreds of folders to analyze. You couldn't create a new worker for each item in the
list—your computer would quickly run out of resources. Instead, you'll create a small,
fixed number of worker isolates and pass them a single work item each. The Directory
Analysis script will create three isolates.

> **TIP** Some tuning is normally required to find the sweet spot for best perfor-
> mance and resource utilization. Too many isolates, and you'll quickly run out
> of memory, and the CPUs will spend as much time switching between isolates
> as they do running them. Too few isolates, and you could be missing out on a
> performance boost. Starting with the number of available cores on your
> machine is usually a good rule of thumb.

Listing 15.9 shows the starting point for your batch Directory Analysis application,
which has a new `getFileListEntryPoint()` function that's used as a worker isolate.
The `getFileListEntryPoint()` function will receive the folder name to process as its
message data. It retrieves the file list and passes it to an analysis function to count the
types of files and return the results. When it returns the results, it also returns its own
`SendPort`, which the default isolate will eventually use to send the next folder to process back to the worker.

Listing 15.9   batchDirAnalysis.dart: starting point for the batch application

```
import "dart:io";
import "dart:isolate";

void main() {
  Queue<String> foldersToProcess = new Queue<String>();
  foldersToProcess.add(r"c:\windows");
  foldersToProcess.add(r"c:\dart");                          Creates list of
  foldersToProcess.add(r"c:\windows\system32");              folders to process
  foldersToProcess.add(r"c:\Program Files");
  foldersToProcess.add(r"c:\work\");

  // todo: process folders with workers                      You'll implement
                                                             the rest of main()
}                                                            in listing 15.10.

void getFileListEntryPoint() {
```

```
    var workerReceivePort = port;
    var workerSendPort = receivePort.toSendPort();
```
Gets SendPort and ReceivePort for worker isolate

```
    workerReceivePort.receive( (folderToProcess, defaultReplyTo) {
        print("Processing folder: $folderToProcess");

        getFileList(folderToProcess).then( (fileList) {
            var results = countFileTypes(fileList);

            defaultReplyTo.send(results, workerSendPort);
        });

    });
}
List<String> getFileList(folderName) {
    // snip implementation
    // returns list of files in the folder
}

Map<String,int> countFileTypes(fileList) {
    // snip implementation
    // returns a count of each file type, such as:
    // .TXT: 3, .DOC: 10, .PDF: 5
}
```
Attaches receive callback handler

Sends results to default isolate, passing in worker's SendPort

Gets list of files in folder and passes them to analysis function

In the default isolate, you need to start a fixed number of worker isolates and send each an item of work to process—in this case, a folder from the queue of folders waiting to be processed is the item of work. Once all the worker isolates have work to complete, the default isolate waits for them to return their work, as shown in figure 15.11.

Listing 15.10 shows spawnFunction() in action, passing three worker isolates an initial data item. Note that you never store a list of all the worker isolates—spawning them and passing data is enough, because each worker isolate returns its own

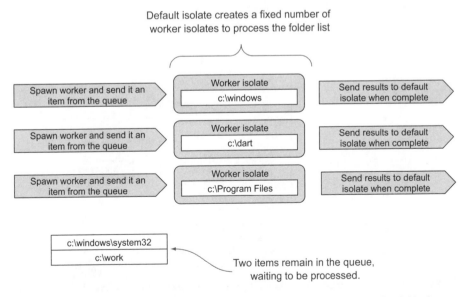

Figure 15.11 The application spawns a fixed number of workers and sends each a folder to process.

SendPort when it returns its results. Each time you send a folder name to a worker isolate, you expect a reply from it, so you also track the number of expected replies. Once the count of replies matches the number of expected replies, you'll close the default isolate ReceivePort and allow the application to exit.

Listing 15.10 Spawning worker isolates and passing initial data items

```
main() {
  // snip creating foldersToProcess queue

  var expectedReplyCount = 0;                           Tracks expected
                                                        number of replies

  var defaultReceivePort = port;                        Gets default isolate's
  var defaultSendPort = defaultReceivePort.toSendPort();  SendPort and ReceivePort

  for (int i=0; i<3; i++) {                             Creates three worker isolates
    SendPort worker = spawnFunction(getFileListEntryPoint);

    expectedReplyCount++;                               Spawns worker
                                                        function
    var folderName = foldersToProcess.removeFirst();
    worker.send(folderName, defaultSendPoint);          Increments
  }                                                     expected reply:
}                            Sends folder to            one reply per send
                             process to the worker
```

Now you have three isolates processing a folder each. The final step is to let your default isolate receive data from each of the three worker isolates and pass each worker isolate its next work item if there's still work waiting to be performed. This is why the worker returns its own SendPort in the replyTo argument: so the default isolate can pass more data into it. Figure 15.12 shows this final sequence of events.

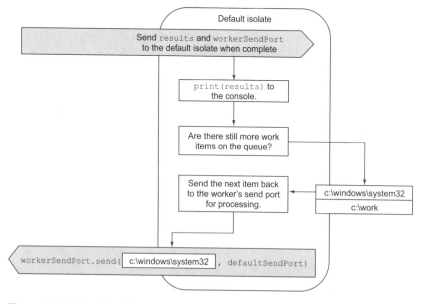

Figure 15.12 The default isolate receives results and sends more work back to the worker isolates.

This loop of the worker returning results and the default isolate sending the next work item continues for all the worker isolates while there's still work on the queue. Because the code in a single isolate only runs in a single thread, you don't need to be concerned with locking access to the queue of work items as you'd do in Java or C#. When the default isolate checks the folder queue and removes an item, no other thread or process has access to the list. This is one of the key benefits of message-passing between isolates: it provides a protected environment for your code to run in, with no other code able to access and modify memory locations that might cause concurrency bugs.

Listing 15.11 puts this last step into action by adding the default isolate's `receive()` callback handler to send more data into the worker while there's still data available. When `expectedReplyCount` matches `actualReplyCount`, you've received all the replies; the application stops waiting for more replies by calling `defaultReceivePort.close()`.

> **Listing 15.11 Implementing the default isolate `receive()` function**

```
main() {
  // snip creating foldersToProcess queue

  var expectedReplyCount = 0;

  var defaultReceivePort = port;
  var defaultSendPort = defaultReceivePort.toSendPort();

  for (int i=0; i<3; i++) {
    SendPort worker = spawnFunction(getFileListEntryPoint);

    expectedReplyCount++;

    var folderName = foldersToProcess.removeFirst();
    worker.send(folderName, defaultSendPoint);
  }

  var actualReplyCount = 0;

  defaultReceivePort.receive( (results, replyToWorker) {    ◁── Attaches default isolate's receive() handler
    print(results);                                          ◁── Outputs returned results

    actualReplyCount++;            ◁── Increments reply counter

    if (foldersToProcess.isEmpty == false) {                 ◁── If queue still contains folders to process, sends next folder back to worker
      expectedReplyCount++;
      var folderName = foldersToProcess.removeFirst();
      replyToWorker.send(folderName, defaultSendPoint);
    }

    if (actualReplyCount == expectedReplyCount) {            ◁── When all replies have been returned, closes default isolate's ReceivePort
      defaultReceivePort.close();
      print("Exiting");
    }
  });
}
```

The application will now keep passing work to the workers while there are still folders to process. In the previous batch direct analysis example, you use a predefined queue, but the previous pattern also works when items are still being added to the queue. Imagine a scenario where each top-level folder that's analyzed returns a list of child folders along with the file-count data, so more folders are added to the back of the queue at the same time other workers are removing items from the front of the queue.

TIP   Although an isolate may be expected to return, it may in fact never return due to some internal condition in the isolate. For this reason, your applications should ensure that they can cope with this scenario.

Remember

- The worker isolate can return its own `SendPort` to the default isolate when it wants more work.
- The list of work items in the default isolate isn't directly accessible by worker isolates.
- Each isolate has access to only its own memory locations, so you don't need to synchronize or lock data when accessing the isolate.

15.4 *Summary*

Isolates, with their separate memory model and message passing, provide a way to achieve concurrency in Dart that's simpler to implement than in Java and C#, because you have only a single thread accessing a memory location at any one time. By spawning isolates to perform multiple different tasks at once, you can use modern hardware to complete work more quickly. And by creating worker isolates, you can distribute the processing of batch tasks across multiple workers in a memory-safe way.

Isolates are spawned as top-level functions from within your code, or by using `spawnFunction()`, or by dynamically loading a Dart source file with `spawnUri()`. Spawning an isolate dynamically from a source file allows you to create a plug-in model to let users of your application provide their own code, which runs as part of your application but about which your app has no prior knowledge. This is a powerful technique for creating extendible, customizable applications for your users to install and use.

You've reached the end of the book. Dart is a fast-moving language, which means you'll have more to learn as the language evolves, but you now know enough to understand the core concepts in the Dart language. Congratulate yourself, and build great applications—and make sure you tell everyone that they're built with Dart.

appendix A
Core language reference

The core Dart language consists of variables and operators, a number of built-in types, flow-control statements, and function blocks. Dart is a dynamically typed language, similar to JavaScript, and type information in variable and parameter declarations is optional. The Dart virtual machine executes Dart code identically whether type information is provided or not. Any type information provided is used by tools to confirm the developer's intention and provides documentation to future developers who may need to read and maintain the code.

A.1 Variable declaration

A variable is declared by prefixing the variable name with one of the following:

- The var keyword (indicating a dynamic type, or no type information is supplied)
- A type name (indicating that type information is provided)
- The final keyword (indicating a dynamic read-only variable)
- The final keyword followed by a type name (indicating a typed read-only variable)

Dynamic variables can contain values of any type, but typed variables are checked by the Dart tools, which ensure that the variable contains a value of the type indicated.

You assign a variable a value using the assignment operator =:

```
var myNumber = 123;         ◁──┐ Assigns variable
                                 myNumber the
                                 value 123

int anInteger = 456;            ◁──┐ Assigns variable
                                     anInteger the
                                     value 456

final otherNumber = 789;                        ◁── Assigns variable
                                                    otherNumber the
final int anotherNumber = 246;   ◁──┐           value 789
                                     Assigns variable anotherNumber
                                     the value 246
```

351

A.1.1   *Declaring variables with the var keyword or type name*

When you use the var keyword to declare a variable, you aren't specifying any specific type information. If you use a type, such as int, instead of var, you're declaring that as a developer you expect the variable to contain an integer value. The Dart tools can validate that the variable only ever contains an integer, but the language itself doesn't enforce this.

> **NOTE**   The var keyword and type names can be used interchangeably without affecting the running of the application.

A variable declared with var or a type name (such as int) doesn't need to contain a value. If you don't provide a value, the variable contains null:

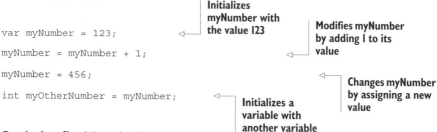

```
var myUninitializedNumber;                    Equivalent and both
var myUninitalizedNumber = null;              assigned the value null

int myUninitializedInt;                       Both int types
int myUninitializedInt = null;                assigned the value null
```

A variable declared with var or a type name is *mutable*. This means its value can be modified or assigned a different value:

```
                                    Initializes
                                    myNumber with
                                    the value 123     Modifies myNumber
var myNumber = 123;                                   by adding 1 to its
                                                      value
myNumber = myNumber + 1;

myNumber = 456;
                                                      Changes myNumber
int myOtherNumber = myNumber;                         by assigning a new
                                    Initializes a     value
                                    variable with
                                    another variable
```

A.1.2   *Declaring final (read-only) variables*

You can replace the var keyword with the final keyword, or use the final keyword in conjunction with a type name to declare a read-only variable. The following rules apply:

- Final variables must be initialized to a value when they're declared.
- Final variables can't be modified after declaration.

Here's an example:

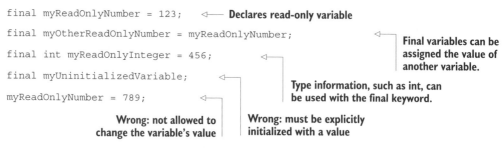

```
final myReadOnlyNumber = 123;      ◄──── Declares read-only variable

final myOtherReadOnlyNumber = myReadOnlyNumber;
                                                    Final variables can be
final int myReadOnlyInteger = 456;                  assigned the value of
                                                    another variable.
final myUninitializedVariable;

myReadOnlyNumber = 789;                    Type information, such as int, can
                                           be used with the final keyword.

       Wrong: not allowed to       Wrong: must be explicitly
       change the variable's value  initialized with a value
```

A.1.3 *Populating variables with literal syntax*

In Dart, all types are objects, and there are no primitive types. Dart has language support for declaring five specific variable types using literal definitions rather than constructing an instance of an object:

- *Numbers*—123, 45.6, 0xAB
- *Strings*—"Hello", 'Dart'
- *Boolean*—true, false
- *Lists*— [123, "Hello", true]
- *Maps*—{"key1":"value1", "key2":"value2"}

All other objects use the new keyword to construct an instance of the object. For example:

```
var myVariable = new Object();          Creates objects and stores
var myDateVariable = new Date();        their reference in a variable
```

NUMBERS

The num type is the base type for numbers. int and double are subtypes of num. Any variable with a decimal point is considered a double; otherwise it's an int:

- Integer values can be of any arbitrary length.
- Double values are 64-bit floating-point numbers.

Here's an example:

```
var myNum = 123;
var myInteger = 234;                     Declares numbers
var myDouble = 123.45;                   using literal values
var myHex = 0xABCD1234;                  with var keyword

num myNum = 123;
num myDoubleNum = 123.45;                Declares numbers
int myInteger = 234;                     using literal values
double myDouble 123.45                   with type information
int myHex = 0XABCD1234;
```

STRINGS

Dart strings are Unicode characters specified in single or double quotes. If you use single quotes to declare a string, you can embed double quotes, and vice versa:

- Single quotes can be embedded in a string declared with double quotes.
- Double quotes can be embedded in a string declared with single quotes.
- Use the escape character \ to add character escape sequences (such as the newline \n escape sequence).
- Prefix a string literal value with the r character to ignore escape characters.

Here's an example:

```
var mySingleQuotedString = 'Hello Dart';        Declares
var myDoubleQuotedString = "Hello Dart";        new string

var embededDoubleQuotes = 'Hello "Dart" World';   Declares new string containing
var embededSingleQuotes = "Hello 'Dart' World";   embedded quotes
```

```
var escapedQuote = 'Hello Dart\'s World';
var newLine = "Hello \nDart";

var rawString = r"Hello \nDart";
```

Escapes embedded single quote

Adds newline-escape sequence: outputs Hello Dart

Ignores newline escape sequence; outputs Hello \n Dart

You can also declare multiline strings enclosed in a pair of triple single-quotes:

```
var myMultiLineString = '''This is a
Multi line
string literal''';
```

To improve formatting and readability, the first new line is ignored if there is no text on it:

```
var myFormattedMultiLineString = '''
This is a
  formatted
    multi-line
      string literal''';
```

DECLARING STRINGS WITH STRING INTERPOLATION

A string can't be concatenated with other strings or other variables using the + operator. This means the following won't work:

```
var foo = "Dart";
var bar = "World";
var foobar = foo + bar;
var helloFooBar = "Hello " + foo " " + bar;
```

Wrong: you can't "add" strings together.

Instead, Dart provides string interpolation to declare strings. A variable can be resolved to its value by prefixing it with a $ (dollar sign):

```
var foo = "Dart";
var bar = "World";
var foobar = "$foo$bar";
var helloFooBar = "Hello $foo $bar";
```

◁—— **"DartWorld"**

"Hello Dart World"

Where the expression needs to be evaluated, such as converting the foo variable to uppercase using the String type's toUpperCase() method, the expression must be wrapped inside a ${ } block:

```
var foo = "Dart";
var helloFooBar = "Hello ${foo.toUpperCase()}";
```

◁—— **"Hello DART"**

All variables of all types have a toString() method (inherited from the base object type), and this is called implicitly if the variable used in string interpolation isn't a string type:

```
var myNumber = 123;
var helloNumber = "Hello ${myNumber.toString()}";
var helloNumber = "Hello $myNumber";
```

◁—— **"Hello 123"**

"Hello 123"; toString() is called implicitly

BOOLEANS

Unlike JavaScript, Dart has exactly one `true` value. Every value other than the literal keyword `true` is considered to be `false`:

```
var myTrueValue = true;
bool myTypedTrueValue = true;
```
There is only
one true value.

```
var myFalseValue = false;
bool myTypedFalseValue = false;
var myNumber = 1;
var myZero = 0;
var myObject = new Object();
var myNull = null;
```
Every other value isn't
true; therefore it's false.

Using the equality operators `==` (equals) and `!=` (not equals), you can produce a boolean value as a result of a conditional comparison:

```
var isTrue = 2 == (1+1);
var isFalse = 123 != 123;
```
Stores
value true

<---— **Stores value false**

> **NOTE** Also unlike JavaScript, conditional statements (like the `if` statement) only allow boolean expressions, so you can't use `myNumber` or `myObject` as a conditional expression. You need to explicitly compare two values, such as `if (myNumber == 1)` or `if (myObject != null)`. The section "Flow control and iterating" has more information about conditional statements.

CREATING LITERAL LISTS (ARRAYS)

Dart has no explicit array type. Instead it has the `List` type, which is an ordered set of objects. A `List` implements the `Collection` interface, as does a `Set` and a `Queue`. The `Collection` interface allows iteration over elements. Only lists, though, have a literal declaration mechanism. A literal list is defined by a comma-separated list of objects, declared in square brackets, which create a fixed-length list:

```
var myList = [123, 'Hello', true];
List otherList = [1,2,3,4,5,6];
```
List containing three elements: a
number, a string, and a boolean

List containing six elements,
all of which are numbers

Lists can also contain other lists:

```
    var listOfLists = [
                    [1,2,3],
                    ['a','b','c','d'],
                    [true, false]
                    ];
```
Outer list containing
multiple inner lists

You access elements in a list by using the variables list indexer `[]` property with a zero-based counter:

```
var myList = [123, 'Hello', true];
var myNumber = myList[0];
var myString = myList[1];
var myBool = myList[2];
myList[1] = 'Hello World';

var notAvailable = myList[3];
```
<---— **Declares list**

Reads values from list
using [ ] indexer syntax

<---— **Updates value in list**

Wrong: no value
at this list index

You can see how many items are in a list by checking the `length` property:

```
int listLength = myList.length;    ⊲— Examines list length
```

The literal syntax creates a fixed-length list object containing a number of prepopulated objects. You can also create a fixed-length list by using the new keyword to create an instance of a `List` object with a fixed number of empty (null) elements:

```
var myList = new List(3);          ⊲— Creates list with three null elements
myList[0] = 123;
myList[1] = 'Hello';               Populates three
myList[2] = true;                  elements with values
```

You can't add new elements to a fixed-length list:

```
var myList = new List(3);   ⊲— Creates fixed-length list      Wrong: can't add a
myList.add(123);                                    ⊲—        fourth element to list
```

If you don't specify the number of elements when creating a list instance, you get a growable list that can be added to:

```
var myList = new List();           ⊲— Creates growable list
myList.add(123);
myList.add('Hello');               Adds three
myList.add(true);                  items into it
print(myList.length);              ⊲— Length is 3
myList.add(456);                   ⊲— Adds fourth item
print(myList.length);              ⊲— Length is 4
```

> **NOTE** The section "Flow control and iterating" has more about accessing multiple list elements sequentially.

You can use a literal list to declare a `Set` or a `Queue` by passing the literal list into their respective `.from(...)` constructors:

```
var set = new Set.from([123,'Hello',true]);
var queue = new Queue.from([123,'Hello',true]);
```

The differences between Lists, Sets, and Queues is shown in Table A.1.

> **NOTE** Lists also support generic typing. See the section "Generic maps and lists" for more information.

Table A.1 Comparison of Lists, Sets, and Queues

List	Set	Queue
Literal definition	No literal definition	No literal definition
Access elements by index	Can't access elements by index	Can't access elements by index
Growable or fixed length	Growable only	Growable only
	Can't contain duplicates	Has methods to enable using it as a Queue (addLast(), removeFirst()) or a Stack (addLast(), removeLast())

CREATING LITERAL MAPS

A map is a set of key/value pairs, and you can define a literal map by using curly braces containing a comma-separated list of these `"key":"value"` pairs. You access the map elements by using the key name in an indexer on the map:

```
Map myMap = {"key1":"value1","key2":"value2"};    ◁── Creates map literal

var value1 = myMap["key1"];                        Reads values from
                                                   map literal by key
var value2 = myMap["key2"];

myMap["key2"] = "a new value 2";        ◁─┐   Updates existing
                                          │   value in map
myMap["key3"] = "a new key value pair";  ◁┘
                                            Inserts new key/
                                            value into map
```

When specifying a literal map, values can be any object:

```
var aValue = new Object();    ◁── Creates object      Uses object as
var myMap = {"key",value};                        ◁──┘ value of map
```

Keys, on the other hand, must be literal strings (not string variables) when you use the literal map syntax to define a map. The following won't work:
                                                    Stores string literal
                                                    inside variable
```
String myKey = "key";                         ◁──┘
var myMap = {myKey: "value"};    ◁─┐
                                   │ Wrong: can't use a variable
                                     to define a map literal's key
```

This restriction only applies when creating the map using the literal syntax. The default implementation of a map is a `HashMap`. Once you've created a map using literal syntax, you can add new keys that implement `Hashable`, which includes string objects:

```
var myMap = {"key1":"value1"};    ◁── Creates literal map

String myKey = "key2";                        ◁── Creates string variable

myMap[myKey] = "value2";    ◁── Uses string variable as map's key
```

You can add to key/value pairs in literal maps after you've created the initial map. If you assign a value to a nonexistent key, the key/value pair is inserted into the map. If you assign a value to an existing key, its value is overwritten. Trying to read a nonexistent key returns `null`:

```
var myMap = {"key1":"value1"};       ◁── Creates map with one key

myMap["key2"] = "value2";            ◁── Adds second key/value pair

myMap["key1"] = "a new value1";      ◁── Updates existing value

var value3 = myMap["key3"];          ◁── Reading nonexistent key returns null
```

When you read a value from a map, it might return `null` because that is the value stored, or it might return `null` because the key doesn't exist. Fortunately, the map interface includes a `containsKey()` function to check for the existence of a key:

```
var myMap = {"key1":"value1"};

var someValue = myMap["someKey"];
```
Reading nonexistent value returns null

```
bool containsSomeKey = myMap.containsKey("someKey");
```
◁—— Returns false

```
myMap["someKey"] = null;
```
◁

```
containsSomeKey = myMap.containsKey("someKey");
```
◁—┐
Setting key to contain value null adds key/ value to map

Returns true

You can also use the constructor syntax rather than the literal syntax to create maps. This means you can use any `Hashable` object as a key, because the constructor creates an empty map. The following creates two identical maps that you can add key/value pairs to:

```
var myLiteralMap = {};
```
◁— Creates empty map using literal syntax

```
var myConstructedMap = new Map();
```
◁
Creates empty map using constructor syntax

You can access the map's collection of keys or values using the `keys` and `values` properties to return a `Collection` interface:

```
var myMap = {"key1":"value1","key2":"value2"};
var keys = myMap.keys;
```
Accesses collection of keys

```
var values = myMap.values;
```
◁
Accesses collection of values

> **NOTE** The section "Flow control and iterating" has more about accessing multiple map keys and values sequentially.

A.1.4   *Generic lists and maps*

Lists and maps can store any combination of objects: for example, a list could store a string, an integer, and a boolean value. You can use Dart's generic typing syntax to declare that a list or a map contains specific types. You specify the specific type information in triangle brackets: `< >`.

The following code defines a list that must contain only strings (or integers, booleans, and so on) and stores that list in a dynamic variable:

```
var myStringList = new List<String>();
```
◁— Declares list that will contain only strings

```
var myIntegerList = new List<int>();
var myBoolList = new List<bool>();

myStringList.add("a string");
```
◁— Adds string to this list

You can also use strongly typed variables to allow the type checker to validate that you're only adding a string into the list:

```
List<String> myStringList = new List<String>();
```
◁
Uses strong typing to declare that myStringList contains only strings

```
myStringList.add("a string");
```
◁—— Adds string to list

```
myStringList.add(123);
```
◁—
Wrong: tools will validate this as an error because it isn't a string.

You can also declare a literal list that only contains a specific type:

```
List<String> myStringList = <String>["item1","item2","item3"];
```

**Declares literal list that tools will
validate to contain only strings**

Maps can also be strongly typed to contain keys and values of a specific type:

```
Map<String,bool> myMap = new Map<String,bool>();
myMap["key1"] = true;
myMap["key2"] = false;
```

**Declares that map will
only contain string keys
and bool values**

**Tools will validate that you're only using
strings as keys and bools as values.**

Finally, just like lists, you can also strongly type literal maps:

```
Map<String,int> myMap = <String,Int>{"key1":123,"key2":456};
```

**Declares literal map that tools will validate
to contain only string keys and int values**

A.2 *Functions*

Functions are the reusable building blocks of all applications. The Dart application begins running with a single top-level function called `main()`, which returns nothing and takes no parameters:

```
main() {

}
```

**Application entry-point
function is called main()**

**Calls other
application code here**

The only mandatory parts of a function are

- Function name (only if you don't want the function to be anonymous)
- Parameter list (may be empty)
- Function body

Dart functions also support the following features:

- Named, optional parameters
- Default optional parameter values
- Assigning a function into a variable
- Referencing a function by name (as opposed to calling the function)
- Lexical closures, allowing functions to wrap over values outside their immediate scope

Dart's optional typing allows many permutations of function declaration. If you provide a return type and parameter type information, the Dart tools will use that to validate your code, and you simultaneously provide valuable documentation to fellow developers. When you provide no type information for parameters and return types, this is equivalent to specifying the type `dynamic`.

NOTE It's good style to provide explicit parameter and return type information on your public interfaces—in other words, code that other developers might have to interact with.

Dart has two versions of a function syntax: the longhand version, which allows multiple lines of code in a { } code block; and a shorthand, one-line version, which automatically returns the value produced by the single-line expression, or `null` if no value is produced.

The smallest function you can produce in either syntax is shown here:

```
() => ;

() {
}
```

⟵ Shorthand syntax with no parameters, no name, and no expression; implicitly returns null

Longhand syntax with no parameters, no name, and no return type

You call a function by specifying its name and passing a list of arguments into it, wrapped in braces:

```
sayHello("Dart");
```

Calls sayHello() function, passing in value "Dart"

A function can optionally return a single value, which can be assigned into a variable:

```
var greeting = getGreeting("Hello","Dart");
```

Stores result of getGreeting() function in greeting variable

If a function doesn't return a value, it generates a `null` value:

```
var message = print("Hello Dart");
```

Message contains null because print() function doesn't return a value

A.2.1 Longhand function syntax

Longhand function syntax encloses the function code in curly braces { }, which appear after the function name and parameter list. The following function shows multiple ways of returning the value of a + b using optional typing. You use the `return` keyword to indicate the return value:

```
sum(a, b) {
    return a + b;
}
```

No return type or parameter information is specified.

```
dynamic sum(dynamic a, dynamic b) {
    return a + b;
}
```

Same as previous, but explicitly declares dynamic

```
num sum(num a, num b) {
    return a + b;
}
```

Specifies num as return type and parameter types

If a function doesn't return a value, you can specify the return type of `void`:

```
void showSum(a, b) {
    print("a is $a, and b is $b");
}
```

No value returned, so void is return type

A.2.2 Shorthand function syntax

The shorthand function syntax uses the => symbol to indicate the expression to return. The following are all valid functions, called `sum`, that return the result of a + b:

```
sum(a,b) => a + b;
dynamic sum(a,b) => a + b;
dynamic sum(Dyanmic a, dynamic b) => a + b;

sum(num a, num b) => a + b
num sum(num a, num b) => a + b;
```

Three functions are equivalent, taking any type and returning the added value

Takes num types as parameters, returns dynamic

Takes num types as parameters, returns num

You can't specify that a shorthand function returns void. This is because all shorthand functions return a value, which is null if no other value is specified:

```
void sum(a,b) => print("a is $a, and b is $b");
```

Wrong: shorthand function still returns null

A.2.3 *Function parameters*

Functions have mandatory parameters and optional parameters. All mandatory parameters must be declared first as a comma-separated list, followed by all optional parameters, which are enclosed in a single block of square brackets. Optional parameters, if not specified, default to null:

```
sum(a, b, [c, b]) {
  if (c == null)  c = 0;
  if (d == null)  d = 0;

  return a + b + c + d;
}

num sum(num a, num b, [num c, num b]) {
  if (c == null)  c = 0;
  if (d == null)  d = 0;

  return a + b + c + d;
}
```

sum() function with optional parameters c and d

Checks to see if c parameter was provided

Same sum() function with type information

PROVIDING DEFAULT VALUES FOR OPTIONAL PARAMETERS

You can also provide a default value to which an optional parameter is initialized, rather than having it automatically initialize to null:

```
sum(a,b, [c=0, d=0]) {
  return a + b + c + d;
}
num sum(num a,num b, [num c=0, num d=0]) {
  return a + b + c + d;
}
```

Sets c and d to default to zero

CALLING FUNCTIONS WITH OPTIONAL PARAMETERS

When you call a function with optional parameters, you must specify all the mandatory parameters first, followed by the optional parameters, either by position or specified explicitly by name and value:

```
sum(a,b,[c=0,d=0]) => a + b + c + d;

sum(1, 2);
```

← c and d not specified, so default to zero

Defines single-line function with optional c and d parameters that default to zero

```
sum(1, 2, 3);
```
c set to 3 by position; d not specified, defaults to zero

```
sum(1, 2, 3, 4);   ◁── c and d specified by position
```

```
sum(1, 2, d:4);
```
d specified by name; c defaults to zero

A.2.4   First class functions

You can declare a function in top-level scope or in another code block, where it can become a closure, closing over other variables that are also in scope.

FUNCTIONS AS VARIABLES

You can reference a function in your code by referring to it by name, without the brackets that specify the argument list:

```
sum(a, b) {
  return a + b;
}
```
Defines sum() function in top-level scope

```
main() {
  var sumFunction = sum;
  var result = sumFunction(1,2);
}
```
Stores sum() function in variable

Calls sum() function using variable reference

You can create a function in the scope of another function:

```
main() {
  sum(a, b) {
    return a + b;
  }
```
Defines sum() function in main() function

```
  var result1 = sum(1,2);   ◁── Calls sum() function
```

```
  var sumFunction = sum;
```
Stores sum() function in another variable

```
  var result2 = sumFunction(1,2);   ◁── Calls sum() function using variable reference
}
```

You can also store a function directly in a variable without giving it a name. This is known as an *anonymous function*:

```
main() {
  var sumFunction = (a, b) {
    return a + b;
  };
```
Stores anonymous function in variable

Stores anonymous function in variable using shorthand function syntax

```
  var shorthandSumFunction = (a, b) => a + b;
}
```

FUNCTIONS AS FUNCTION ARGUMENTS

In the same way you can store a function in a variable, you can also pass a function as an argument to another function that accepts a function in its parameter list:

```
doCalculation(calcFunction, a, b) {
```
Defines doCalculation() function, which accepts another function as its first parameter

```
  return calcFunction(a, b);
}
```
Uses passed-in function to return a value

```
main() {
  sum(a, b) => a + b;   ◁── Defines sum() function
```

```
    var multiply = (a, b) => a * b;
    var result1 = doCalculation(sum, 1, 2);
    var result2 = doCalculation(multiply,1,2);
    var result3 = doCalculation((a, b) => b - a, 1, 2);
}
```

◁── **Defines multiply() function stored in a variable**

◁── **Passes sum() function to doCalculation() function**

◁── **Passes multiply() function to doCalculation() function**

◁── **Passes anonymous subtract() function to doCalculation() function**

FUNCTIONS AS RETURN TYPES

A function can also be returned as a return type from another function:

```
getSumFunction() {
  var sum = (a, b) => a + b;
  return sum;
}

main() {
  var sum = getSumFunction();
  var result = sum(1,2);
}
```

◁── **Declare sum() function**

◁── **Returns it**

◁── **Stores return value in sum variable**

◁── **Calls sum() function using variable reference**

FUNCTIONS AS CLOSURES

Functions close over variables in their surrounding scope. In the following example, getSumFunction() declares a multiplier value (unknown to callers of getSumFunction()), which is referenced in the returned sum() function. The sum() function maintains a reference to the multiplier even though getSumFunction() has exited and is no longer in scope:

```
getSumFunction() {
  var multiplier = 100;

  sum (a, b) {
    return (a + b) * multiplier;
  }

  return sum;
}

main() {
  var sum = getSumFunction();
  var result = sum(1,2);
}
```

sum() function closes over multiplier variable, which is outside sum()'s own scope

◁── **Returns (I + 2) * I00 = 300**

A.3 *Flow control and iterating*

Flow control in Dart is very similar to flow control in JavaScript and Java. For decision making, Dart has

- `if/else` statements
- The conditional `?` operator
- `switch` statements

And for looping around collections of objects, Dart has

- for loops
- for/in loops
- do while loops
- while do loops
- Breaking and continuing inside a loop
- forEach() map method

A.3.1 *Decision making for controlling flow*

Applications make decisions all the time. if/else statements form the backbone of this decision making, with the conditional operator being used for shorter decision making and switch being used to select from multiple possible options.

IF/ELSE STATEMENTS

The basic structure of an if statement is to check that a variable is a boolean true or false value, executing code in the following block if the condition is true:

```
var someCondition = true;                    Checks condition
if (someCondition) {                         and executes code
  print("was true");                         Executes code in block if
  print("multiple lines of code");           condition evaluates to true
}
```

If the code to execute consists of only a single line, then it's acceptable to provide the code to execute on the same line, without the curly braces to specify the block:

```
                                             Prints "was true" if
if (someCondition) print("was true");        someCondition is true
```

The condition that is checked must evaluate to a boolean; otherwise an error is raised. For instance, the following check for a null value, which works in JavaScript, doesn't work in Dart, which raises an error:

```
var myValue = new Object();                  A myValue isn't boolean,
if (myValue) {                               so error is raised
  print("value is not null");
}
```

The correct way to check this explicitly is to use comparison operators, shown in table A.2, to compare two values:

```
var myValue = new Object();                  Explicit check that myValue isn't
if (myValue != null) {                       null returns boolean true
  print("value is not null");
}
```

Table A.2 Relational operators

Operator	Explanation
a == b	Are the values considered equal (not necessarily the same instance)?
a != b	Not equal.

Table A.2 Relational operators *(continued)*

Operator	Explanation
`a > b`	Greater than.
`a >= b`	Greater than or equal to.
`a < b`	Less than.
`a <= b`	Less than or equal to.
`a is String`	Is an instance of a specific type.
`a is! String`	Isn't an instance of a specific type.
`identical(a,b);`	Is the same instance.

You can add an optional `else` statement to execute when the `if` statement's condition evaluates to `false`. This follows either the block or line containing the `if` statement's code that executes when the value is `true`:

```
var someCondition = false;
if (someCondition) {                    Checks for true
  print("was true");                    condition
}
else {                                  Else
  print("was false");                   clause
}

if (someCondition) print("was true");   Single-line if
else print("was false");                else check
```

NOTE Although the language allows it, it's considered bad style to mix the curly brace with the single line in `if`/`else` statements.

You can combine `else` with `if` to produce an `else if` statement to chain multiple conditions together:

```
var someValue = 3;

if (someValue == 1) {
  print("value is 1");
}
else if (someValue == 2) {              Chains multiple if / else if
  print("value is 2");                  / else statements to check
}                                       multiple conditions with
else if (someValue == 3) {              block syntax
  print("value is 3");
}
else {
  print("value is $someValue");
}
```

```
if (someValue == 1) print("value is 1");
else if (someValue == 2) print("value is 2");
else if (someValue == 3) print("value is 3");
else print("value is $someValue");
```
Uses single-line syntax to chain multiple if / else if / else statements

As long as the end result is a boolean value, you can compare multiple conditions using the logical operators (shown in table A.3) and parentheses ( ) to combine multiple conditions.

Table A.3   Logical operators

Logical operator	Explanation
||	OR
&&	AND
!	NOT (`true` becomes `false`, `false` becomes `true`)

Here are some examples of using logical operators and brackets:

```
var value1 = 1;
var value2 = 200;

if (value1 == 1 || value2 == 200) print("true");

if (value1 < 10 && value2 > 100) print("true");

if ( !(value1 > 0= && value1 =< 100) || value2 == 200) {
  print("true");
}
```
value1 equals 1 OR value2 equals 200

value1 is less than 10 AND value2 is greater than 100

value1 ISN'T between 0 and 100 OR value2 equals 200

USING THE CONDITIONAL OPERATOR FOR CONDITIONAL SHORTHAND

Often you want to specify the value of a single variable as a result of a decision. For example:

```
var myColor = null;
var myValue = 23;

if (myValue == 23) {
  myColor = "blue";
}
else {
  myColor = "red";
}
```
Set value of myColor depending on value of myValue

This is verbose. You can simplify it by using the conditional ? operator to return a value if a condition evaluates to `true` or `false`. Here's the syntax:

```
condition ? return value if true : return value if false;
```

For example, the previous code can be rewritten as follows:

```
var myColor = null;
var myValue = 23;

myColor = (myValue == 23) ? "blue" : "red";
```
If myValue equals 23, return "blue"; else, return "red"

USING THE SWITCH STATEMENT FOR MULTIPLE COMPARISONS

The switch and case keywords let you check multiple values. Consider the following conditional check, which contains multiple if / else if / else statements:

```
var someValue = 3;
if (someValue == 1) {
  print("value is 1");
}
else if (someValue == 2) {
  print("value is 2");
}
else if (someValue == 3) {
  print("value is 3");
}
else {
  print("value is $someValue");
}
```

This can be rewritten using a switch statement, which checks each case value to see if it's equal to the switched value. Every condition that contains a body must also have a break statement that causes the switch check to end:

```
var someValue = 3;                    Compares value
switch (someValue) {                  of someValue

  case 1:                             Does it equal 1?

    print("value is 1");             If yes, executes code
                                                              Exits switch block
    break;                                                    following successful match

  case 2:                             Does it equal 2
    print("value is 2");             (and so on...)?
    break;
  case 3:
    print("value is 3");
    break;                            Uses default if it doesn't
  default:                            match any case statement
    print("value is $someValue");
}
```

It's an error not to include a break statement if there is any other code matching a case statement. For example:

```
var someValue = 3;
switch (someValue) {
  case 1:                             There is a value
    print("value is 1");             to match 1.

                                      Wrong: break statement missing.
  case 2:                             This is reported as an error.
    print("value is 2");
    break;
}
```

But you can have multiple empty case statements without a break. This allows matching on multiple cases:

```
var someValue = 3;
switch (someValue) {
  case 1:
  case 2:
  case 3:
    print("value is 1, 2 or 3");
    break;
}
```

Multiple case statements with no other code are allowed to fall through.

A.3.2   *Loops and iterating*

Dart has four language-level ways of iterating, and maps provide their own function for iterating key and values. The first three loop while a condition is true:

- do while loops
- while loops
- for loops

Support for the "for in" loop is provided by the the Iterable and Iterator interfaces, which are implemented by the Collection types such as List, Set, and Queue.

Maps provide a method of iterating each key/value pair in the list in addition to providing access to the collection of keys and values.

DO WHILE LOOPS

A do while loop performs the code block first and then checks to see if a condition is true. This means a do while loop executes at least one iteration.

The following loop will iterate only once:

```
var someCondition = true;
do {
  someCondition = false;
} while (someCondition);
```

Specifies code block to execute first

After each execution, repeats if condition is still true

You can include a counter, which increments each iteration:

```
var counter = 0;
do {
  counter ++;
} while (counter < 100);
```

Increments counter by 1

If you need to exit a loop immediately, use the break statement:

```
var counter = 0;
do {
  counter ++;
  if (counter == 42) {
    break;
  }
} while (counter < 100);
```

If counter equals 42, breaks out of loop

WHILE LOOPS

While loops are similar to do while loops, except that the condition is checked before the loop is entered. This means a while loop may not iterate at all:

```
var counter = 0;
while (counter < 100) {                    ◁── If condition is true, performs iteration
  counter ++;
}
```

Using the break statement works the same as previously discussed.

FOR LOOPS

A for loop also uses a counter, but the for loop has a three-part construction that lets you initialize the counter variable, specify the condition, and increment the counter:

```
for (int counter = 0; counter < 100; counter ++) {     ◁── Sets up looping
  print("Hello Dart");                                  ◁─┐ Prints "Hello
}                                                           │ Dart" 100 times
```

For loops are often used with lists, because the counter can also be used as a list index. You can check the list length by reading the length property:

```
var myList = ["Dart","JavaScript","Java"];       ◁── Defines literal list

for(int i = 0; i < myList.length; i++) {         ◁─┐ Defines zero-based
  var language = myList[i];              ◁─┐        │ counter and iterates
  print(language);                         │        │ for length of list
}                         Extracts each list │
                          item by element    │
```

Like while loops, you can break out of a for loop using the break statement. There is a better way to iterate through a list, though, and that is the for/in loop.

FOR/IN LOOPS

The for/in loop uses the Iterator and Iterable interfaces. That is, any object that can provide an iterator can be iterated with the for in keywords. This type of loop effectively says "for each element in the list, loop," and looks like the following snippet:

```
var myList = ["Dart","JavaScript","Java"];       ◁── Defines literal list

for (var language in myList) {                   ◁─┐ Assigns each item
  print(language);                     ◁─┐          │ in list to language
}                                        │          │ variable
              For each iteration, uses   │
              language variable
```

ITERATING MAPS WITH FOREACH()

Maps have two ways of iterating the key and value pairs. You can get the keys collection using the keys property and iterate it like any list to access the values:

```
var myMap = {"key1","value1","key2","value2"};   ◁── Defines literal map

for (var key in myMap.keys) {                    ◁─┐ Iterates for each
                                                    │ key in map's keys
  var value = myMap[key];              ◁─┐ Uses key to access
                                          │ key's value
  print(value);                      ◁─┐
                                        │ Uses value
}
```

Maps also provide a function called `forEach()` that takes a callback function that can receive the key and value objects for each pair in the map. In the following example, the anonymous function

```
(key, value) {
  print(key);
  print(value);
}
```

is passed into the map's `forEach()` function. The anonymous function is highlighted in bold and executes for each key/value pair in the map:

```
var myMap = {"key1","value1","key2","value2"};        ⊲—— Defines literal map


myMap.forEach( (key, value) {                     ⊲—┐  Passes anonymous function
  print(key);                    | Uses key            that is passed each key and
  print(value);                  | and value           value as parameters, in turn
});
```

appendix B
Defining classes and libraries

This appendix discusses building classes and using libraries and privacy.

B.1   *Classes and interfaces*

Dart is a class-based, object-orientated language with single inheritance and multiple interfaces. Dart has explicit classes and implicit interfaces: that is, a class definition implicitly defines an interface on its public properties and methods that other classes can implement.

> **NOTE**   In the initial release of Dart, there were explicit interfaces defined using the interface keyword. After feedback from Dart's early adopters, it was discovered that because an abstract class definition also defines an interface, the interface keyword was redundant.

B.1.1   *Defining classes*

The class keyword is used to define a class. Classes must be defined in top-level scope (that is, you can't define a class in a function, method, or other class):

```
class MyClass {            ◁── Defines class
                           ◁┐  Properties and methods
}                           │  defined in class body
```

You create an instance of a class by using the new keyword:

```
main() {                                      ┐ Creates instance
  var anInstanceOfMyClass = new MyClass();   ◁┘ of MyClass
}
```

You use the class name as type information throughout your application when assigning an instance into a variable or defining a function parameter. Just as with the built-in types (String, int), using that type information is optional, but the Dart tools will validate your code if you annotate your variables and parameters with type information:

371

```
class MyClass {              <--- Defines class called MyClass
}
void someFunction(untypedParameter, MyClass typedParameter) {    <--- Specifies MyClass as parameter type
  print(untypedParameter is MyClass);
  print(typedParameter is MyClass);                              Both print true when MyClass passed as an argument
}
main() {
  var anInstanceOfMyClass = new MyClass();
  MyClass aTypedInstance = new MyClass();                        Creates typed or untyped, final and non-final instances of MyClass
  final aFinalInstance = new MyClass();
  final MyClass aTypedFinalInstance = new MyClass();

  someFunction(anInstanceOfMyClass, aTypedInstance);             Typed or untyped has same effect
  someFunction(aTypedInstance, anInstanceOfMyClass);
}
```

PROPERTIES

Classes can have properties, which are attributes that describe the class. The following class describes an animal that has a number of legs and a color. The number of legs is strongly typed to be an integer, and the color is dynamically typed and can contain any type:

```
class Animal {               Integer legCount property
  int legCount;
  var color;                 Dynamically typed color property (see Note)
}
```

NOTE Early in your application's development, it's acceptable to use dynamic typing for properties in classes, especially when you haven't decided what type a property will become. As development progresses, though, you should aim to change dynamic types, such as the color property, into strong types that can be validated by the tools. The following example shows how dynamic typing is useful in early stages of development.

You access the properties on an instance of a class using dot notation syntax, similar to that used in Java and JavaScript. The syntax for reading and writing properties is identical:

```
main() {
  var dog = new Animal();           Creates instance of an animal
  dog.legCount = 4;                 Sets leg count to a value; tools will validate that only an int value is used
  dog.color = 0xFFF;                Any type can be used for color; here you use hex value

  var bird = new Animal();
  bird.legCount = 2;
  bird.color = "blue";              Here color is a string

  var snake = new Animal();
  snake.legcount = 0;
  snake.color = "diamond patterned";  Here color is also a string

  var totalLegs = dog.legCount + bird.legCount + snake.legCount;   Reads property values from each animal object
}
```

You can initialize properties with an initial value and make properties constant by using the final keyword. Again, you can mix strong typing and optional typing. Every instance of the class will have the same starting values. If you don't initialize a property, its starting value is null, just like a variable:

```
class Animal {
  final isVegetable = false;          Final properties can't be modified and
  final bool isAnimal = true;         must be initialized before the class is
  final bool isMineral = false        constructed.

  var int legCount = 4;               Other properties can be initialized
  var color = "black";                but can be modified by code later.

}
```

NOTE   See the section on constructors for more on providing initial and final values at runtime rather than in the class definition.

GETTERS AND SETTERS

A class's properties can be represented by getters and setters, which proxy for the underlying property. This allows you to write code that's invoked when a user tries to access a property: for example, code to validate the value that's being written or generate a value in the getter. The following example stores legCount in the property called _legCount; the getter and setter code is invoked when legCount is accessed. The setter validates that the number of legs is zero or greater:

```
class Animal {
  int _legCount;          <── Underlying property        Getter uses shorthand
                                                         syntax to return
  get legCount => _legCount;                             _legCount value

  set legCount(value) {                                  Setter takes a value
    if (value < 0) _legCount = 0;                        and assigns it to
    else _legCount = value;                              _legCount property
  }
}
```

You can also use strong typing on getters and setters:

```
class Animal {
  int _legCount;                                         Strongly typed getter lets
                                                         tools validate that int is
  int get legCount => _legCount;                         returned
  set legCount(int value) => _legCount = value < 0 ? 0 : value;

}
                                                         Strongly typed setter lets
                                                         tools validate that int is set
```

Accessing a getter and setter in calling code is identical to accessing a property directly. This means when you create your class, you can start with properties and then change to getters and setters without affecting other code that uses your class:

```
main() {                           Sets legCount;
  var dog = new Animal();          doesn't matter if it's       Reads legCount;
  dog.legCount = 4;                a setter or a property        doesn't matter if it's a
  int totalLegs = dog.legCount;                                  getter or a property
}
```

By providing only a getter or a setter, it's possible to create read-only or write-only properties:

```
class Animal {
  int _legCount;

  int get legCount => _legCount;
}
```

No setter, so legCount property is read-only

```
class Animal {
  int _legCount;

  set legCount(int value) => _legCount = value;
}
```

No getter, so legCount property is write-only

> **NOTE** The underscore in `_legCount` represents a private property. Privacy exists in Dart at a library, rather than a class, level. See the section on libraries for more information.

METHODS

Classes can have functions called *methods* associated with them. Methods work like normal functions, except that they can access properties and methods on the specific instance of the class. Method definition is the same as function definition, except that methods are defined in the top-level scope of the class declaration. The `this` keyword is implied when it isn't explicitly used and refers to the specific instance of the object:

```
class Animal {
  int legCount;

  void printLegCount() {
    print(legCount);
    print(this.legCount);
  }
}
```

Declares method called printLegCount() with no return value and no parameters

Prints value stored in each instance's legCount property

Use of this keyword is optional but can sometimes improve readability.

Methods, like functions, can also use the shorthand function syntax:

```
class Animal {
  int legCount;

  void printLegCount() => print(legCount);
}
```

Shorthand function syntax

You can use the `this` keyword to help when there would be name clashes, such as when a method parameter name is the same as a property name:

```
class Animal {
  int legCount;

  void addLegs(int legCount) {
    this.legCount += legCount;
  }
}
```

legCount property

addLegs() method defines parameter also called legCount

Uses this to distinguish between class's property and parameter

You use dot notation to call a method of a class instance, just as with properties, but you must also provide the parentheses ()—again, just as with function calls:

```
main() {
  var dog = new Animal();
  dog.legCount = 1;                    ◁— Sets legCount      Calls legCount()
  dog.addLegs(3);                                            method
  dog.printLegCount();                 ◁┐ Calls printLegCount()
}                                         method
```

Just as with functions, if you leave off the parentheses on the function call, you access the function object itself, which you can store in a variable:

```
main() {
  var dog = new Animal();                           Stores addLegs()
  var addLegsMethod = dog.addLegs;     ◁—           method in a variable
  addLegsMethod(4);                    ◁┐ Calls addLegs() method,
}                                         which adds 4 legs to dog
```

Methods have full access to other methods and properties in the instance of the class:

```
class Animal {
  int legCount;

  void addLegs(int legCount) {
    this.legCount += legCount;

    printLegCount();              One method can call another method;
    this.printLegCount();         use of this keyword is optional.
  }

  void printLegCount() => print(legCount);
}
```

Methods have the same parameter rules as functions and can take mandatory and optional parameters with default values. Parameters and return types are optional but provide documentation to tools and fellow developers:

```
class Animal {
  String sayHello([String greeting="woof") {      ◁— Defines single optional parameter
    return "$greeting $greeting $greeting";           with default value "woof"
  }                                               ◁┐ Returns string containing
}                                                    greeting parameter 3 times

main() {
  var dog = new Animal();           ◁┐ Prints "woof woof woof"
  print(dog.sayHello());               (uses default value)

  var bird = new Animal();                      ◁┐ Prints "tweet tweet tweet"
  print(bird.sayHello("tweet"));                   (uses passed-in value)
}
```

CONSTRUCTORS

When you use the new keyword to create an instance of a class, this calls the class's constructor method. The constructor method uses the same name as the class. If no constructor is defined, this is equivalent to an empty constructor.

The following

```
class Animal {

}
```
◁—— **No constructor defined**

is equivalent to

```
class Animal {
  Animal() {

  }
}
```
Empty constructor defined

You can use the constructor to perform an initialization step in the class:

```
class Animal {
  int legCount;

  Animal() {
    legCount = 4;
  }
}
```
Constructor sets value

CONSTRUCTOR PARAMETERS

Like other methods, the constructor can take parameters with optional and default values. You can use this to define property values as the class is initialized:

```
class Animal {
  int legCount;

  Animal([int legCount=0]) {
    this.legCount = legCount;
  }

}
main() {
  var dog = new Animal(4);
  var snake = new Snake();
}
```
Optional constructor parameter with default value of zero

Sets legCount property to parameter value

Passes in legCount value to constructor

◁—— **Uses default value**

Dart also provides a useful shorthand for populating properties in the constructor. When you use the this keyword in the constructor's parameter definition, Dart knows you want to set the property with the same name:

```
class Animal {
  int legCount;

  Animal([this.legCount = 0]) {

  }
}
main() {
  var dog = new Animal(4);
  print(dog.legCount);
}
```
Automatically populates class's legCount property

Empty constructor body

◁—— **Prints 4**

CONSTRUCTOR INITIALIZATION

Dart also has another initialization block in the constructor, which you can use to populate `final` values that need some calculation. Final values must be populated before the constructor starts executing.

The initialization block appears after the argument list and before the constructor-opening curly bracket defining the code block. It's a comma-separated list of statements beginning with a colon. Code in the initialization block is bold:

```
class Animal {
  final int legCount;            Final properties can't
  final bool hasBackLegs;        be modified once class
  final bool hasFrontLegs;       has been created.
                                                          Begins initialization
  Animal(frontLegCount, backLegCount) :                   block with a colon
    legCount = frontLegCount + backLegCount,   Initializes final
    hasBackLegs = backLegCount > 0,            property values before
    hasFrontLegs = frontLegCount > 0 {         constructor body

    print(legCount);              Inside constructor
    print(hasFrontLegs);          body, final values
    print(hasBackLegs);           are populated.
  }
}

main() {                          Calling code is
  var dog = new Animal(2,2);      unchanged.
  dog.hasBackLegs = false;                 Wrong: can't modify
}                                          final properties
```

NAMED CONSTRUCTORS

A class can have multiple named constructors in addition to the default constructor. For example, you might want to create an animal instance by reading values out of a map:

```
class Animal {
  int legCount;
  var color;
                                  Default constructor
  Animal() { }                    with empty body
                                               Declares named constructor
  Animal.fromMap(Map values) {                 called fromMap()
    this.legCount = values["legCount"];
    this.color = values["color"];   Sets properties from
  }                                 passed-in map values
}

main() {                                       Declares
  var dogMap = {"legCount":4,"color":0xFFF};   literal map
  var dog = new Animal.fromMap(dogMap);

  var snake = new Animal();                    Creates new dog using
  snake.legCount = 0;                          named constructor
  snake.color = "diamond pattern";
}                                 Creates new snake
                                  using default
                                  constructor
```

If you don't provide a default constructor, then you can only use named constructors to create instances of the class. Named constructors share all the same rules relating to optional parameters and initialization blocks as the default constructor.

FACTORY CONSTRUCTORS

A factory constructor allows your class to decide how the class is instantiated, such as returning an instance of a class from a cache rather than creating a new instance. It uses the factory keyword as a prefix and must return an instance of a class, but you can have named factory constructors in the same way as other constructors. Calling code uses them just like normal constructors, and the code has no knowledge that it's calling a factory:

```
class Animal {
  String name;

  factory Animal.withName() {          ⊲──┘  Named factory
    var animal = new Animal("fido");           constructor
    return animal;                             Responsible for creating and
  }                                            returning instance of animal

  Animal(this.name) {  }               ⊲── Default constructor
}
main() {
  var dog = new Animal.withName();     ⊲──┘  Calling syntax is identical
  print(dog.name);                           for other constructors.
}
```

This is useful for maintaining a cache of objects and loading them from a cache:

```
class Animal {                         Factory constructor with optional
  String name;                              animalCache parameter

  factory Animal.fromCache(String name, [List animalCache = []) {  ⊲──┘
    for (var existingAnimal in animalCache) {
      if (existingAnimal.name == name) {
        return existingAnimal;                 If animal with same name
      }                                        is in cache, return it.
    }

    return new Animal(name);           ⊲──┐  Not found in cache, so
  }                                         return new instance.

  Animal(this.name) {  }
}
                                       Creates new
main() {                               instance of fido
  var fido = new Animal.fromCache("fido");   ⊲──┘
  List animalCache = new List();             Creates new instance
  animalCache.add(fido);      ⊲── Adds fido to cache    of fido; returns
                                                        cached version
  var fido2 = new Animal.fromCache("fido", animalCache);  ⊲──┘
  print(fido === fido2);             ⊲──┐  Prints true; they're
}                                         the same instance.
```

B.1.2 *Class inheritance*

Classes can form an inheritance hierarchy. For example, all animals have legs, but a dog has different methods and properties than a bird (birds fly; dogs run). You can use class inheritance to define a base class, such as `Animal`, which has properties and methods common to all animals, and then define subclasses that inherit the base class and add their own methods and properties. This creates an is-an relationship between the subclass and the parent class: for example, a `Dog` is-an `Animal`. This doesn't work the other way around—an `Animal` isn't a `Dog`.

You use the `extends` keyword to extend an existing class:

```
class Animal {                          ⟵— Defines base class
  int legCount;

  void eat() {                          Method in
    print("nom nom nom");               base class
  }
}

class Dog extends Animal {              ⟵— Dog is-an Animal
  void run() {                          New method
    print("I'm running - fun");         specific to Dog
  }

}

class Bird extends Animal {   ⟵— Bird is-an Animal    New property
  int wingCount;                                       specific to Bird

  void fly() {                                         New method
    print("Fly away, there's a dog chasing me");       specific to Bird
  }
}
main() {                              Creates instance
  var dog = new Dog();            ⟵— of Dog
  dog.legCount = 4;               Uses inherited properties
  dog.eat();                      and methods from Animal
  dog.run();                                      Uses method that
                                                  only exists on Dog

  var bird = new Bird();          ⟵— Creates instance of Bird
  bird.wingCount = 2;                             Uses property that
  bird.legCount = 4;              Uses inherited properties    only exists on Bird
  bird.eat();                     and methods from Animal
  bird.fly();                                     Uses method that
}                                                 only exists on Bird
```

With the is-an relationship, you can get strong typing at multiple levels:

```
main() {
  Dog fido = new Dog();           Strong typing on
  Bird tweety = new Bird();       instantiated class
  Animal someDog = new Dog();
  Animal someBird = new Bird();   Strong typing on base class
}
```

```
print(fido is Dog);
print(someDog is Dog);
print(fido is Animal);          Prints "true"
print(tweety is Animal);
print(someDog is Animal);

print(tweety is Dog);           Prints "false"; tweety and
print(someBird is Dog);         someBird aren't Dogs.

Dog someDogAnimal = new Animal();    <—— Wrong: Animal isn't a Dog.
}
```

Type inheritance is also useful when you're strongly typing lists, maps, and functions or methods:

```
void eatFood(Animal animal) {        Function takes an
  animal.eat();                      Animal as a parameter.
  animal.fly();
}                                    Can use any property or method
                                     on Animal base class ...
main() {
  Dog fido = new Dog();              ... but can't use methods
  Bird tweety = new Bird();          from subclasses.

  eatFood(fido);                     Both fido and
  eatFood(tweety);                   tweety are Animals.

  List<Animal> animals = new List<Animal>();
  animals.add(fido);                 List of Animals happily
  animals.add(tweety);               contains fido and tweety.
}
```

There's no limit to the depth of inheritance. For example, you might define specific classes of Dog, such as `Poodle` and `Husky`, which extend from `Dog`.

OVERRIDING METHODS

Subclasses can also provide their own implementation of methods and properties defined in the parent class. For example, a bird might "peck" when eating:

```
class Animal {
  int legCount;

  void eat() {                       Animal defines base nom
    print("nom nom nom");            nom implementation
  }
}

class Bird extends Animal {          Overrides read-only
  int _legCount = 2;                 implementation of legCount
  int get legCount => _legCount;     property by implementing getter

  void eat() {                       Overridden
    print("peck peck peck");         implementation of eat
  }
}

void eatFood(Animal animal) {        When bird is passed in, uses
  animal.eat();                      bird-specific eat() method
}
```

```
main() {
  var tweety = new Bird();
  eatFood(tweety);
}
```

◁── **Prints "peck peck peck"**

B.1.3 *Abstract classes*

Sometimes you want the strong typing provided by a base class but with completely different implementations in each of the subclasses. For example, dogs and birds don't eat food the same way, so it might make more sense to force Dog and Bird to provide their own implementations. You can do this with an abstract class, which doesn't define a specific implementation but instead forces subclasses to provide an implementation. The optional abstract keyword is used to define an abstract class or method:

```
abstract class Animal {
  int legCount;

  abstract void eat();
}
```

◁── **abstract keyword documents that this is intended to be an abstract class**

◁── **No body provided for eat() function, so subclasses must provide implementation**

```
main() {
  var dog = new Animal();
}
```

◁── **Wrong: can't create instance of abstract class**

The abstract keyword is optional, so the following class has the same effect:

```
class Animal {
  int legCount;

  void eat();
}
```

◁── **No abstract keyword**

◁── **No abstract keyword on method, so absence of method body implies that it's abstract**

This means subclasses must provide an implementation. If they don't, then that class is also implicitly abstract and can't be instantiated:

```
class Dog extends Animal {
  void eat() => print("chomp");
}
```

◁── **Provides implementation of eat()**

```
class Bird extends Animal {

}
```

◁── **Doesn't provide implementation, so is also abstract**

```
main() {
  var dog = new Dog();
  var bird = new Bird();
}
```

◁── **Can create instance of Dog**

◁── **Can't create instance of Bird**

Abstract classes are useful for providing some functionality but mostly for forcing subclasses to provide their own specific implementations for other functionality. For example, the Animal class might provide a default sleep() implementation but force subclasses to provide their own eat() implementation:

```
class Animal {
  int legCount;

  void sleep() {
    print("zzzz");
  }

  void eat();
}
```

Implementation of sleep() is provided

eat() has no implementation, so class becomes abstract

B.1.4   *Implicit interfaces*

Every class has an implicit interface. An *interface* is the list of the properties and methods that a class promises it will have. Other code can rely on this promise when executing.

This is especially useful when you don't want to subclass a specific implementation; instead you want to provide a different alternative implementation, such as a mock. Imagine a third-party library that contains an enterprise dog that connects to a server somewhere for food. It looks like this:

```
class EnterpriseDog {
  String eat(String connectionString, String food) {
    // connect to database
    // do something with food
    return foodResult;
  }
}
```

Does something complex that relies on external dependencies

If you write a method in your code to print the result of the eat() method, and you want to test it, you can pass in an EnterpriseDog instance, but that involves setting up a database and all the external dependencies:

```
void showFoodResult(EnterpriseDog dog) {
  var result = dog.eat("192.168.2.99:8080","dogfood");
  print(result);
}

main() {
  showFoodResult(new EnterpriseDog());
}
```

Server needs to be running for this to work.

You just want to check that your result is printed.

Using interfaces, you can provide your own mock implementation of the Enterprise-Dog from the other library by using the implements keyword:

```
class MockDog implements EnterpriseDog {
  String eat(String connectionString, String food) {
    return "yum";
  }
}

main() {
  showFoodResult(new MockDog());
}
```

Implements EnterpriseDog

Provides its own implementation

MockDog can be used anywhere EnterpriseDog is used.

IMPLEMENTING ABSTRACT CLASSES

All classes have an implicit interface, and this includes abstract classes. This is analogous to defining and implementing an interface in Java or C#:

```
class IEater {                          Abstract class has
  void eat();                           implicit interface
}

class Dog implements IEater {           Implements interface
  void eat() {                          from abstract class
    print("chomp");
  }
}
```

MULTIPLE INTERFACES

A class can implement multiple interfaces. For example, your `Dog` might implement two different interfaces:

```
class IEater {                          Defines
  void eat();                           abstract class
}

class IRunner {                         Defines
  void run();                           abstract class
}
                                        Implements two
class Dog implements IEater, IRunner {  abstract classes
  void eat() => print("chomp");         Implementation of IEater

  void run() => print("I'm running...");       Implementation
}                                              of IRunner
```

B.1.5 *Static methods and properties*

Classes can have static methods and properties. A *static* method or property belongs to a class but acts independently from any instances of that class. Use the `static` keyword to indicate that the property or method is static. You use the class name to access static properties and methods rather than the name of a specific instance:

```
class Animal {                          Static property belongs to class as
  static int animalCount = 0;           a whole, not a specific instance.

  static void incAnimalCount() {               Static method can act
    animalCount++;                             on static properties.
  }

  Animal() {                            Default constructor
    incAnimalCount();                   calls static method.
  }
}
main() {
  var dog = new Animal();                      Accesses static
  print(Animal.animalCount);                   property, prints 1

  var bird = new Animal();                     Accesses static
  print(Animal.animalCount);                   property, prints 2
}
```

B.2   Libraries and privacy

A *library* is one or more Dart files linked together. Libraries are the smallest unit of privacy in Dart. A library can contain multiple source files, multiple functions, and multiple classes. A library that contains a `main()` function can also be used as an entry-point Dart script.

B.2.1   Defining libraries

A library is defined with the `library` statement, which must appear at the top of the file and defines the library name. Your library can be composed of multiple source files, which contain classes and functions that form your library, but the library file itself can also contain classes and functions. Your library is the aggregate of the library file and any source files it contains.

You can also import other libraries into your library by using the `import` statement and providing a path to that library. Imported libraries provide external code that your library can use. Listings B.1, B.2, and B.3 show two library files and a source file. `my_library` is defined in my_library.dart (listing B.1), is made from one other source file called source.dart (listing B.2), and imports another library called other_library.dart (listing B.3).

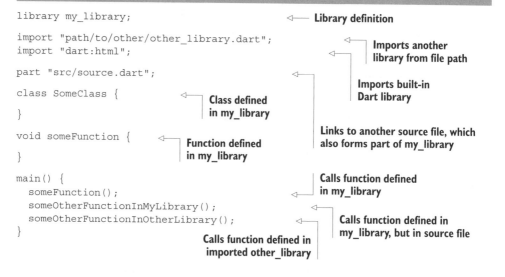

Listing B.1   my_library.dart

```
library my_library;                                    ⟵── Library definition

import "path/to/other/other_library.dart";            ⟵──┐ Imports another
import "dart:html";                                    ⟵──┘ library from file path

part "src/source.dart";                                ⟵──  Imports built-in
                                                             Dart library
class SomeClass {              ⟵──┐ Class defined
}                                 └ in my_library       Links to another source file, which
                                                        also forms part of my_library
void someFunction {           ⟵──┐ Function defined
}                                 └ in my_library

main() {                                                Calls function defined
  someFunction();                              ⟵──      in my_library
  someOtherFunctionInMyLibrary();              ⟵──┐
  someOtherFunctionInOtherLibrary();   ⟵──       └ Calls function defined in
}                                                  my_library, but in source file
                      Calls function defined in
                      imported other_library
```

Listing B.2   source.dart

```
part of my_library;             ⟵──  Indicates library the source file is part of

class SomeOtherClassInMyLibrary {
}                                        Functions and classes defined in source
                                         file form my_library just like functions
void someOtherFunctionInMyLibrary {      and classes defined in main library file.
}
```

Listing B.3   other_library.dart

```
library other_Library;                   ⟵── Defines other_library

class SomeClassInOtherLibrary {

}                                         Functions and classes belong to
                                          other_library but are publically
void someFunctionInOtherLibrary {         accessible to other libraries.

}
```

B.2.2   Library privacy

Anything prefixed with an underscore is defined as private to that library. Listing B.4 shows other_library.dart, which contains a private class, a private function, and a public class with private methods and properties. None of the private elements are accessible to the importing my_library.

Listing B.4   other_library.dart with private elements

```
library other_library;

class SomeClassInOtherLibrary {

}

void someFunctionInOtherLibrary {

}
                                              Private function isn't
void _aPrivateFunction() {                    accessible by code
  print("In a private function");        ⟵── outside library
}
                                              Private class isn't
class _SomePrivateClass {                ⟵── accessible outside library
  _SomePrivateClass () {                 ⟵
    print("In a private class constructor");   Private constructor
  }
}

class SomePublicClass {
                           Calls private method          Calls private
  aPublicMethod() {         from public method           function in library
    print("In a public method");
    _aPrivateMethod();                 ⟵
    _aPrivateFunction();               ⟵                Creates instance
    var aPrivateClass = new _SomePrivateClass();  ⟵     of private class
  }

  _aPrivateMethod() => print("In a private method");  ⟵── Defines private method

  int _aProperty;                                     ⟵── Defines private property
  int get aProperty => _aProperty;
  set(value) => _aProperty = value;
}                                           Provides public getter
                                            and setter to access
                                            private property
```

index